PIANO • VOCAL • GUITAR

TREASURY of STANDARDS

VOLUME 2 – I (I Said . . . .) to O

the
ULTIMATE
series

HAL LEONARD
PUBLISHING
CORPORATION

Home Office:
960 East Mark Street
Winona MN 55987

National Sales Office:
8112 West Bluemound Road
Milwaukee WI 53213

TREASURY of STANDARDS

VOLUME 2 – I (I Said . . .) to O

Contents

I SAID MY PAJAMAS

Words and Music by EDDIE POLA
and GEORGE WYLE

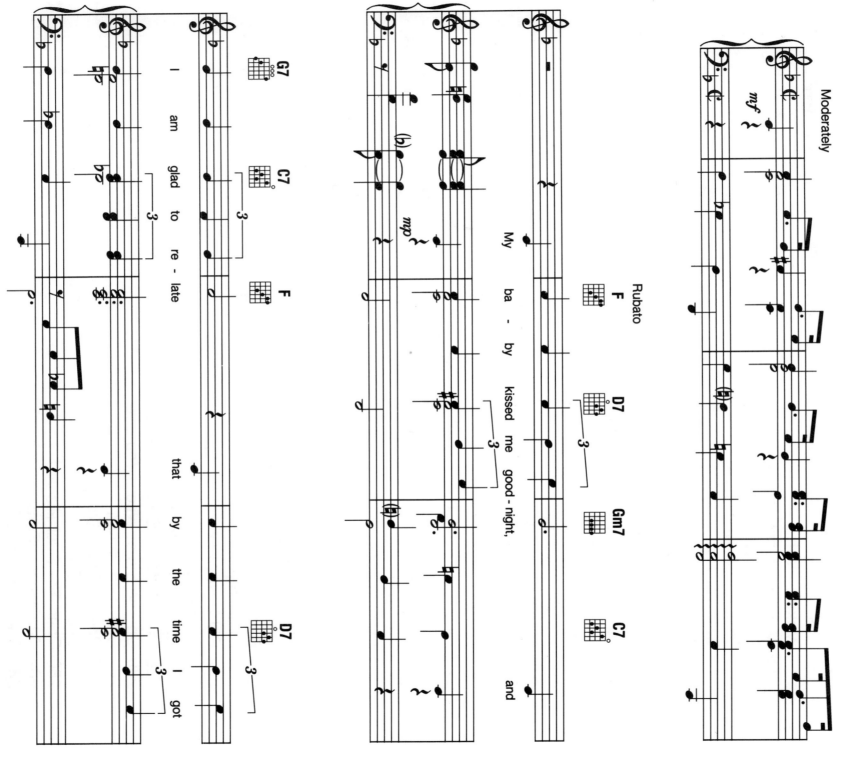

Gm7 C7 G7 Gm7 C7
home, I was feel - ing great!
3
Rhythmically
F D7 Gm C7
I climbed up the door and o - pened the stairs. I said my pa - ja - mas and
pow - dered my hair and pinned up my nose. I hung up the bath and I
mp-mf
F D7 Gm
put on my pray'rs. I turned off the bed and crawled in - to the light,
turned on my clothes. I put out the clock and wound the cat up tight,
and
F G7 C7 F D7
all be-cause you kissed me (Kiss) good - night. Next morn - ing, I woke and
I ran up the shade and
3

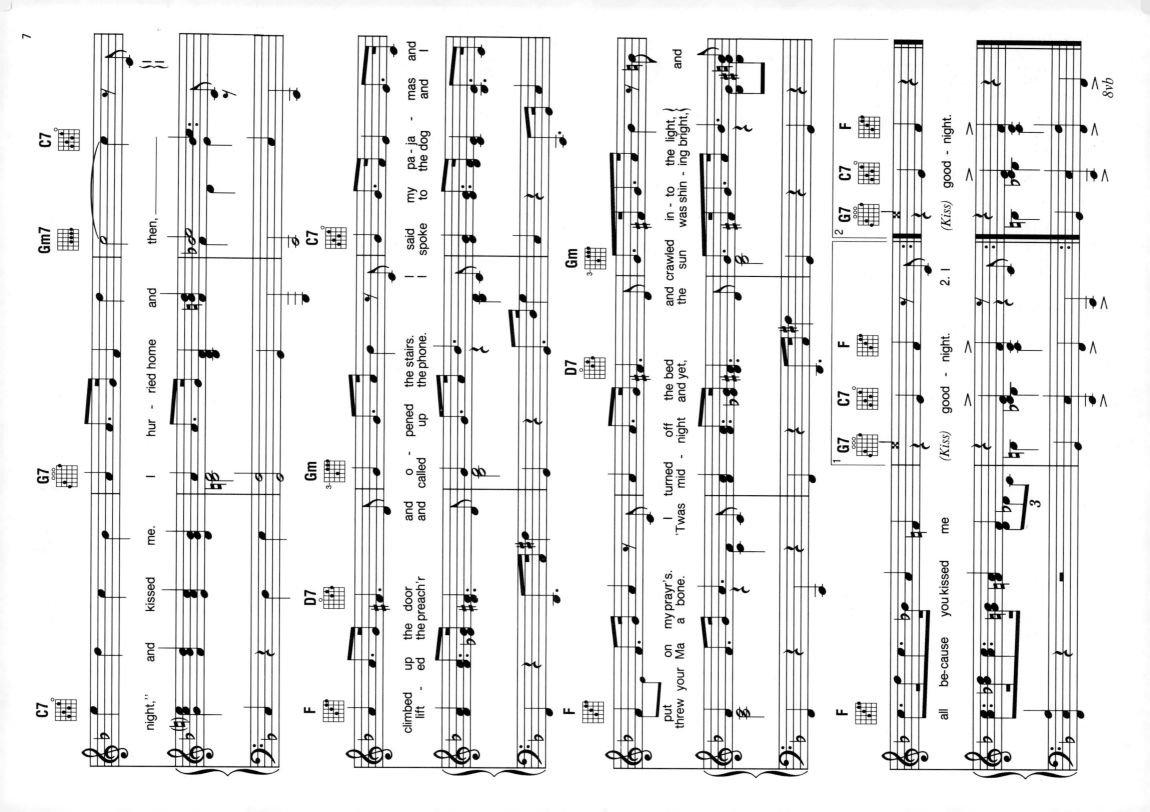

I SEE YOUR FACE BEFORE ME

Words by HOWARD DIETZ
Music by ARTHUR SCHWARTZ

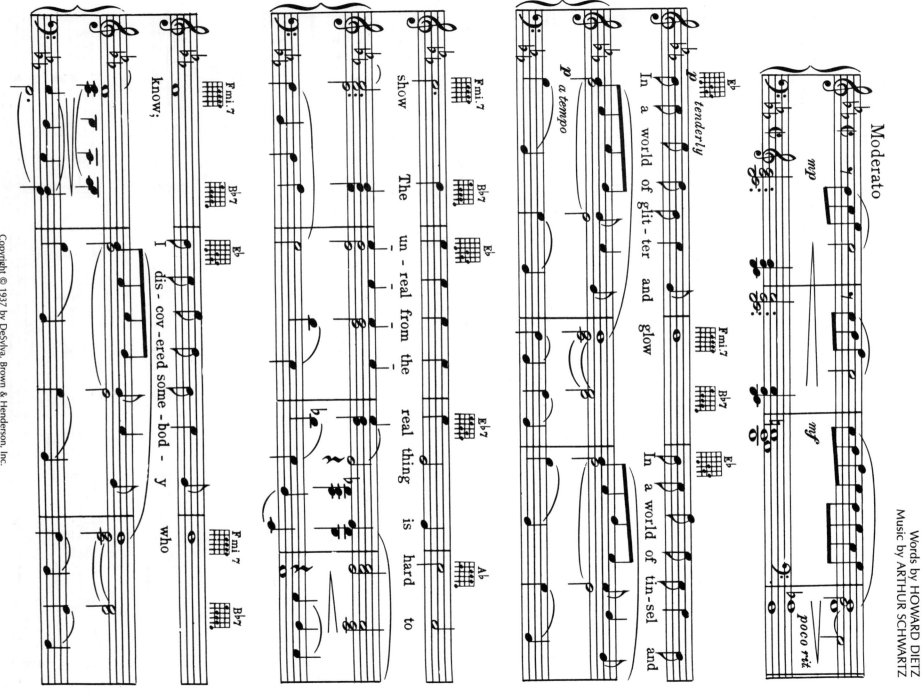

9

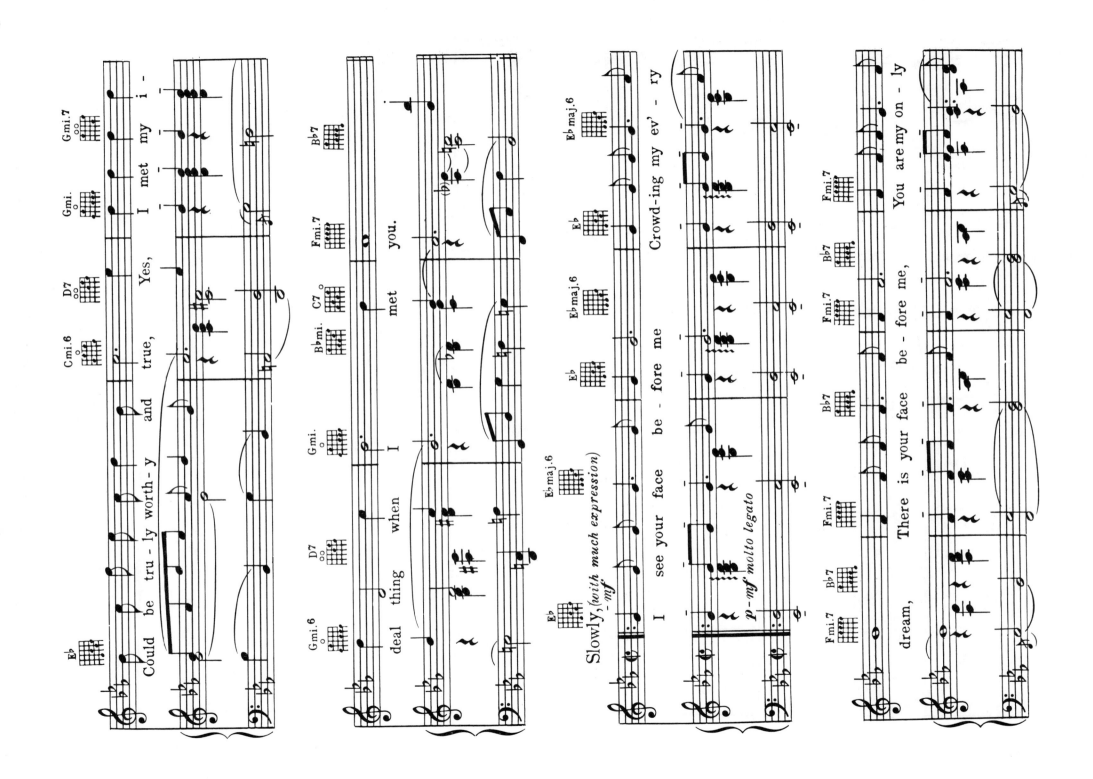

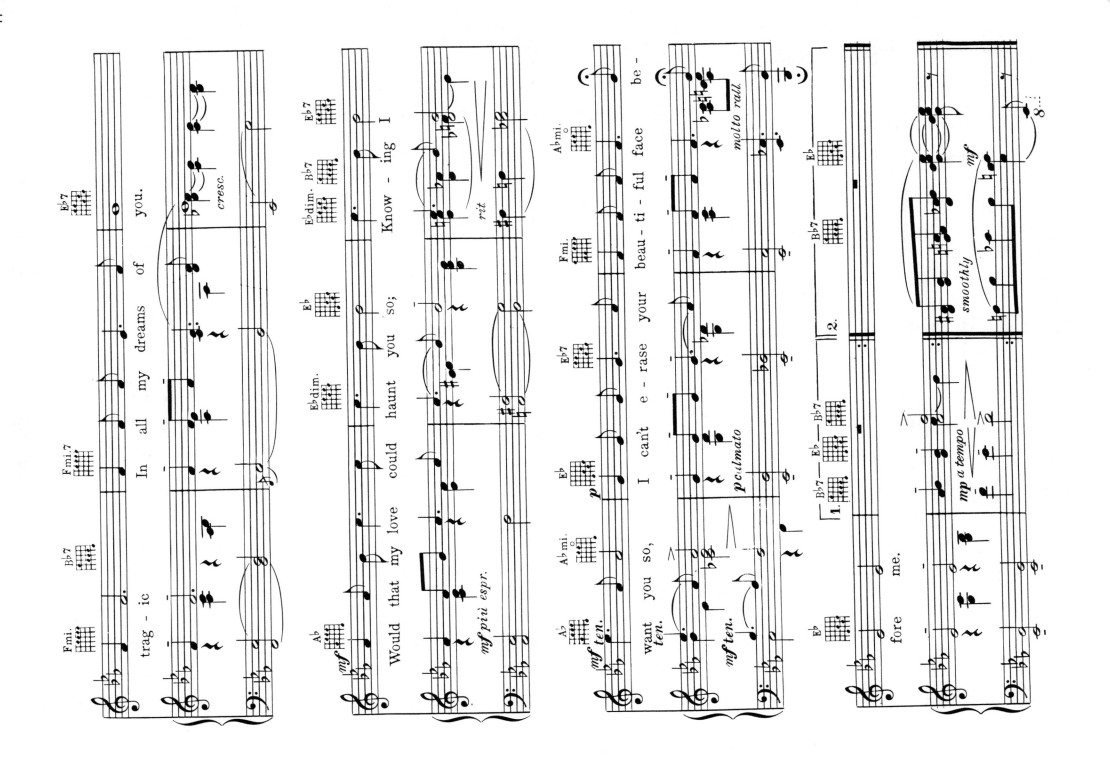

I TALK TO THE TREES
(From "PAINT YOUR WAGON")

Words by ALAN JAY LERNER
Music by FREDERICK LOEWE

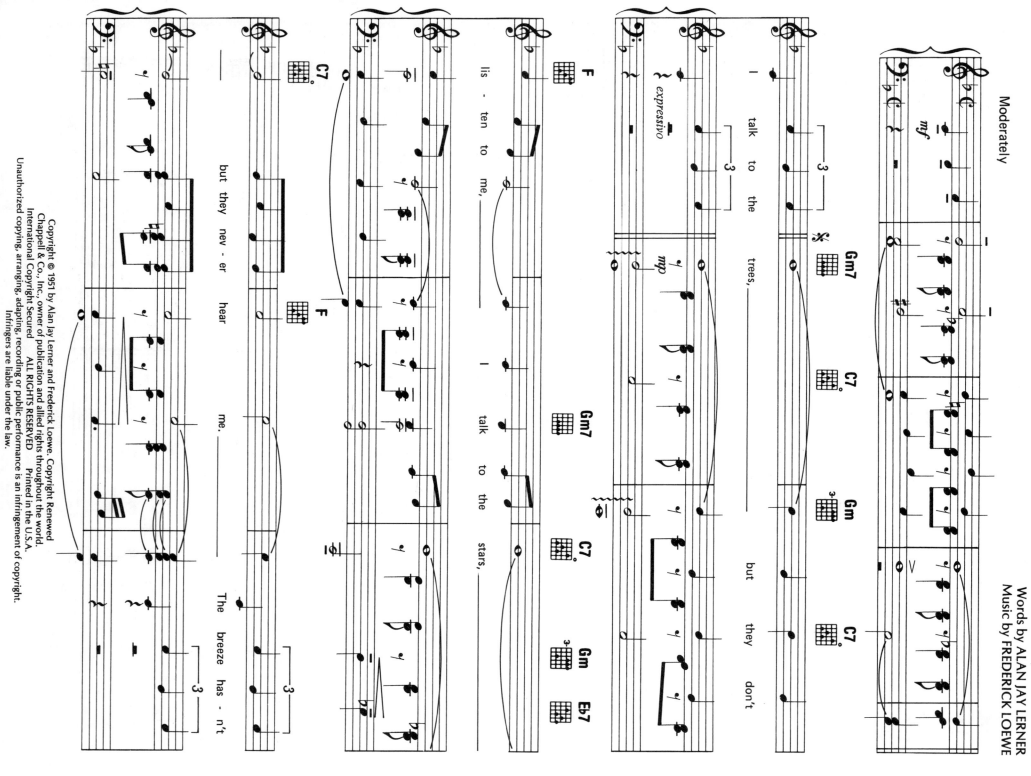

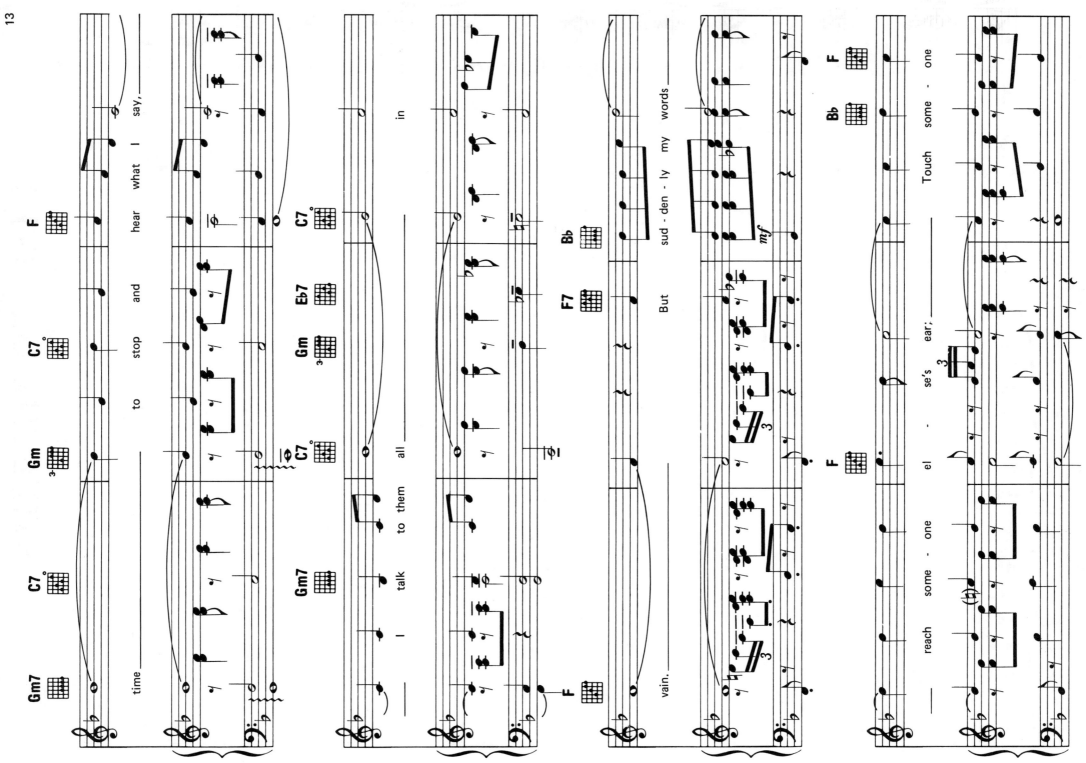

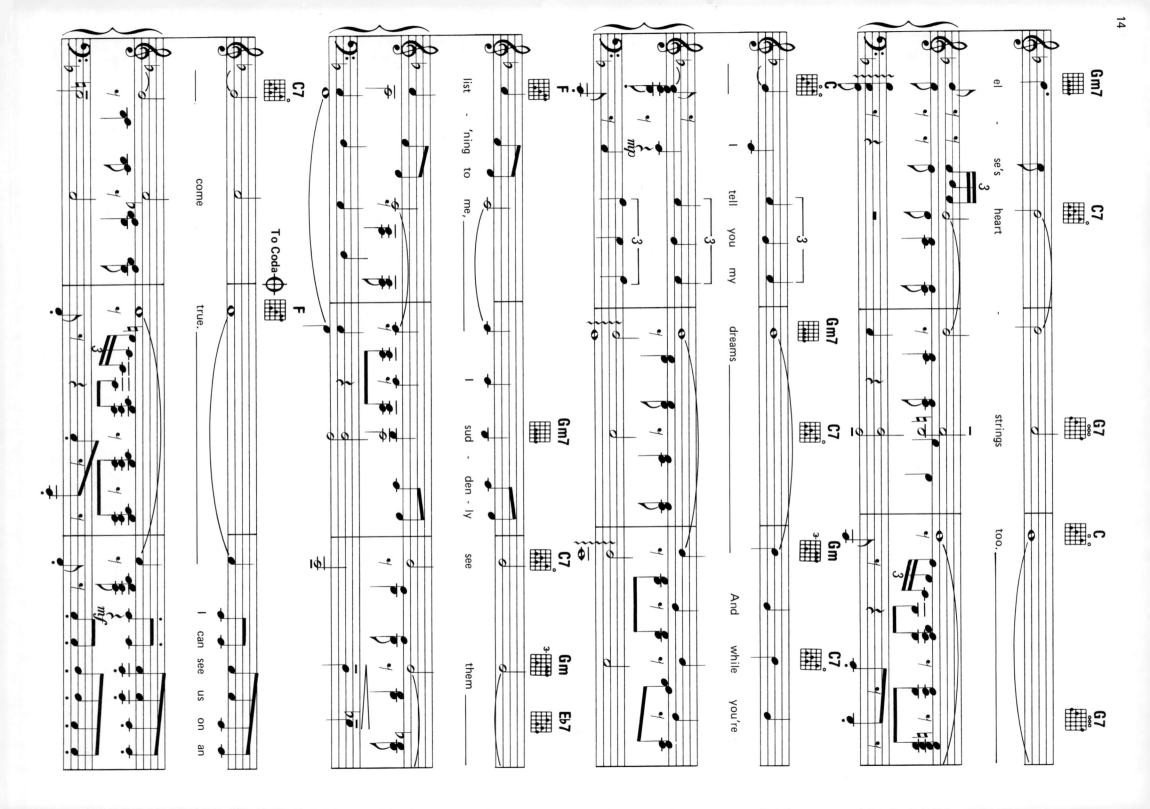

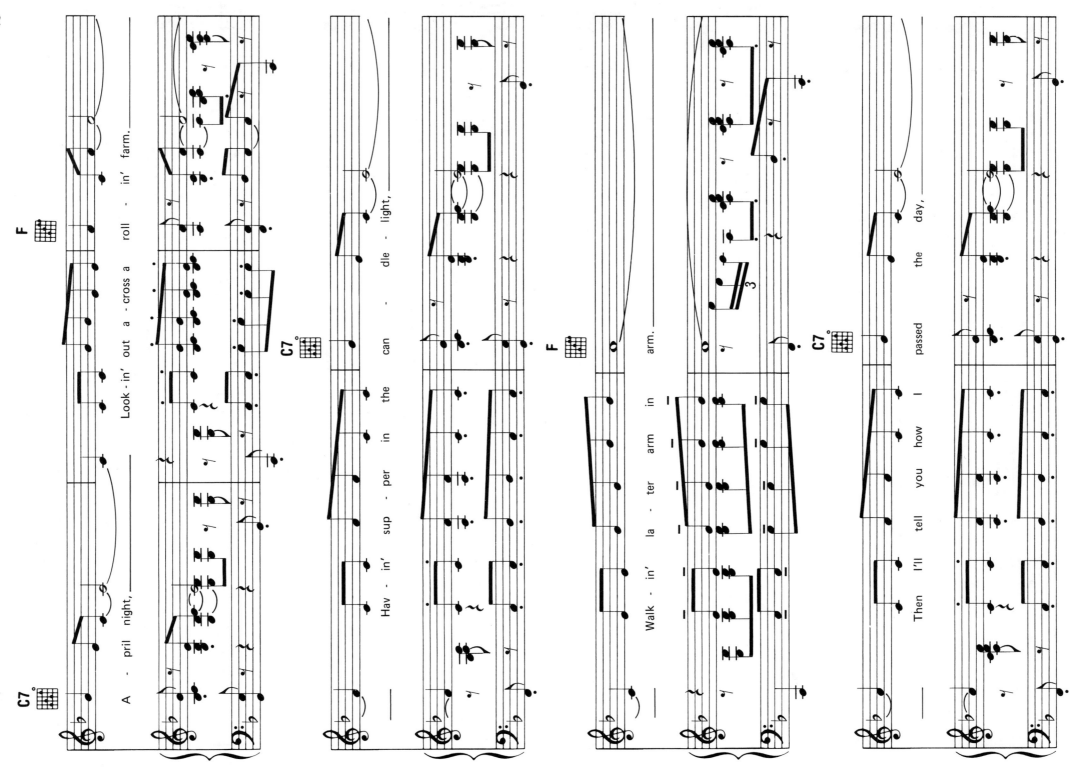

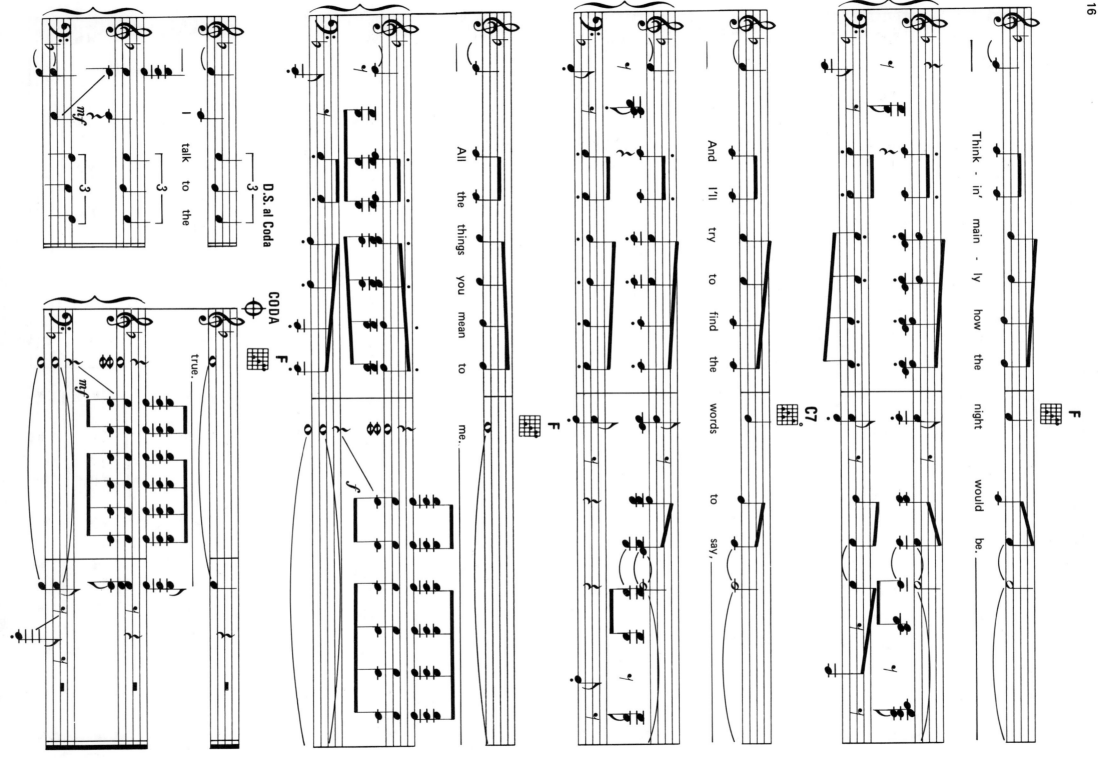

I WHISTLE A HAPPY TUNE

(From "THE KING AND I")

Words by OSCAR HAMMERSTEIN II
Music by RICHARD RODGERS

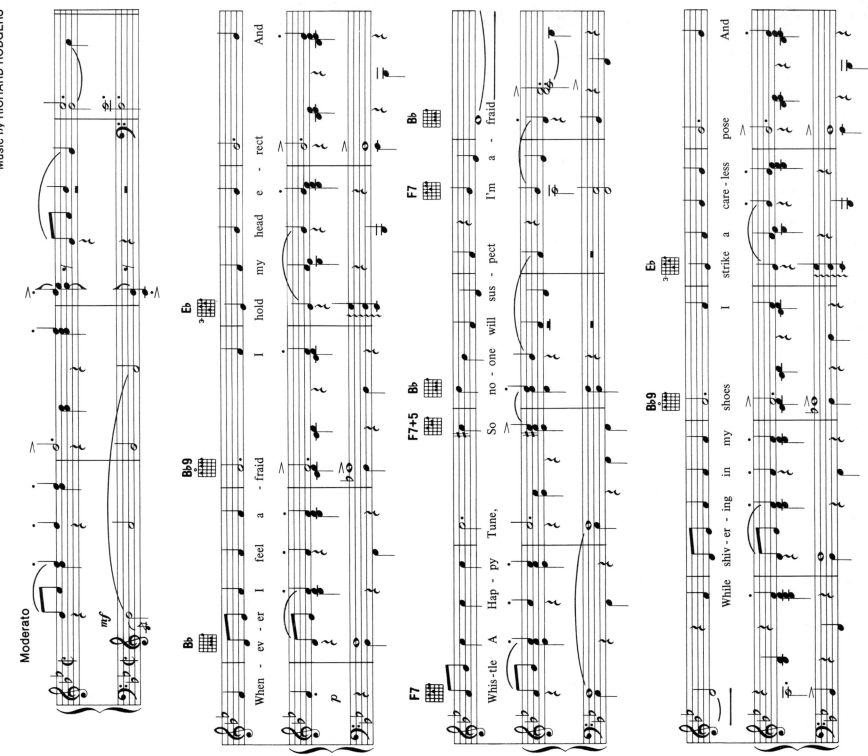

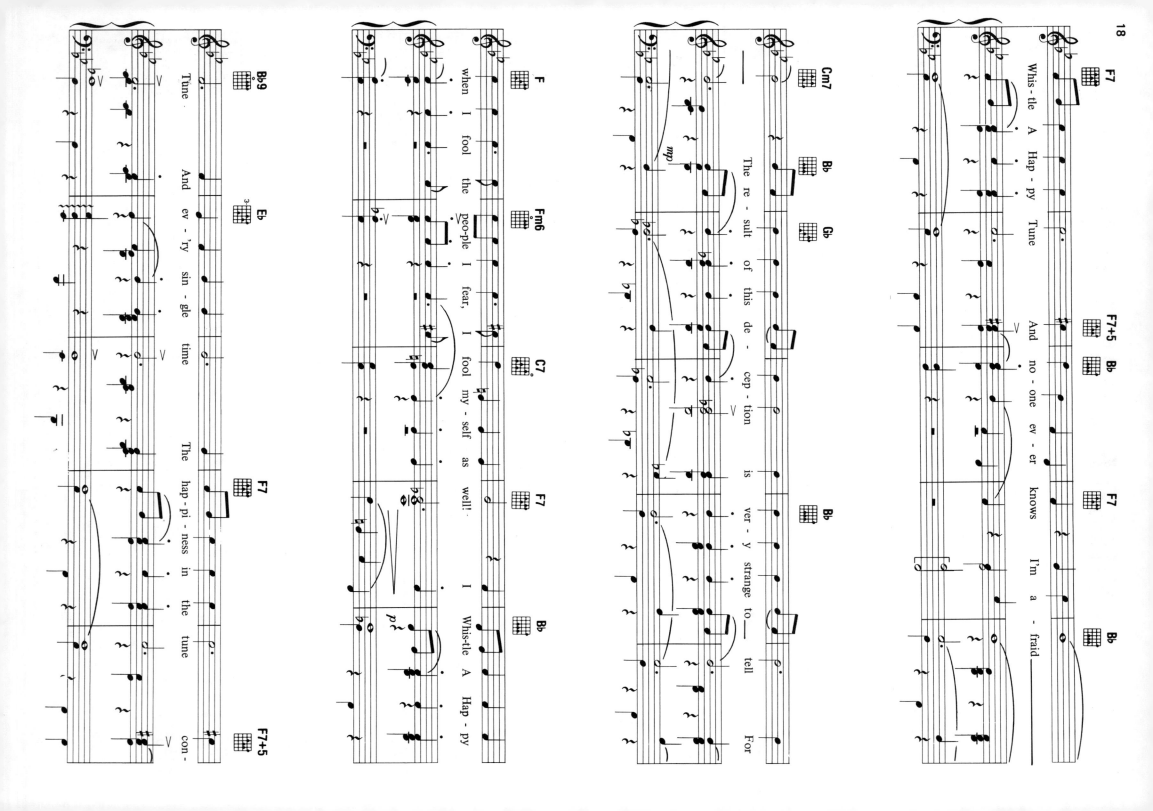

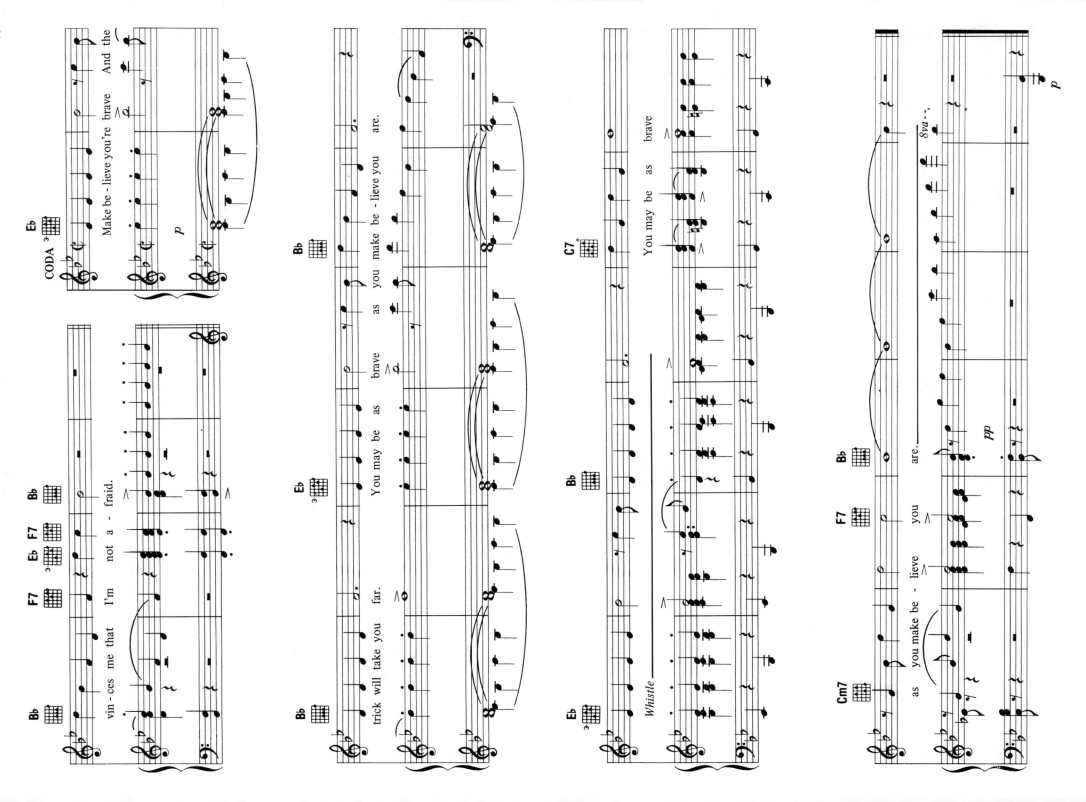

I WANT A GIRL
(Just Like The Girl That Married Dear Old Dad)

By WILL DILLON
and HARRY VON TILZER

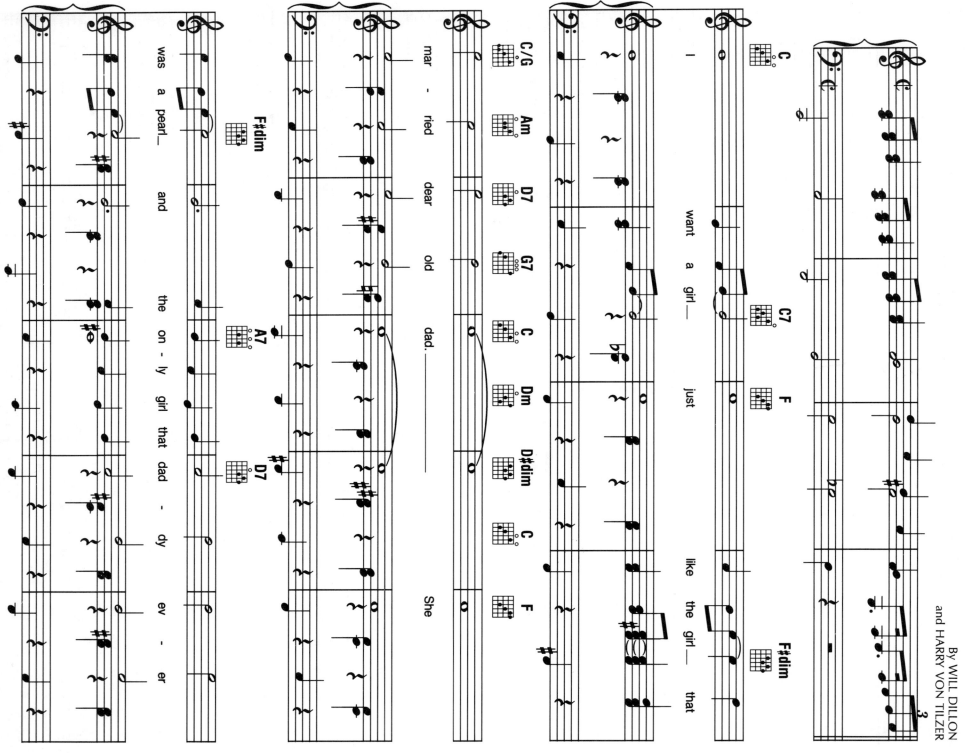

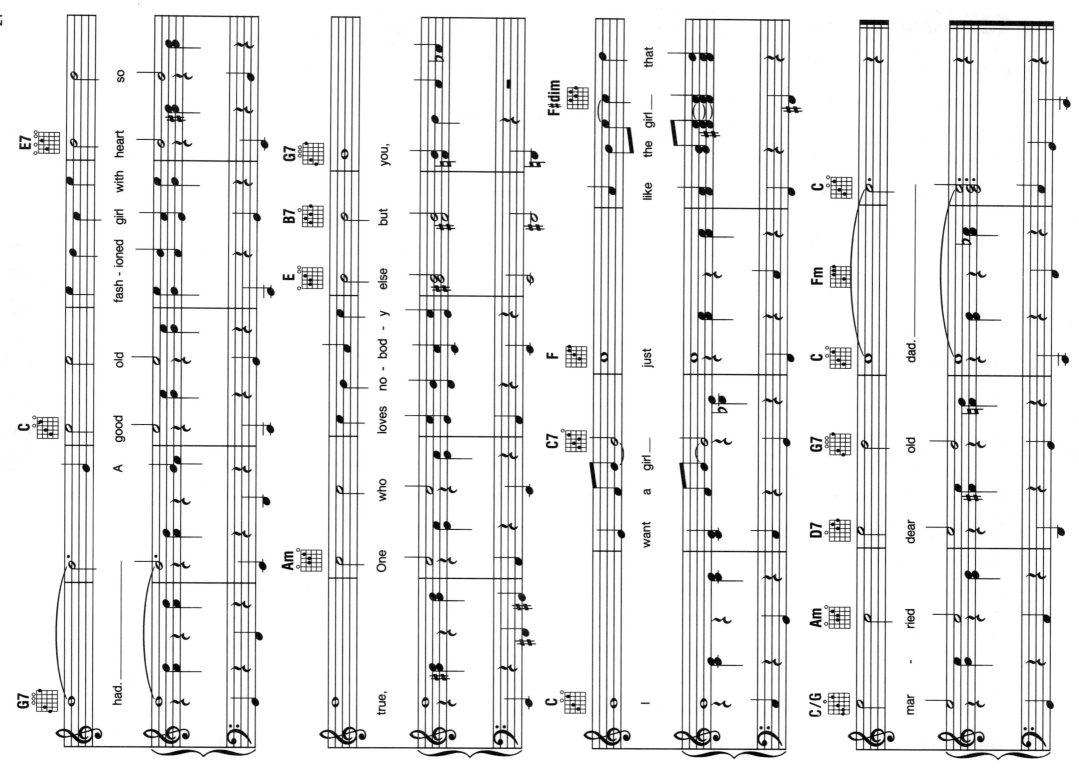

I WILL WAIT FOR YOU

English Words by NORMAN GIMBEL
Music by MICHEL LEGRAND

Moderate tempo

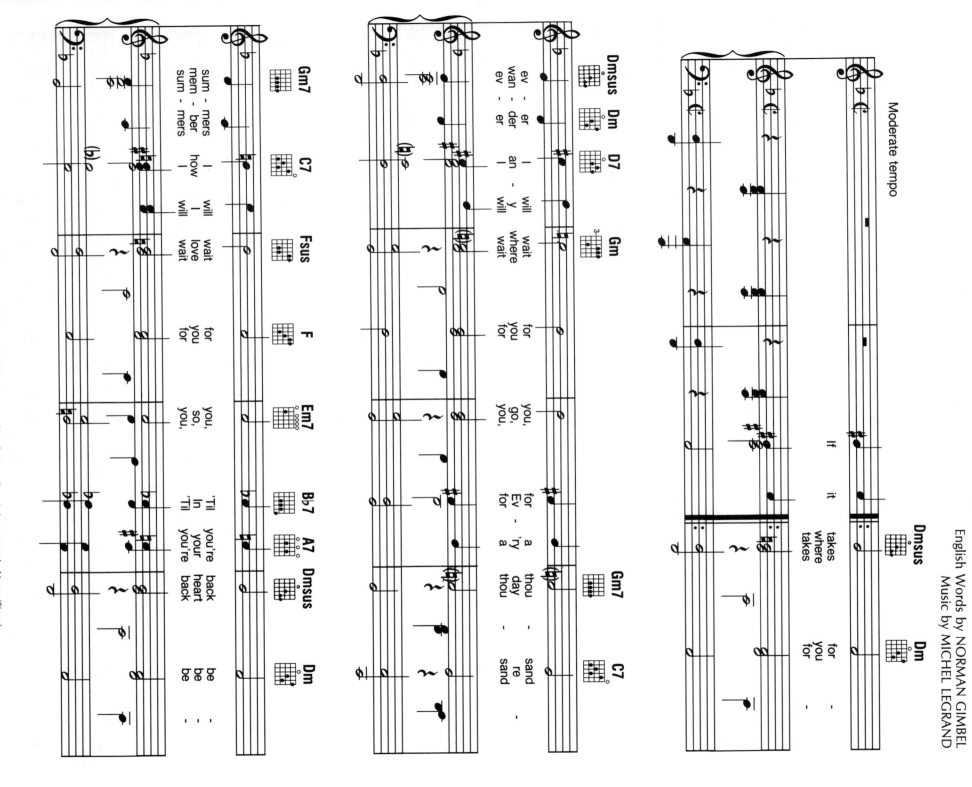

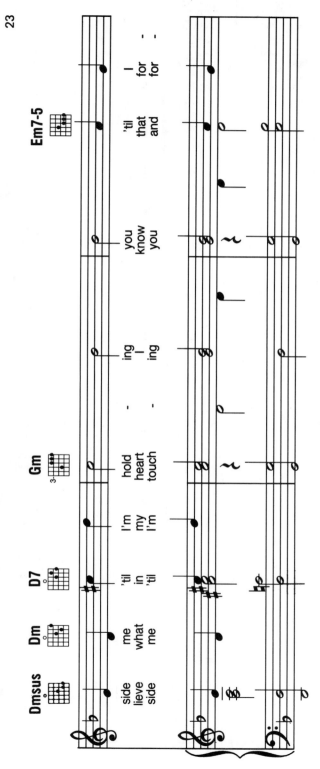
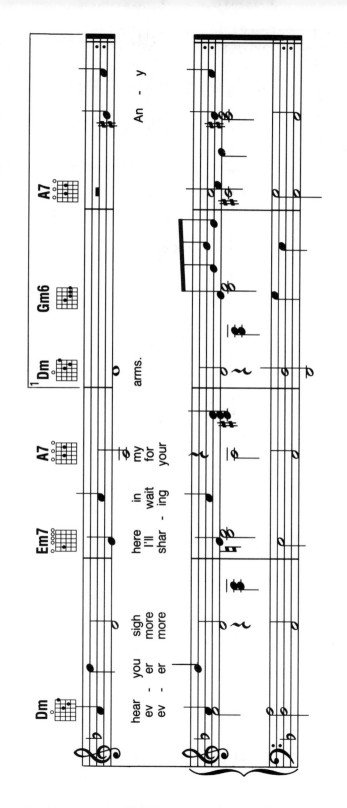
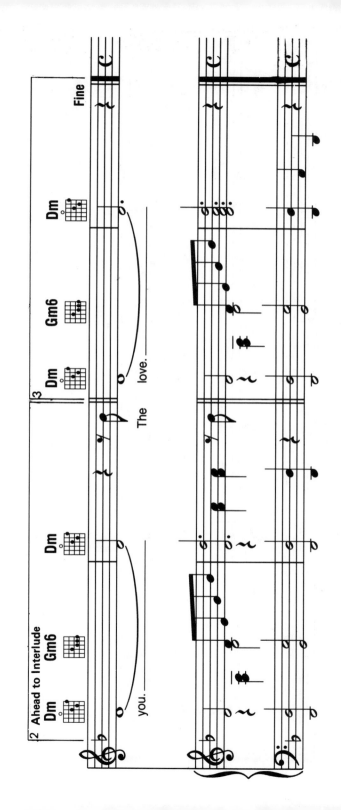

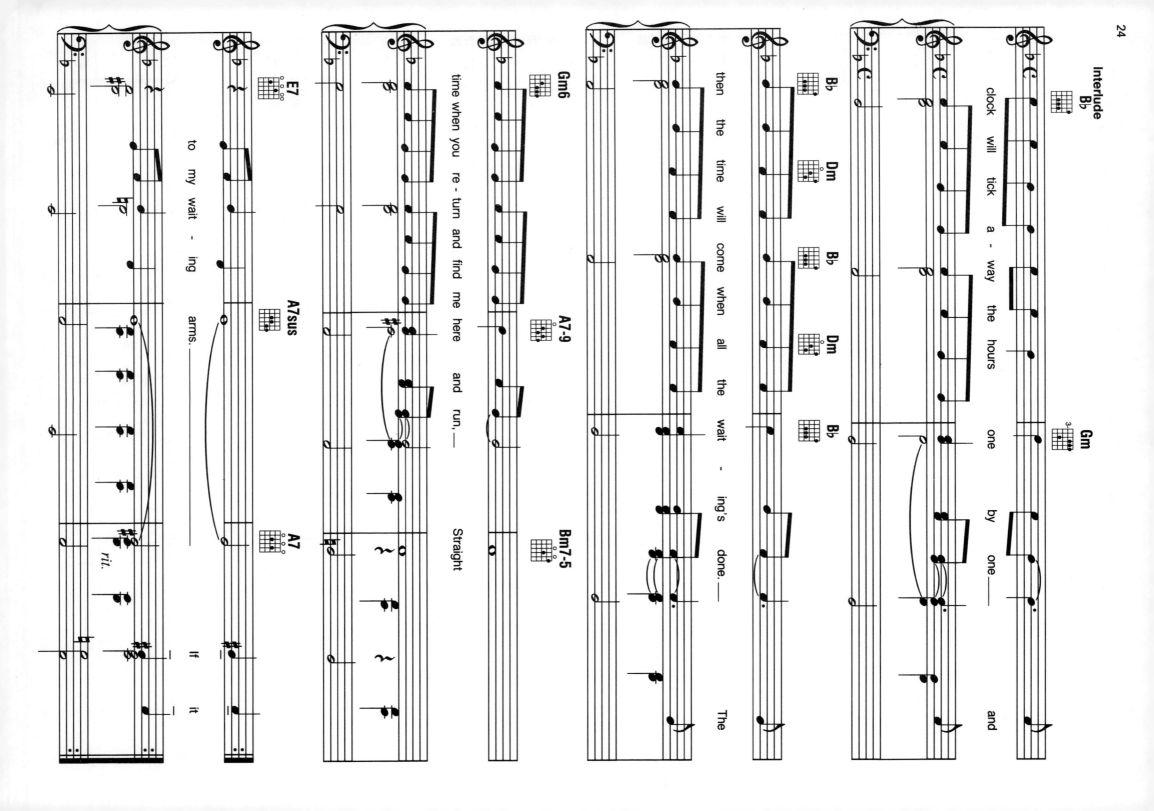

I WISH I WAS EIGHTEEN AGAIN

Words and Music by SONNY THROCKMORTON

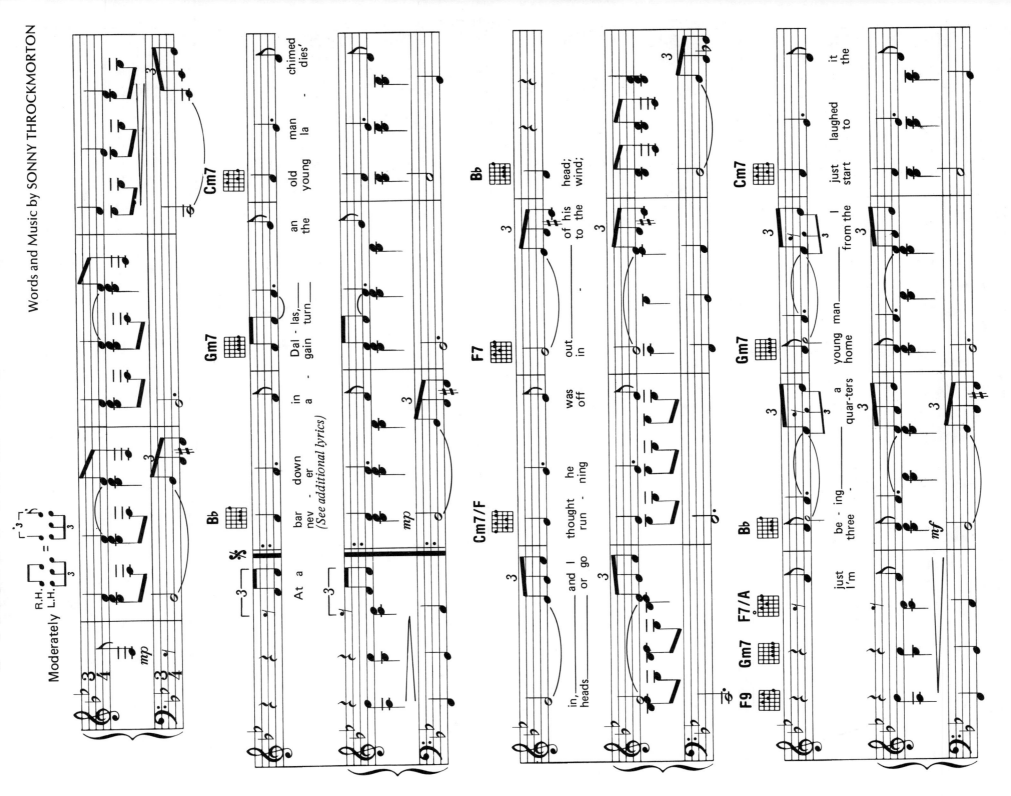

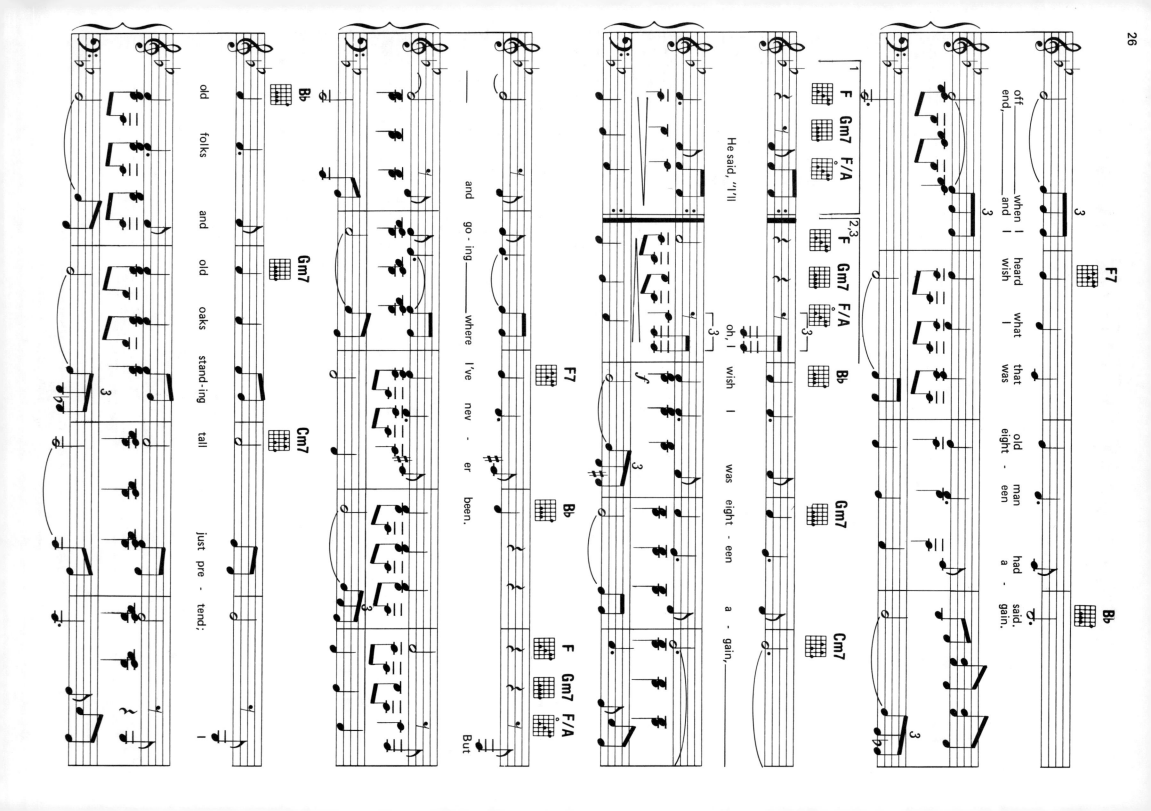

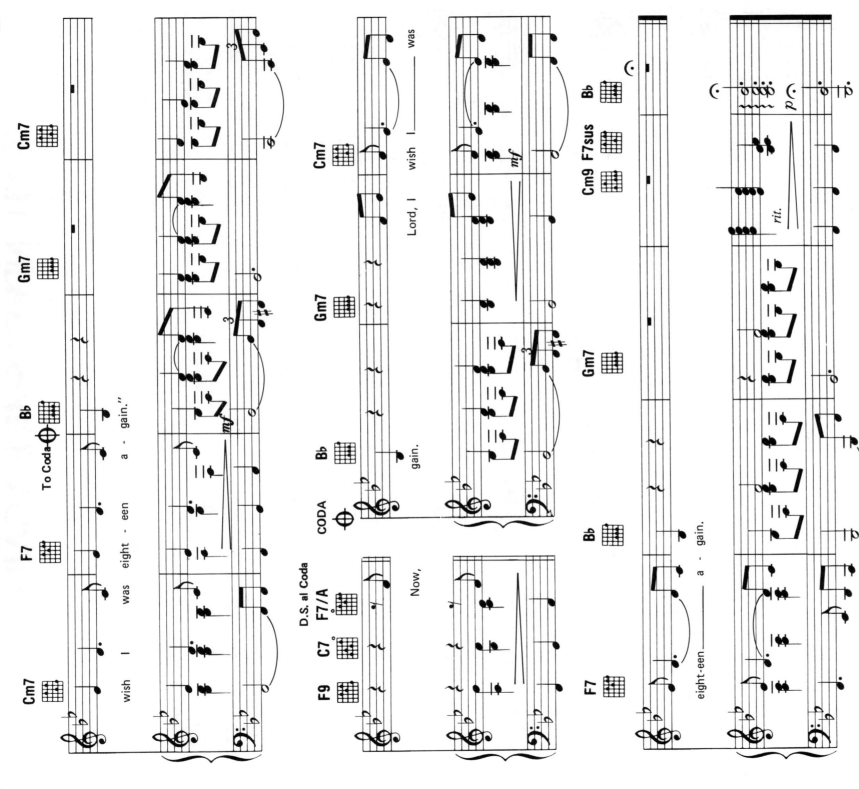

3. (Now,) time turns the pages
   And, oh, life goes so fast;
   The years turn the black hair all gray.
   I talk to some young folks;
   Hey, they don't understand
   The words this old man's got to say.

   (Third ending)

I'LL NEVER SMILE AGAIN

Words and Music by
RUTH LOWE

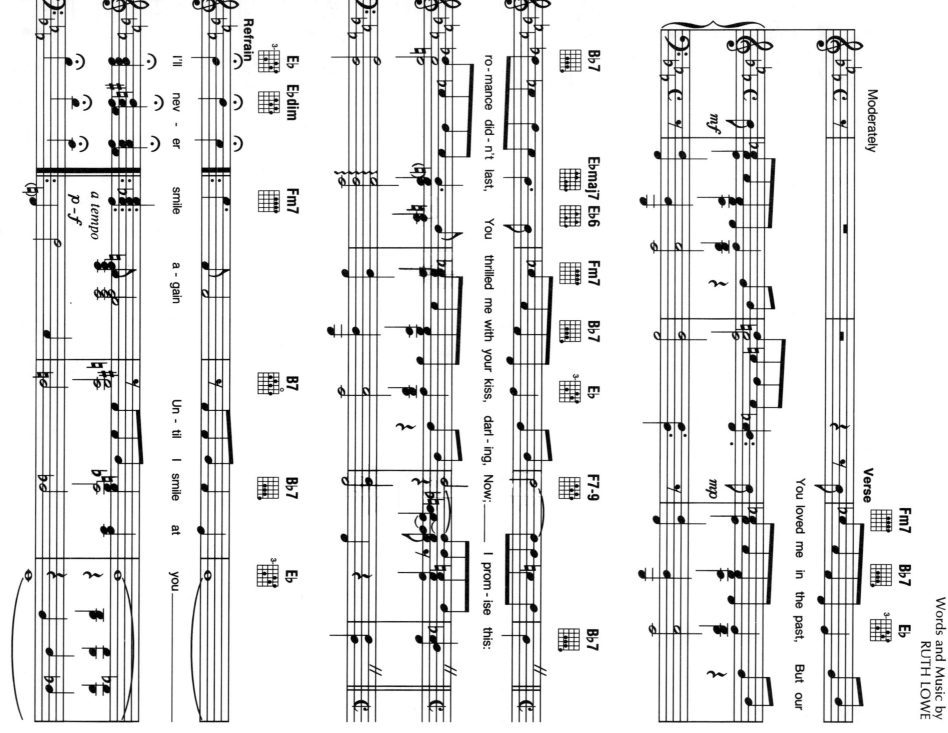

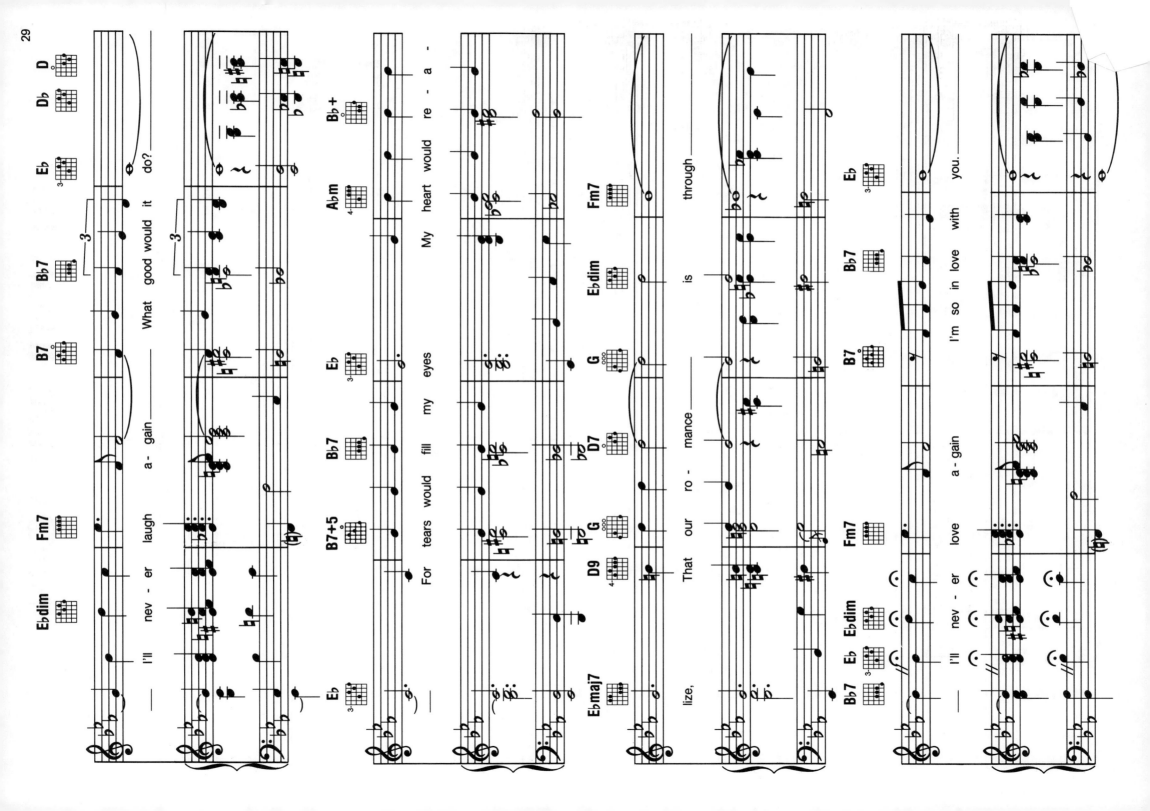

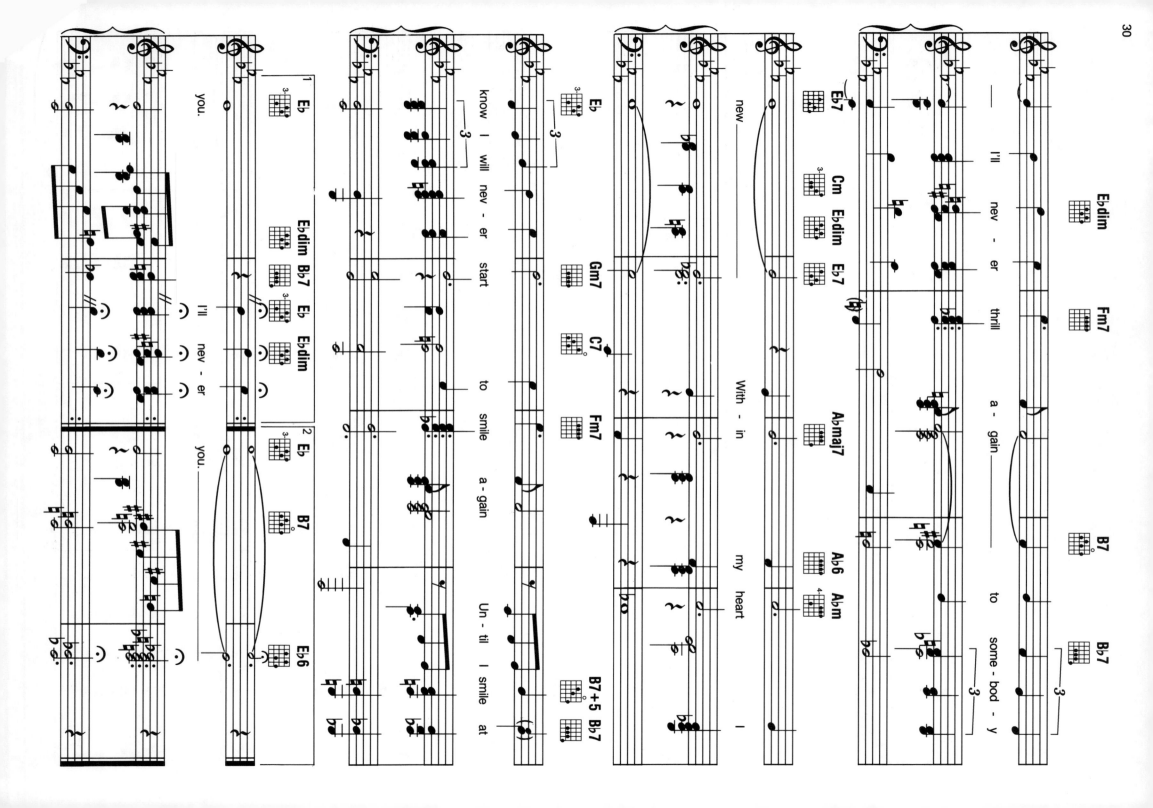

I'M EASY

Words and Music by KEITH CARRADINE

With feeling

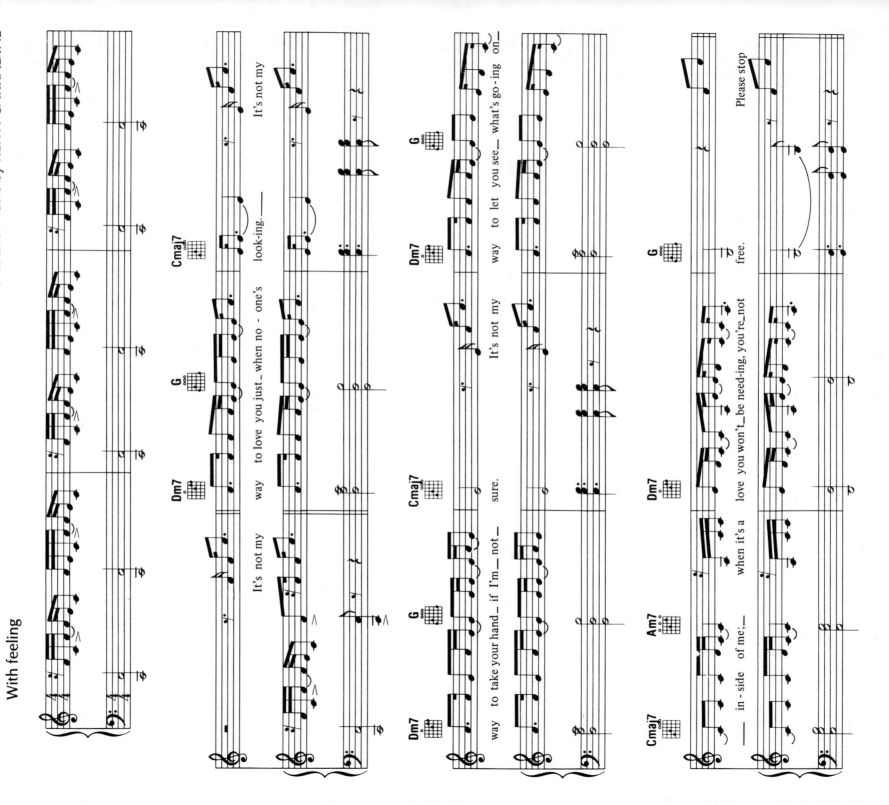

MCA MUSIC

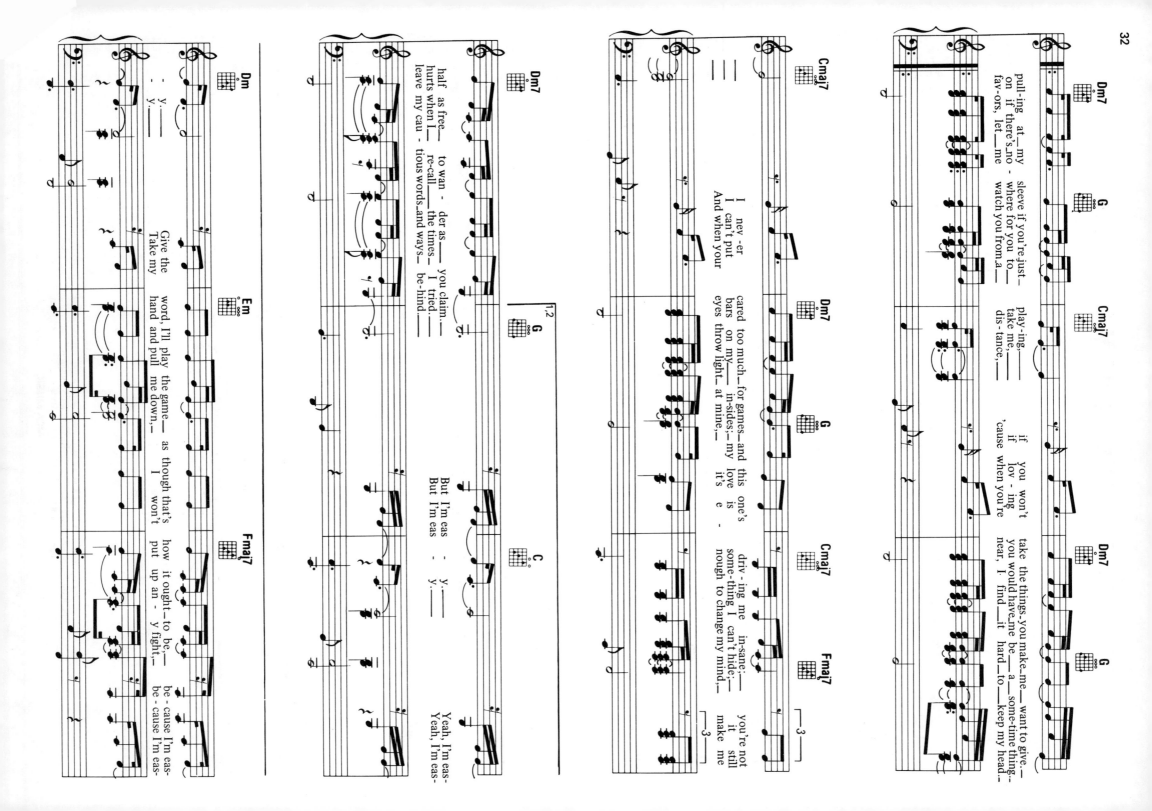

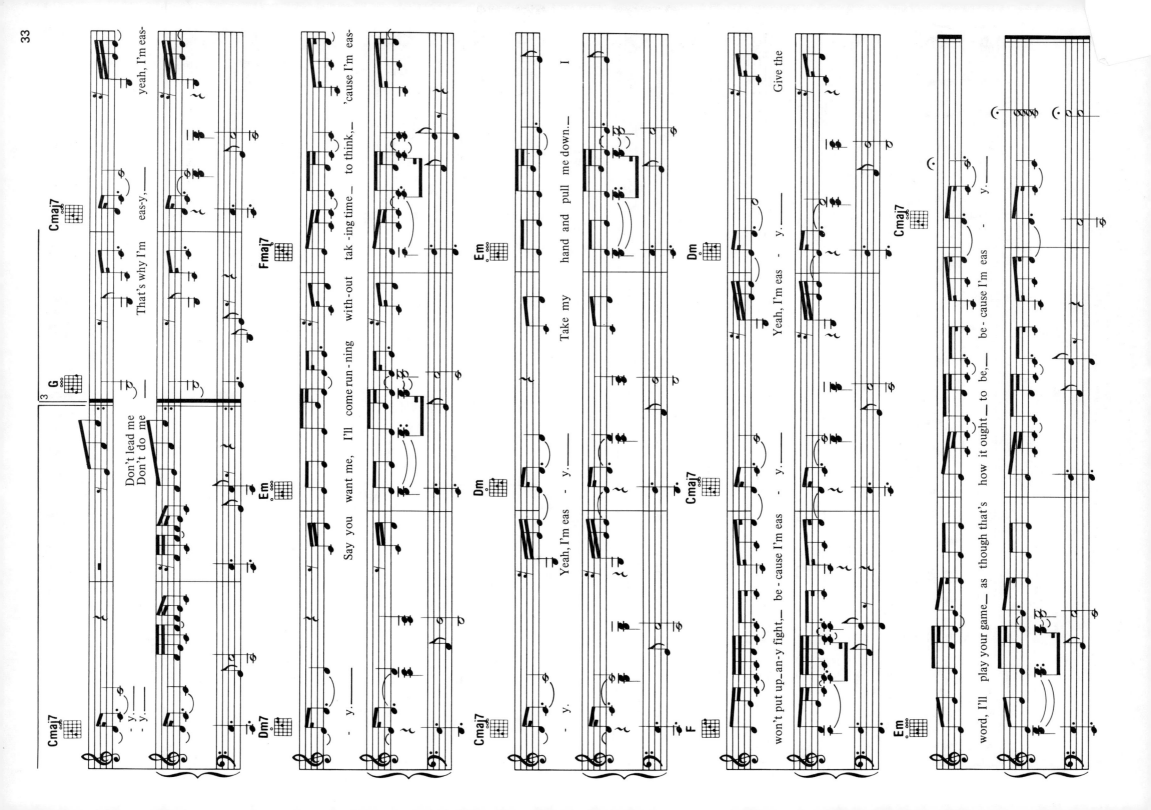

IF EVER I WOULD LEAVE YOU

(From "CAMELOT")

Words by Alan Jay Lerner
Music by Frederick Loewe

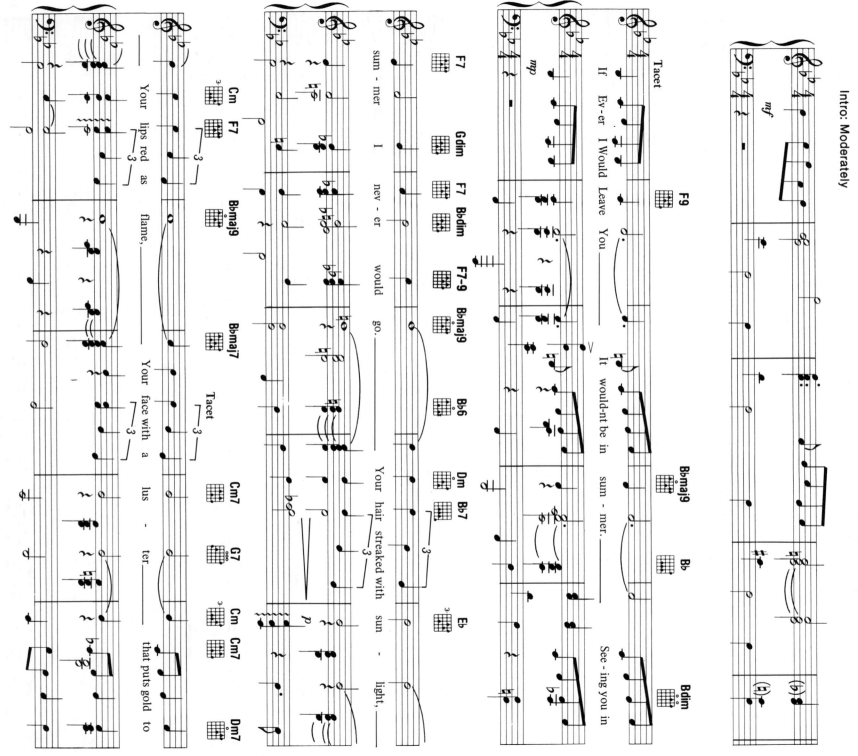

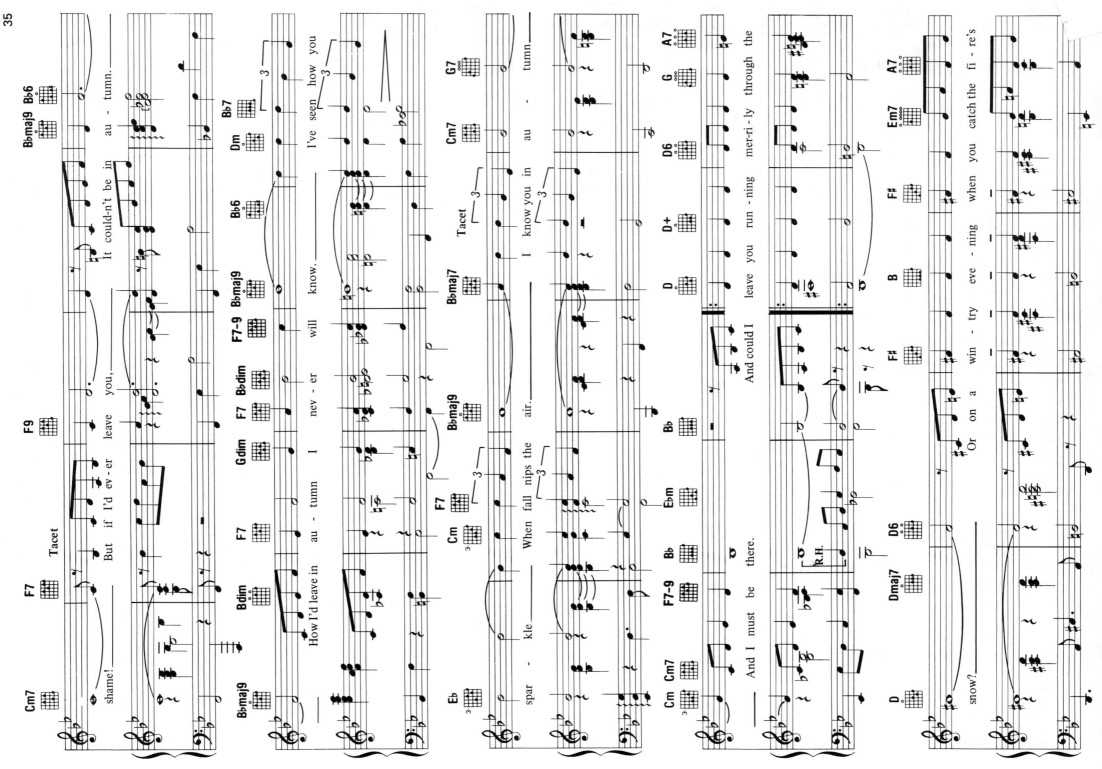

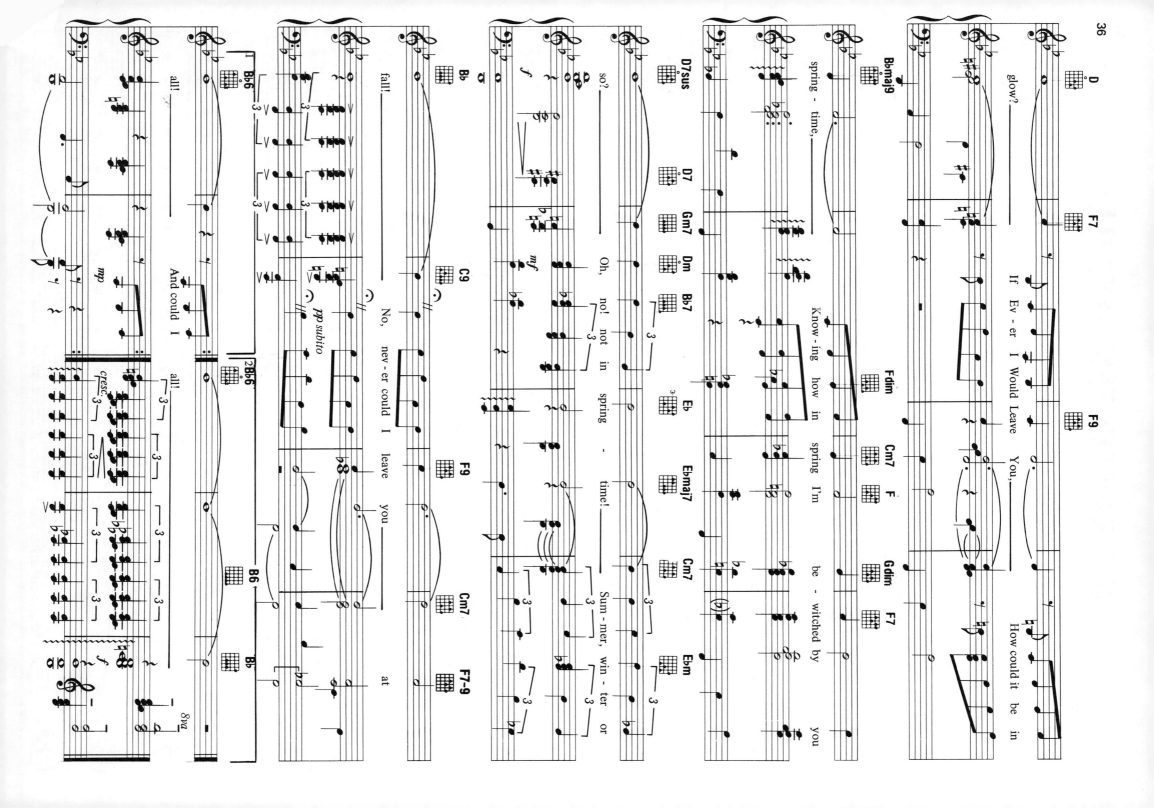

IF I RULED THE WORLD

Words by LESLIE BRICUSSE
Music by CYRIL ORNADEL

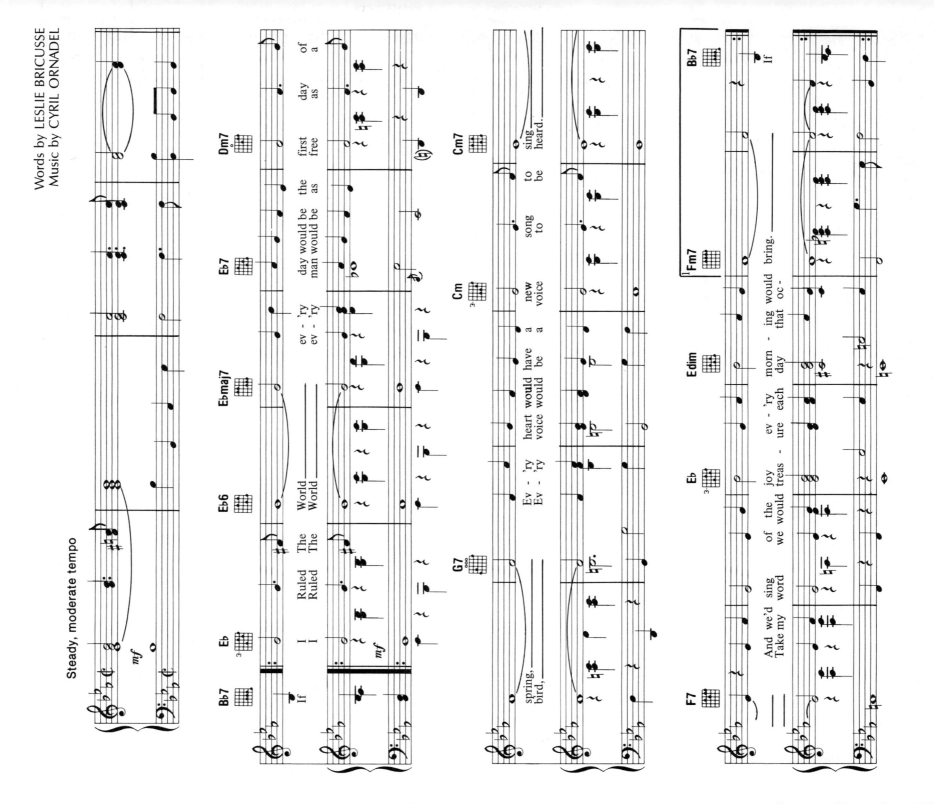

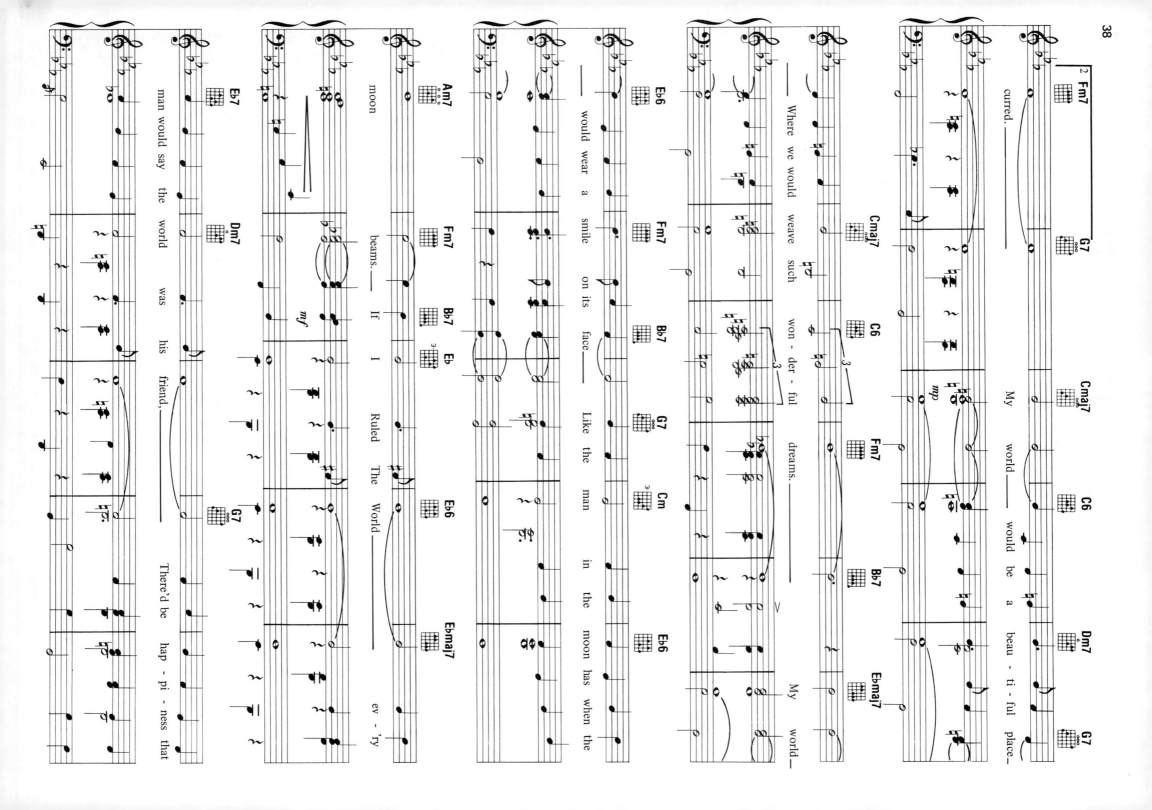

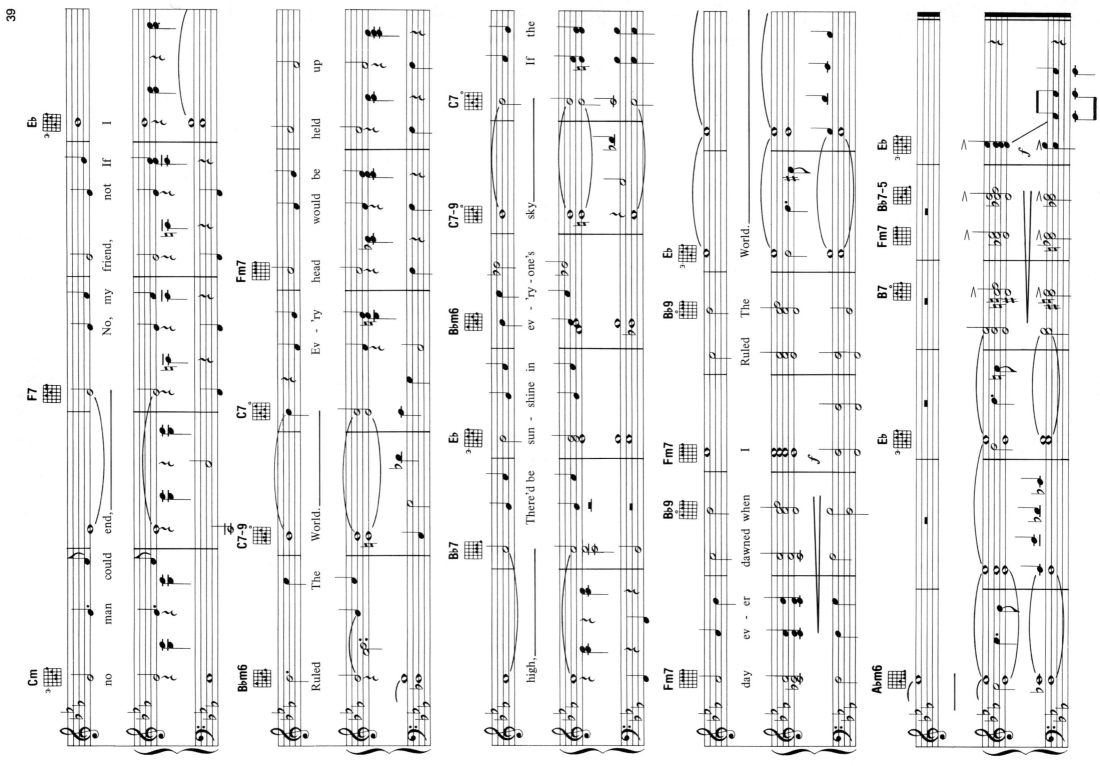

IF I LOVED YOU

(From "CAROUSEL")

Words by OSCAR HAMMERSTEIN II
Music by RICHARD RODGERS

Moderately

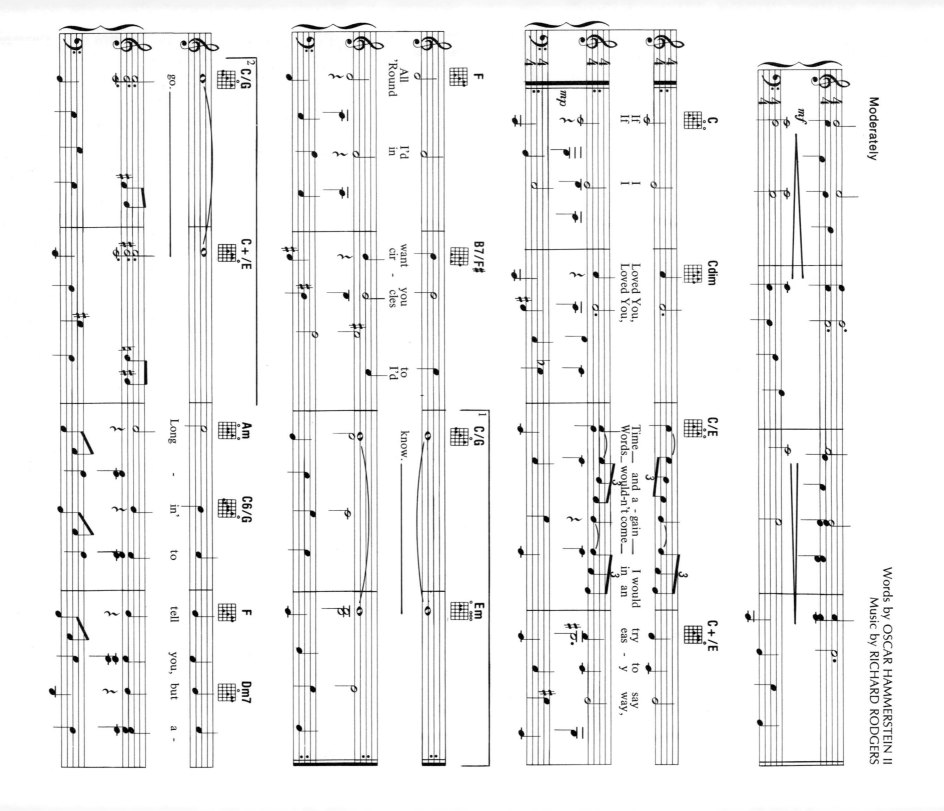

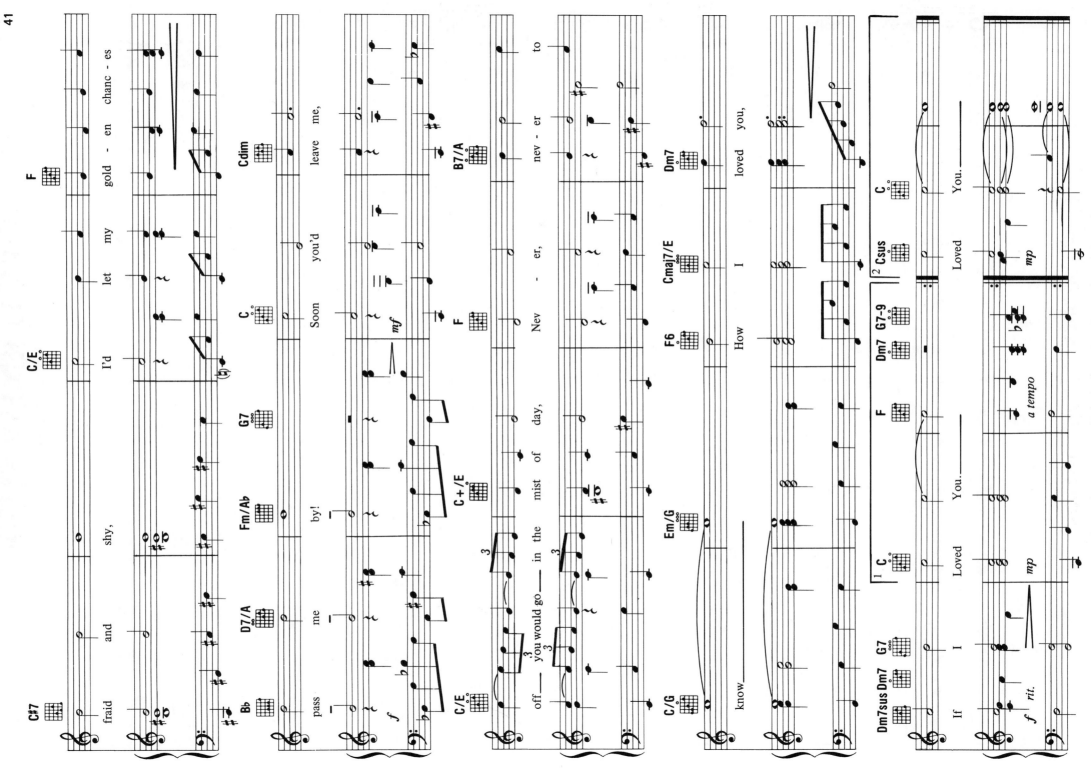

IF YOU KNEW SUSIE
(LIKE I KNOW SUSIE)

Words and Music by B.G. DESYLVA
and JOSEPH MEYER

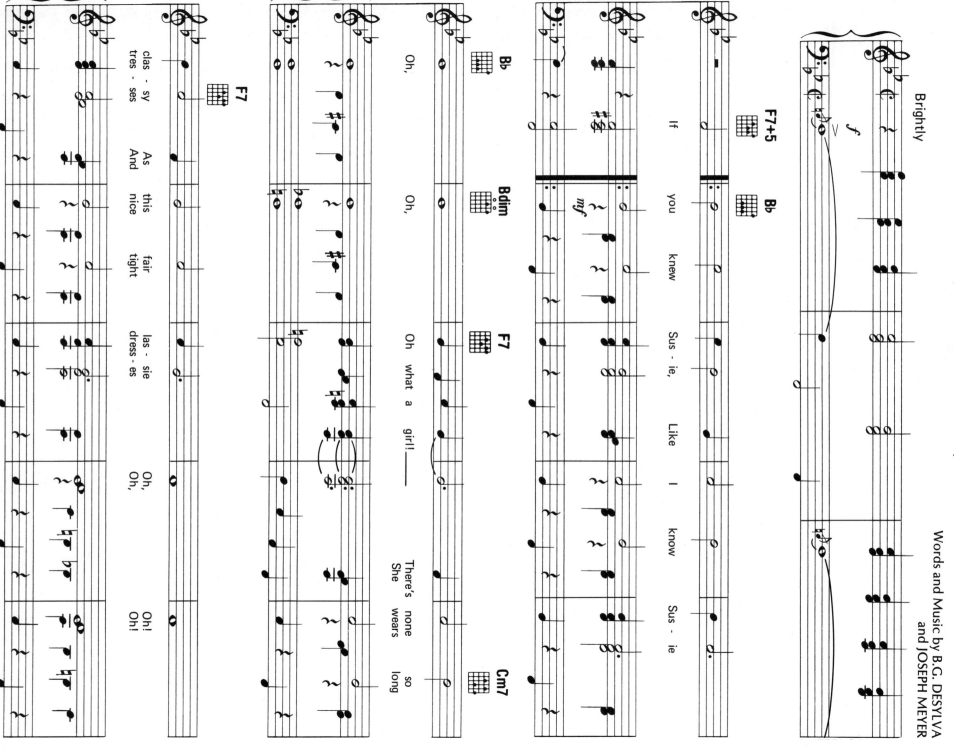

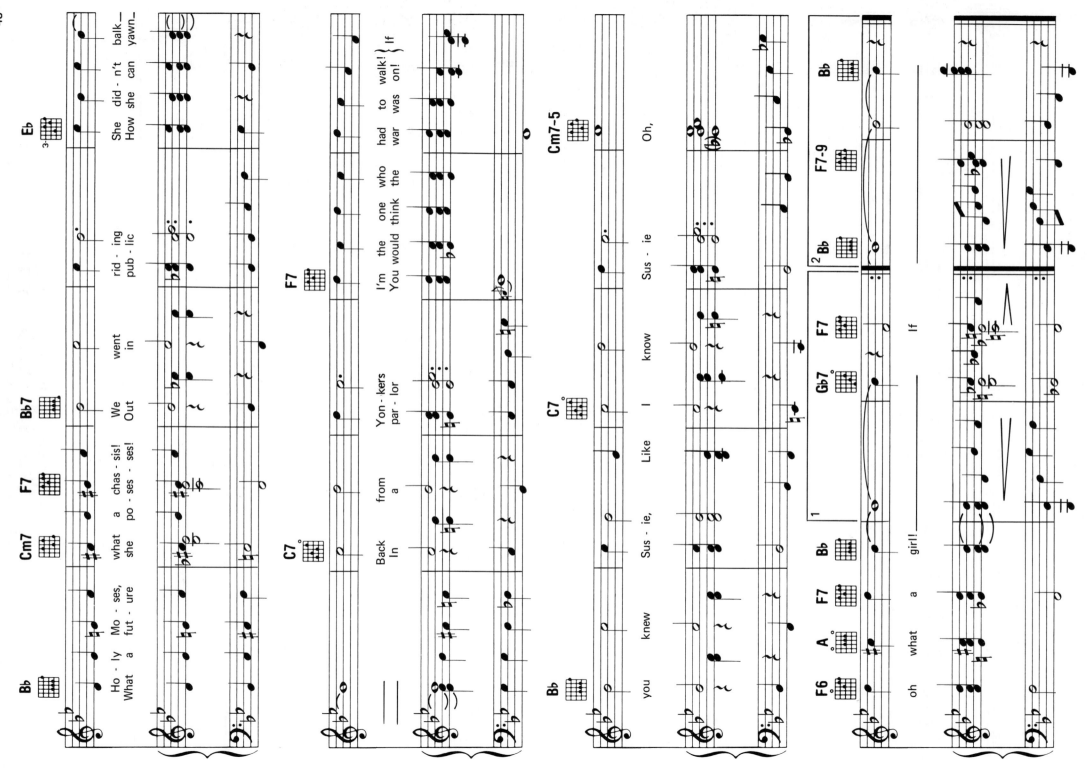

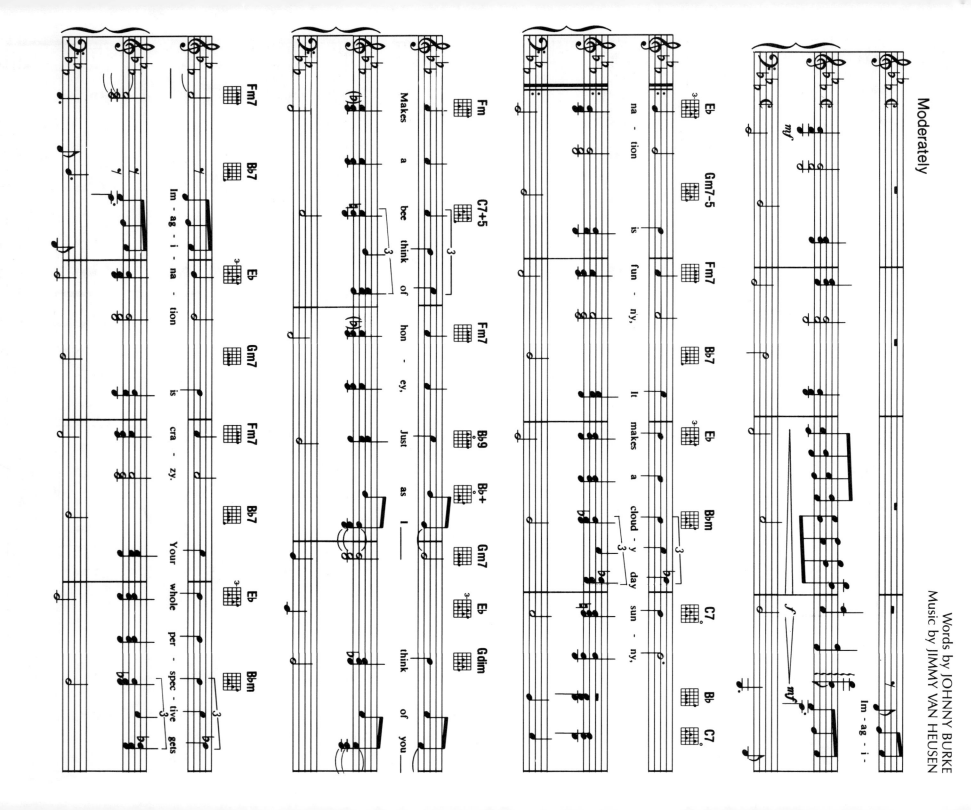

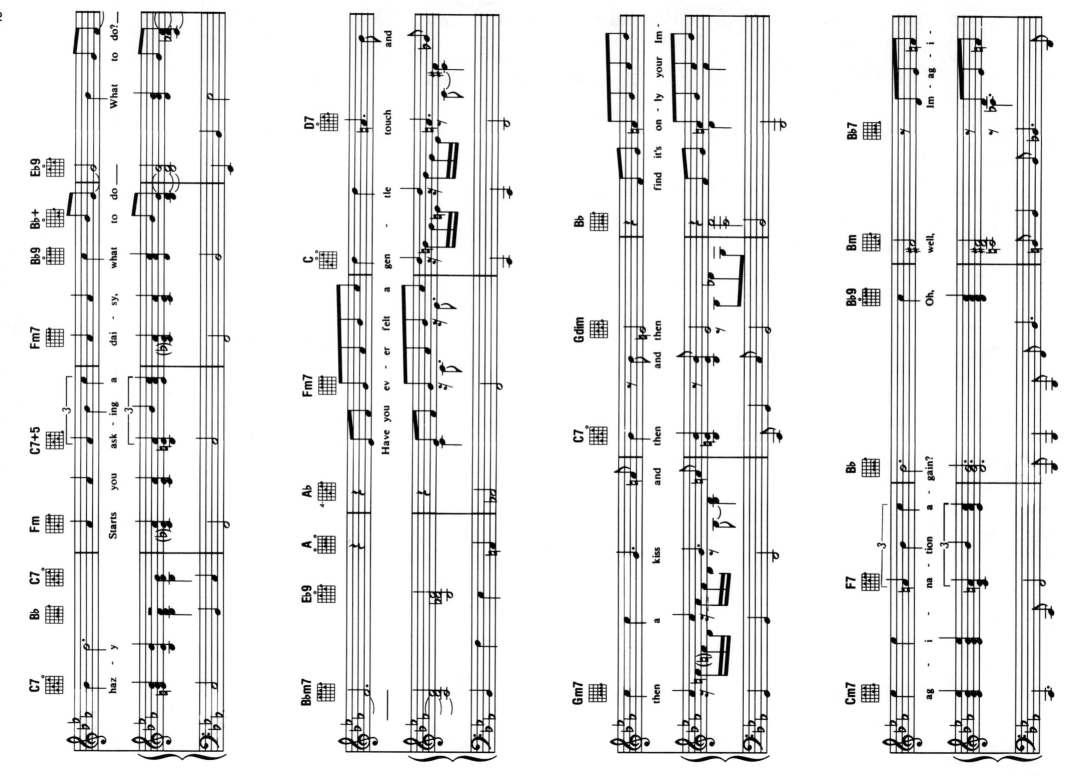

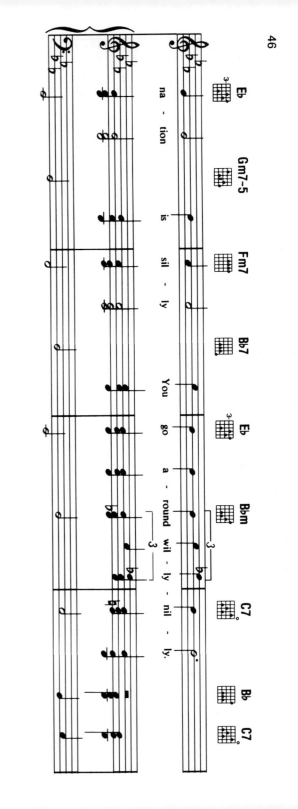

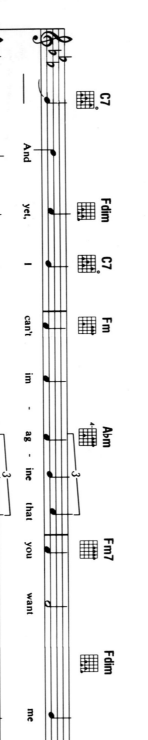

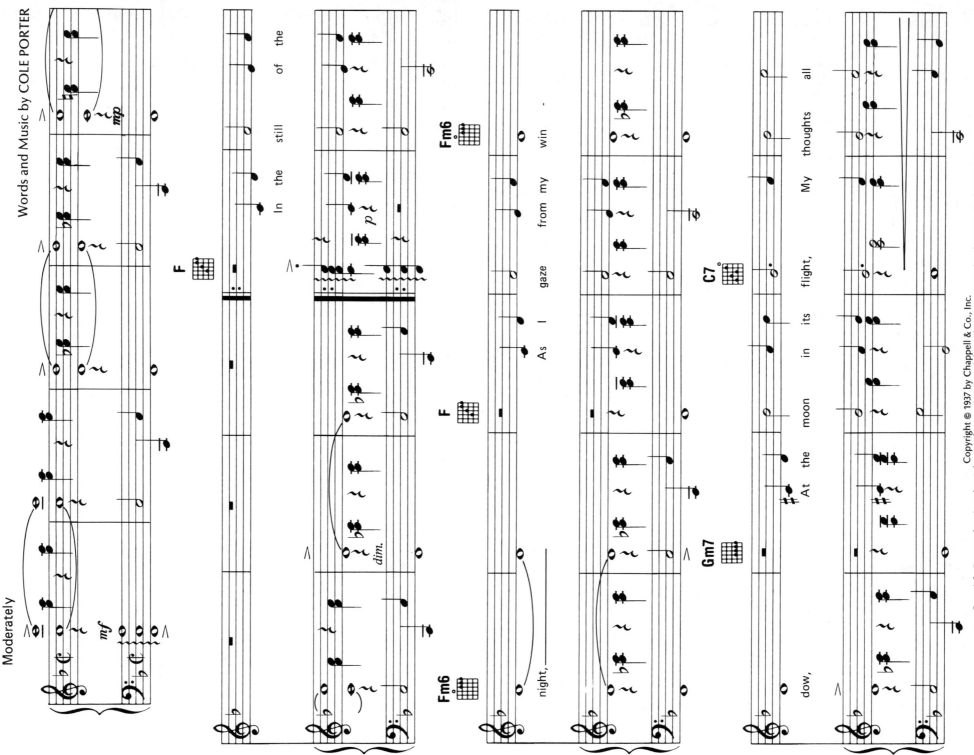

IN THE STILL OF THE NIGHT
(From "ROSALIE")

Words and Music by COLE PORTER

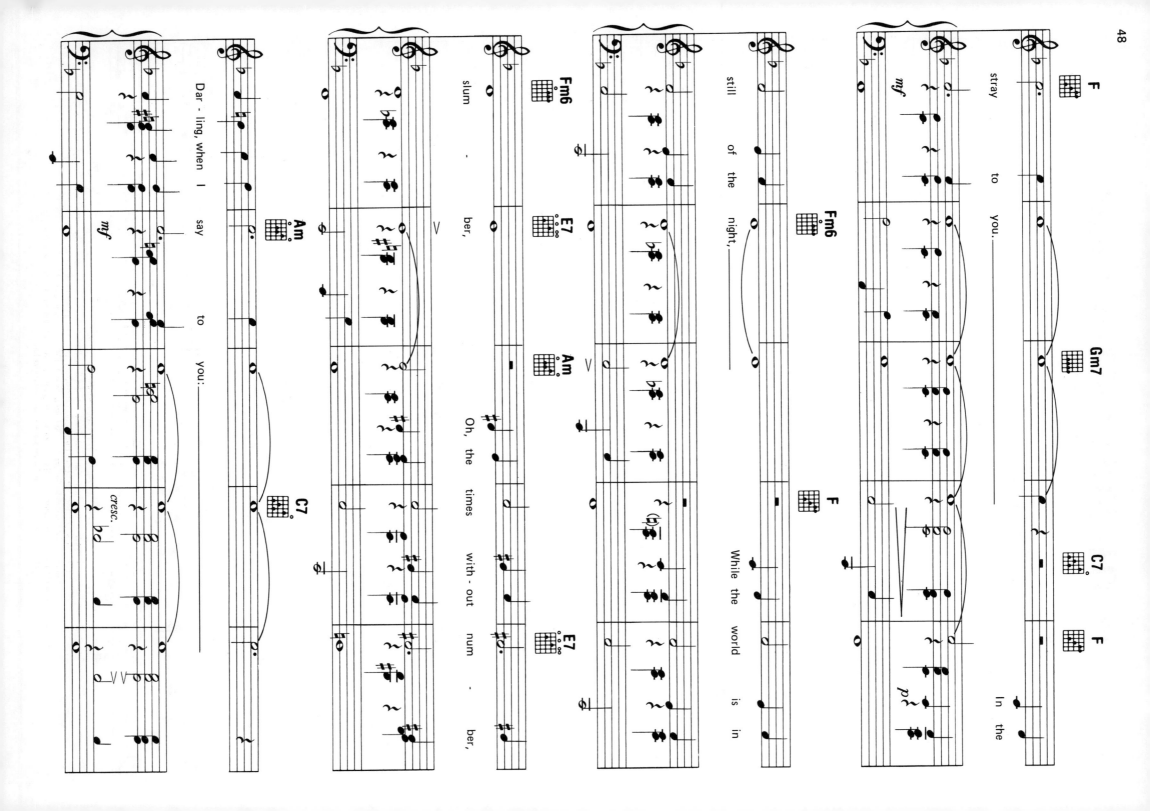

F
Bb
Gm7
C7
"Do you love me
As
F
I love you?
Are
F+
Bb
C7
you my life - to - be,
My
Cm6
Am7
D7
dream come true?"
Or
f
sf
mf

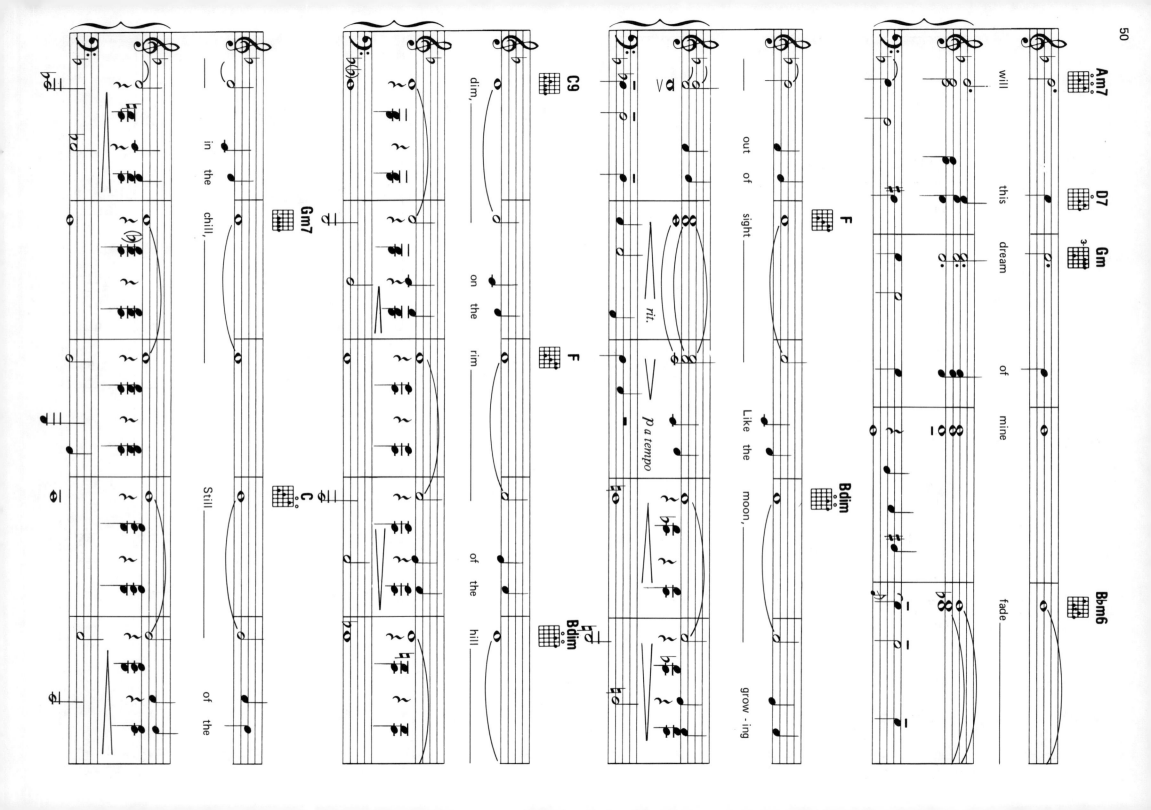

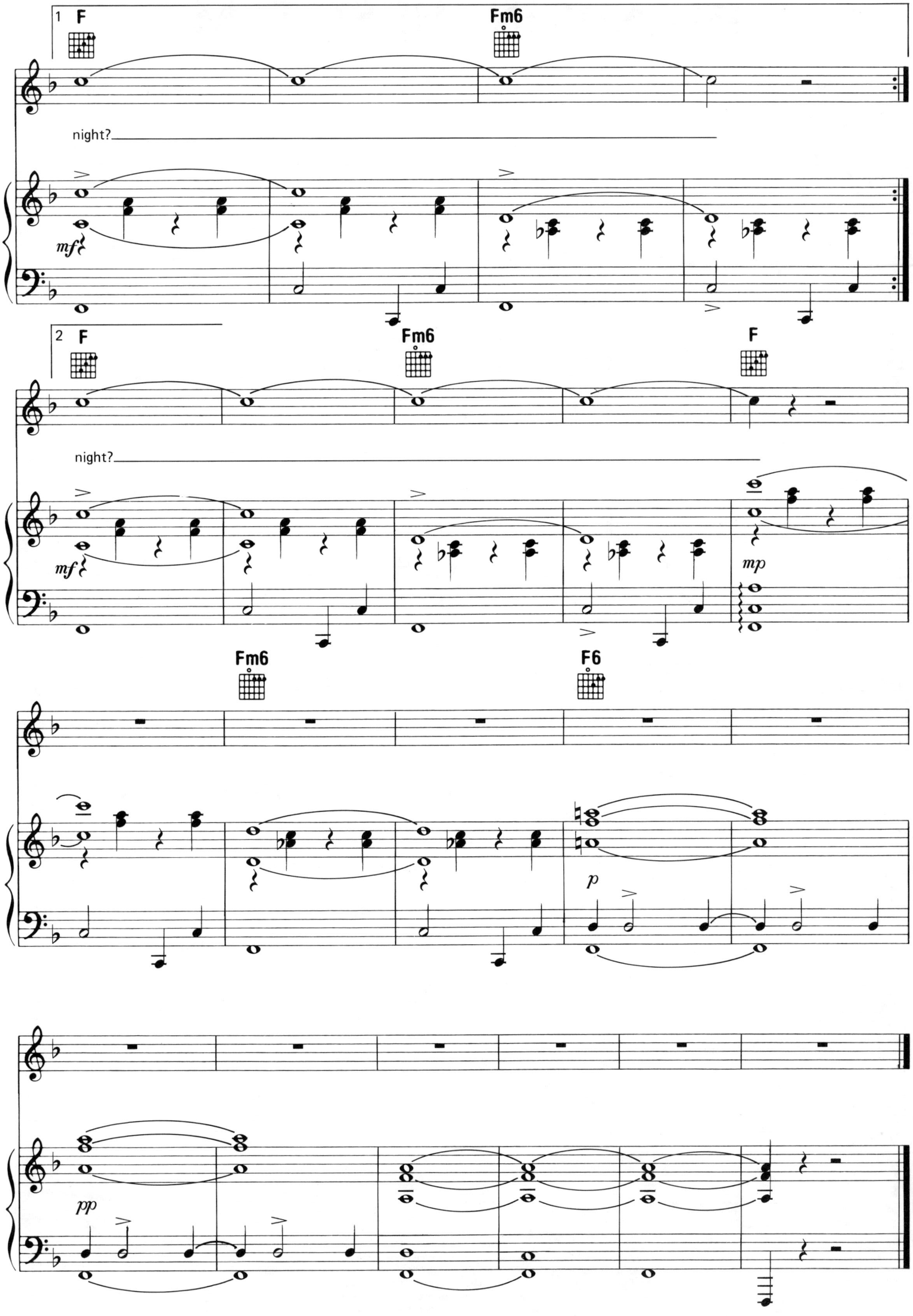
1
F
Fm6
night?
mf
2
F
Fm6
F
night?
mf
mp
Fm6
F6
p
pp

ISLANDS IN THE STREAM

Moderately Slow Rock

Words and Music by BARRY GIBB,
MAURICE GIBB and ROBIN GIBB

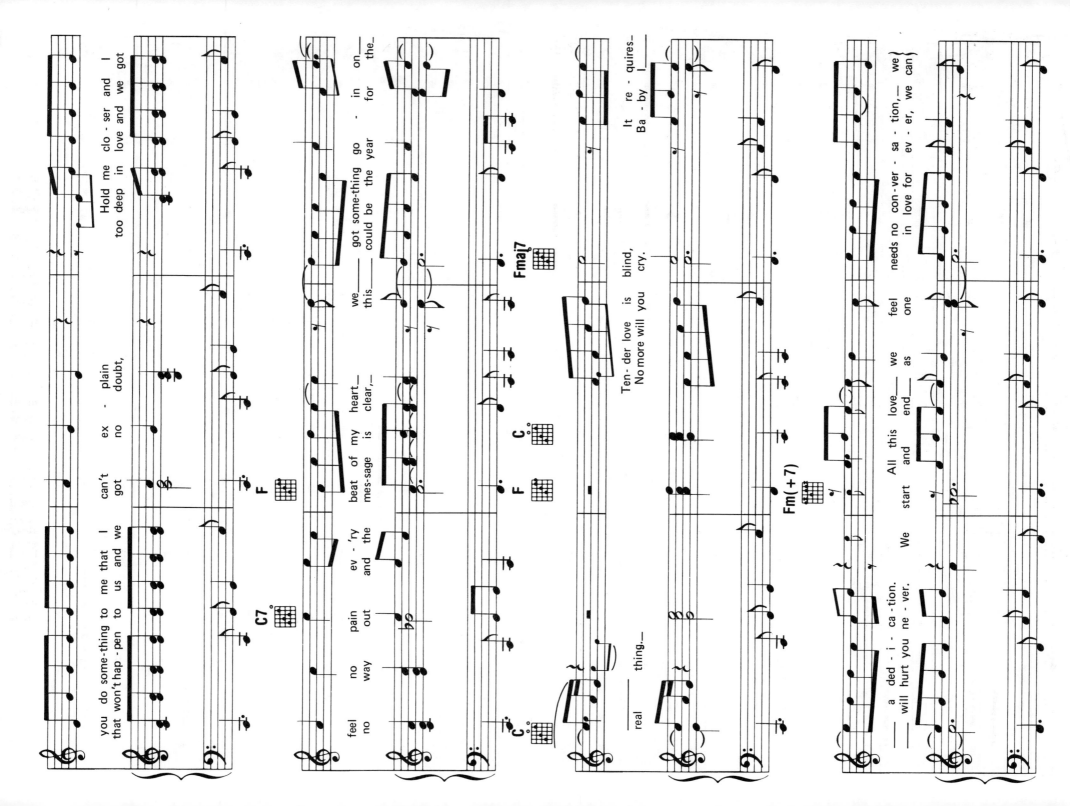

IT'S A PITY TO SAY "GOODNIGHT"

Words and Music by
BILLY REID

Moderately with a relaxed beat

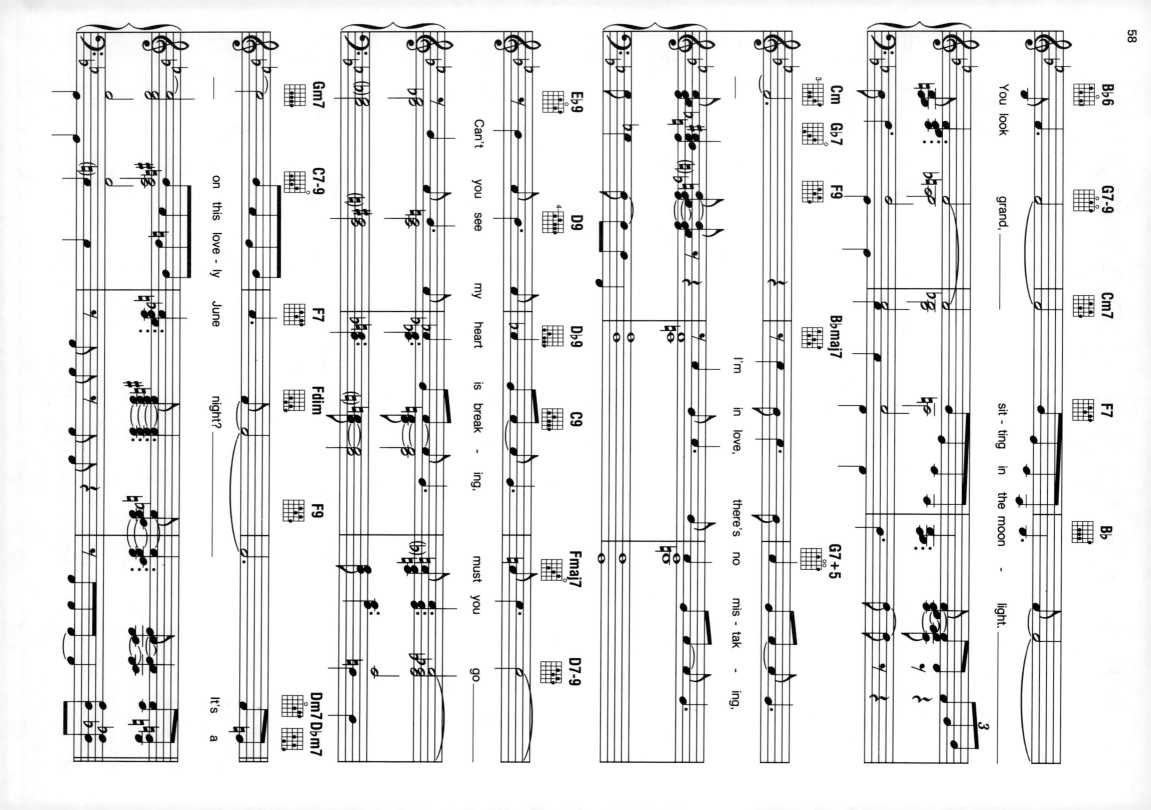

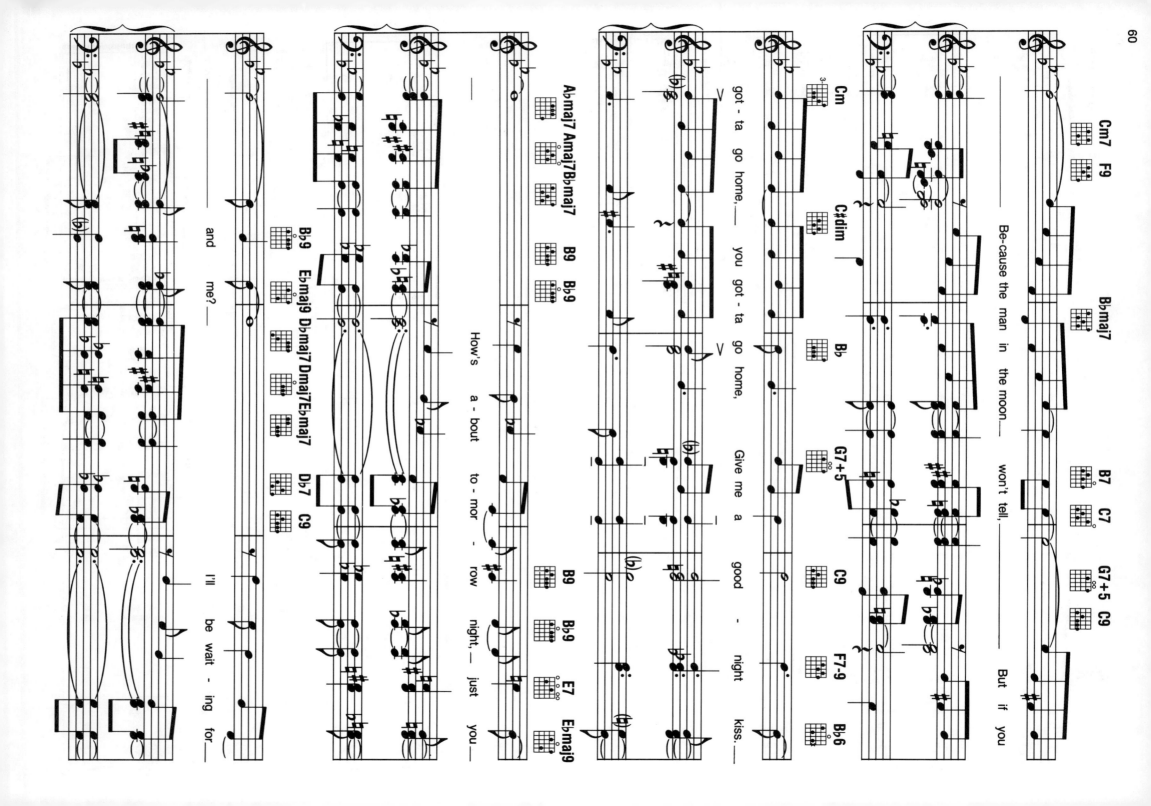

Db9 C9 C9+5 F9 Cm7 F7 Fdim F9 Dm7 Dbm7
— you, dar - ling, Un - der - neath the ap - ple tree, — It's a
Cm7 Gb7 F9 Cm7 F9 Bbmaj7 B7 C7
pi - ty to say — "good - night," — Be-cause I want you to hold — me tight, —
G7+5 C7 Cm C#dim Bb G7+5
— But if you got - ta go home, — you got - ta go home, Give me a
C9 F7-9 Bb6 Ab7 Amaj7 Bbmaj7 Dm7 Dbmaj7 Cm7 C#m7 Bbmaj7
good - night kiss. — It's a —

IT AIN'T NECESSARILY SO

Words by IRA GERSHWIN
Music by GEORGE GERSHWIN

Sporting Life

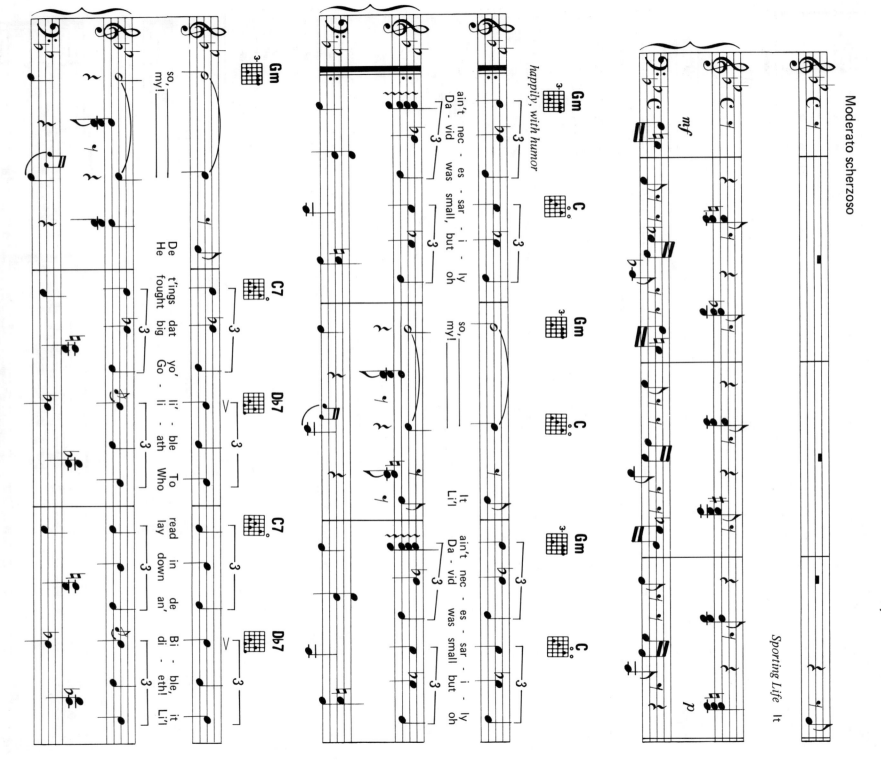

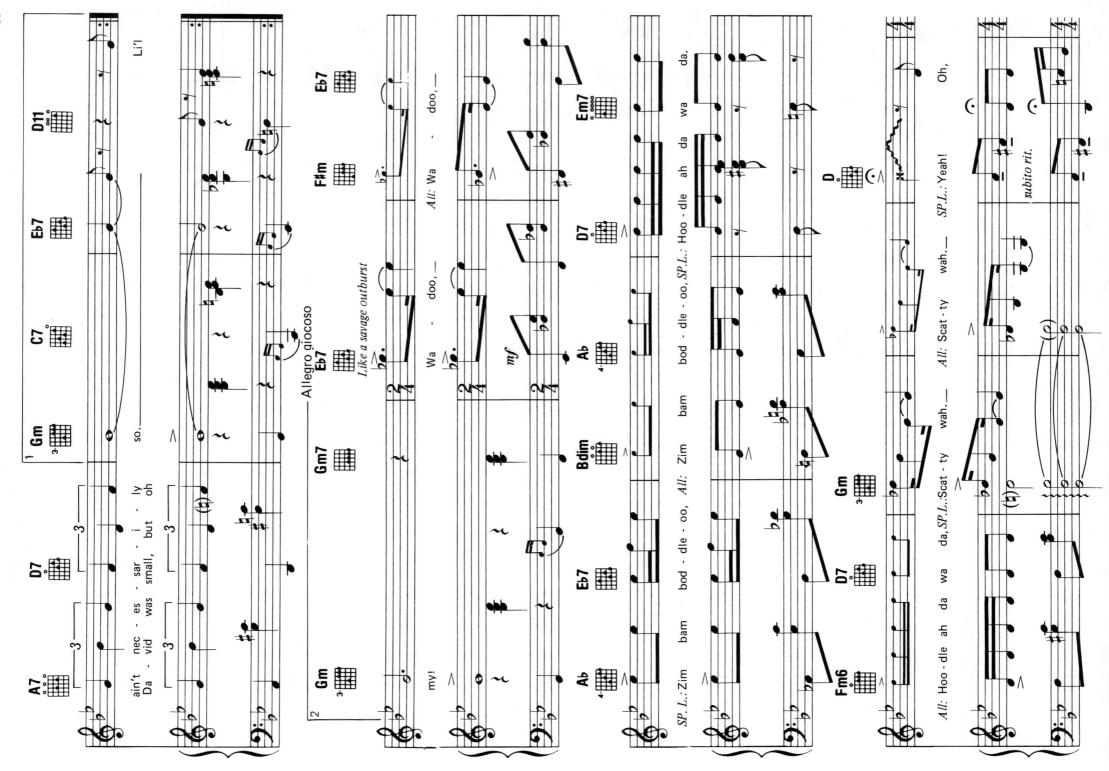

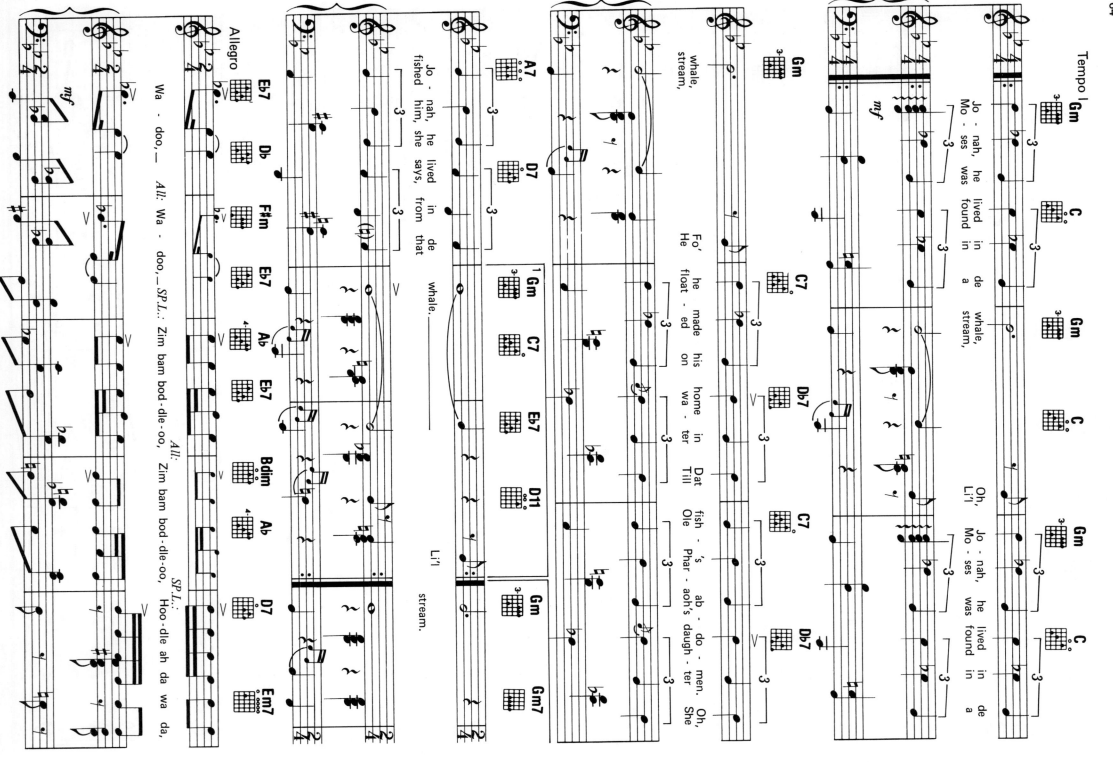

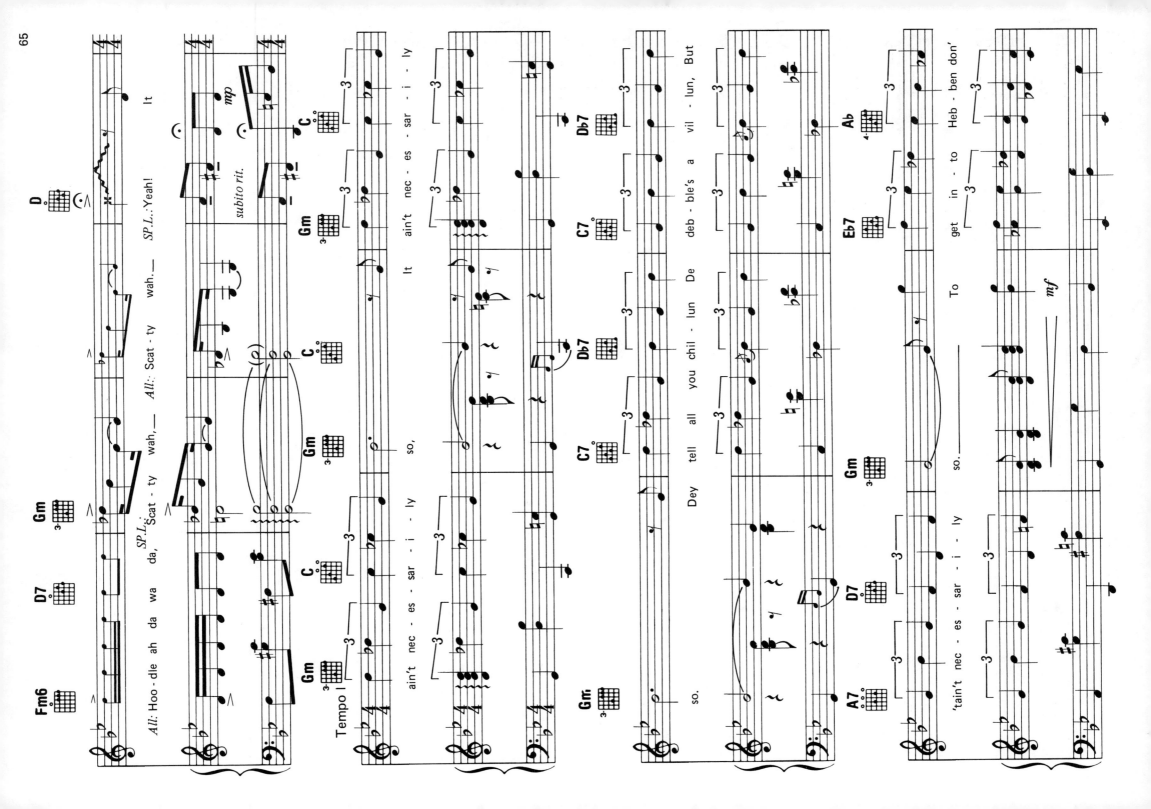

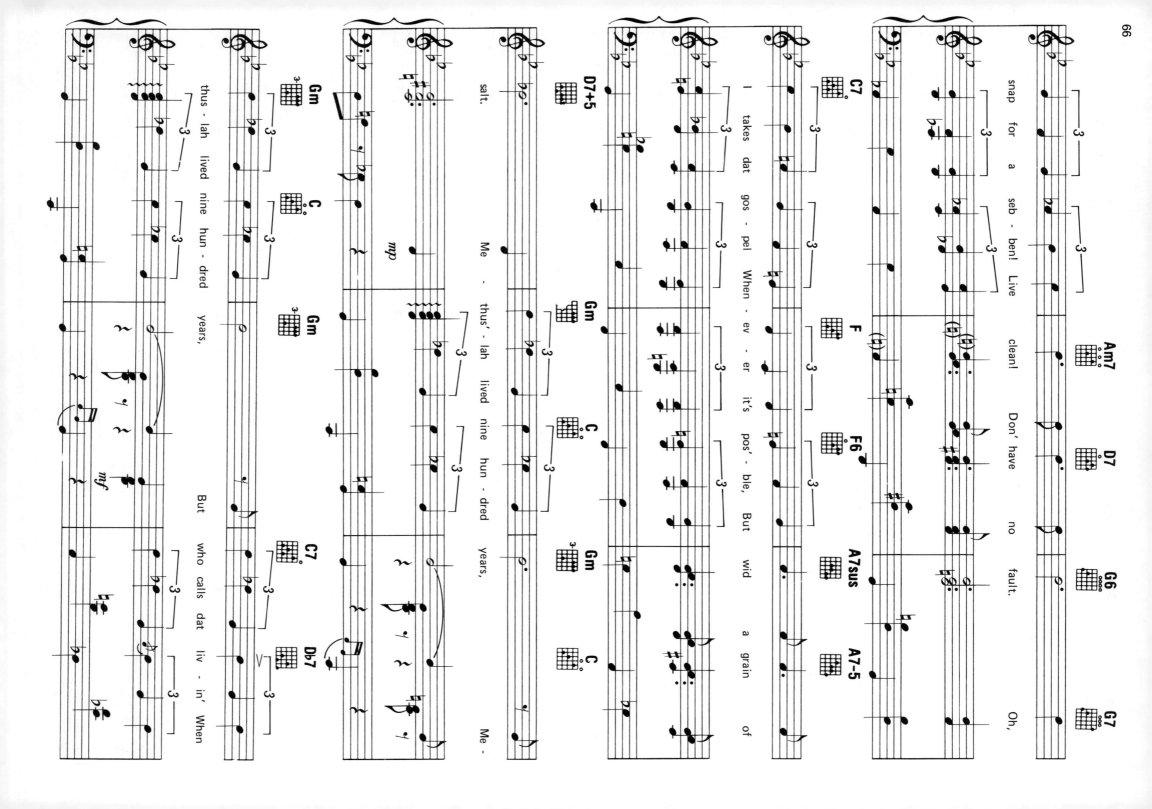

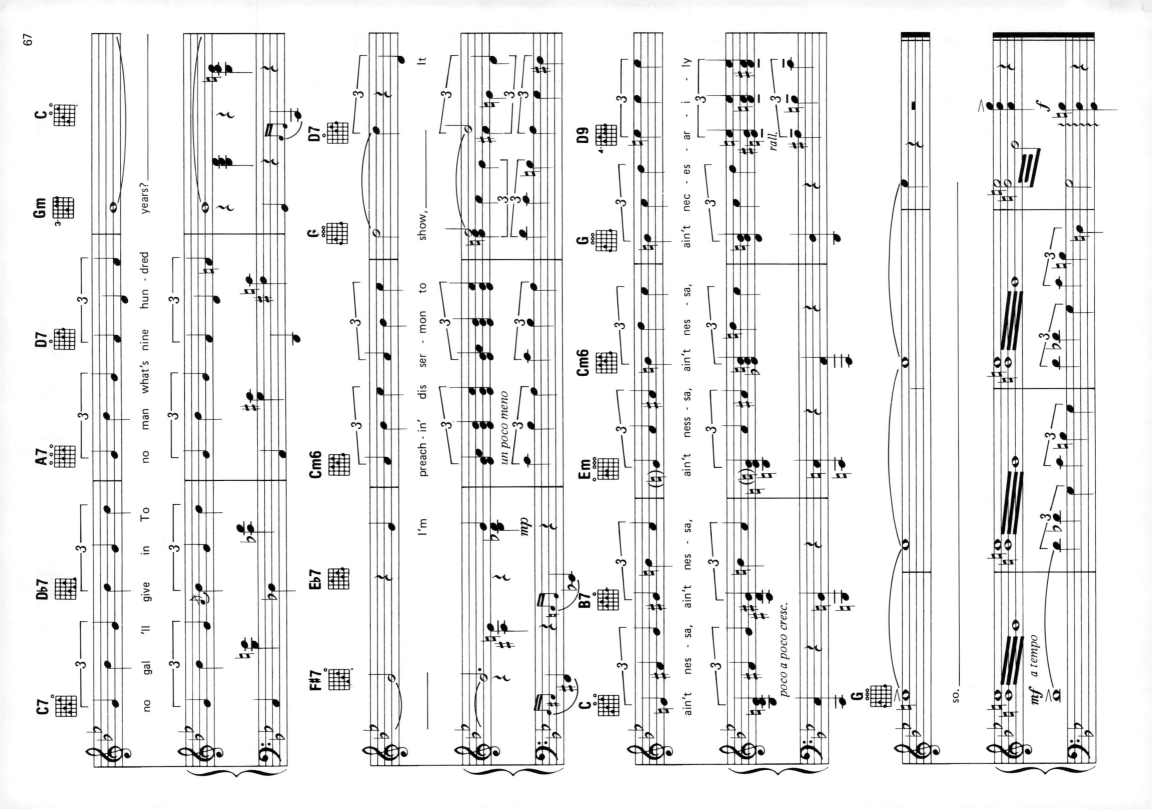

IT MIGHT AS WELL BE SPRING

(From "STATE FAIR")

Words by OSCAR HAMMERSTEIN II
Music by RICHARD RODGERS

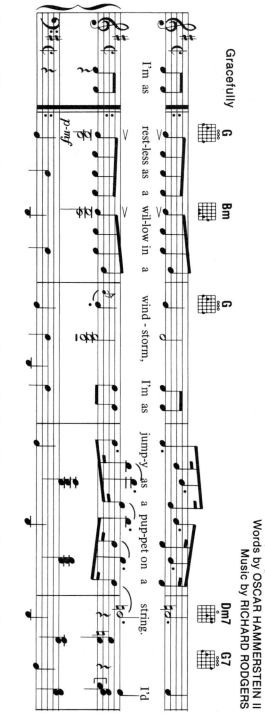

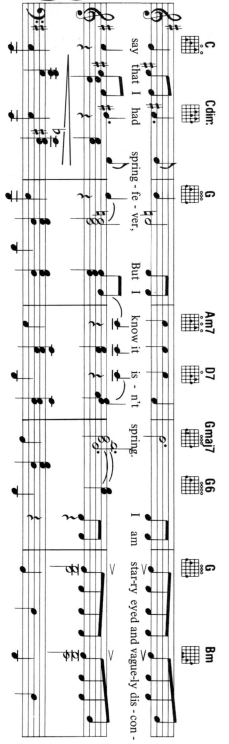

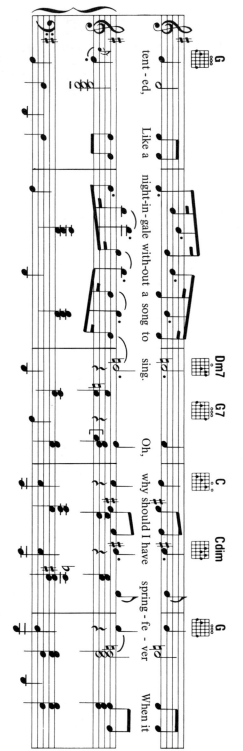

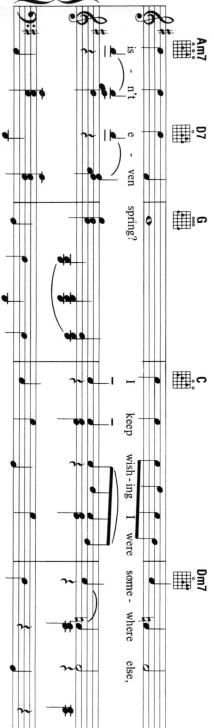

Gdim G7 C F♯m7 B7
Walk-ing down a strange new street, Hear - ing words that I have nev - er heard from a
cresc.
Em A7 G D7 G D7 G Bm G
man
girl
I've yet to meet. I'm as bus-y as a spi-der spin-ning day dreams, I'm as gid-dy as a ba-by on a
mf
p
Dm7 G7 C Cdim G Am D9 B+ B7 E7-9
swing. I have-n't seen a cro-cus or a rose-bud, or a rob-in on the wing, But I
A7 D9 G7 A7 G
feel so gay in a mel-an-cho-ly way That It Might As Well Be Spring. It Might as
D7sus D7 G Em C D7 G C G
Well Be Spring! Spring!
mf
mf

IT'S ALL RIGHT WITH ME

(From "CAN-CAN")

Words and Music by
COLE PORTER

Steadily moving fox trot

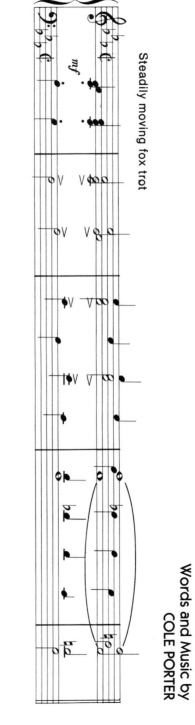
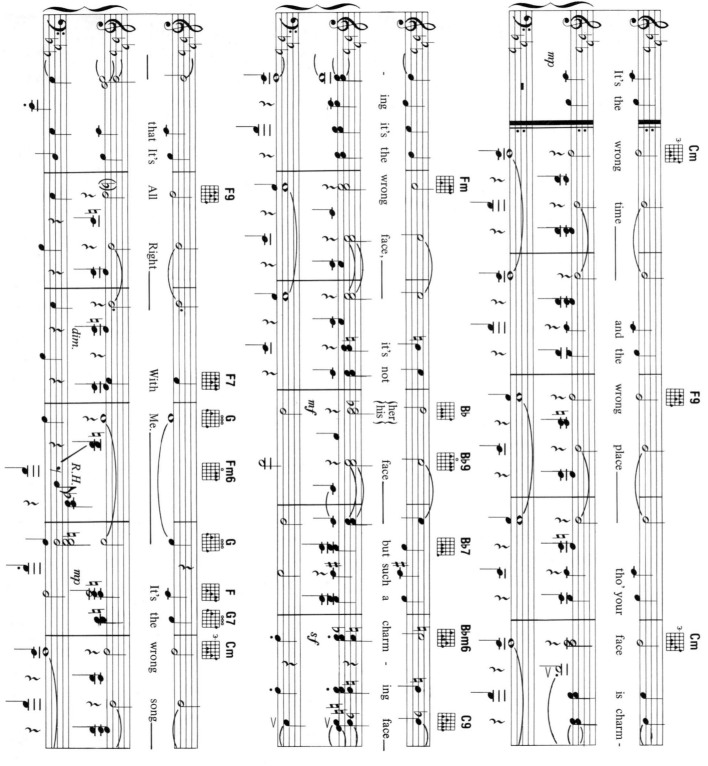

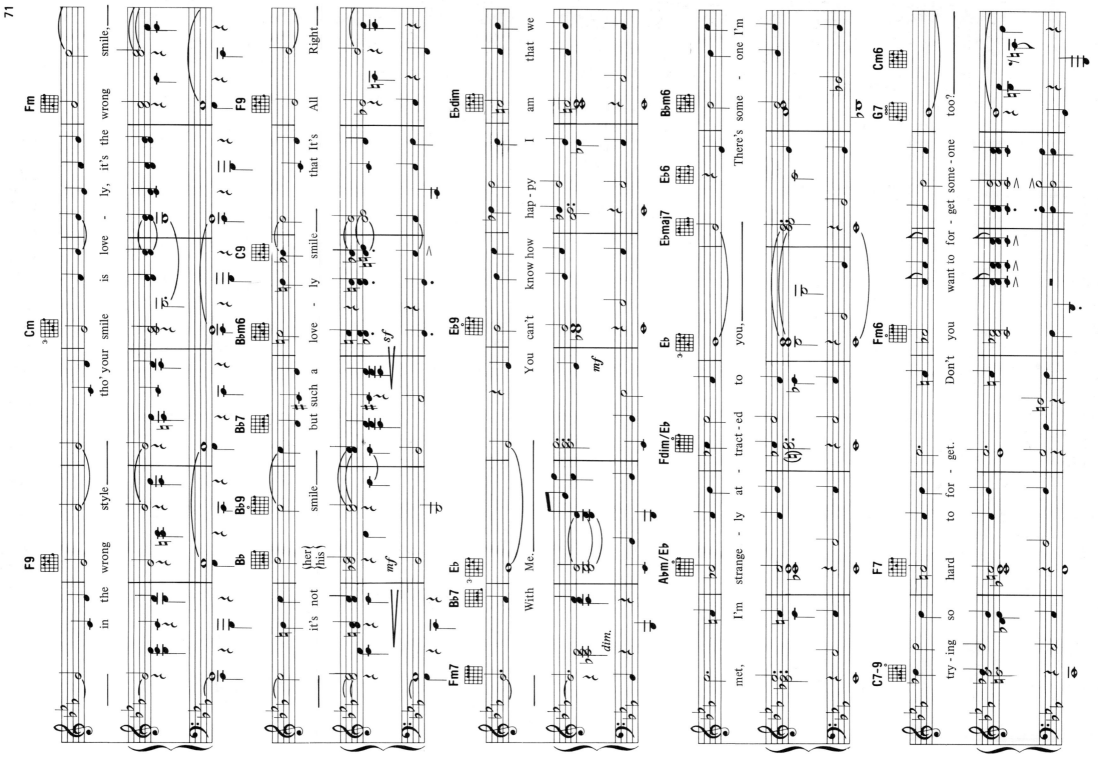

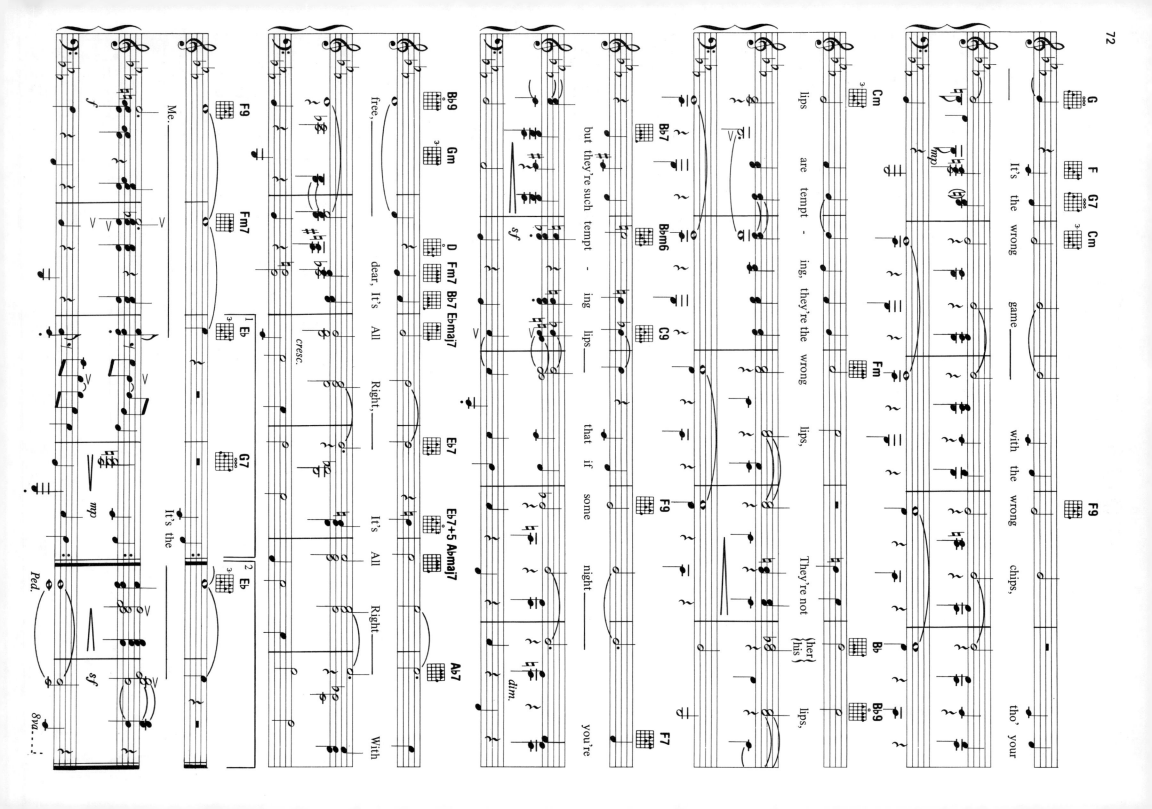

JERSEY BOUNCE

Words by ROBERT B. WRIGHT
Music by BOBBY PLATER,
TINY BRADSHAW and EDWARD JOHNSON

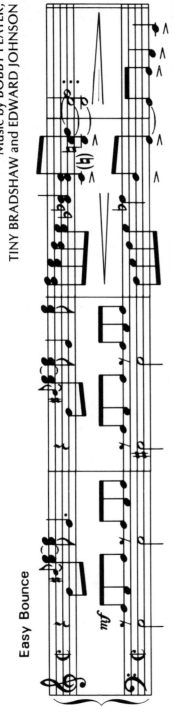

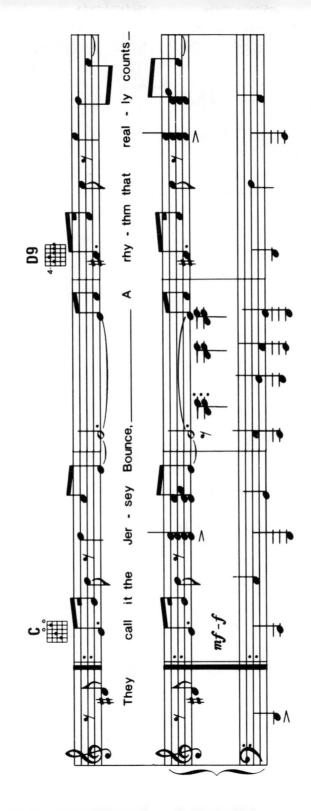

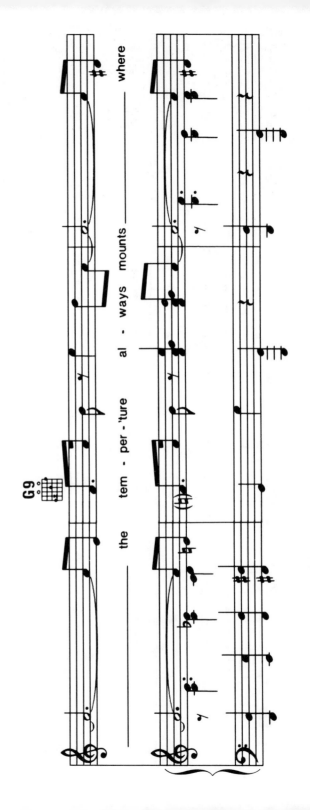

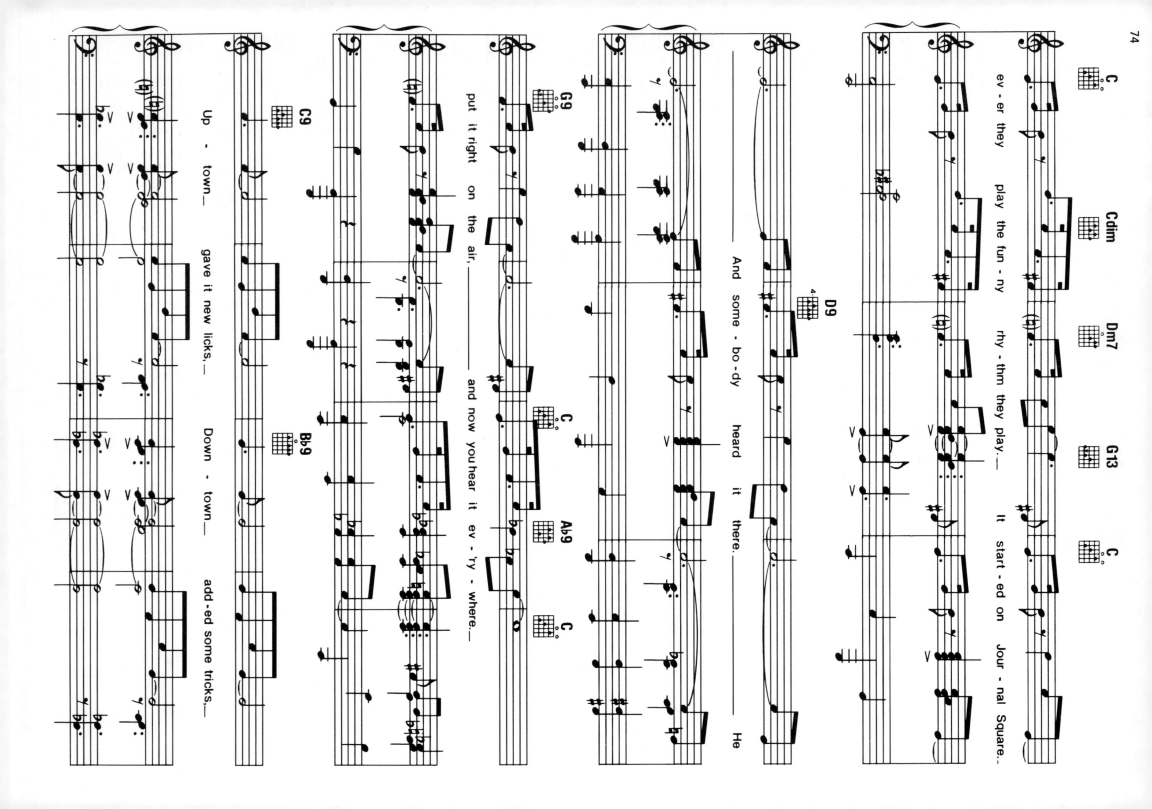

IT'S DE-LOVELY
(From "RED, HOT AND BLUE!")

Words and Music by
COLE PORTER

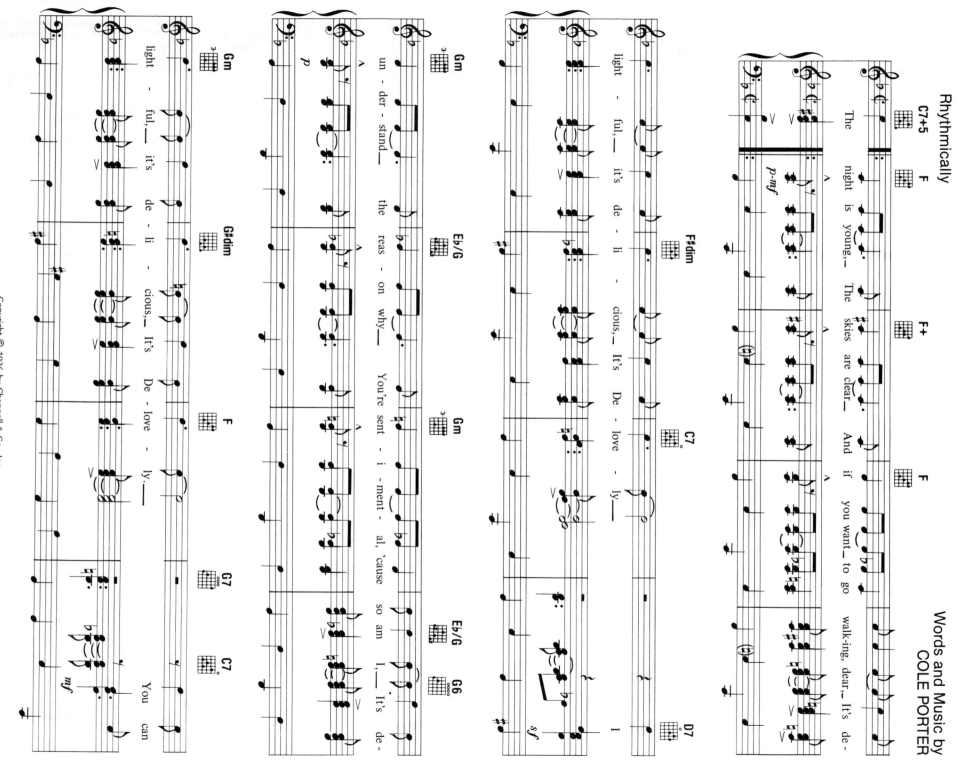

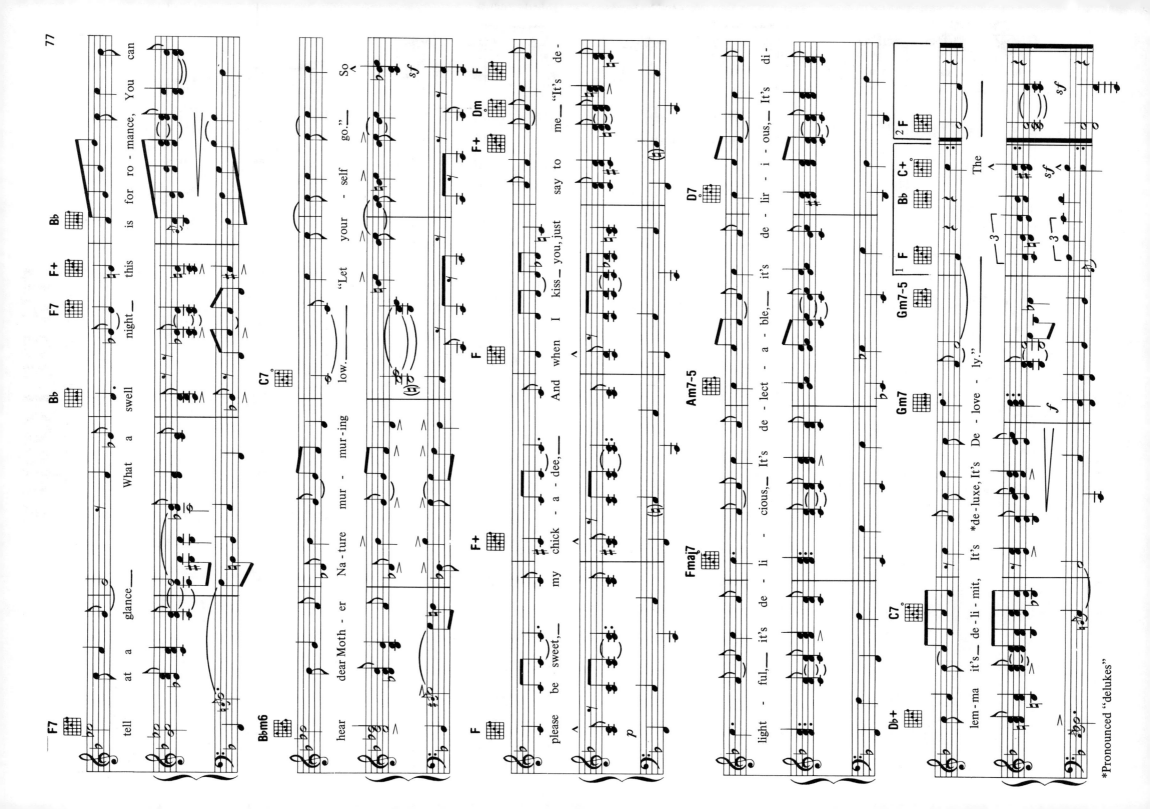

*Pronounced "delukes"

IT'S MAGIC

Words by SAMMY CAHN
Music by JULE STYNE

Slowly

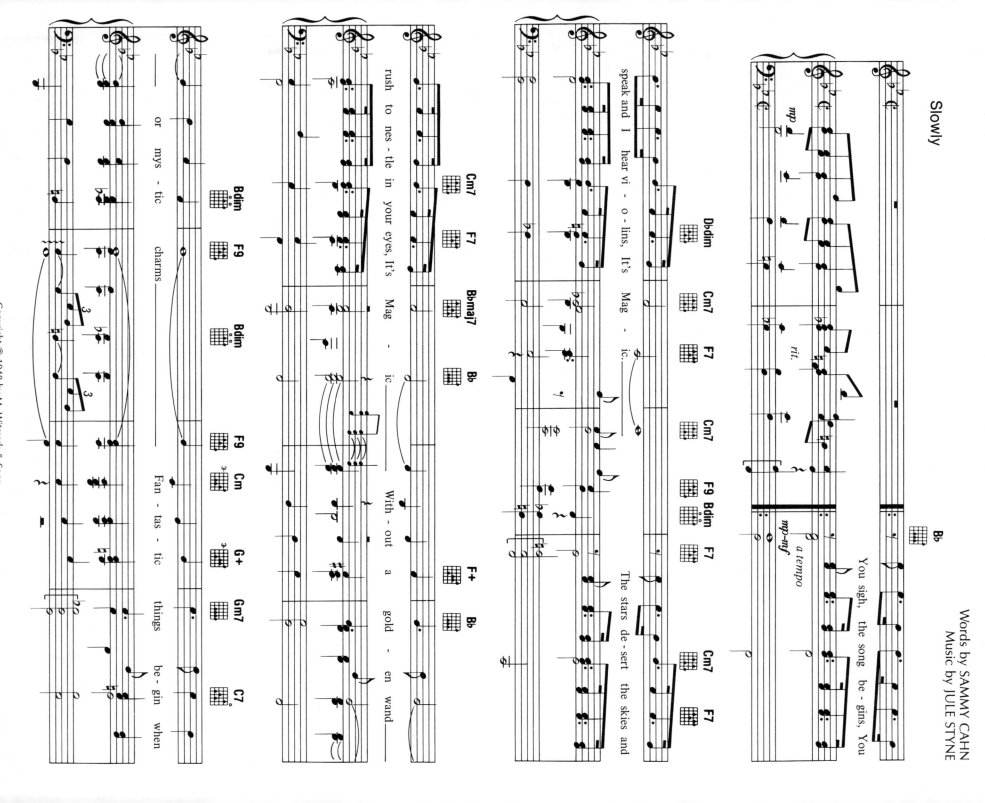

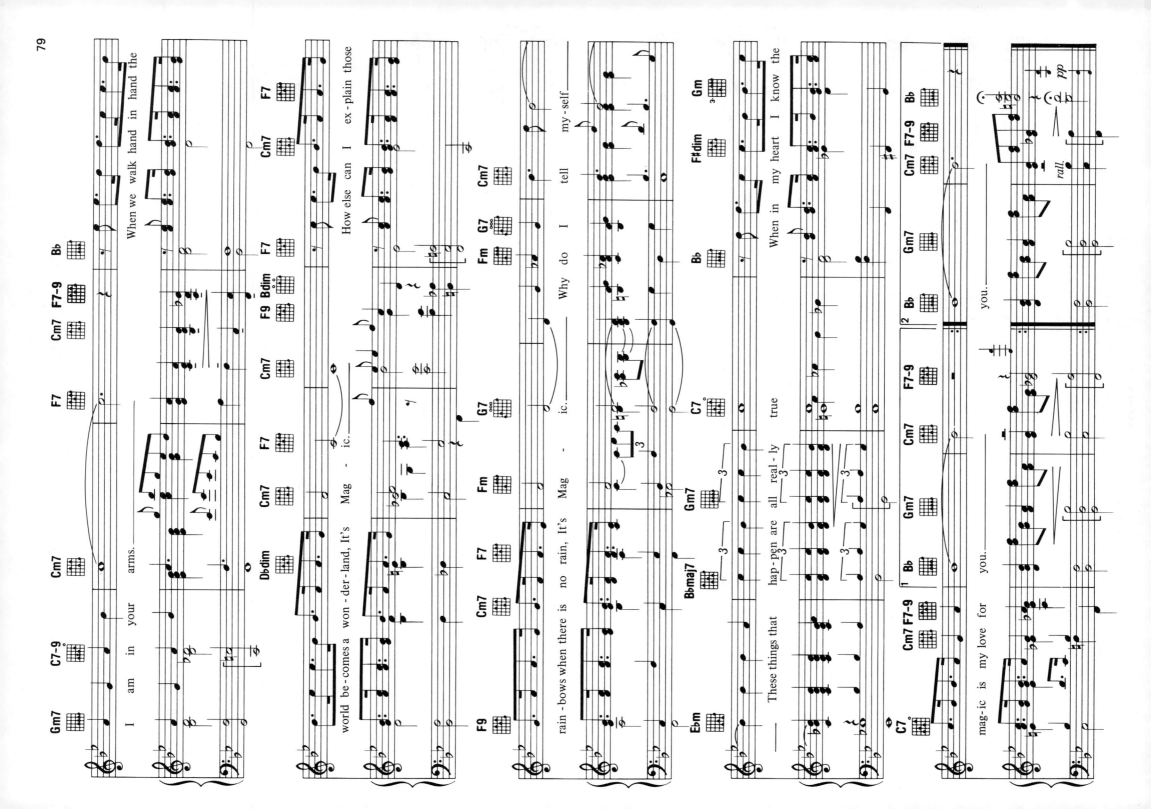

IT'S NOT UNUSUAL

With a beat

Words and Music by GORDON MILLS
and LES REED

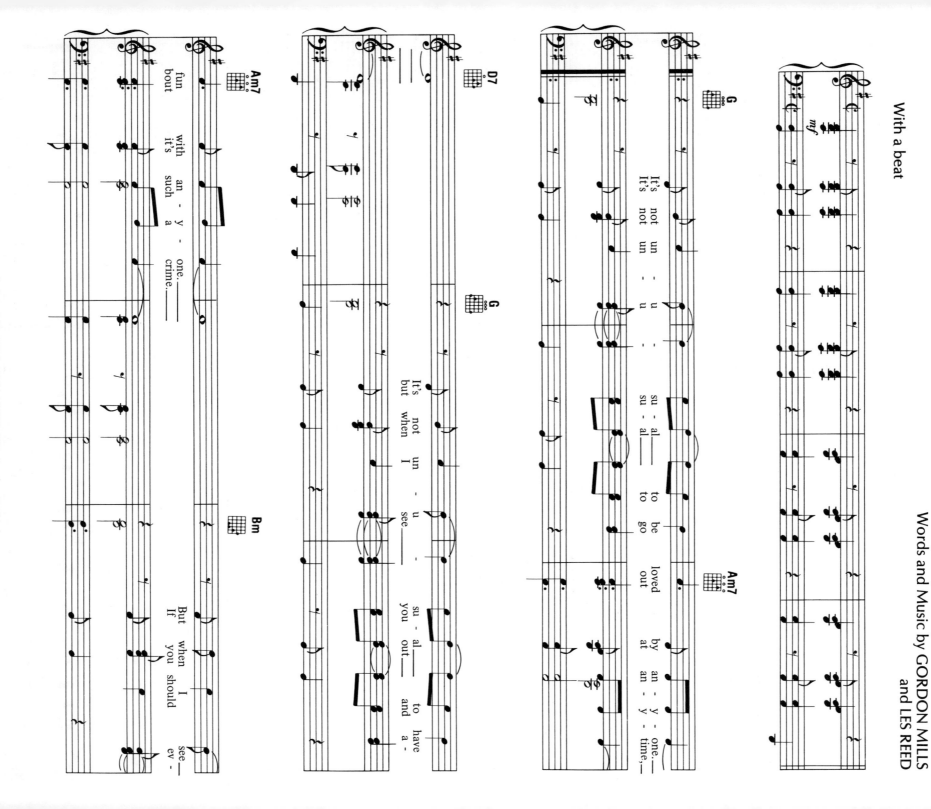

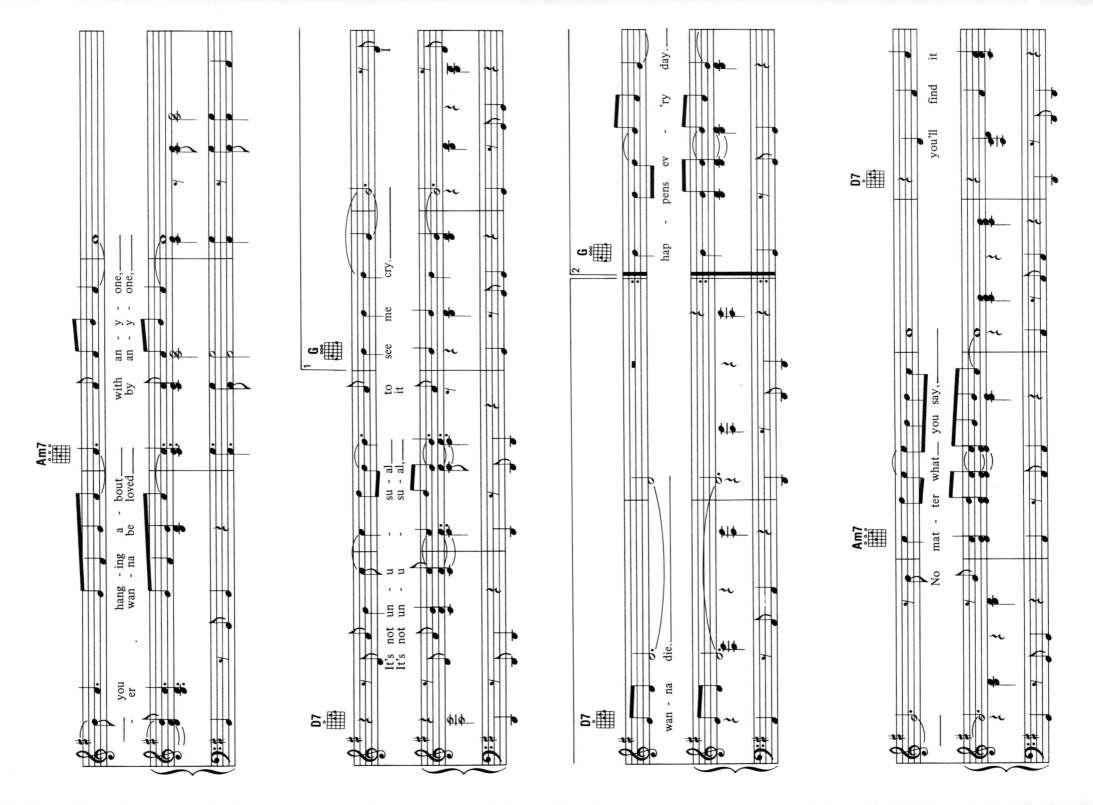

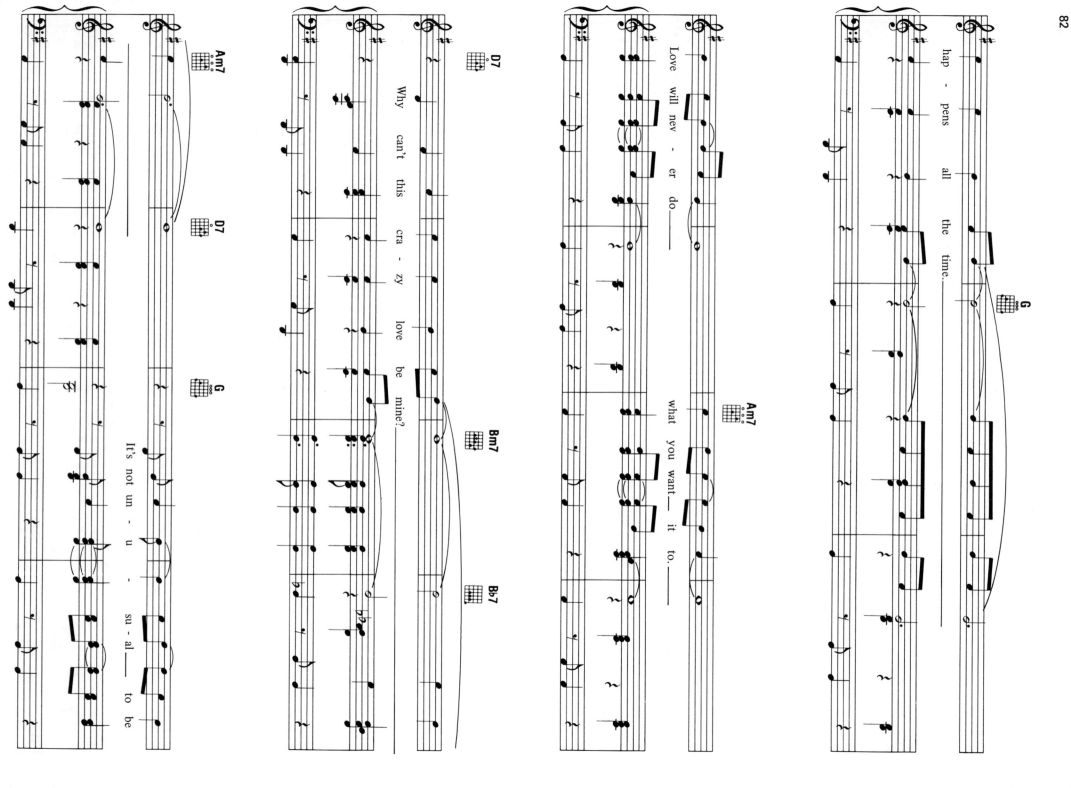

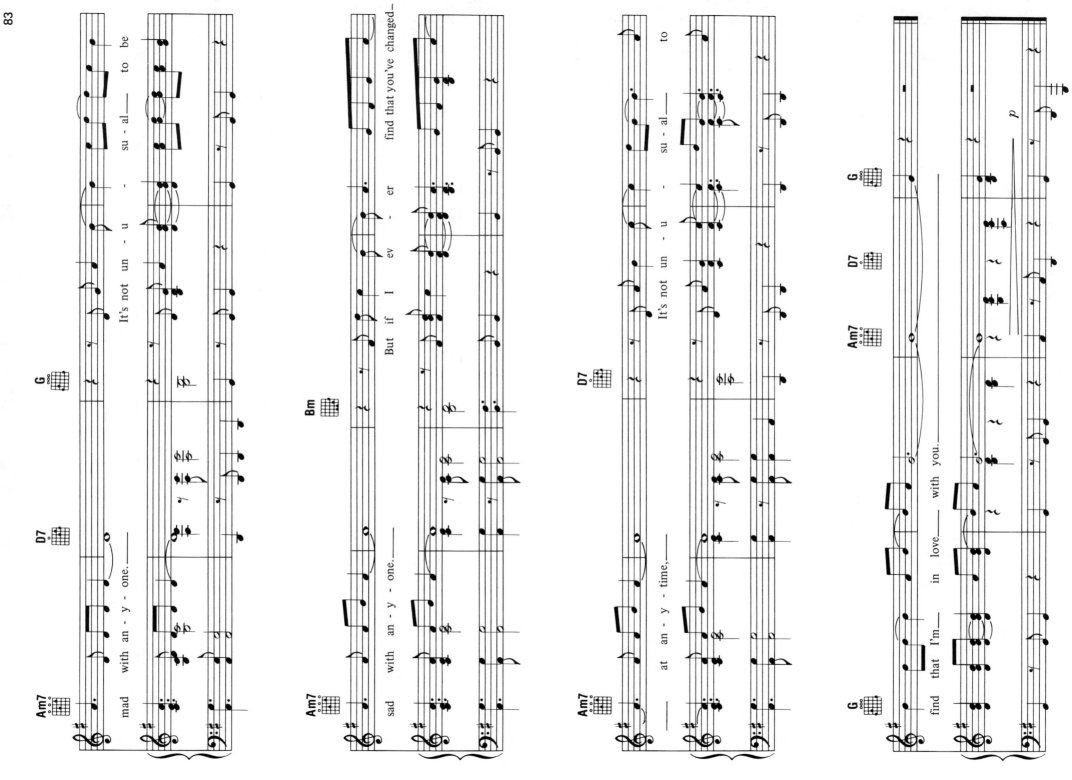

JOHNNY ONE NOTE

Words by LORENZ HART
Music by RICHARD RODGERS

Moderately

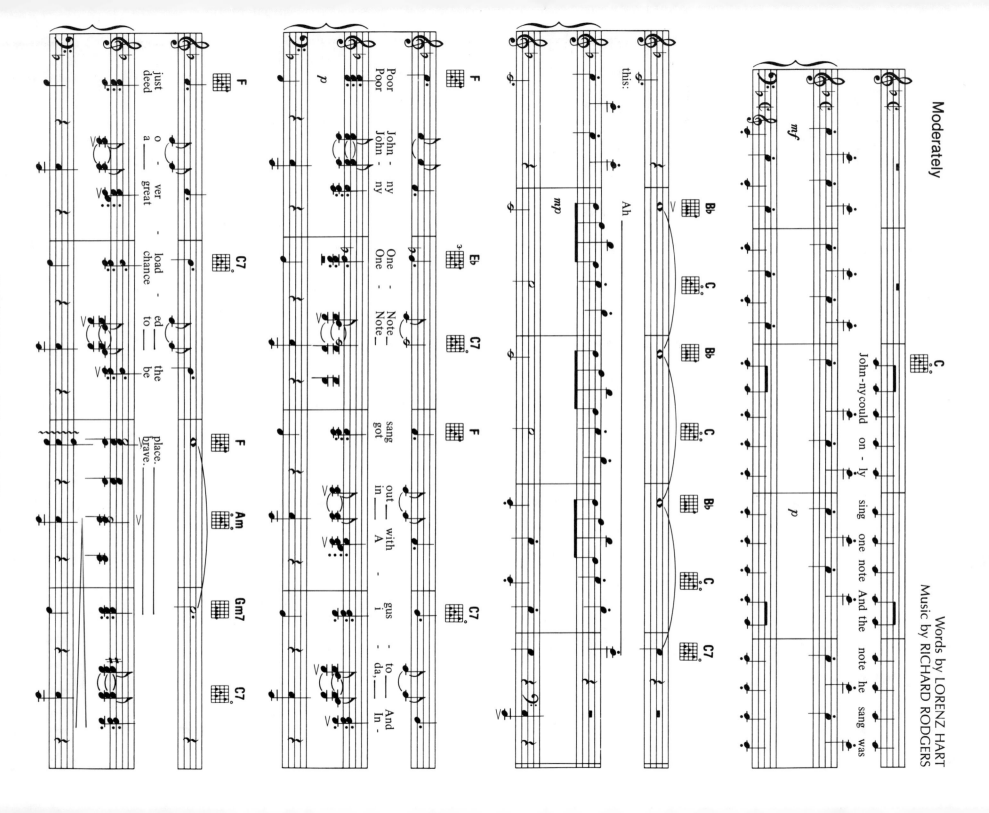

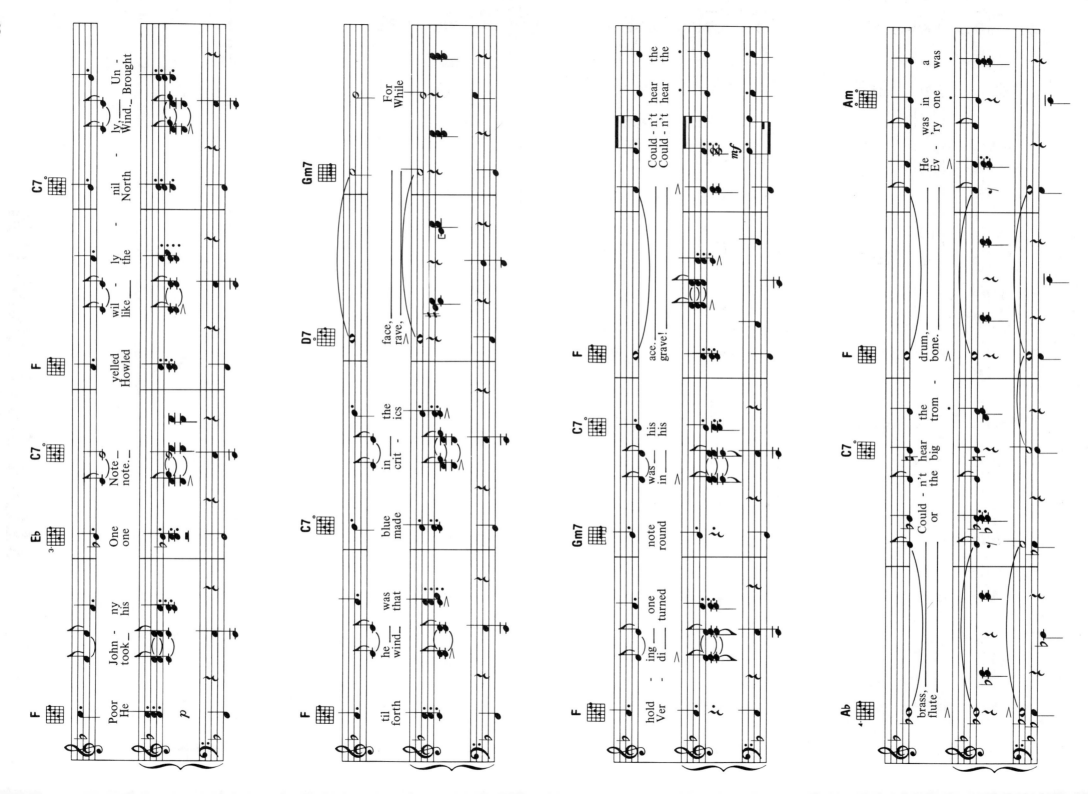

85

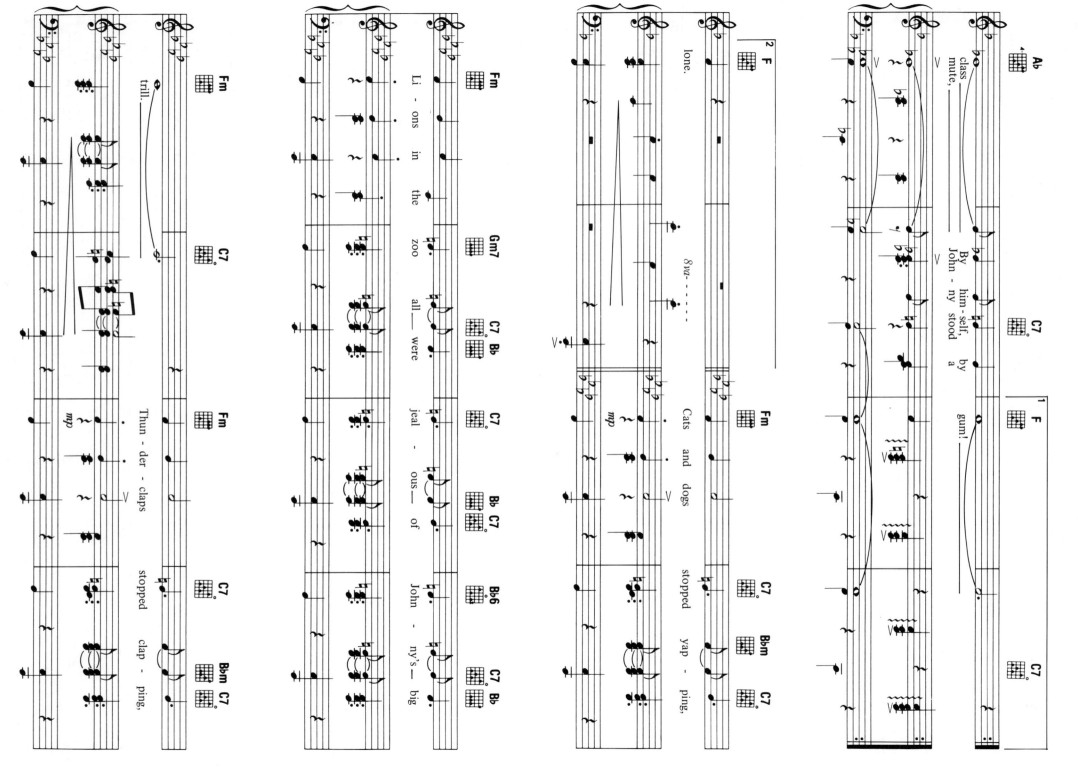

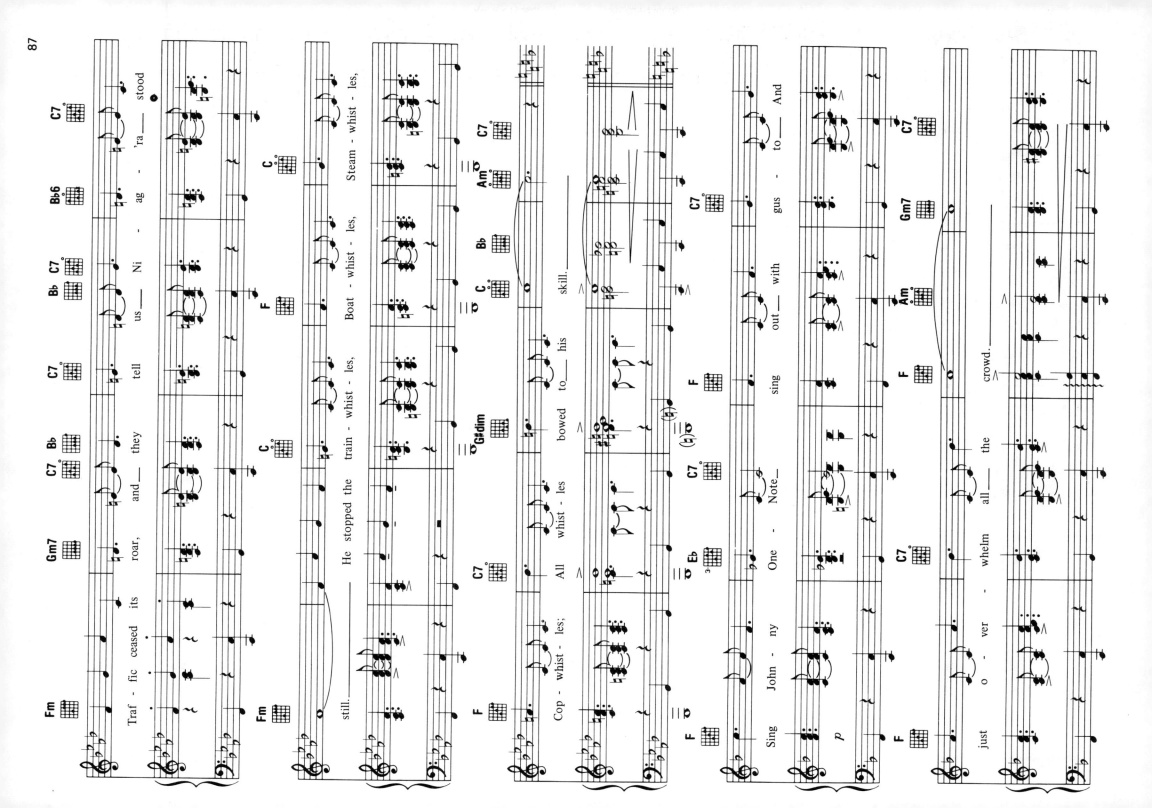

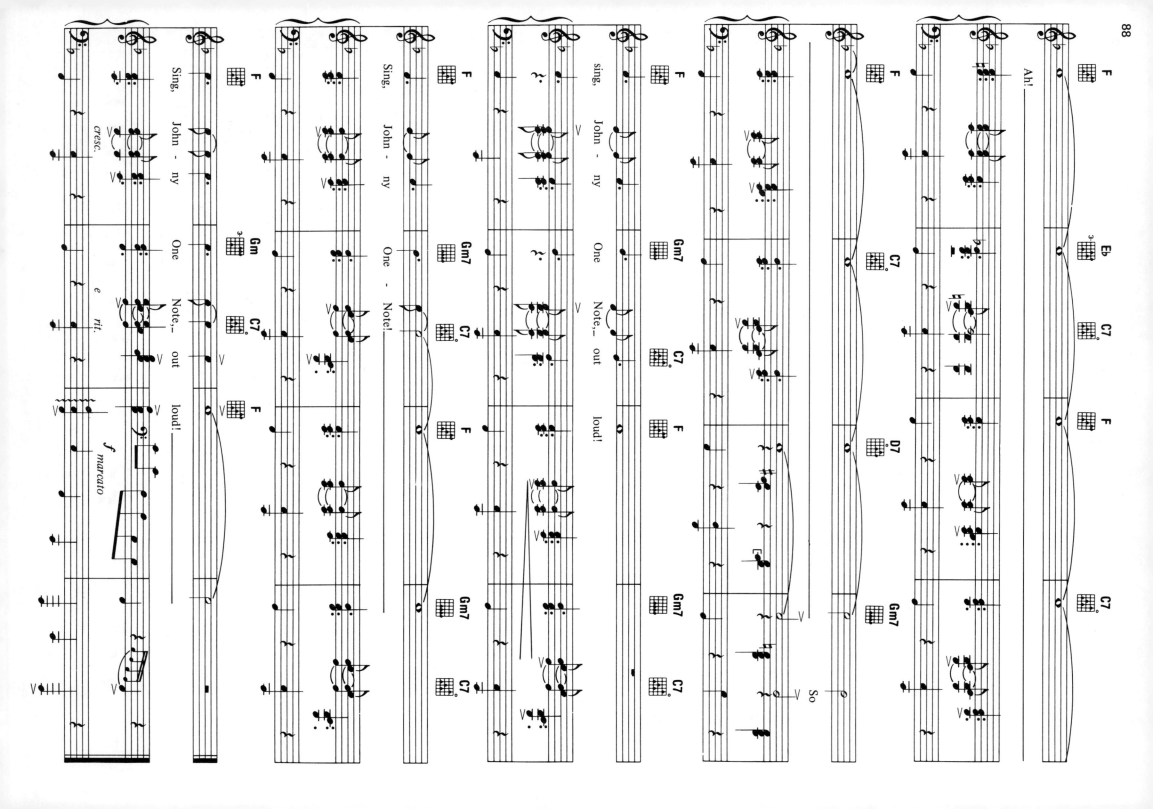

LADY

Words and Music by GRAHAM GOBLE

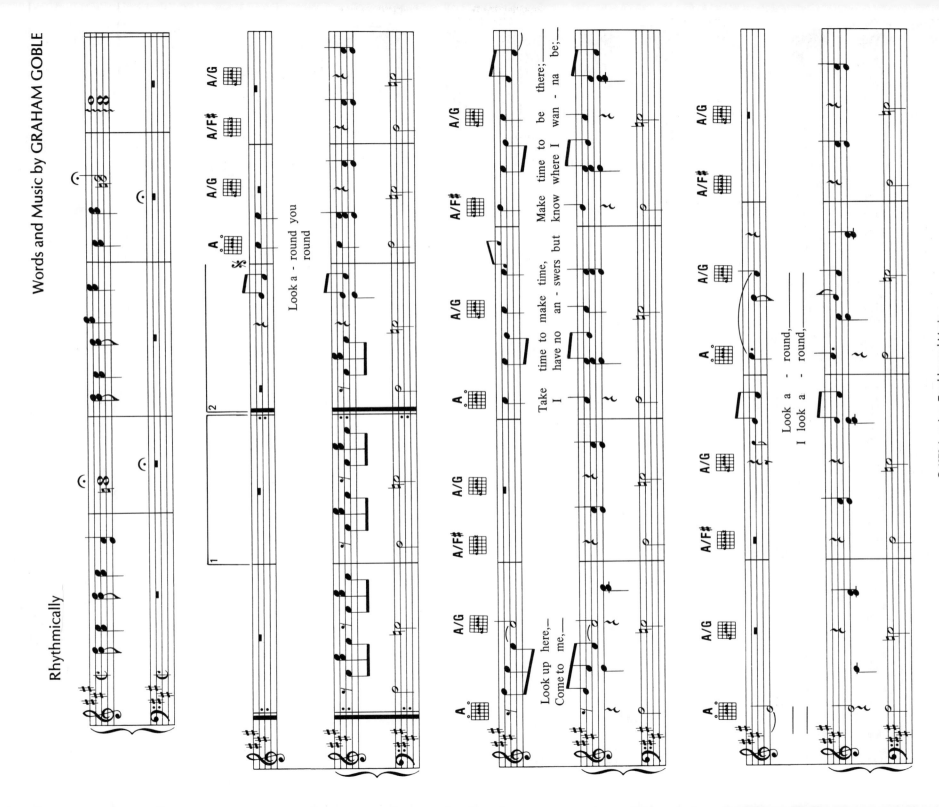

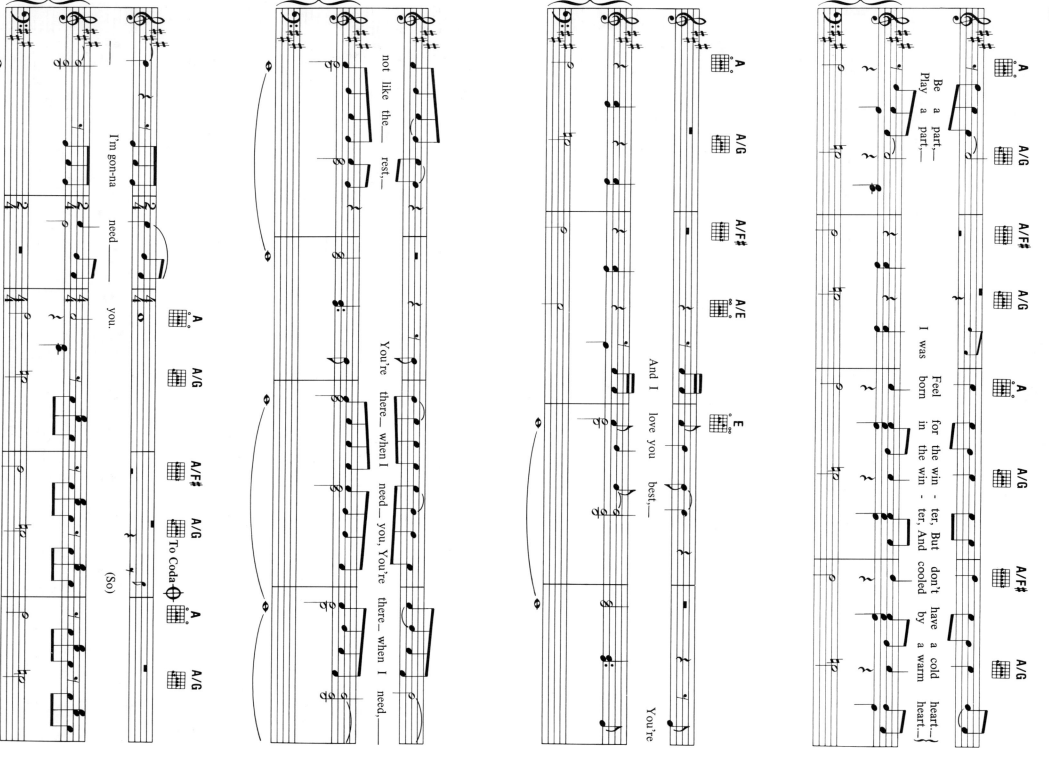

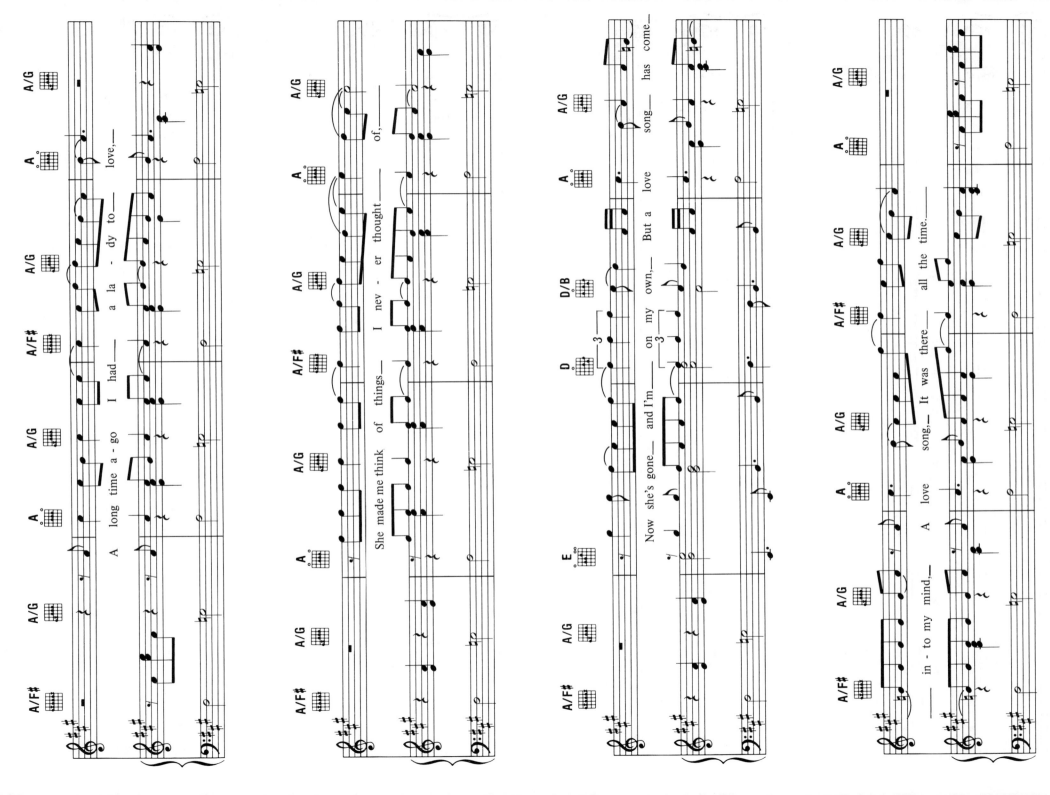

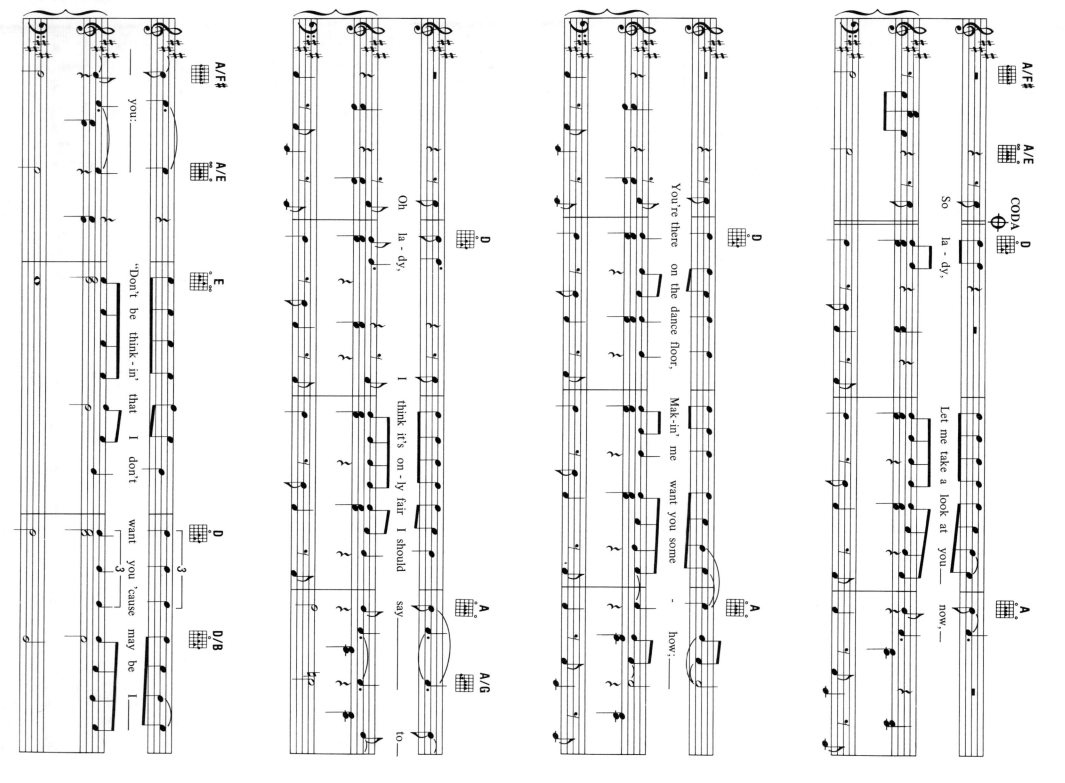

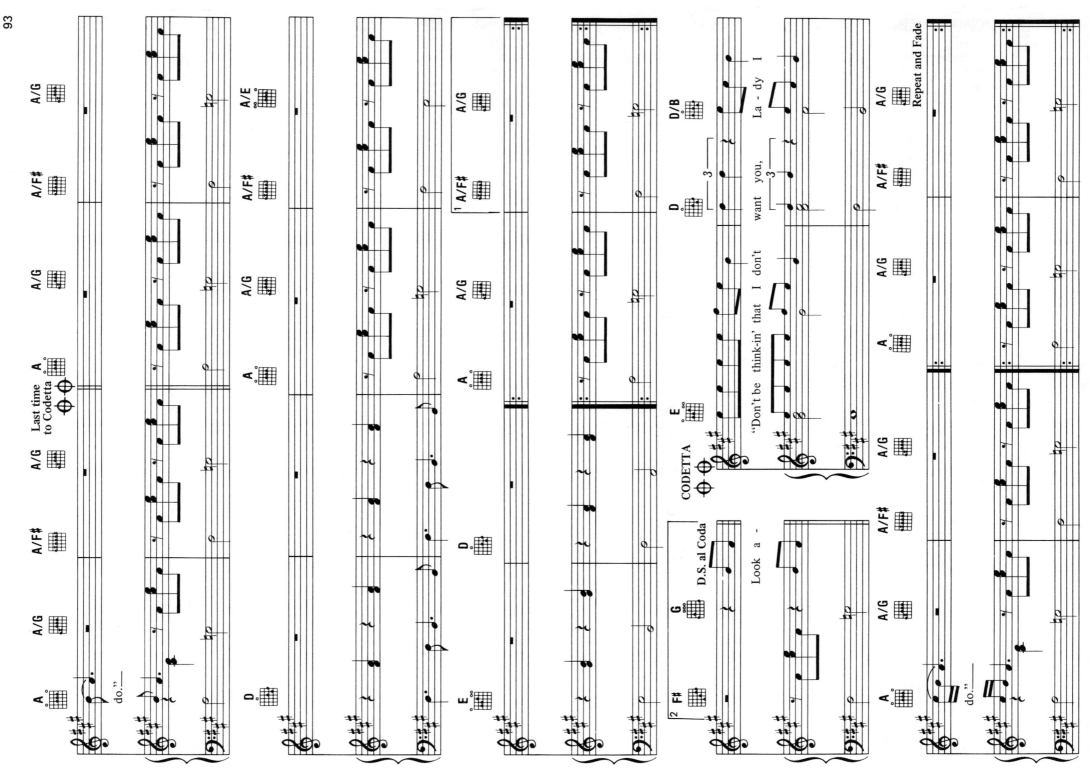

JUKE BOX SATURDAY NIGHT

Words by Al Stillman
Music by Paul McCrane

Medium Swing

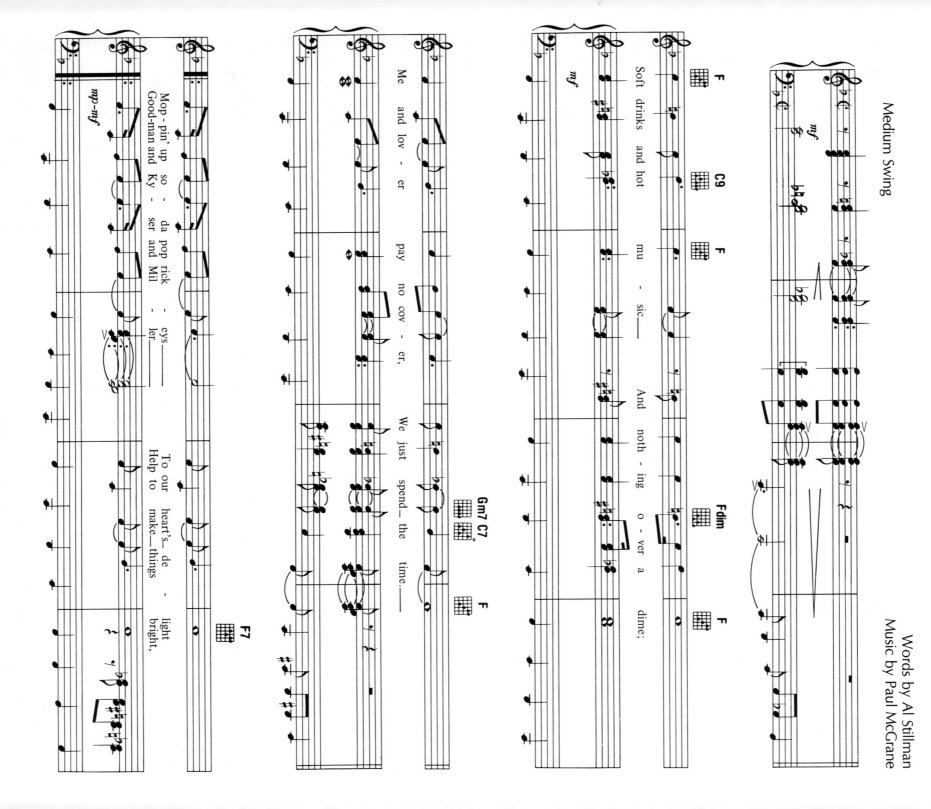

JUNE IS BUSTIN' OUT ALL OVER

(from "CAROUSEL")

Words by OSCAR HAMMERSTEIN
Music by RICHARD RODGERS

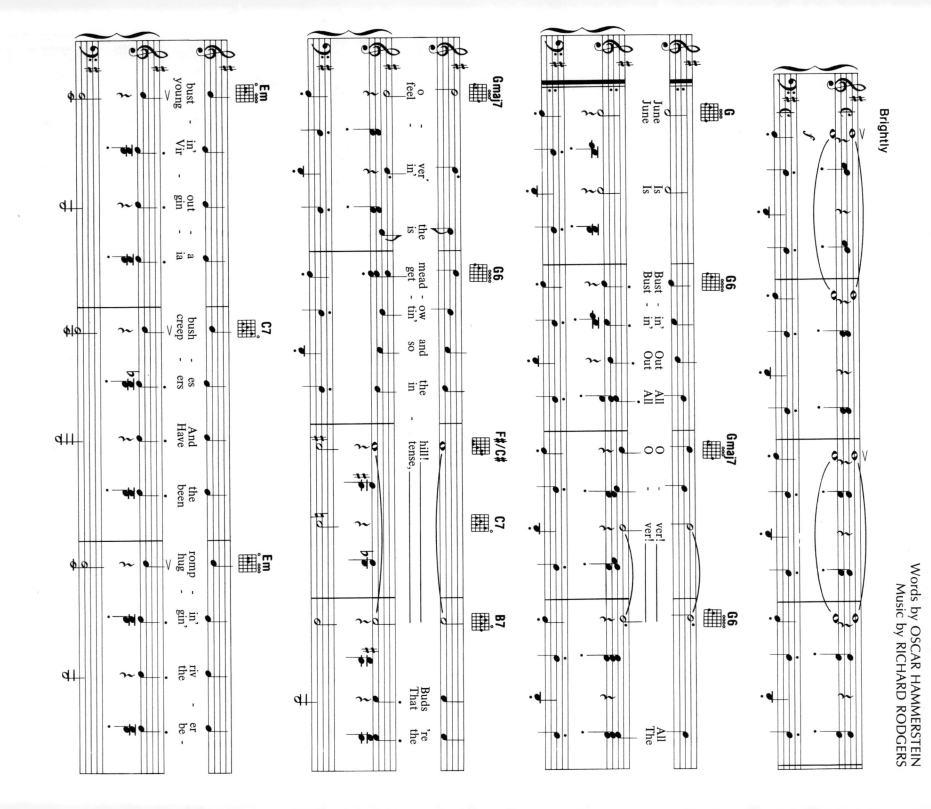

Bb7 A7 F#m7 B7 Em7 A11 A7 D Em
push - es ev - 'ry lit - tle wheel that wheels be - side a mill!
jeep - ers Out - a all the morn - in'
R.H.
Fdim D7/F# Em7 A7 D Cm/Eb D7
glor - ies on the fence! Be - cause it's
Gmaj7 G6 G Fm6 E7
June! June, June, June,
Am7 E7 Eb7 Am7 D13
Tacet
Jest be - cause it's June! June!
ff
Gmaj9 G Ab6/9 Gmaj9
June!

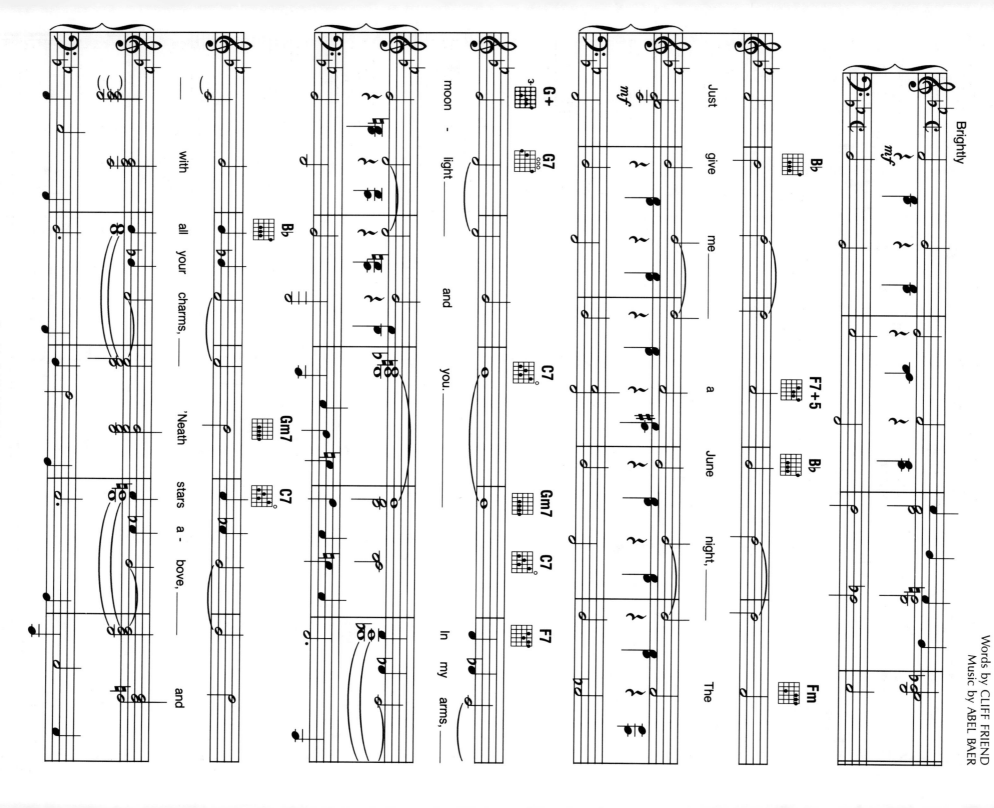

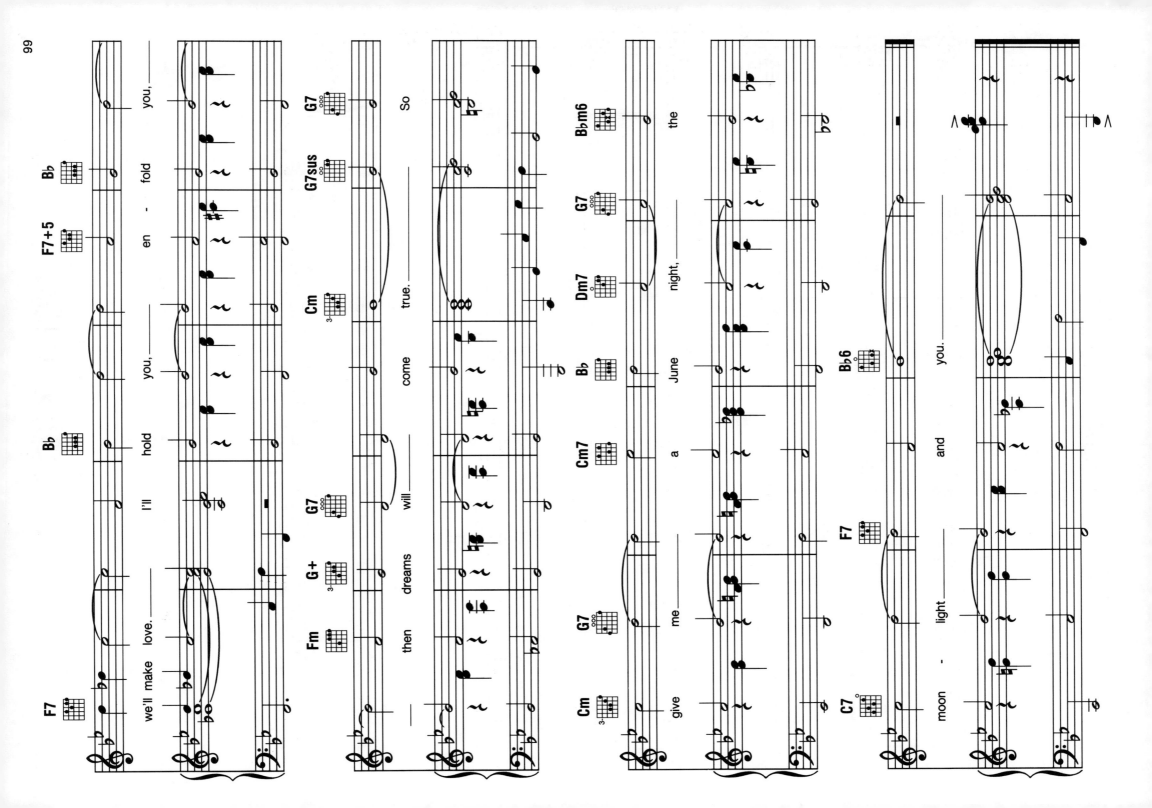

JUST A GIGOLO
(SCHÖNER GIGOLO)

Original German Text by JULIUS BRAMMER
English Words by IRVING CAESAR
Music by LEONELLO CASUCCI

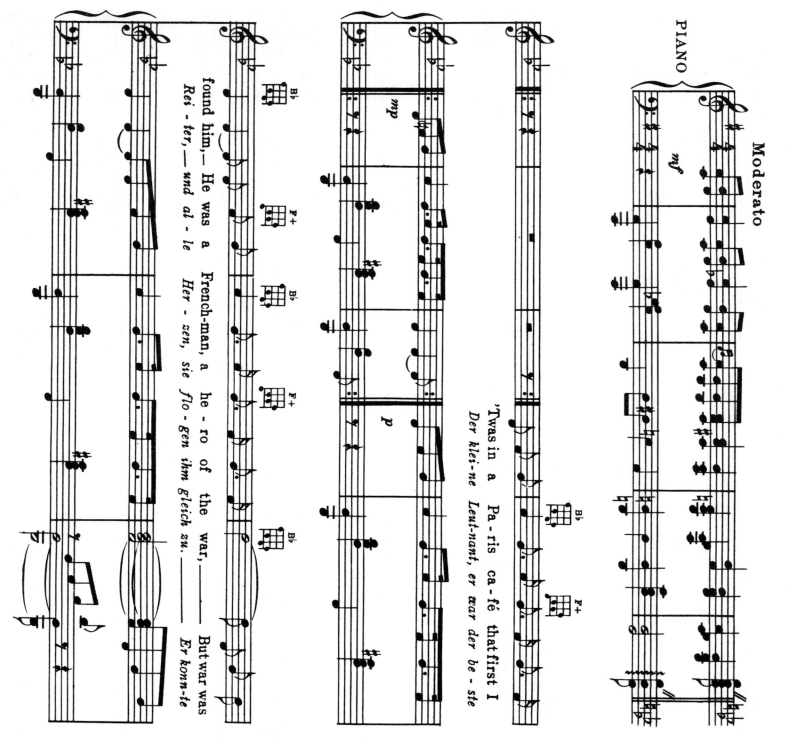

Moderato

PIANO

'Twas in a Pa - ris ca - fé that first I
Der klei - ne Leut - nant, er war der be - ste

found him, — He was a French - man, a he - ro of the war, — But war was
Rei - ter, — und al - le Her - zen, sie flo - gen ihm gleich zu. — Er konn - te

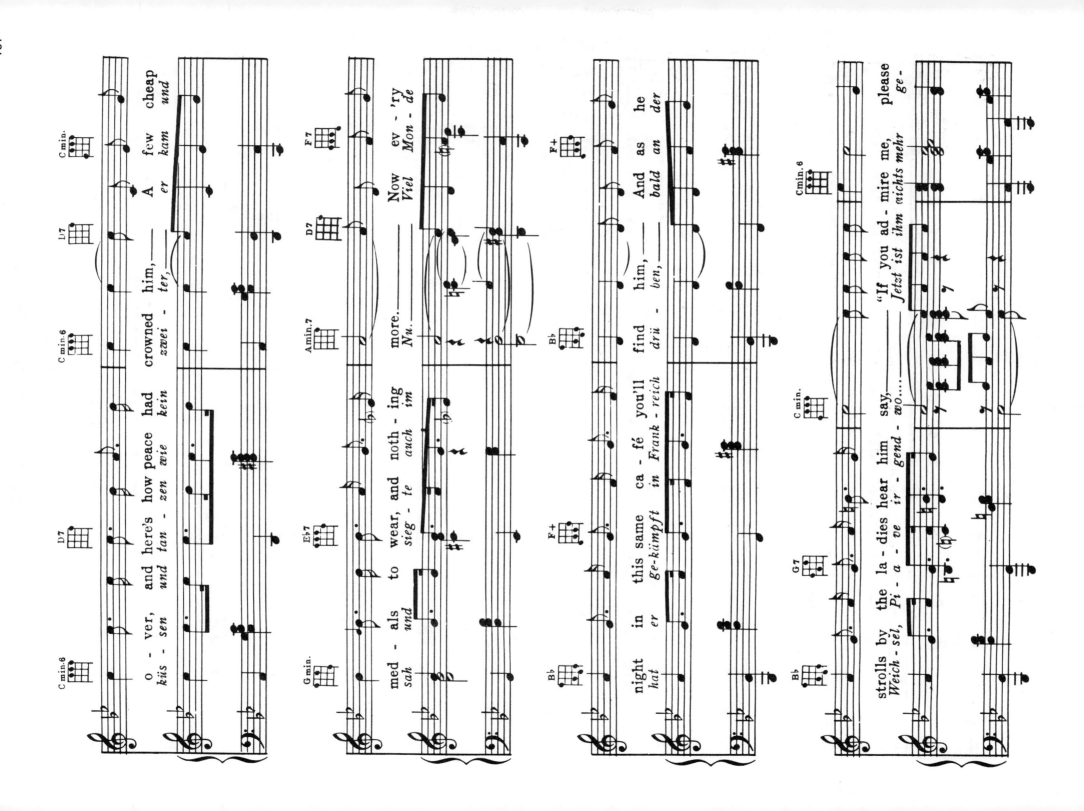

101

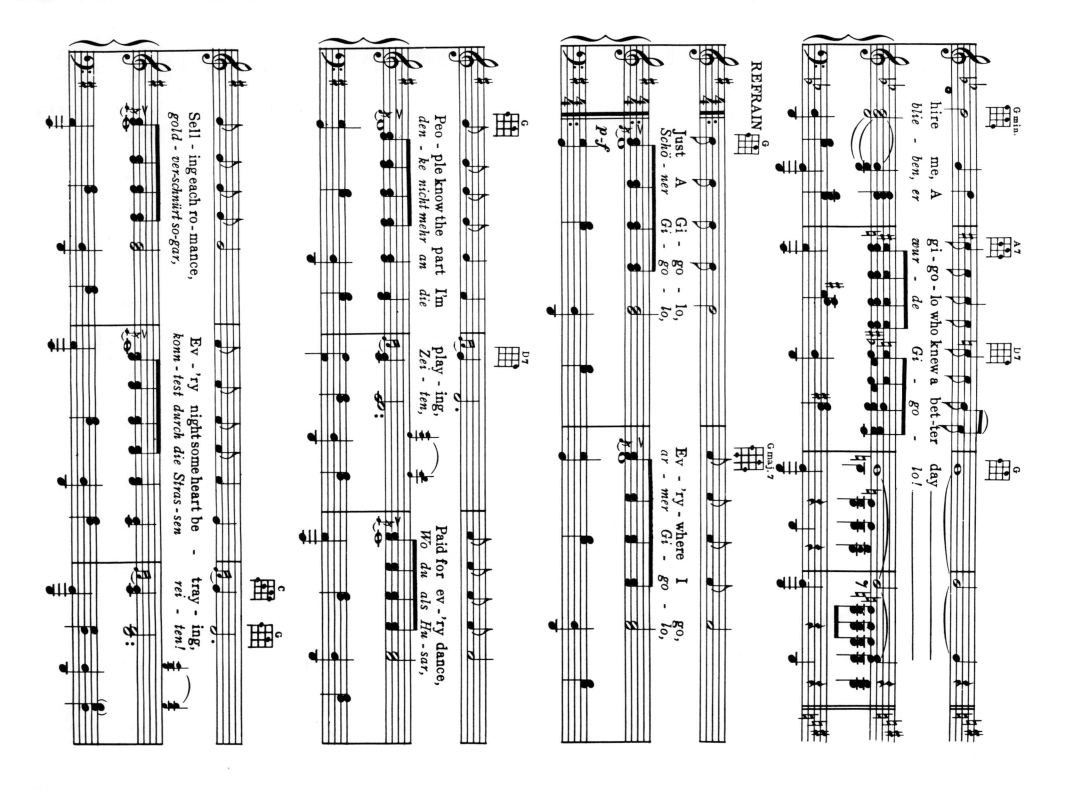

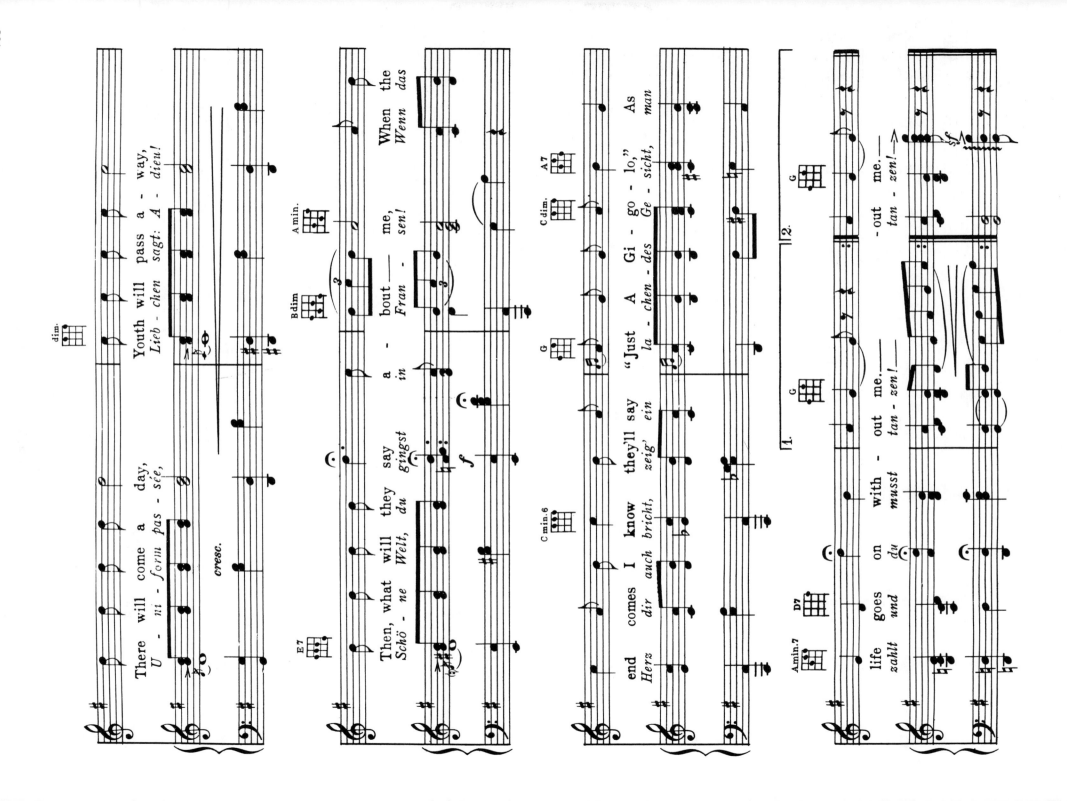

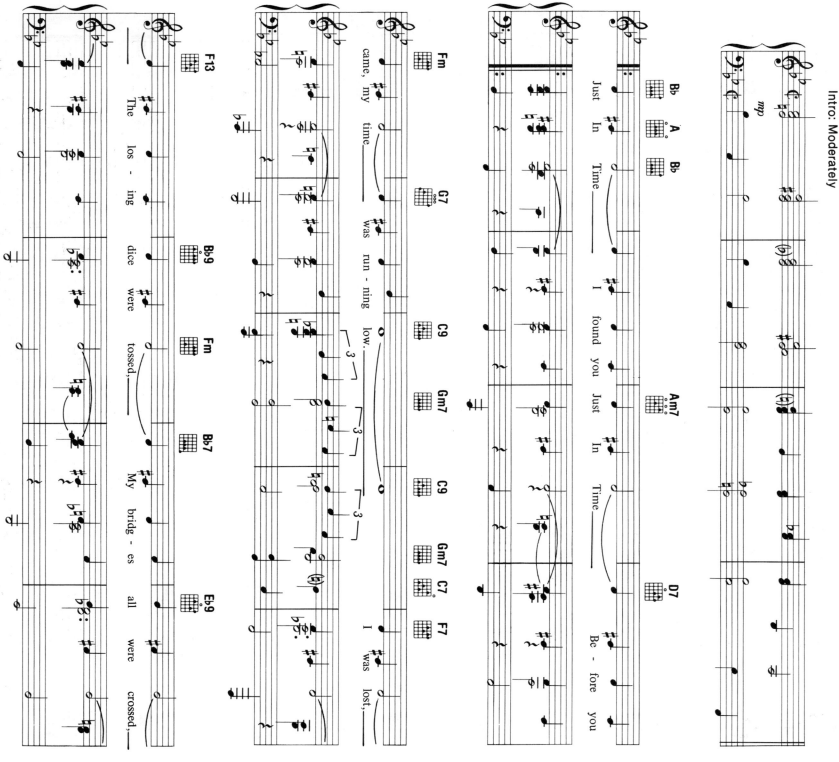

JUST IN TIME
(From "BELLS ARE RINGING")

Words by BETTY COMDEN and ADOLPH GREEN
Music by JULE STYNE

Intro: Moderately

KING OF THE ROAD

Words and Music by ROGER MILLER

Moderately, with a bounce

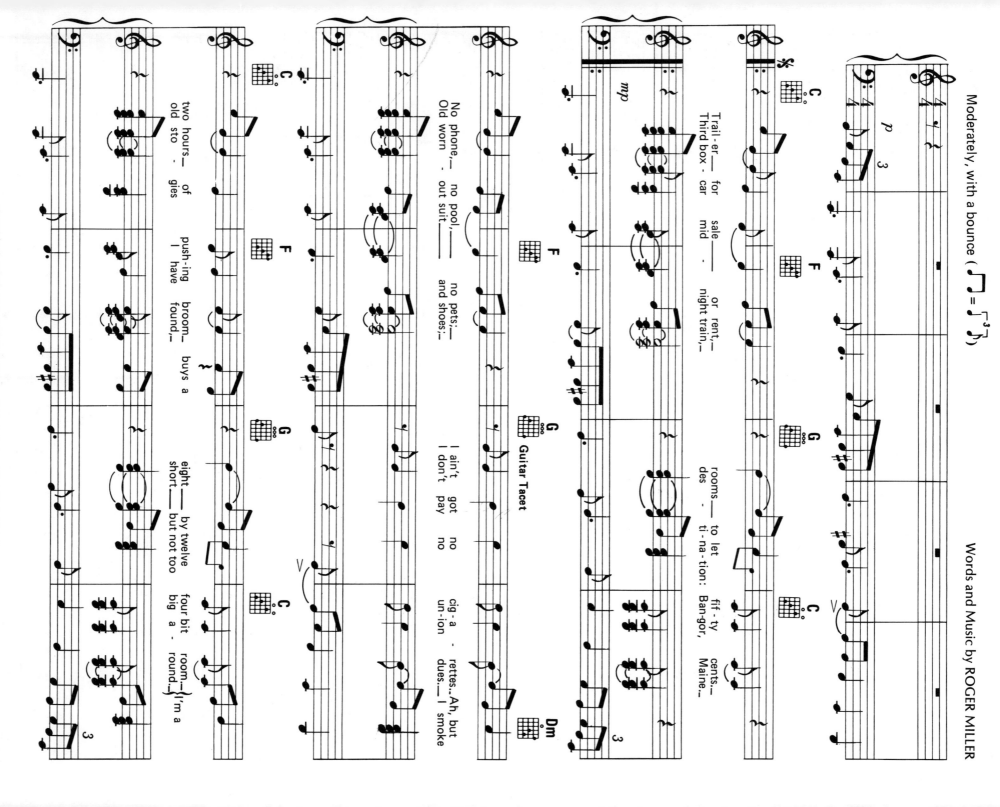

LA MER
(BEYOND THE SEA)

Music by CHARLES TRENET

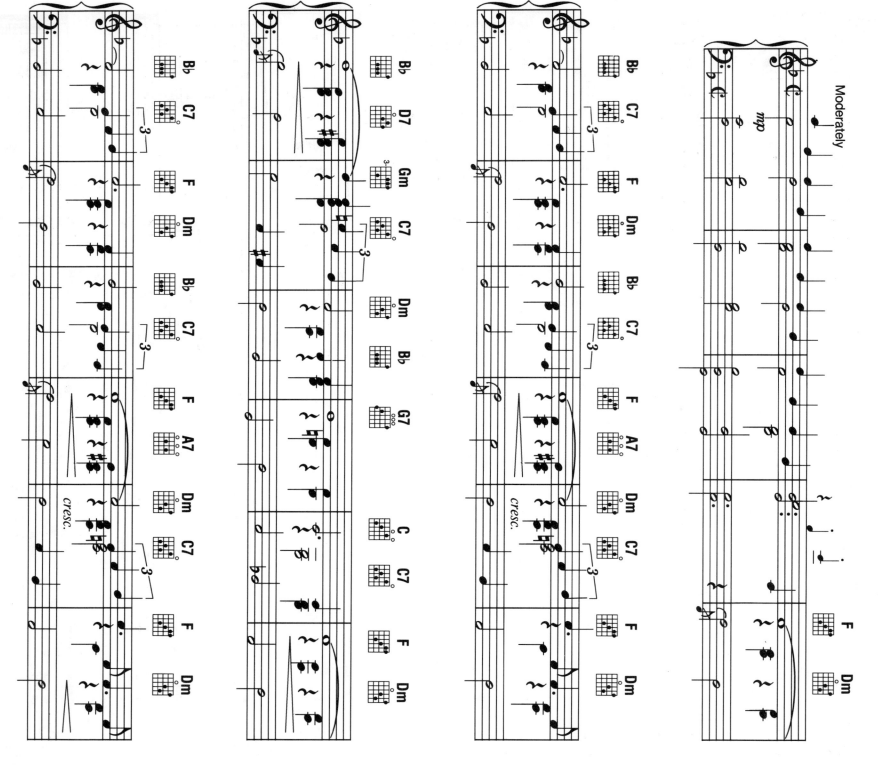

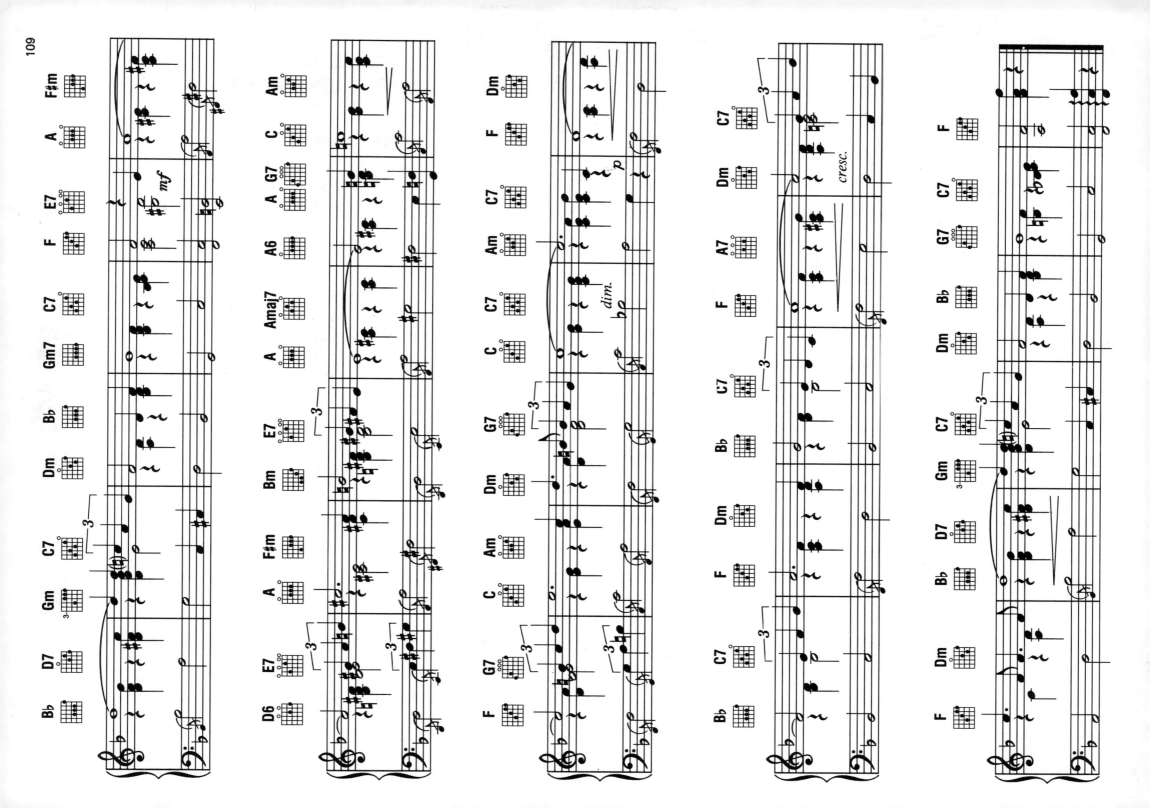

THE LAST TIME I SAW PARIS

Words by OSCAR HAMMERSTEIN II
Music by JEROME KERN

Briskly

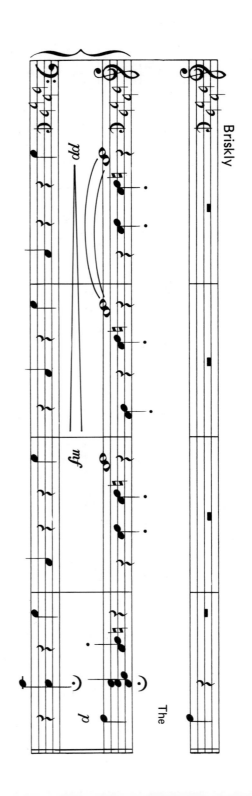

The

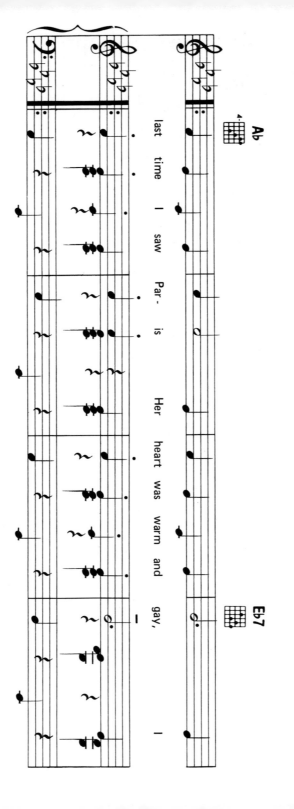

last time I saw Par - is Her heart was warm and gay, I

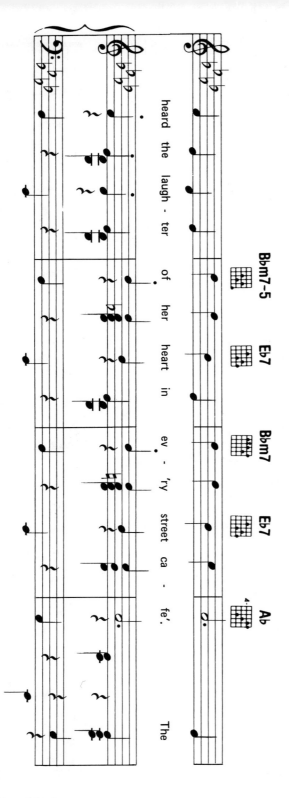

heard the laugh - ter of her heart in ev - 'ry street ca - fe'. The

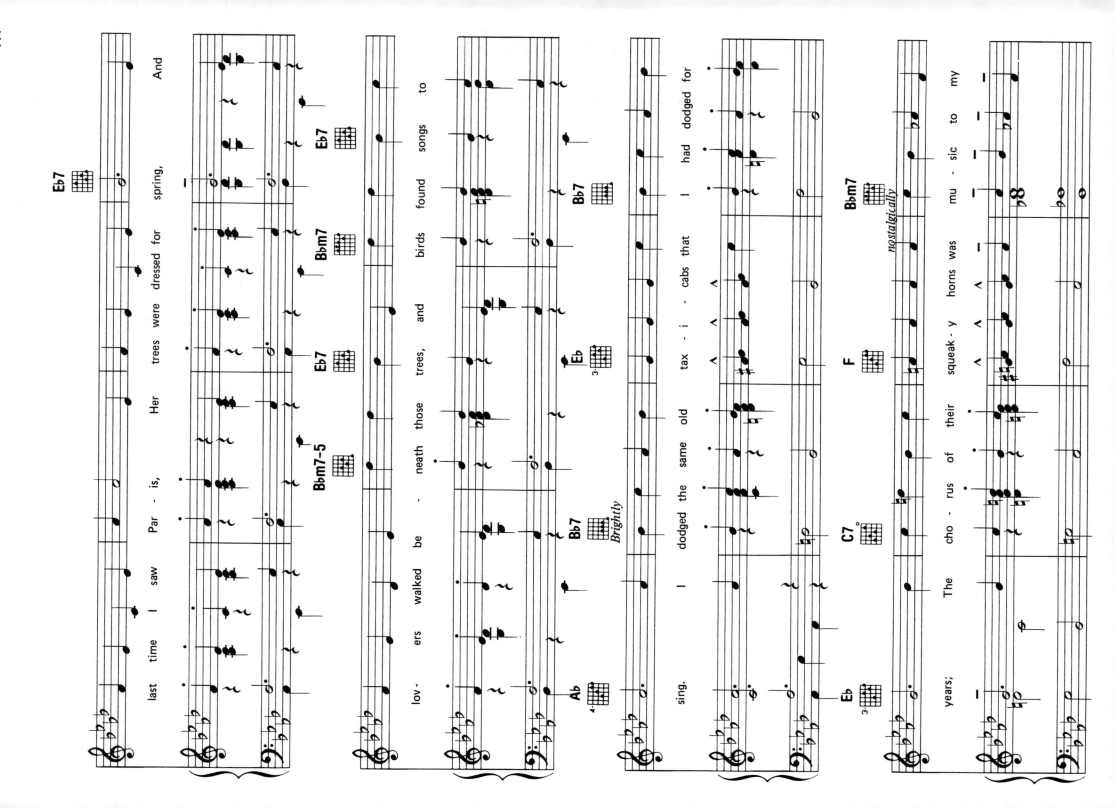

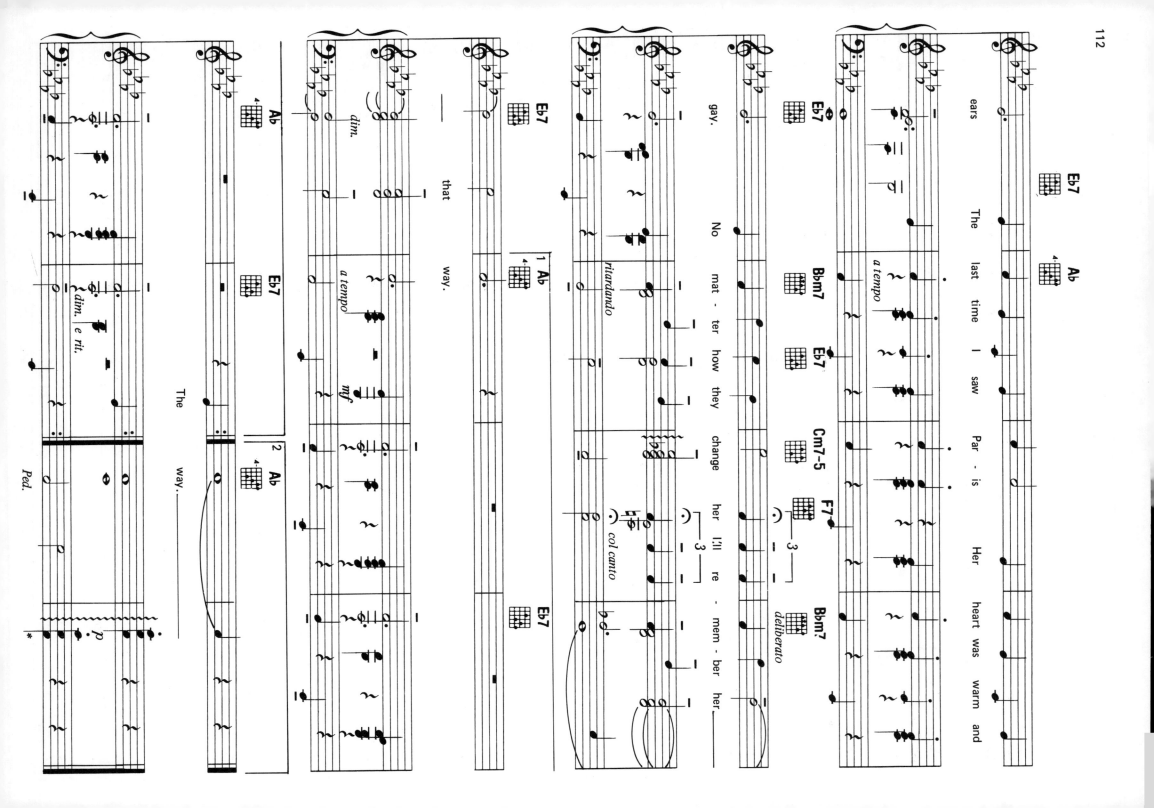

112

LEFT IN THE DARK

Words and Music by JIM STEINMAN

Medium Slow Rock Ballad

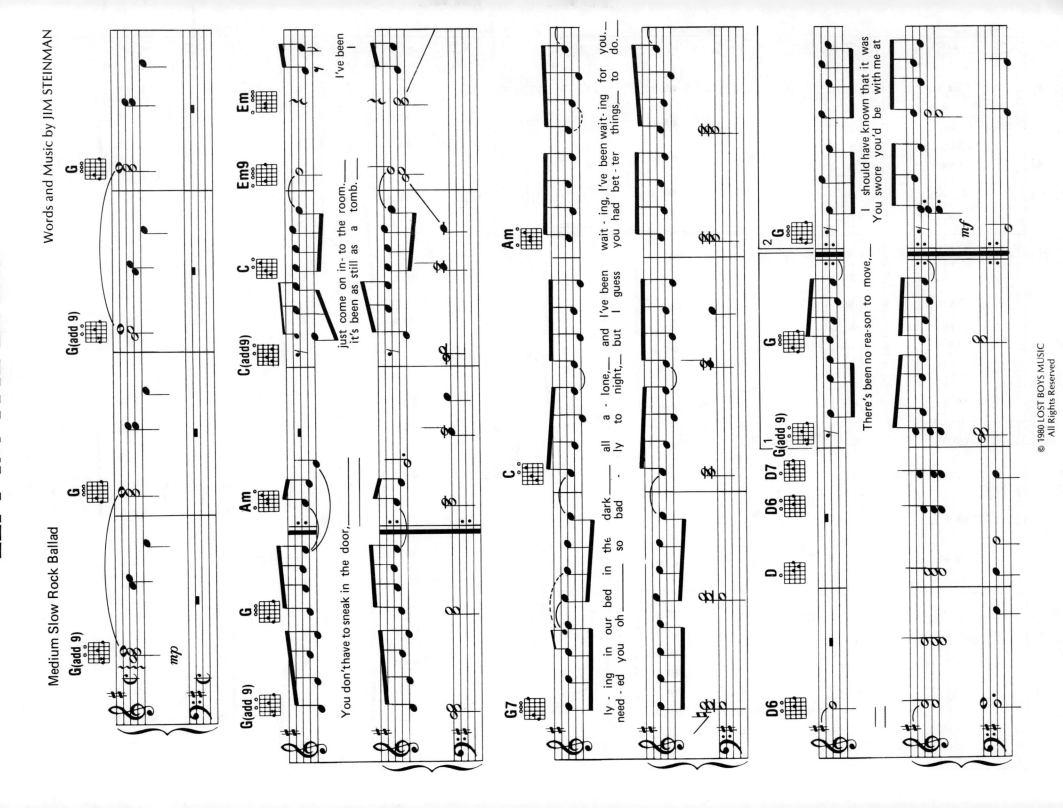

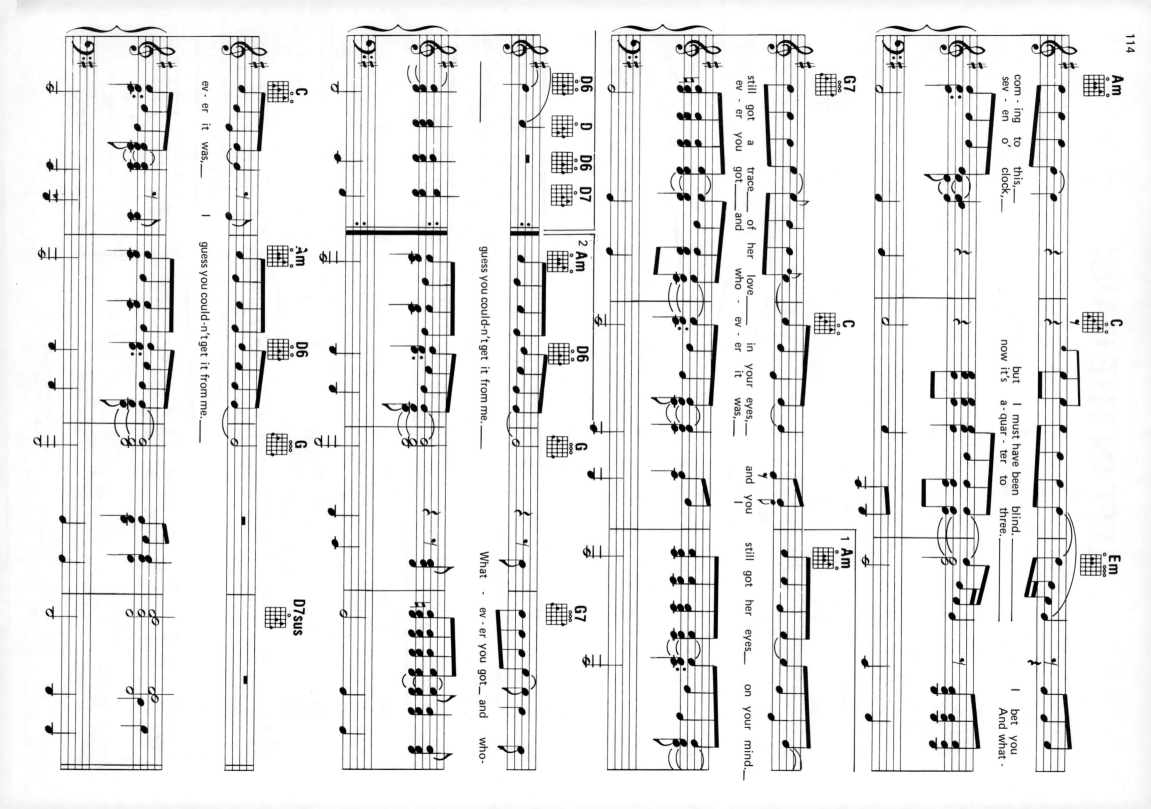

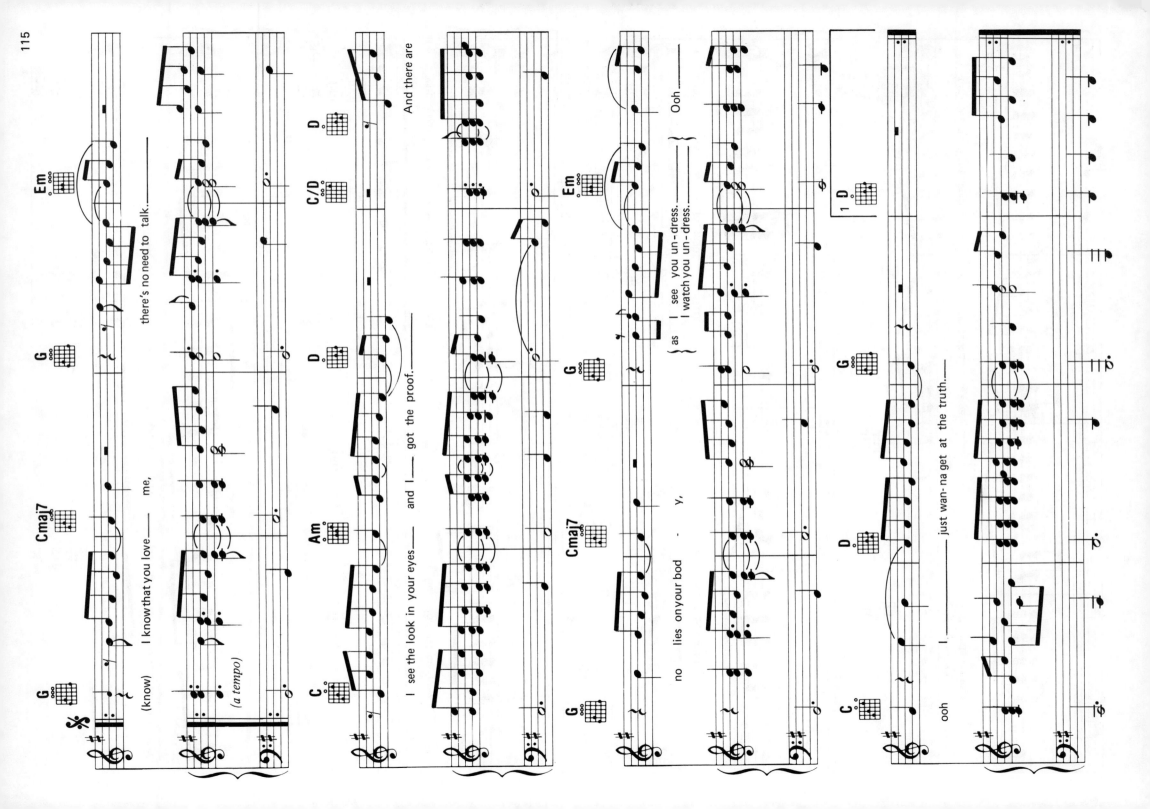

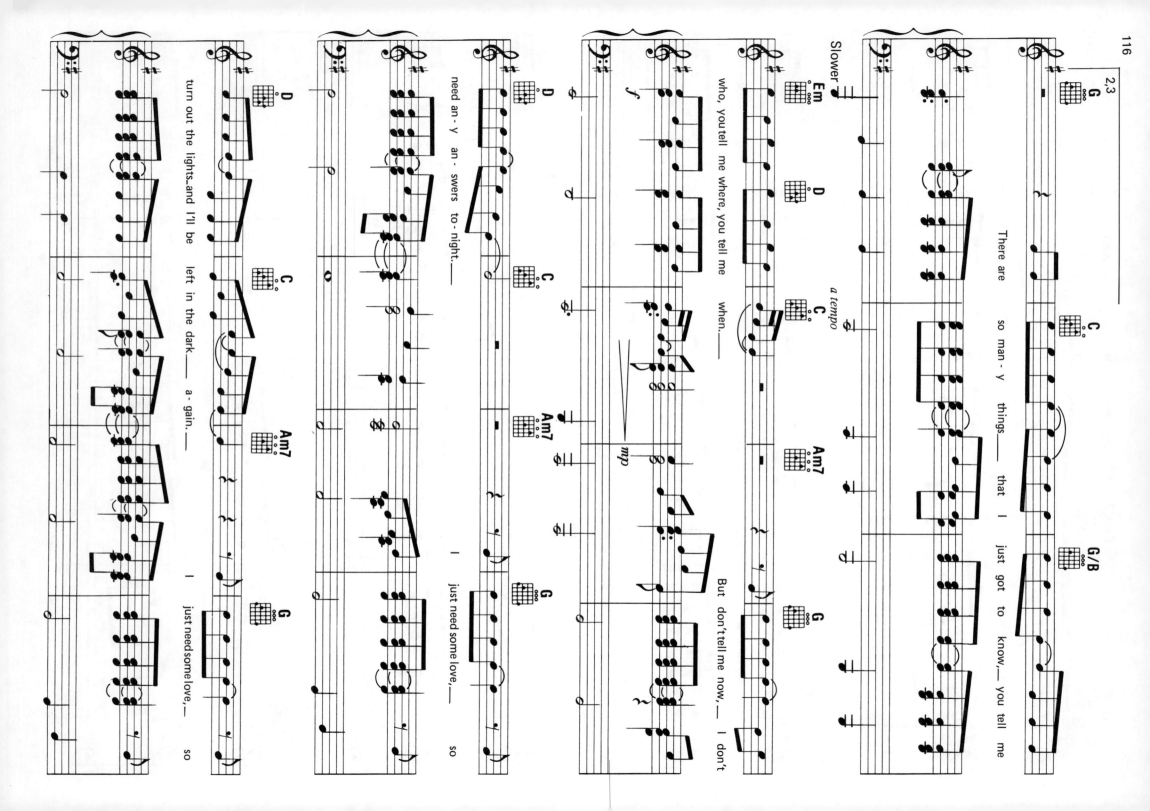

To Coda
D
C
Am7
turn out the lights__ and I'll be left in the dark____ a - gain.____ I
G
D
Em
just need some love,__ so turn____ out the lights__ and I'll be left in the dark____ a - gain,__
mf
C
G
Am7
3
left in the dark__ a - gain.
G/B
C
D
Am7
G/B

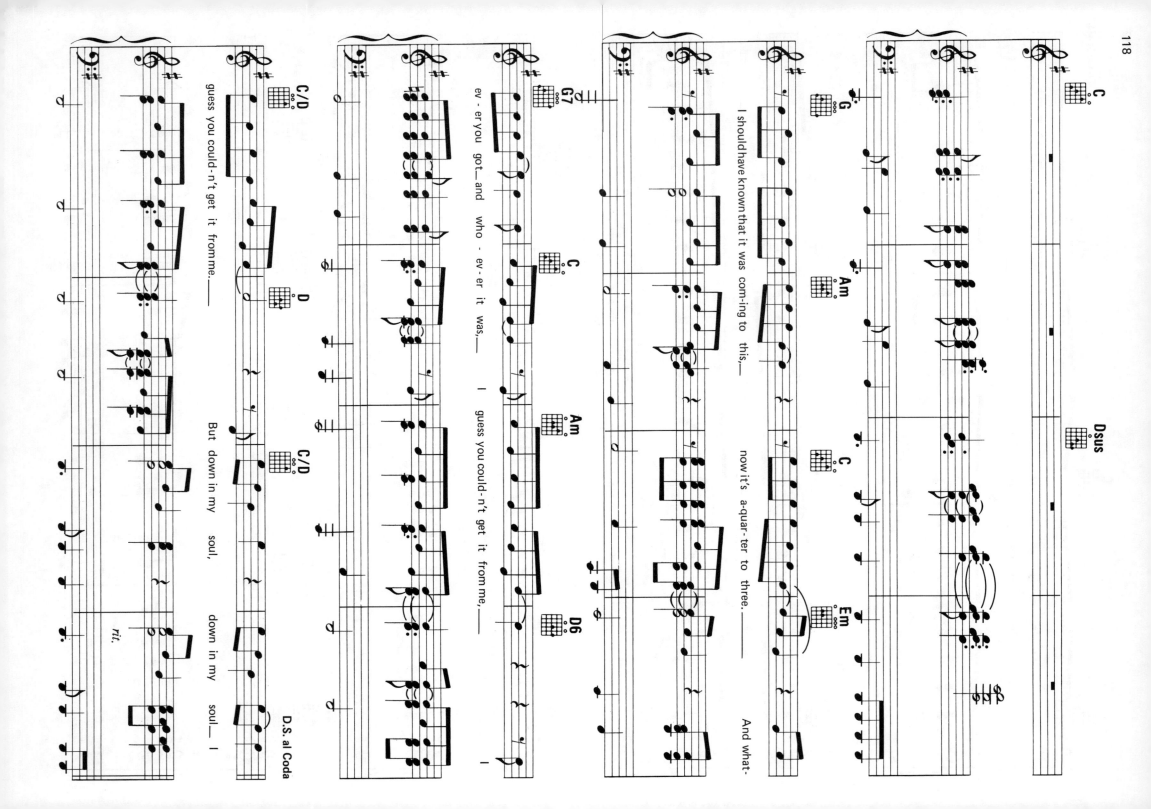

119

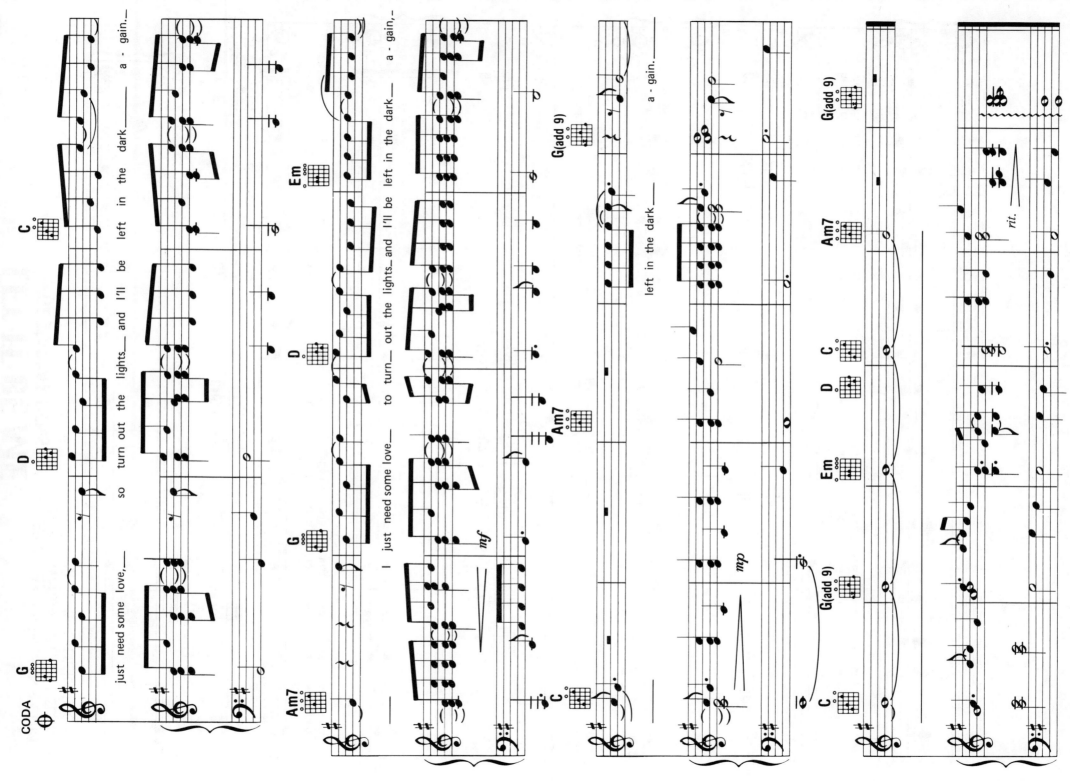

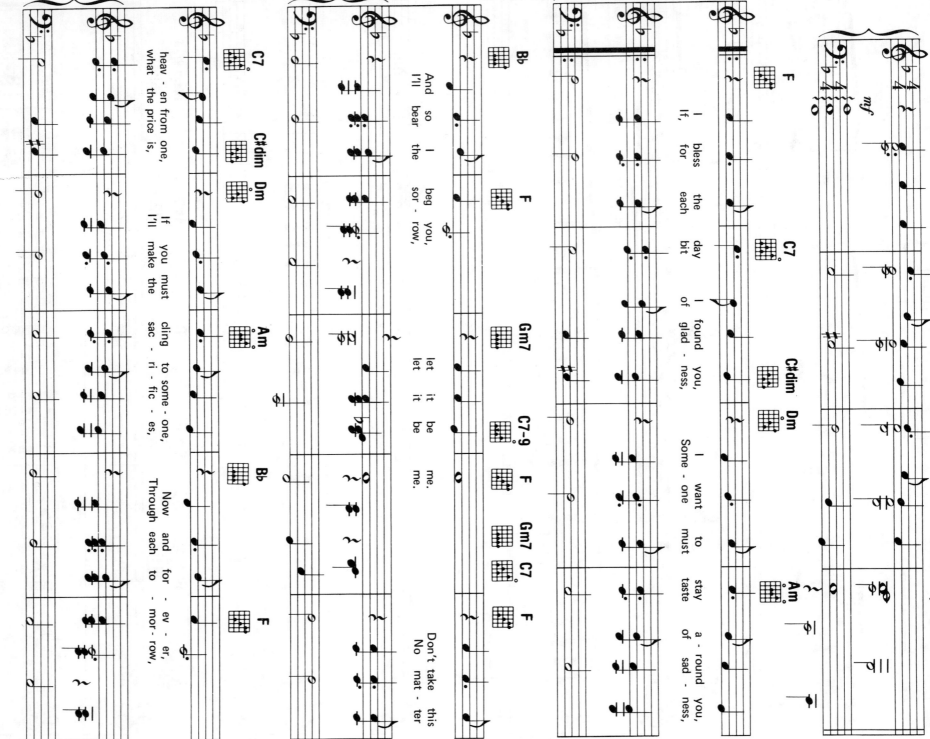

LET IT BE ME
(JE T'APPARTIENS)

English Words by MANN CURTIS
French Words by PIERRE DELANOE
Music by GILBERT BECAUD

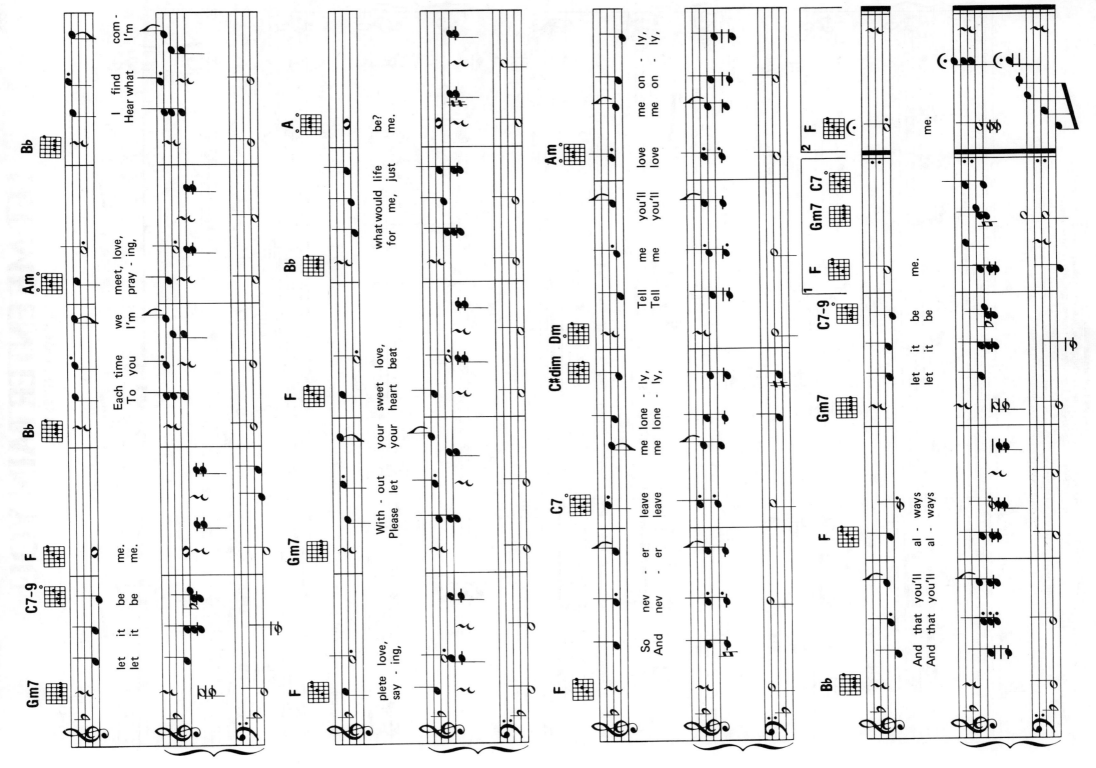

LET ME ENTERTAIN YOU
(From "GYPSY")

Words by STEPHEN SONDHEIM
Music by JULE STYNE

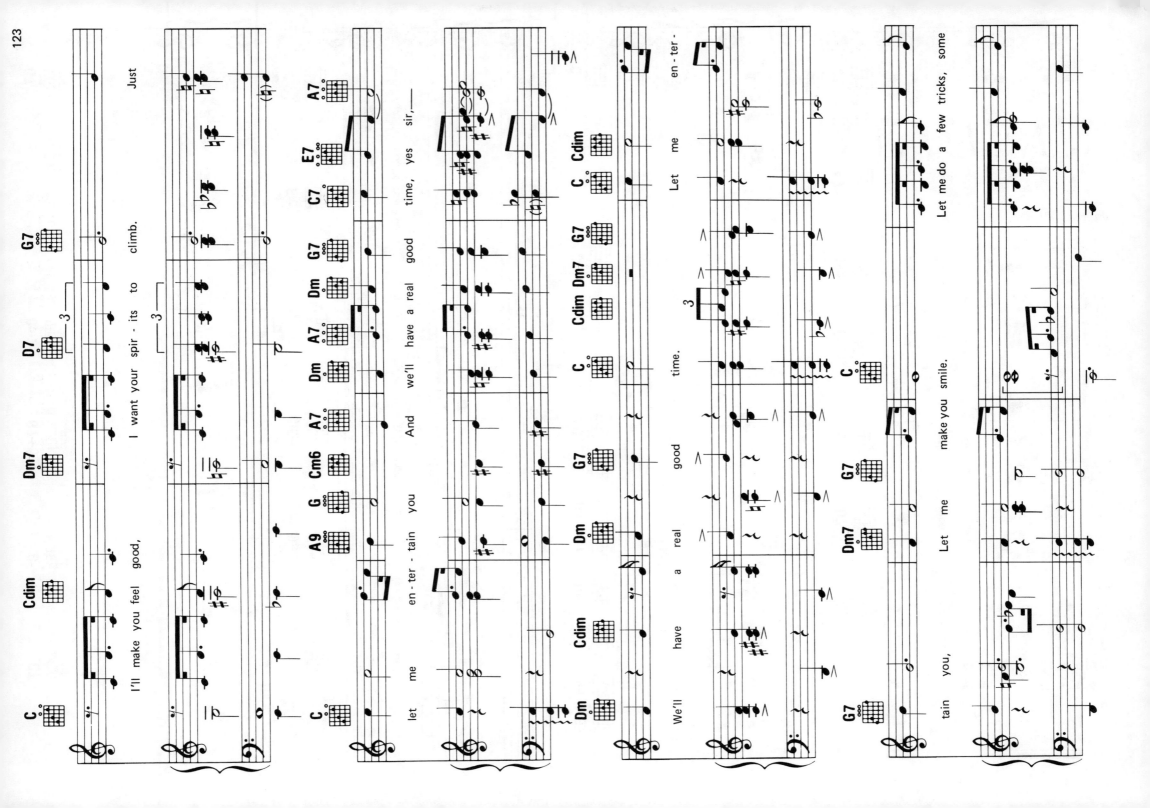

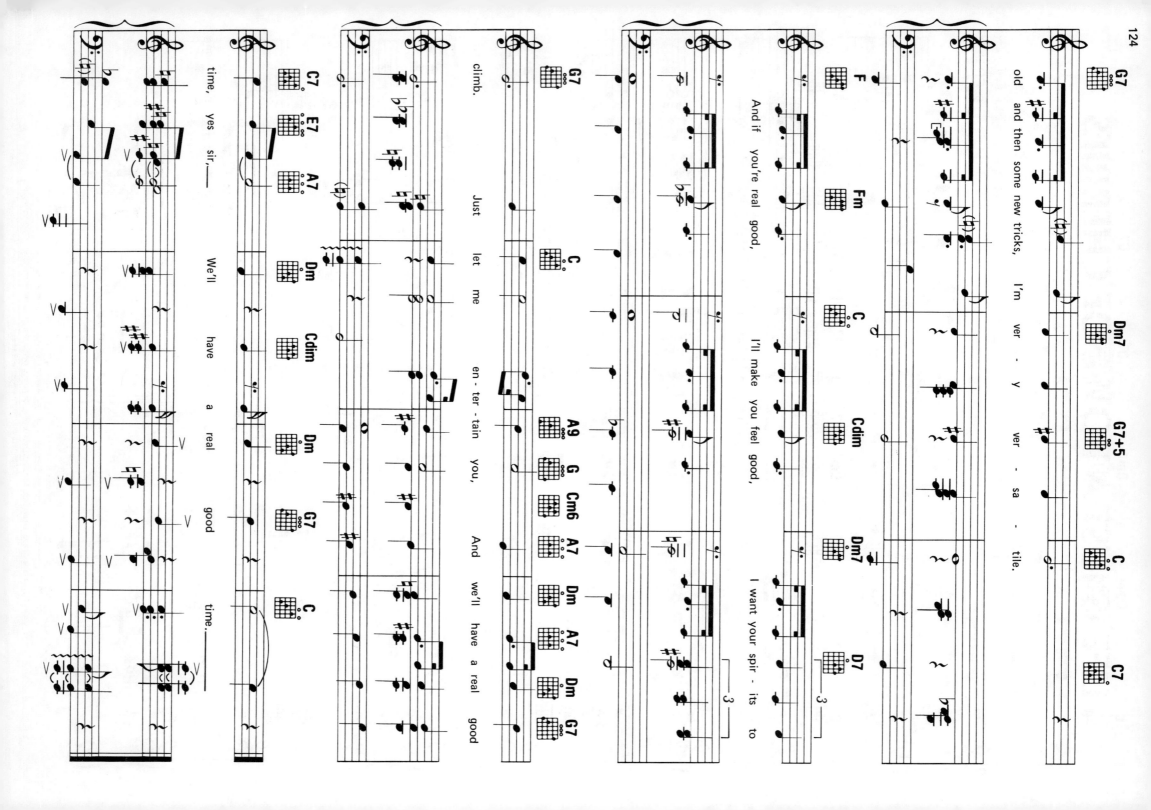

124

LIFE IS JUST A BOWL OF CHERRIES

Words and Music by LEW BROWN
and RAY HENDERSON

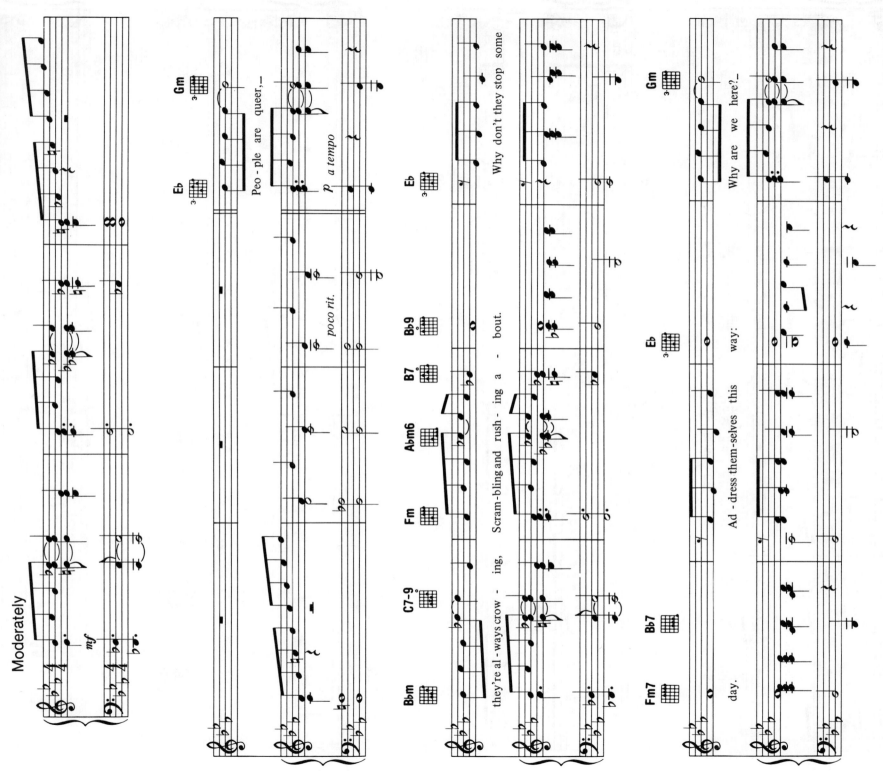

126

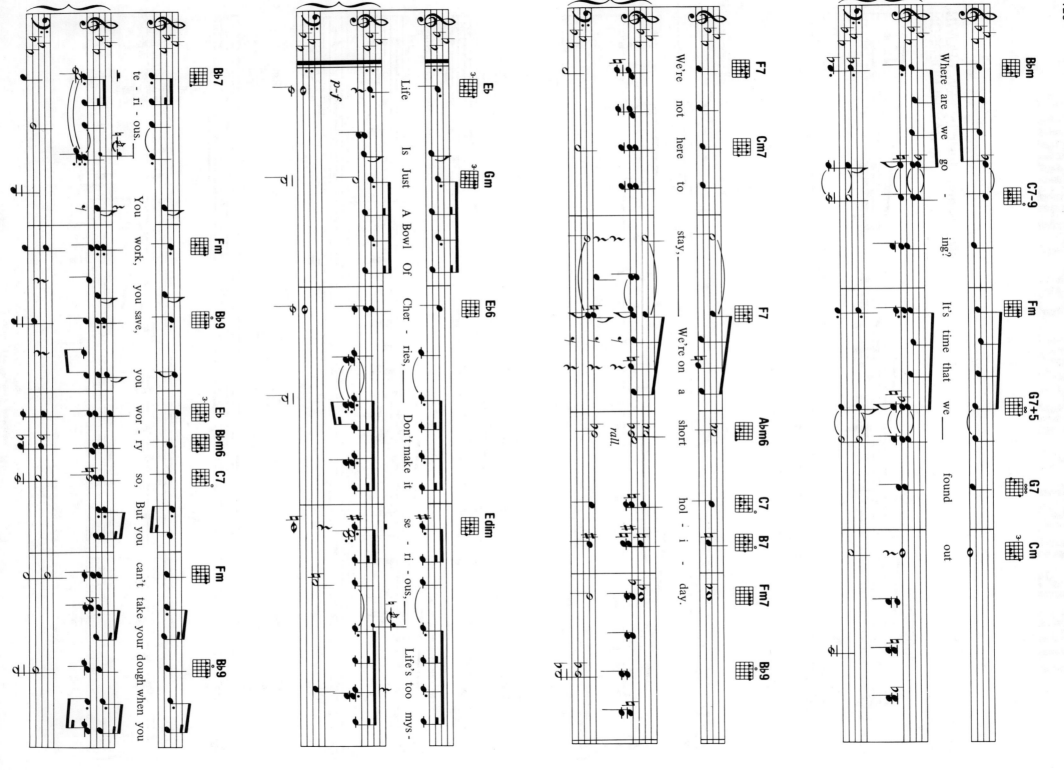

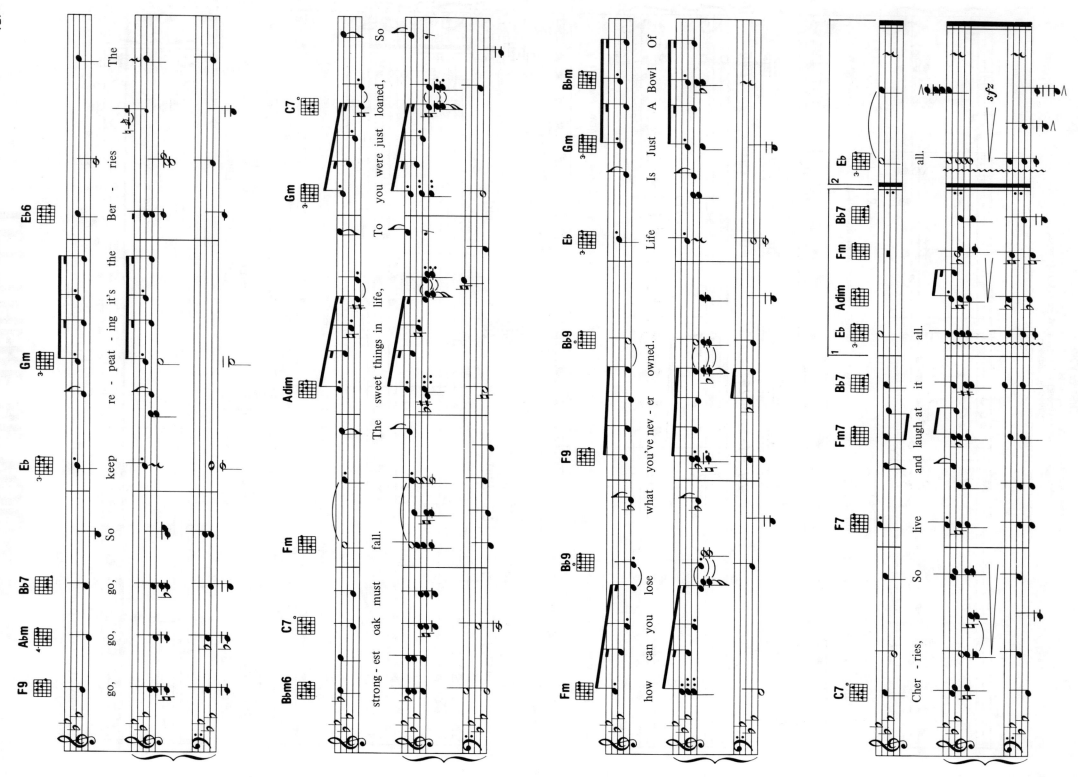

LET THERE BE YOU

Slowly and Lightly Rhythmical

Words and Music by VICKI YOUNG
and DAVE CAVANAUGH

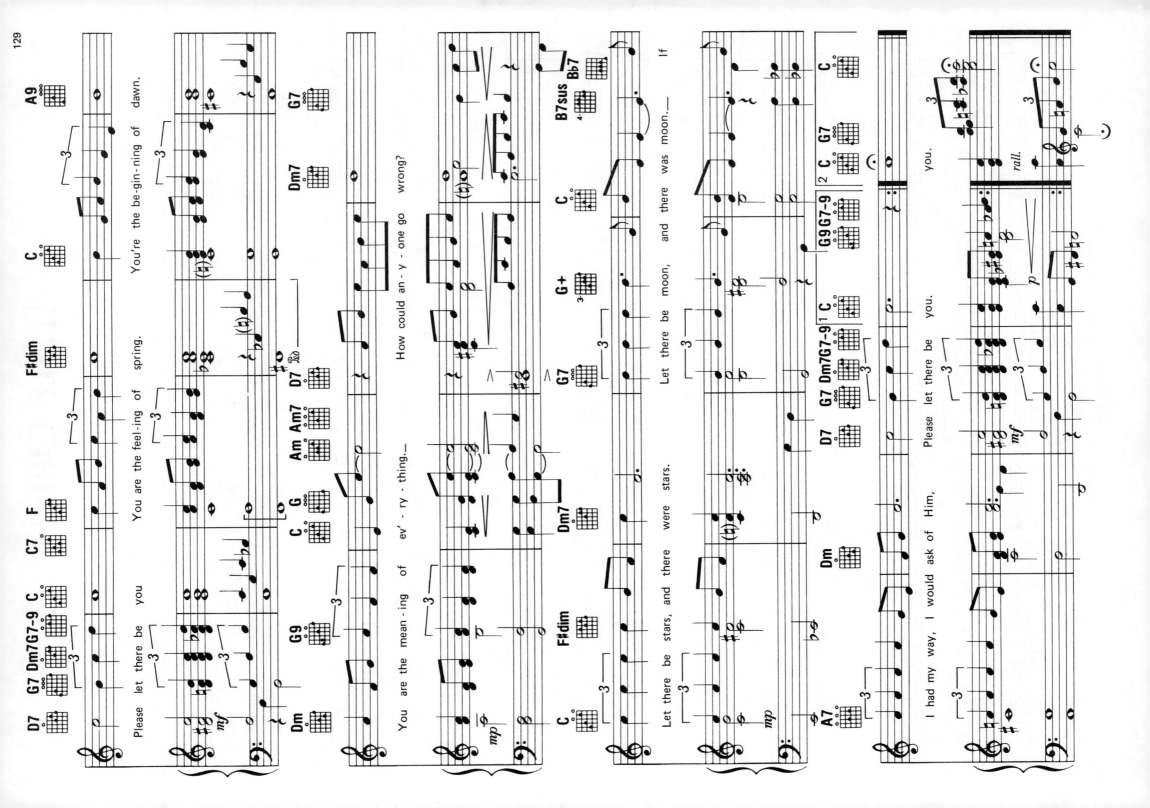

LITTLE GIRL

Words and Music by MADELINE HYDE
and FRANCIS HENRY

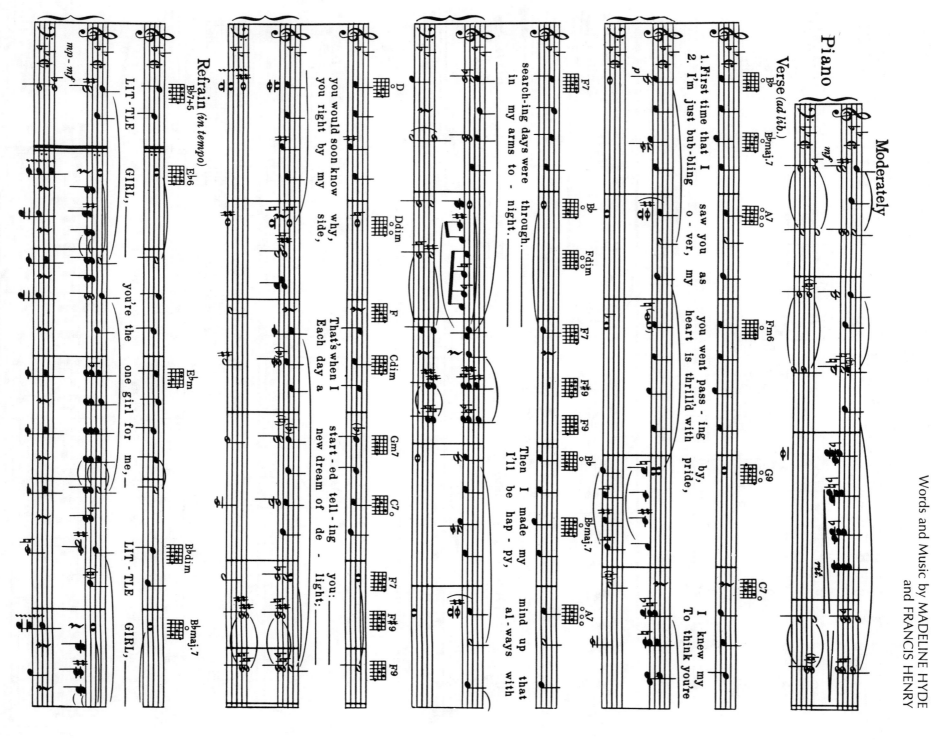

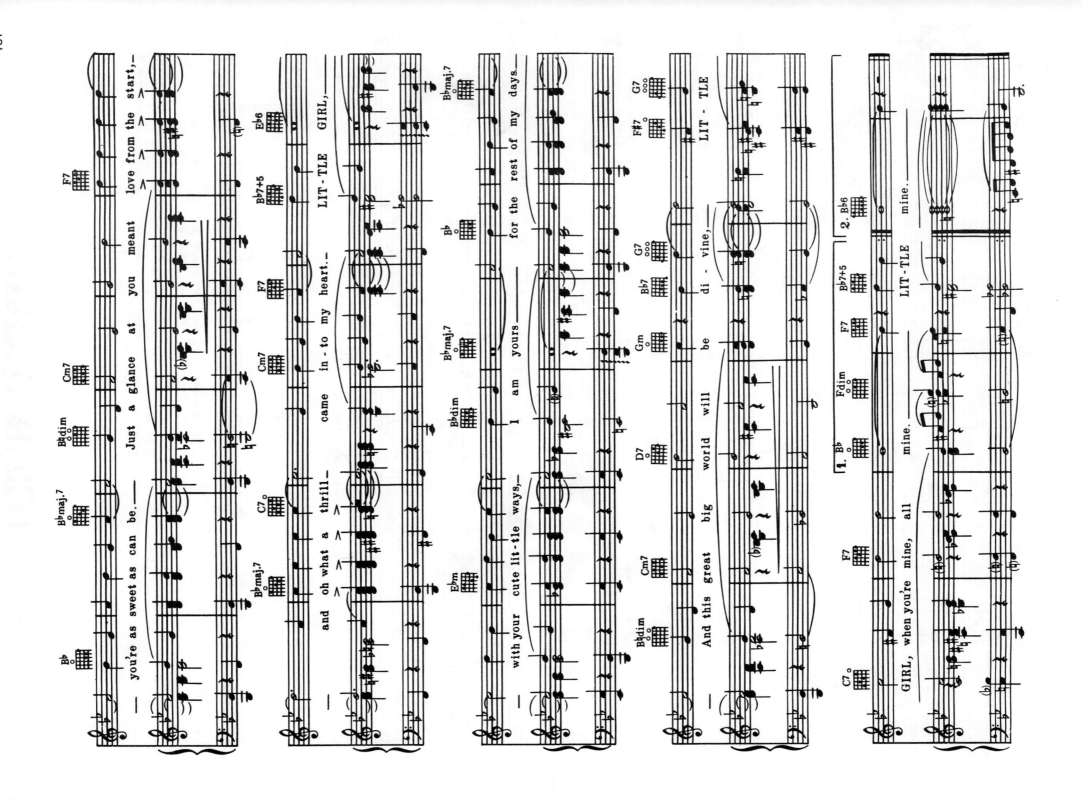

LITTLE GIRL BLUE

Words by LORENZ HART
Music by RICHARD RODGERS

Moderately

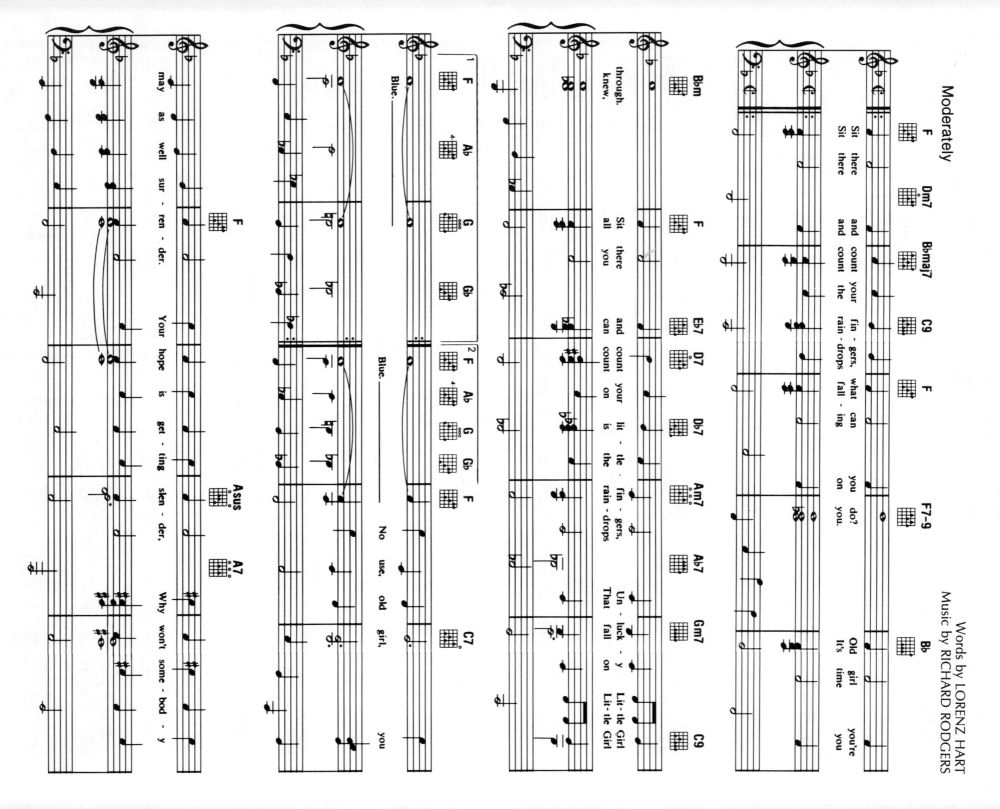

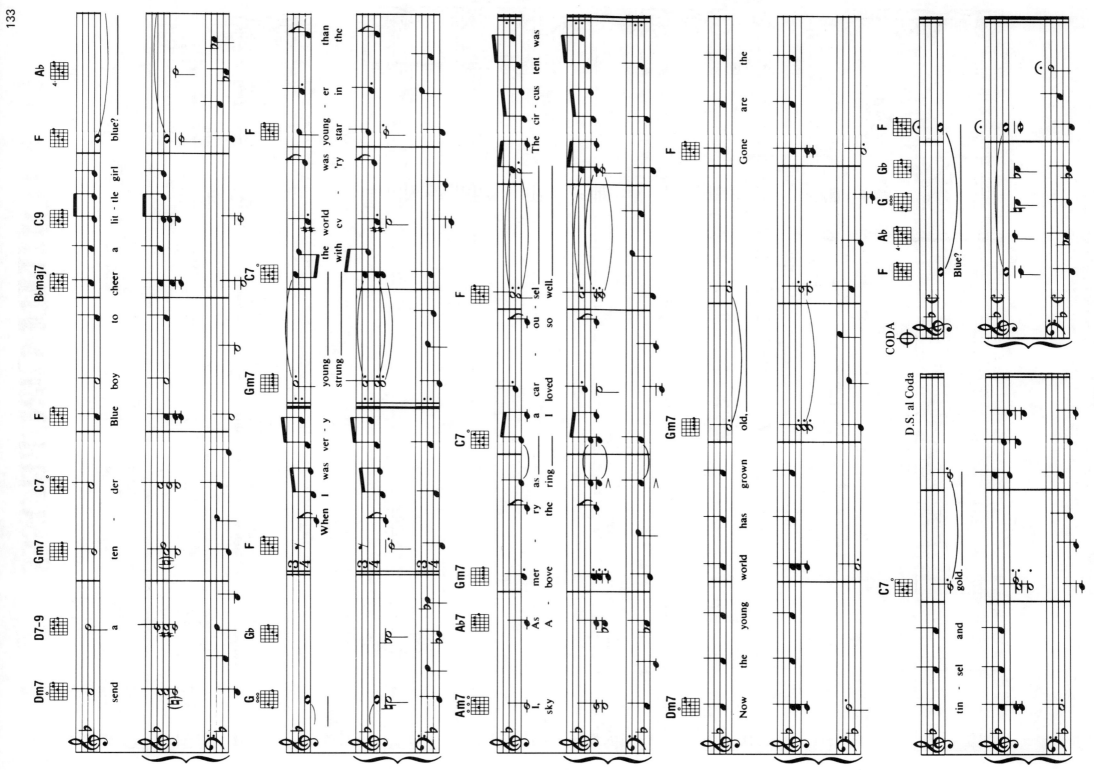

LOLLIPOPS AND ROSES

With movement

Words and Music by TONY VELONA

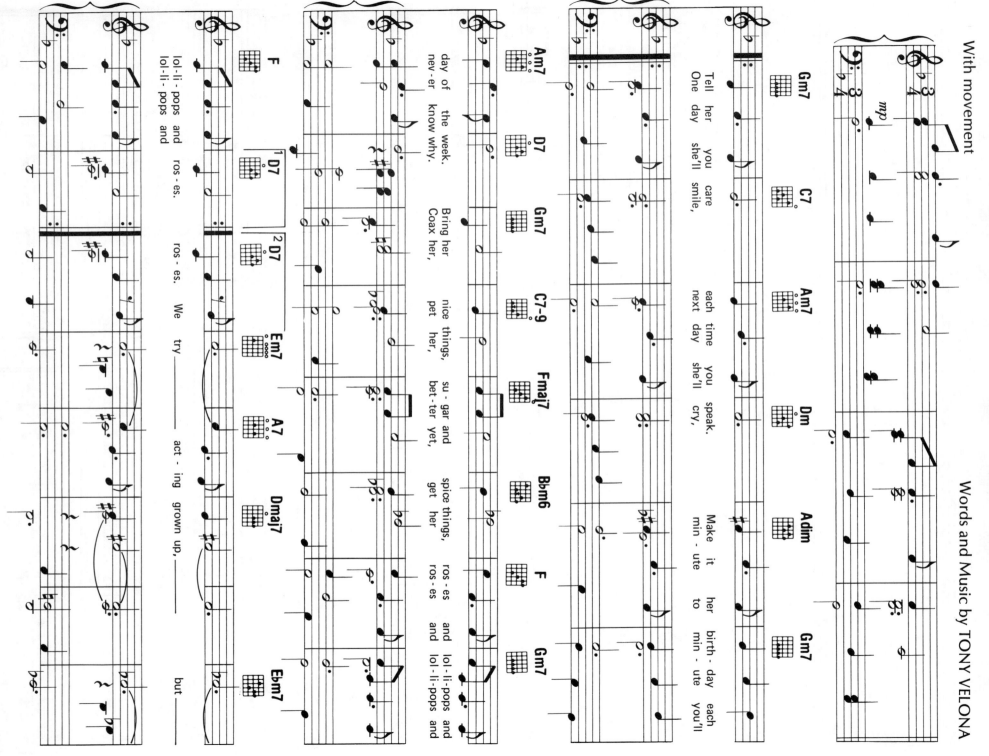

MCA MUSIC

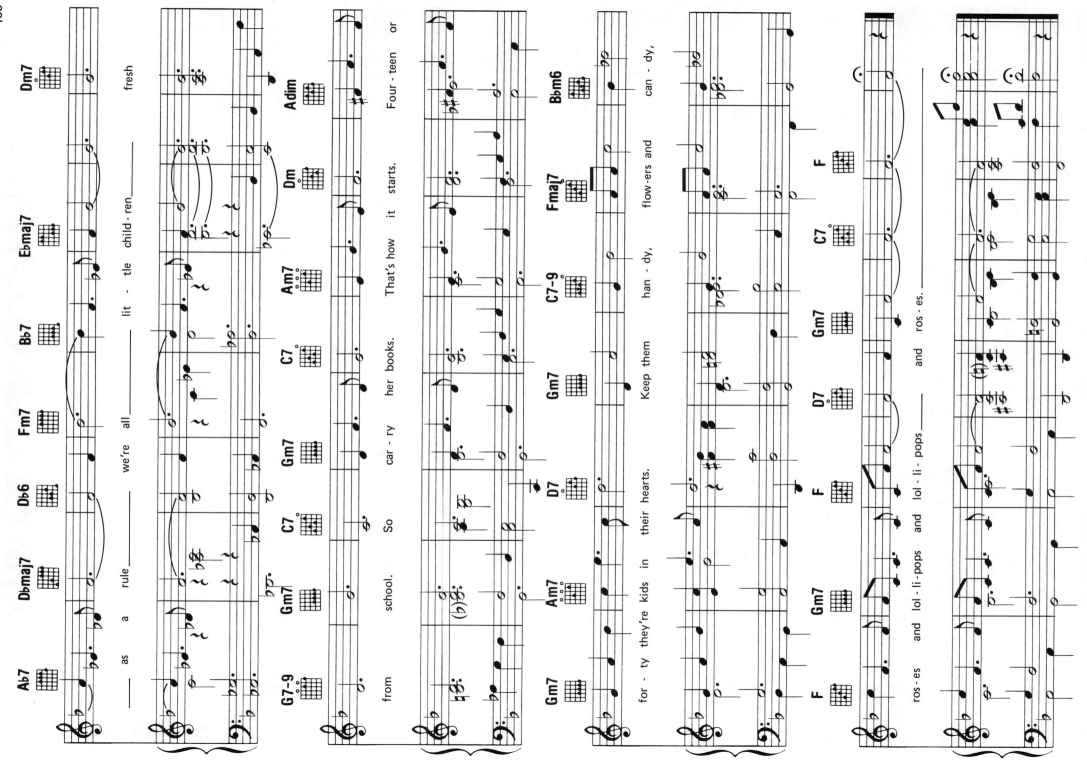

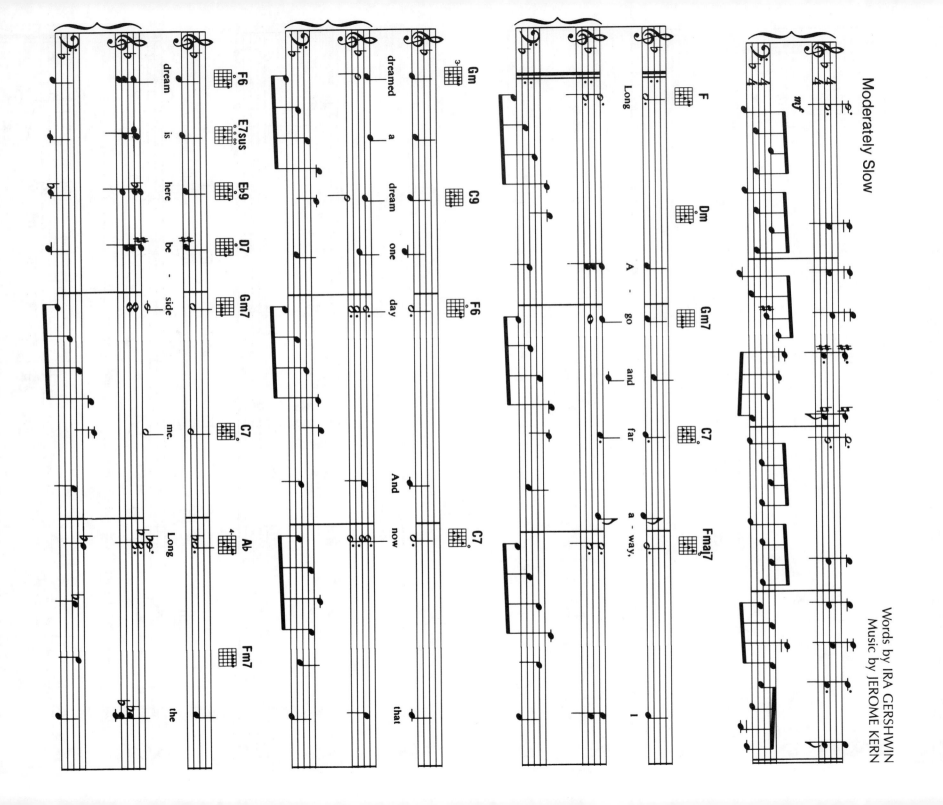

LONG AGO AND FAR AWAY

Words by IRA GERSHWIN
Music by JEROME KERN

Moderately Slow

136

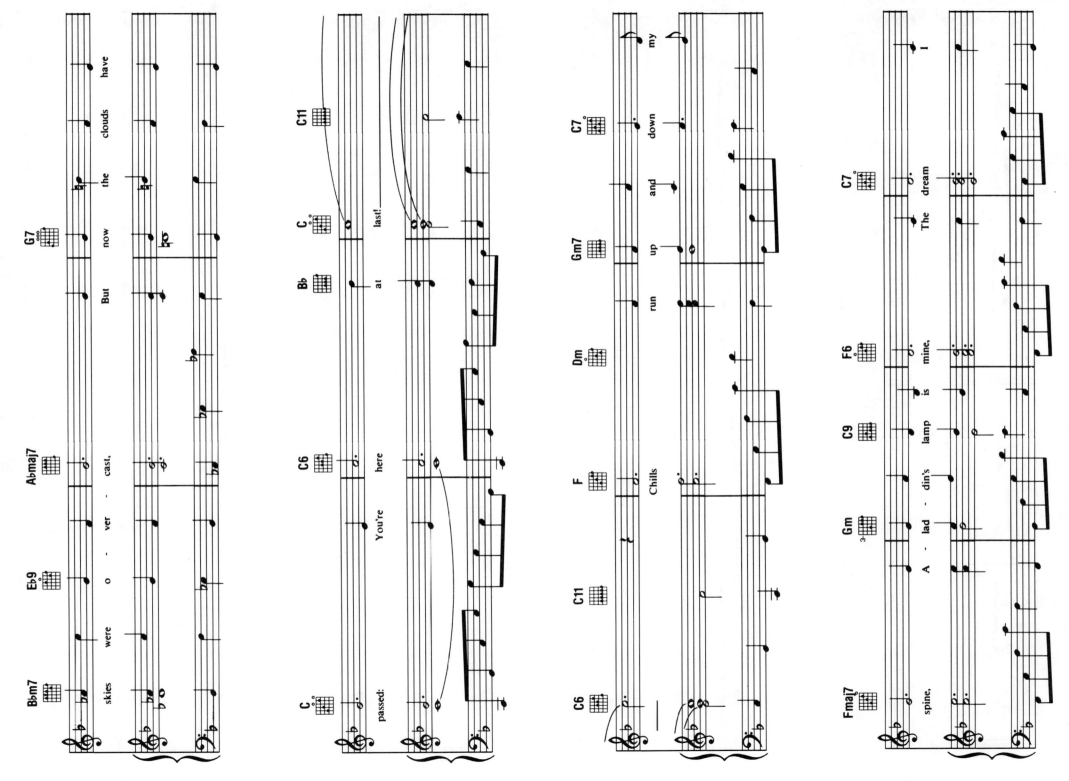

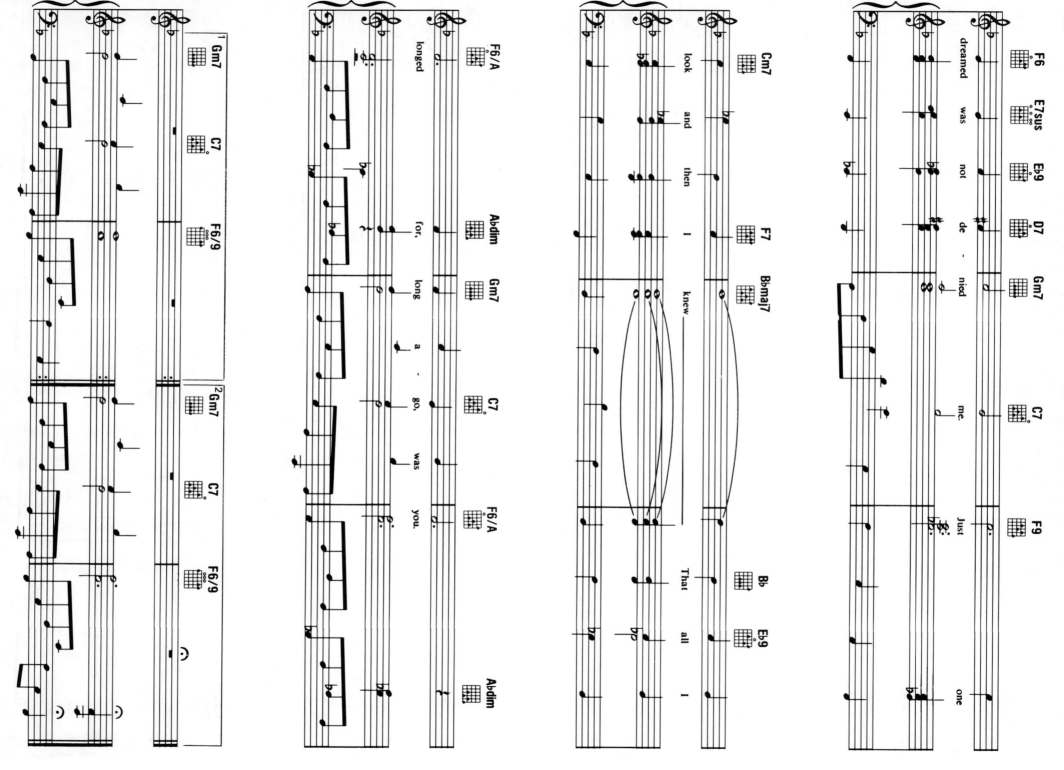

LOVE IS HERE TO STAY
(From GOLDWYN FOLLIES)

Words by IRA GERSHWIN
Music by GEORGE GERSHWIN

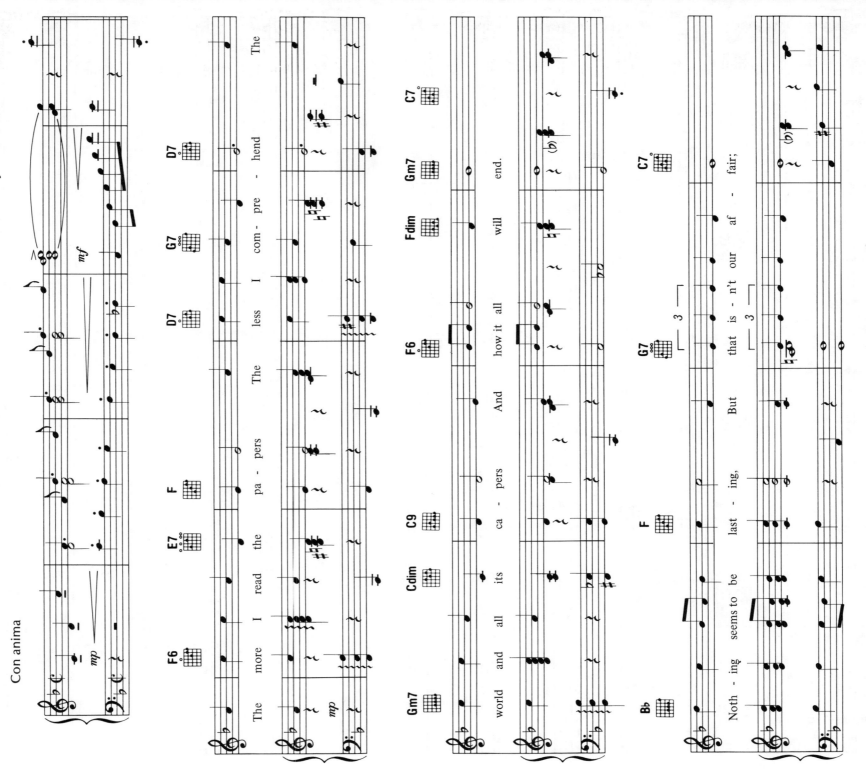

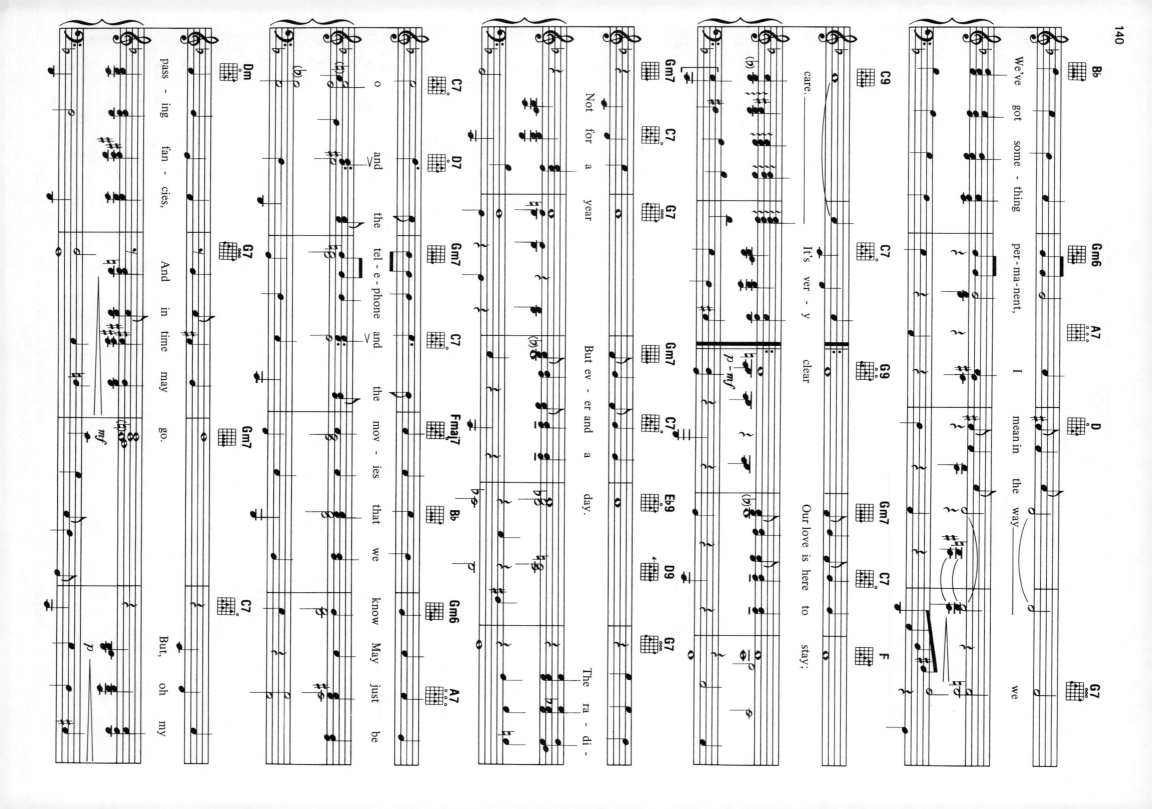

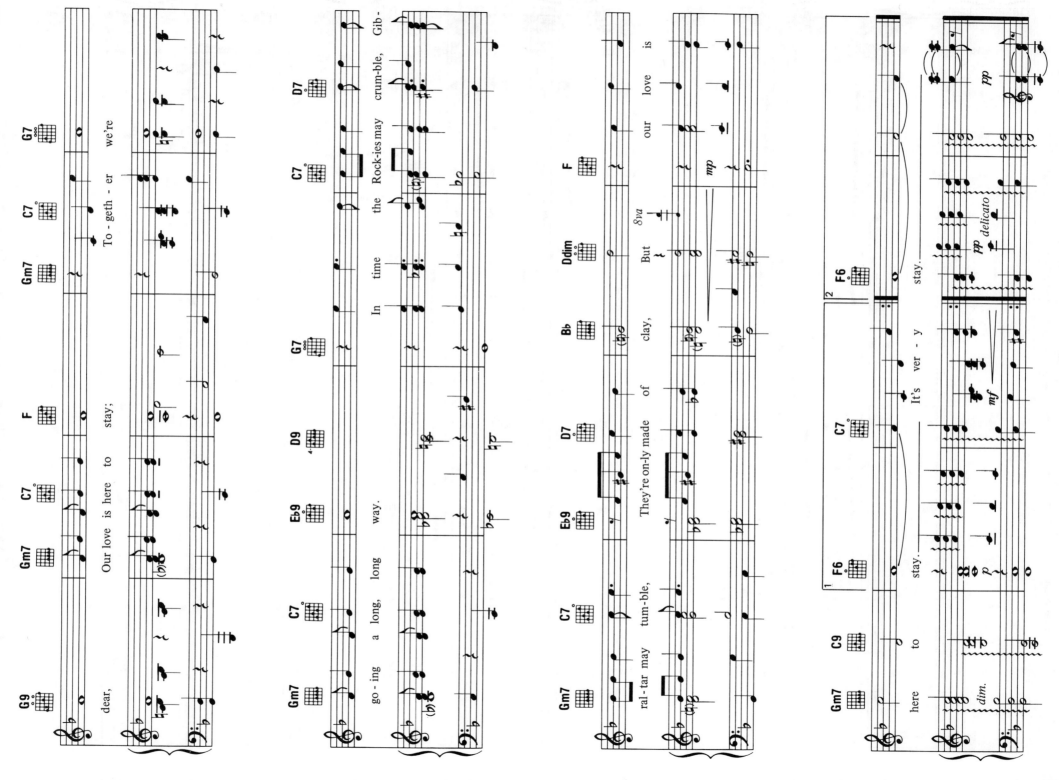

LOOK FOR THE SILVER LINING

Words by BUD DESYLVA
Music by JEROME KERN

Moderately

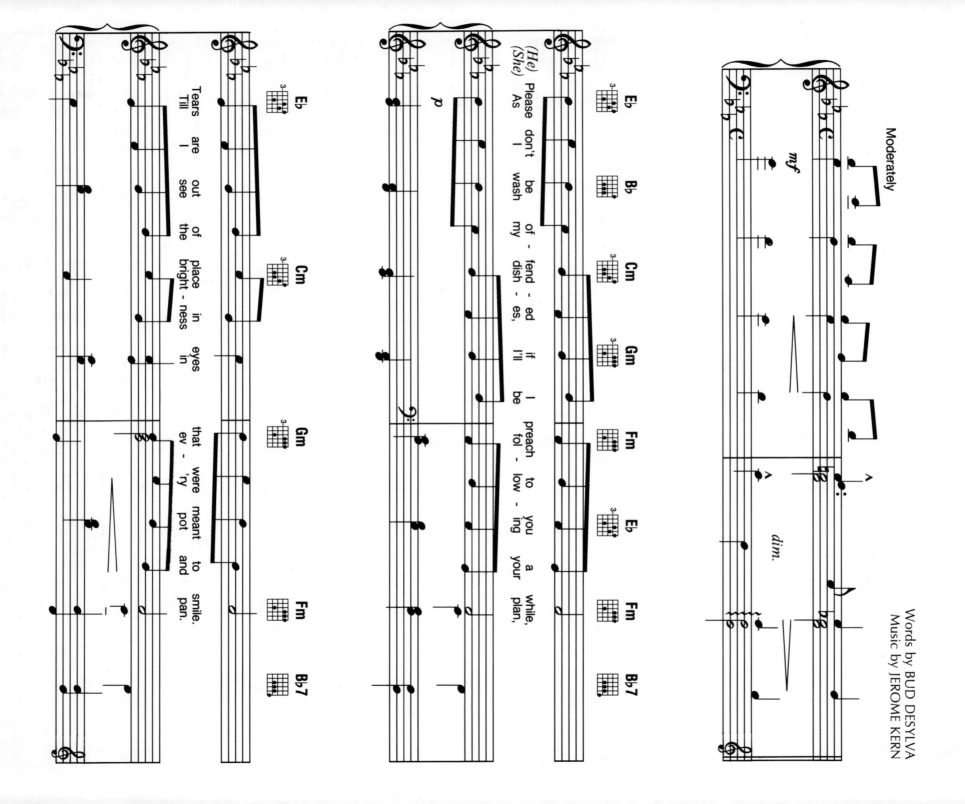

Eb
Bb
Cm
Gm
Fm
Eb
Fm
Bb7
There's a way to make your ver - y big - gest troub - les small,
I am sure your point of view will ease the dai - ly grind,
Eb
F7
Bb7
Eb
Bb7
Here's the hap - py se - cret of it all.
So I'll keep re - peat - ing in my mind.
Slowly
Eb
Bb7
Eb
Look for the sil - ver lin - ing
p-f
Ab
When - e'er a cloud ap - pears in the

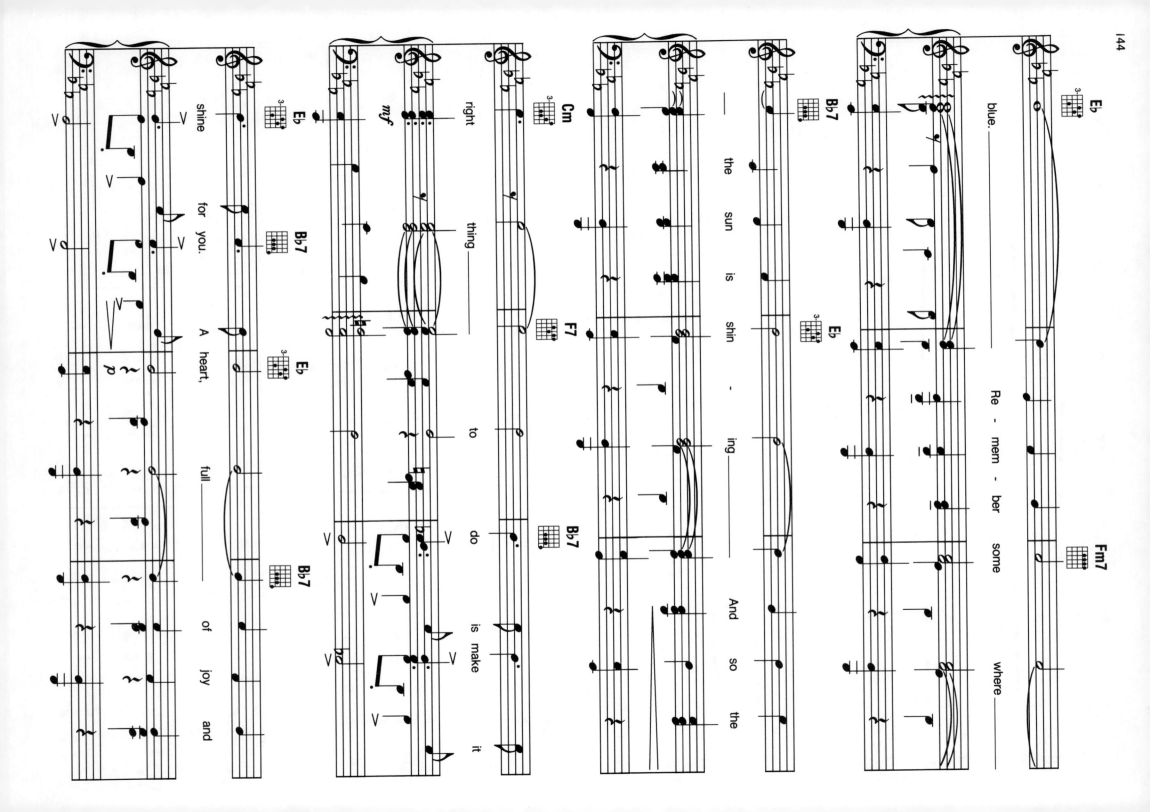

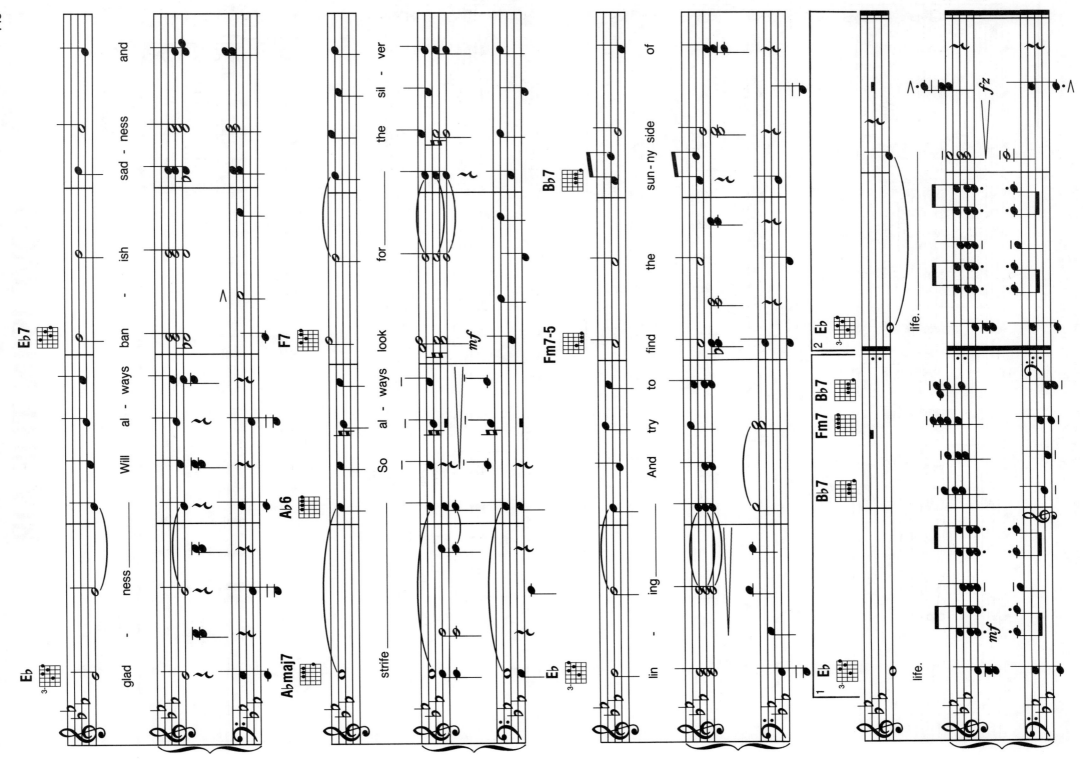

LOVE IS IN THE AIR

Words and Music by HARRY VANDA
and GEORGE YOUNG

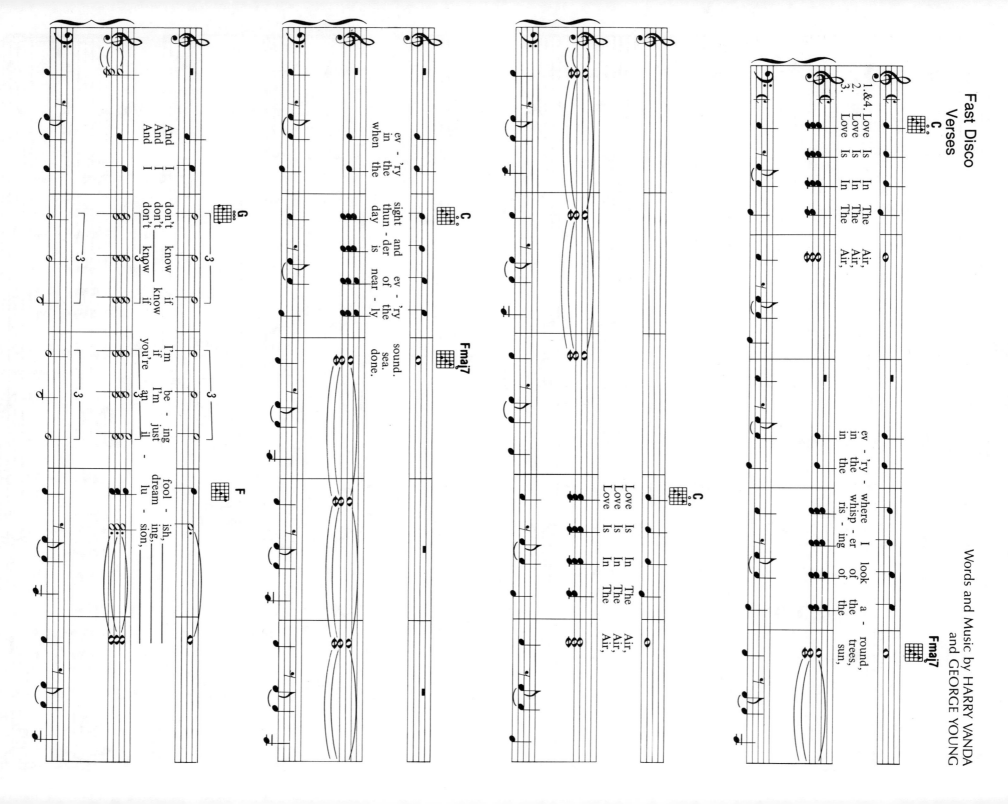

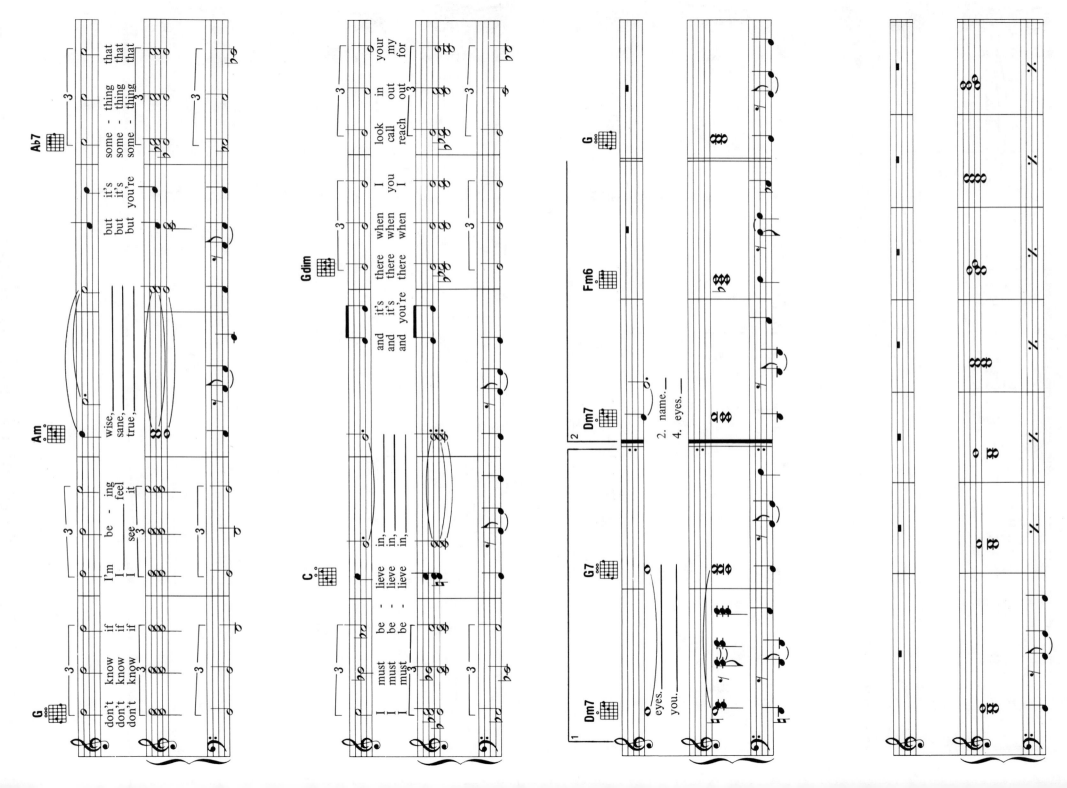

147

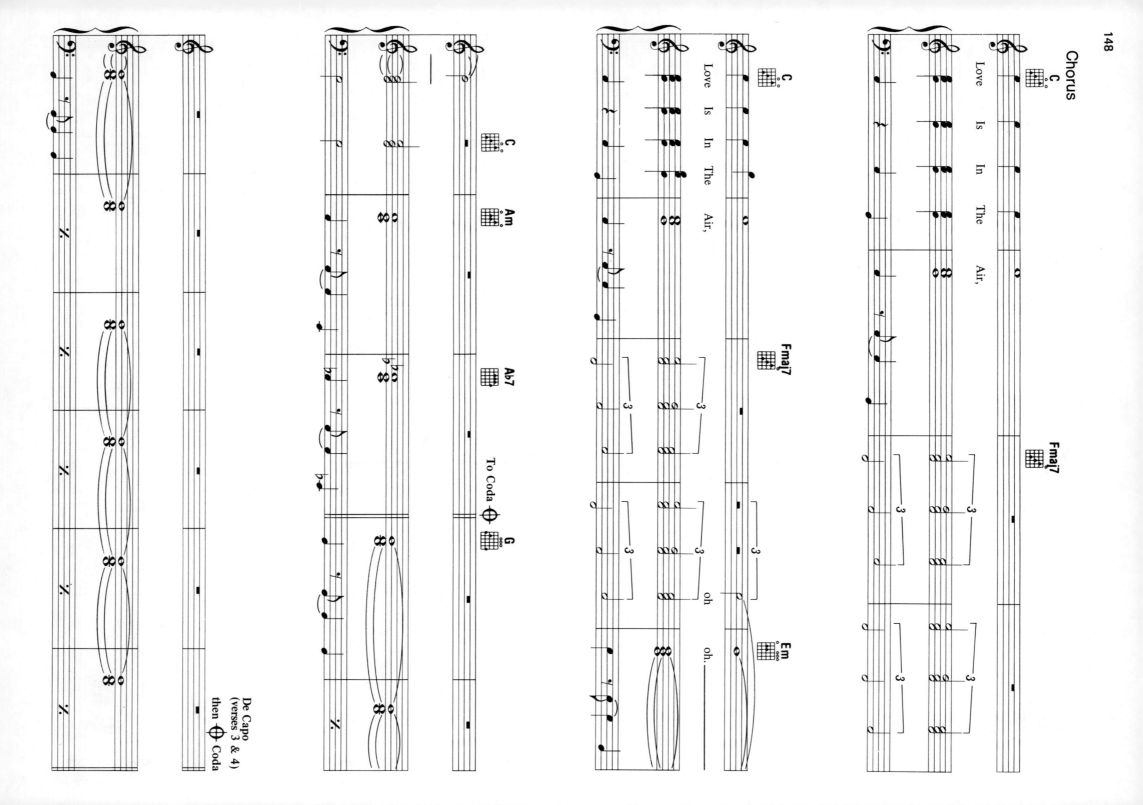

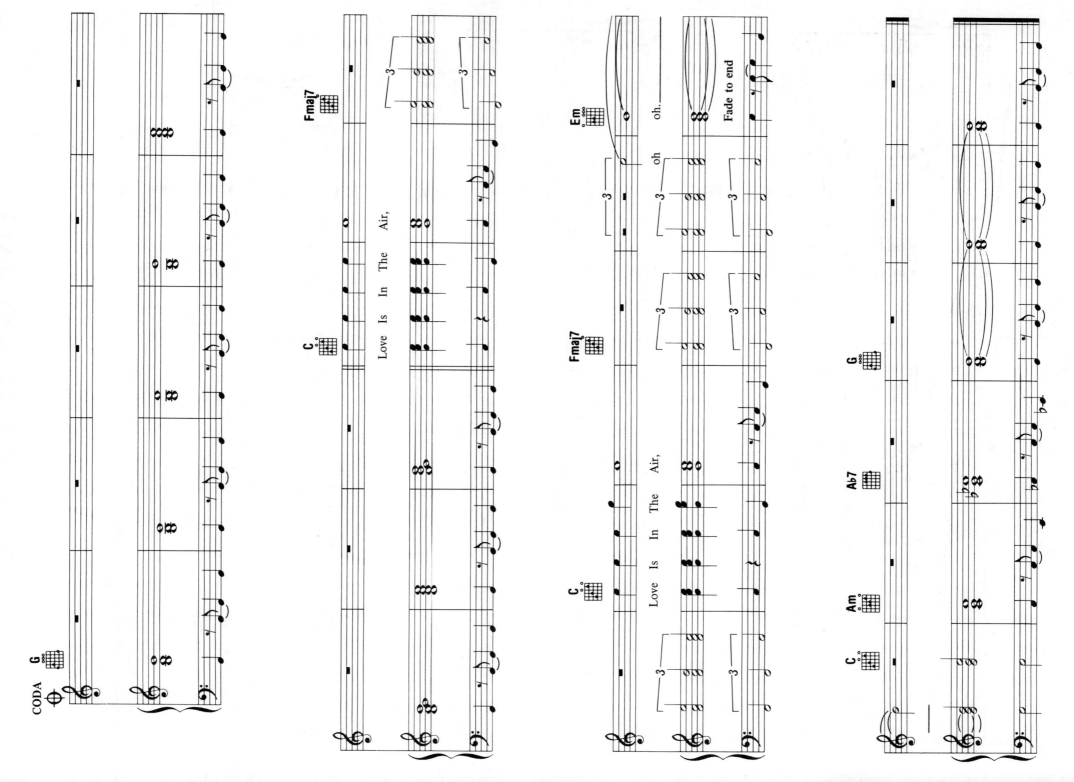

LOVE ON THE ROCKS

Words and Music by NEIL DIAMOND
and GILBERT BECAUD

Moderately slow Ballad

mp legato

Love on the rocks   ain't no sur - prise.

Pour me a drink,—   and I'll   tell you some lies.—

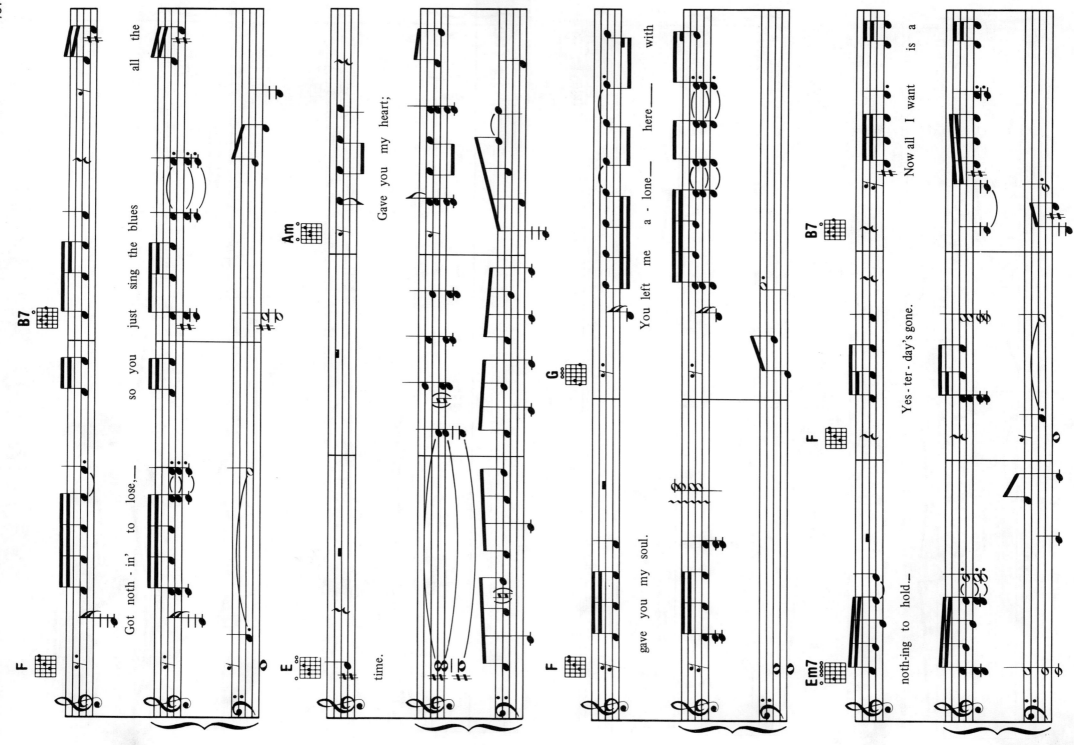

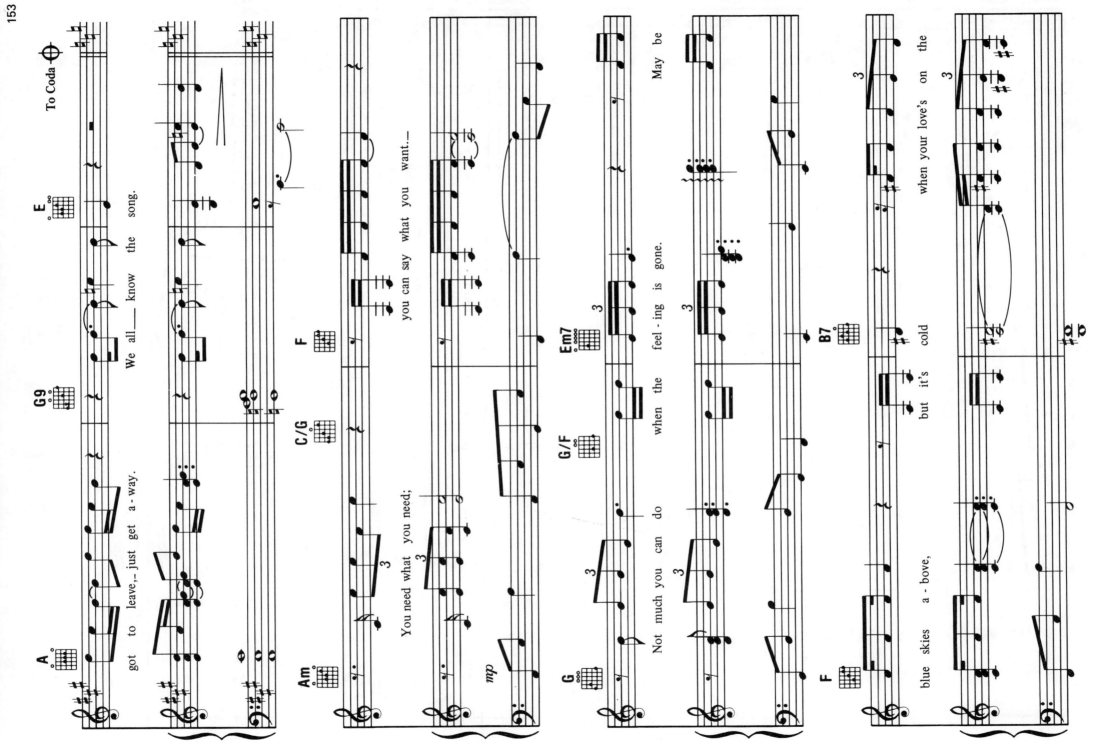

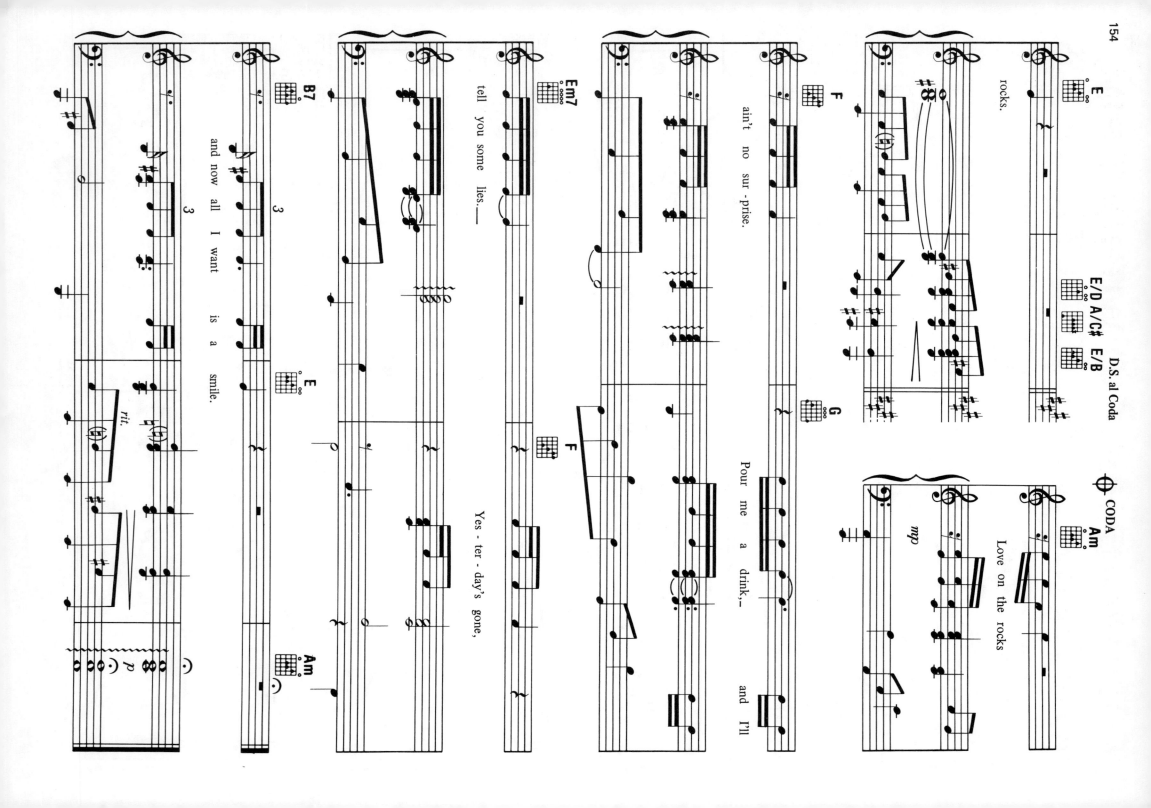

MAD ABOUT HIM, SAD WITHOUT HIM, HOW CAN I BE GLAD WITHOUT HIM BLUES

Words and Music by LARRY MARKES
and DICK CHARLES

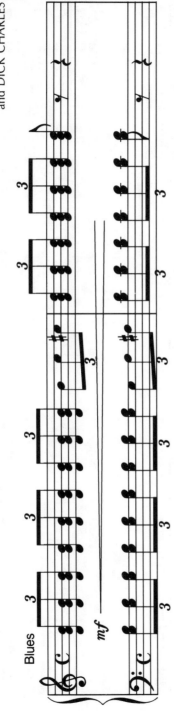
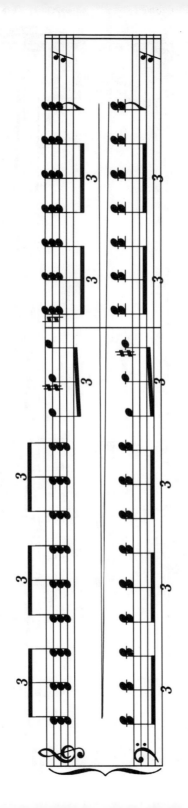
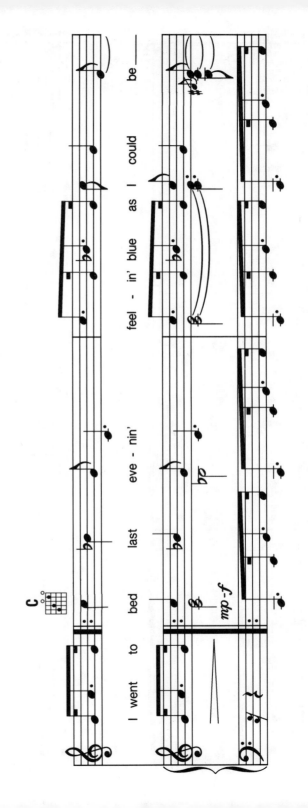

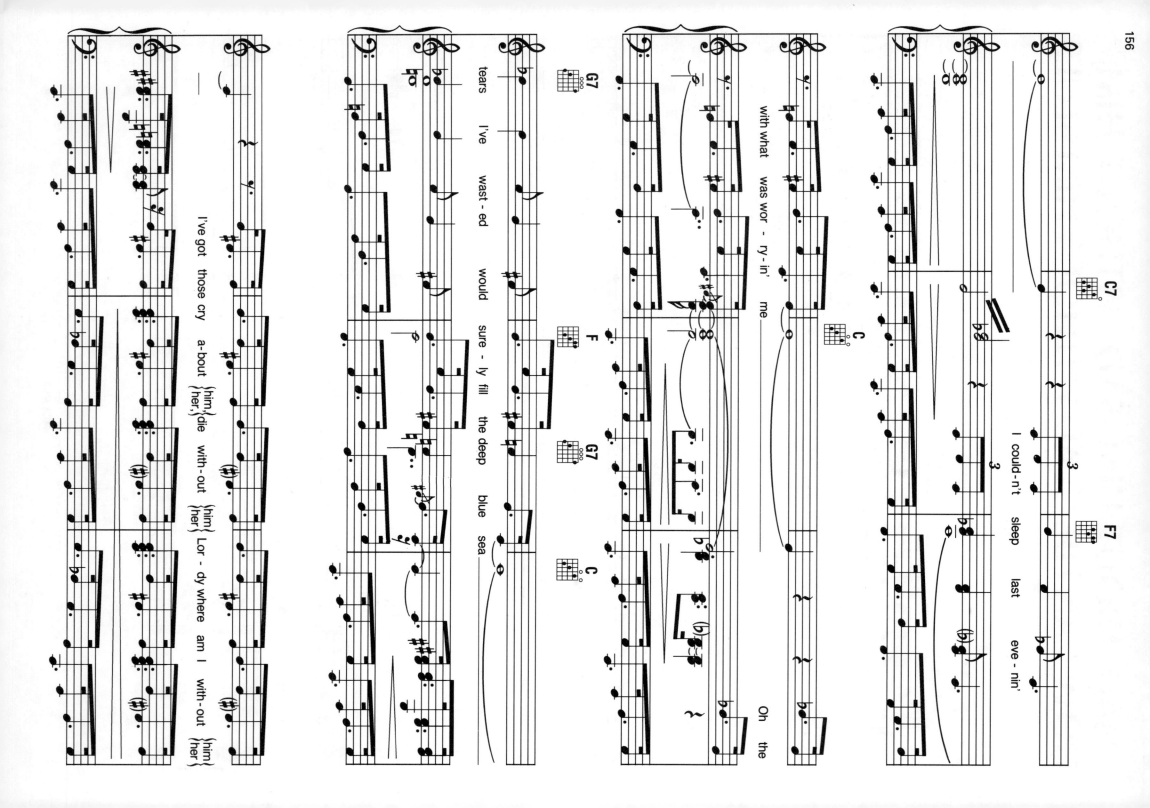

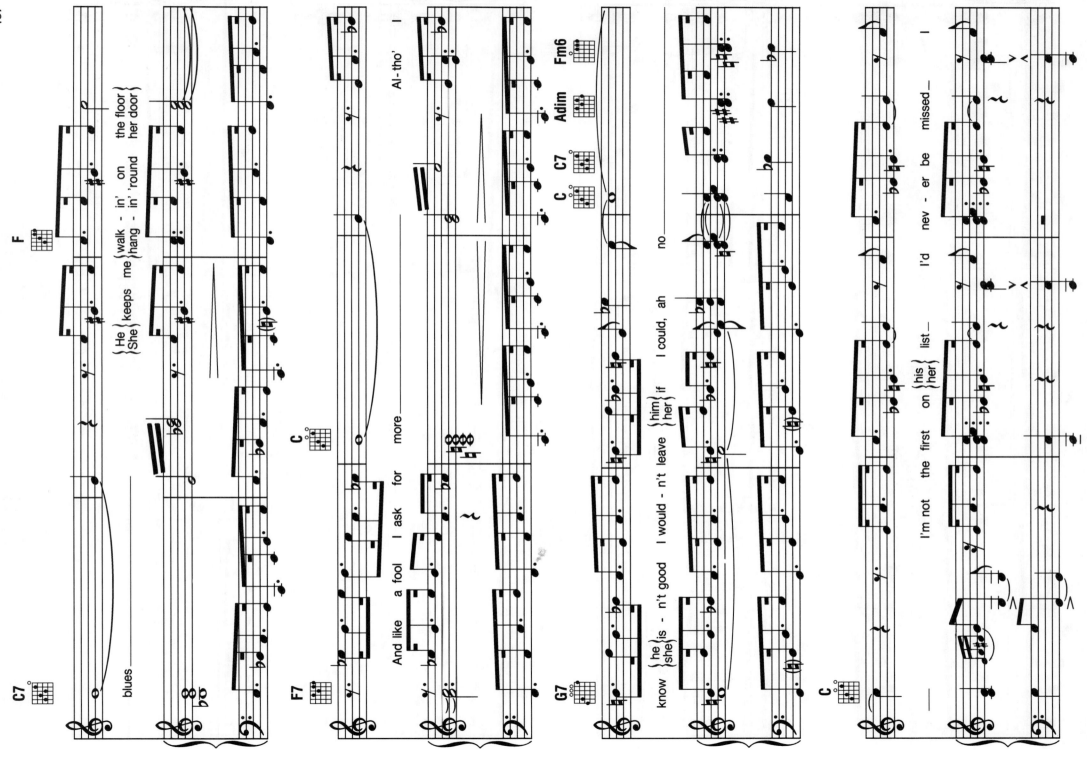

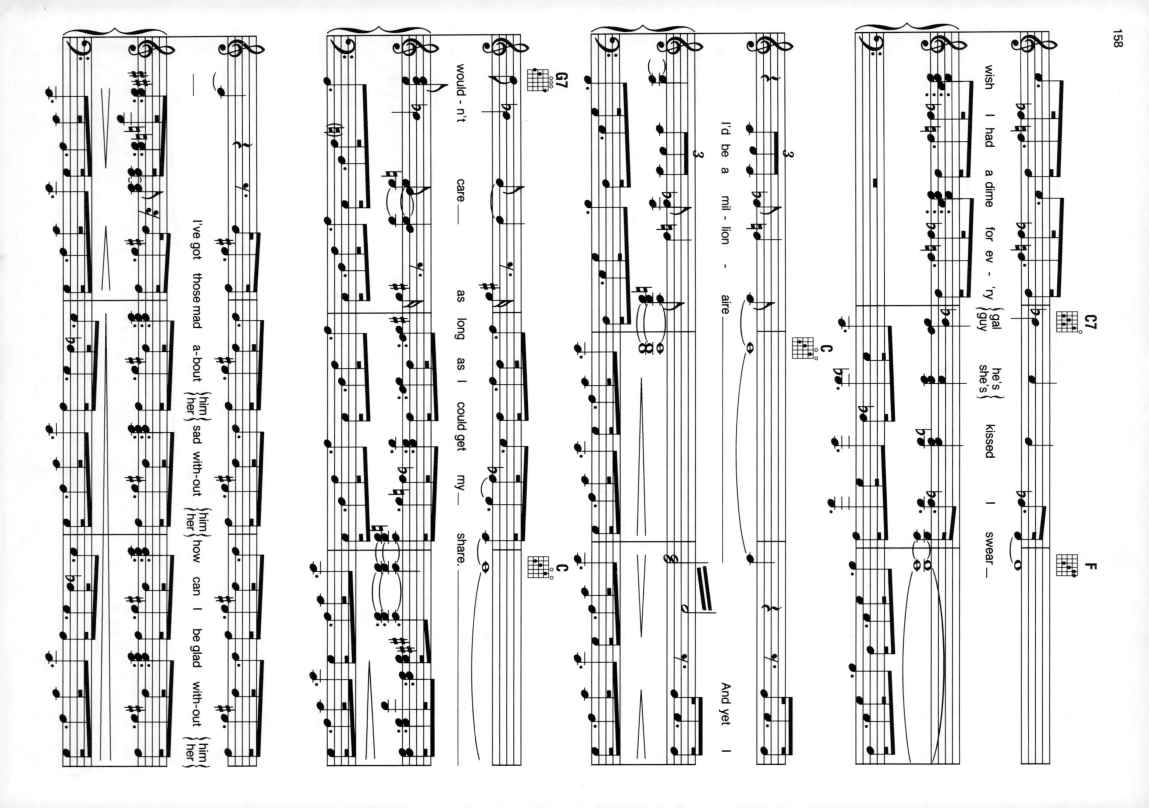

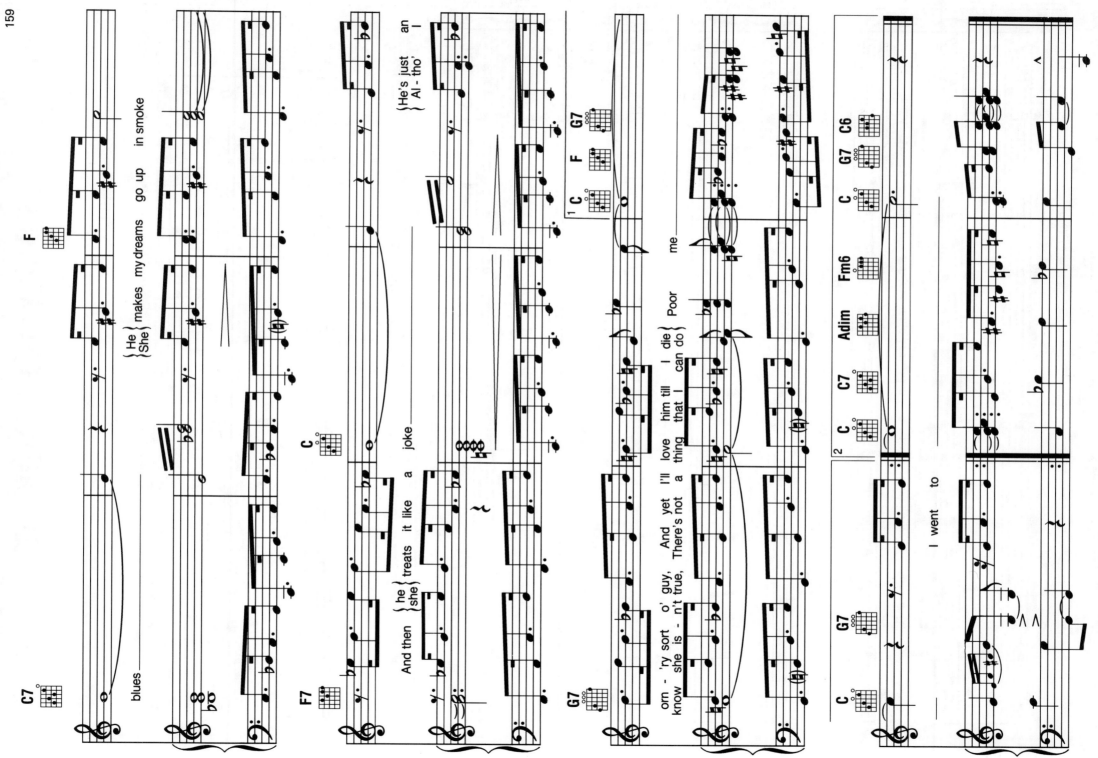

LOVELY TO LOOK AT

Words by DOROTHY FIELDS and JIMMY McHUGH
Music by JEROME KERN

Moderately

Love - ly to look at, De - light - ful to know and

heav - en to kiss. A com - bin -

a - tion like this, Is quite my

most im - pos - si - ble scheme come true, Im - a - gine find - ing a dream like you! You're

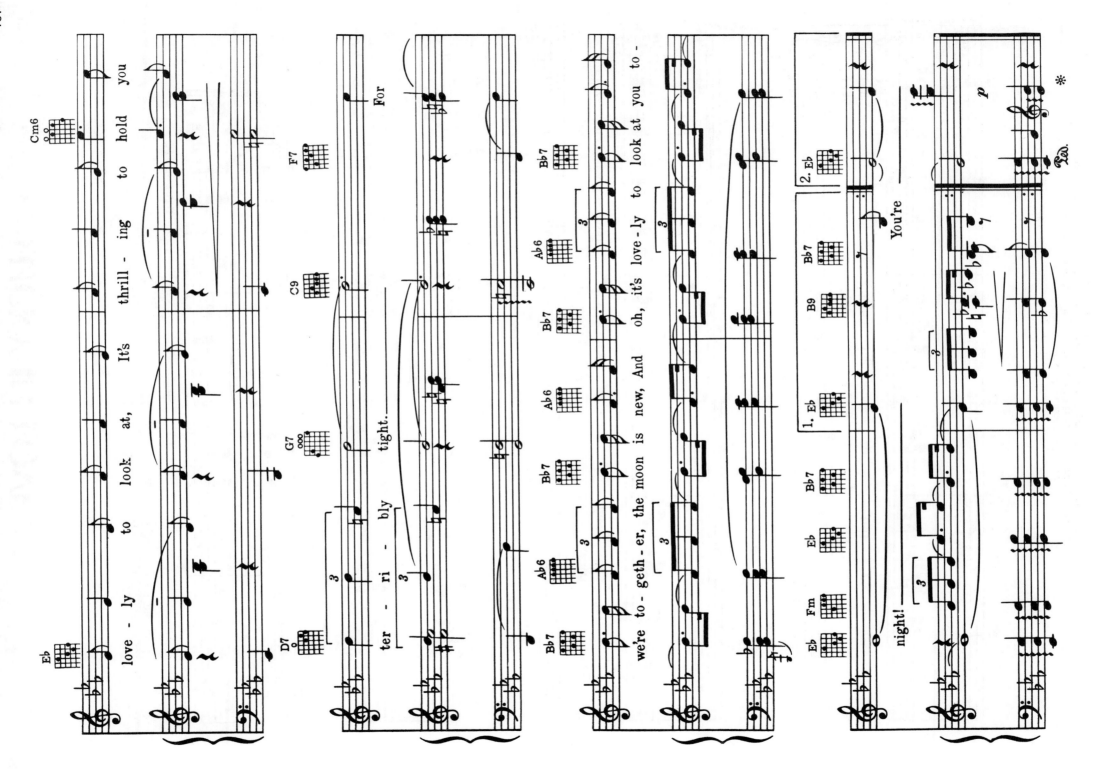

LUCKY IN LOVE

Words and Music by B.G. DeSYLVA,
LEW BROWN and RAY HENDERSON

Moderato

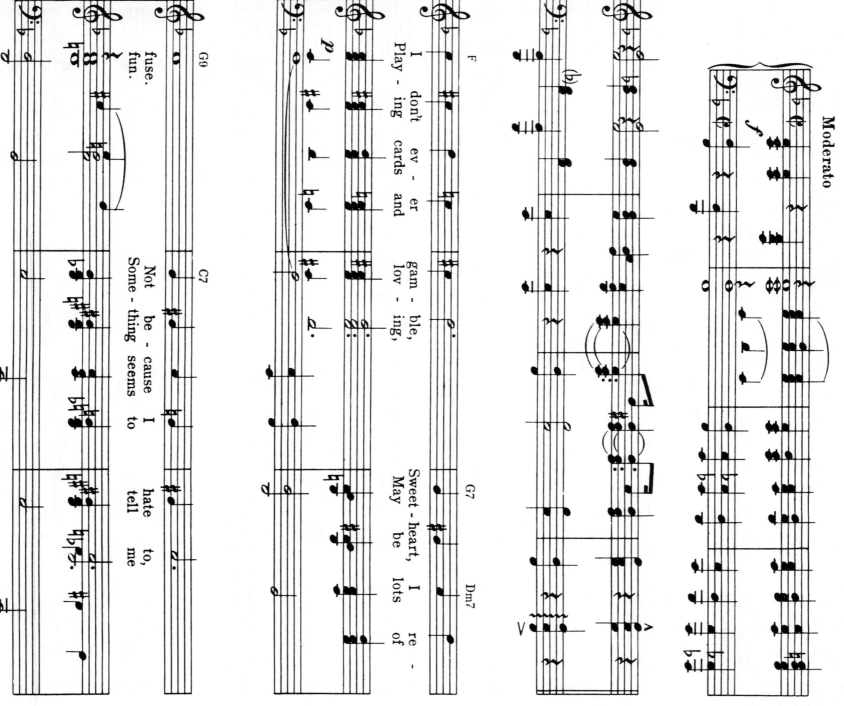

Lyrics: I don't ev - er Play - ing cards and gam - ble, lov - ing, Sweet - heart, May be lots of I re - Not be - cause I Some - thing seems to hate to, tell me fuse. fun.

163

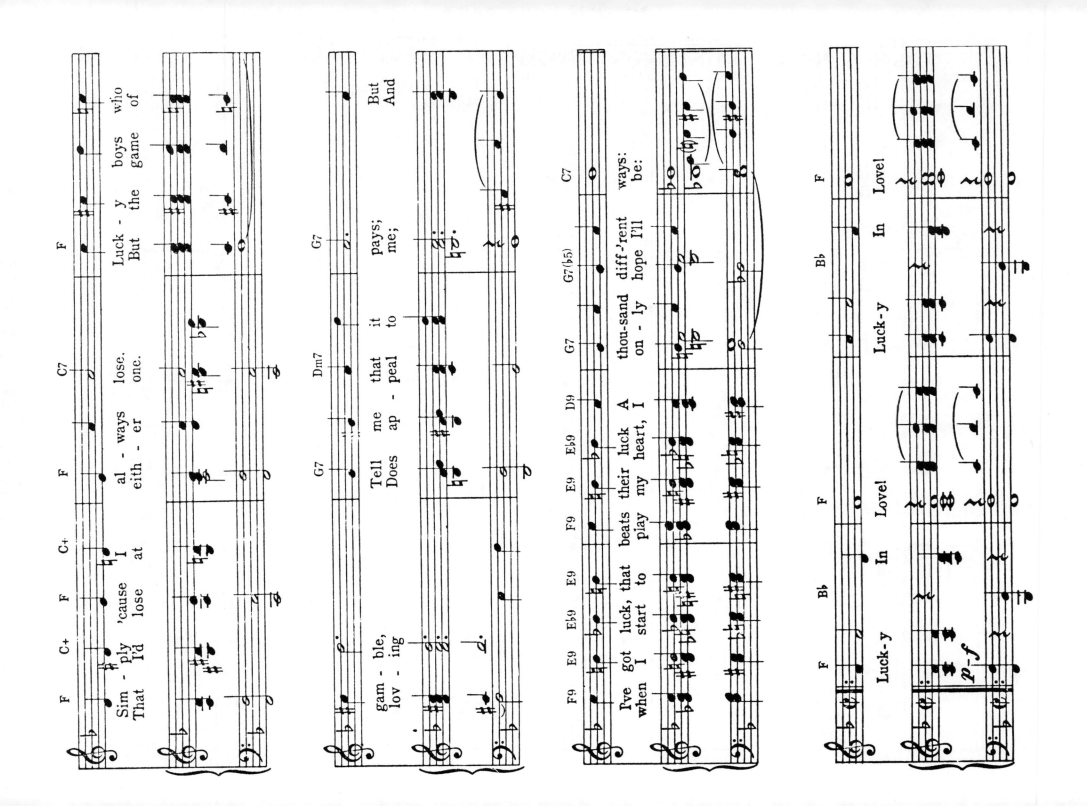

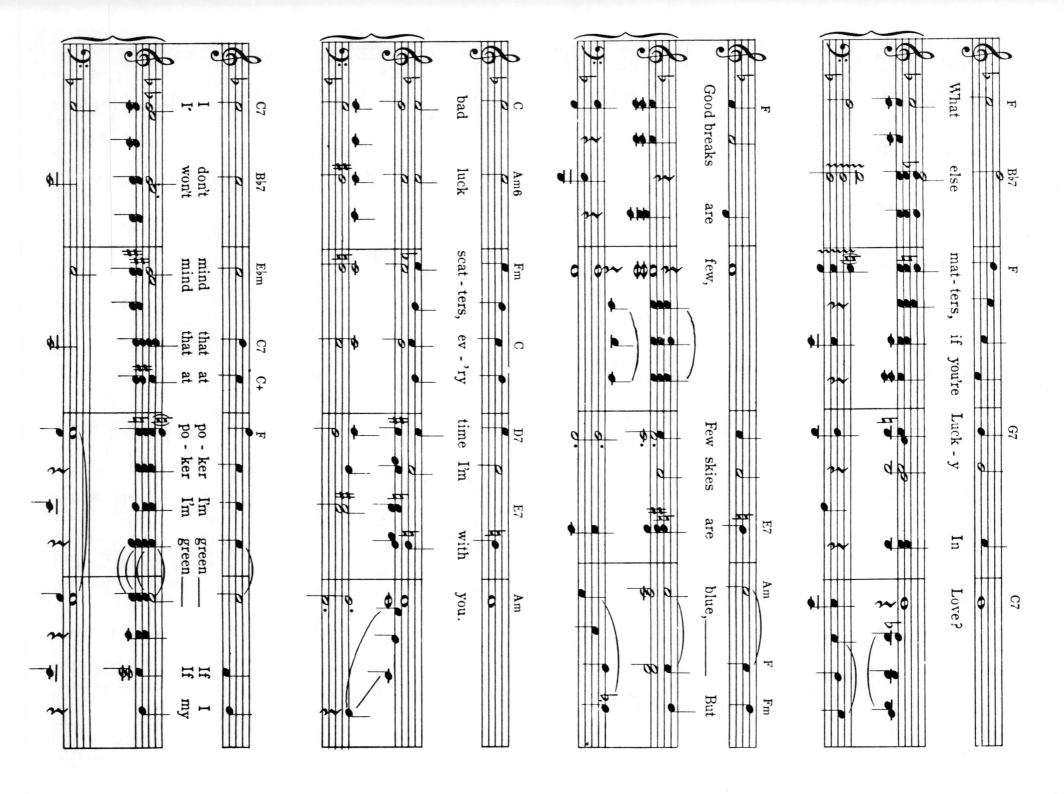

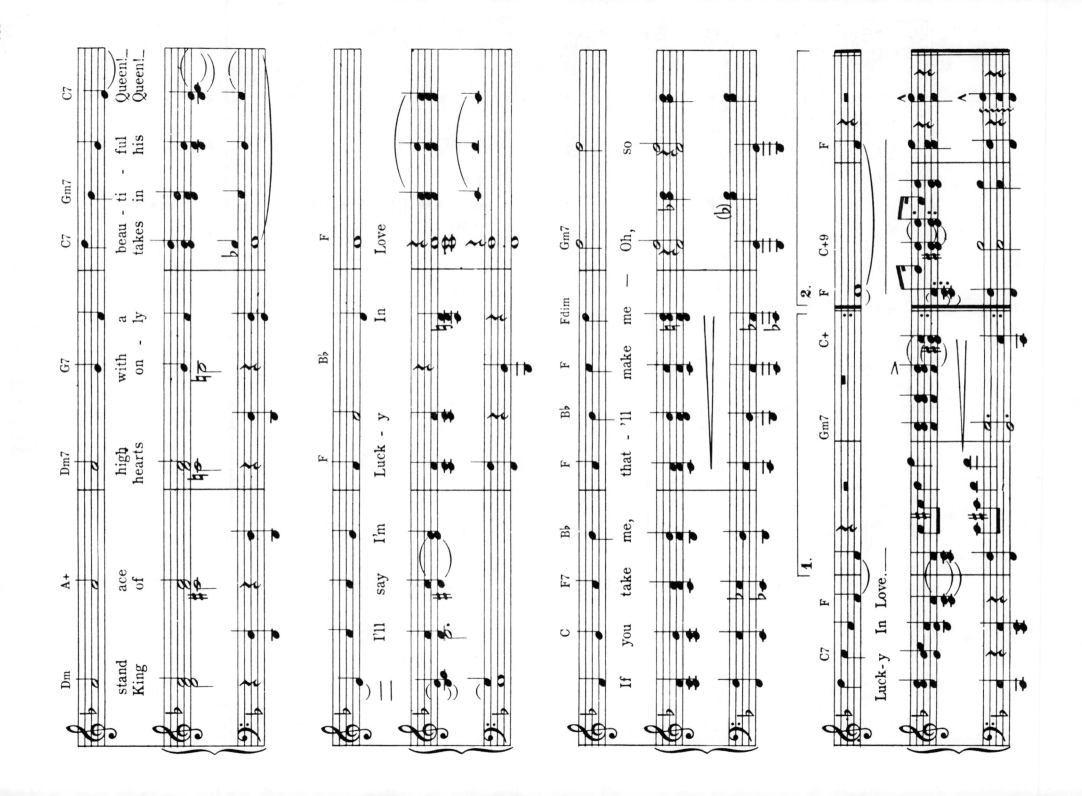

MAKE BELIEVE
(From "SHOW BOAT")

Words by OSCAR HAMMERSTEIN II
Music by JEROME KERN

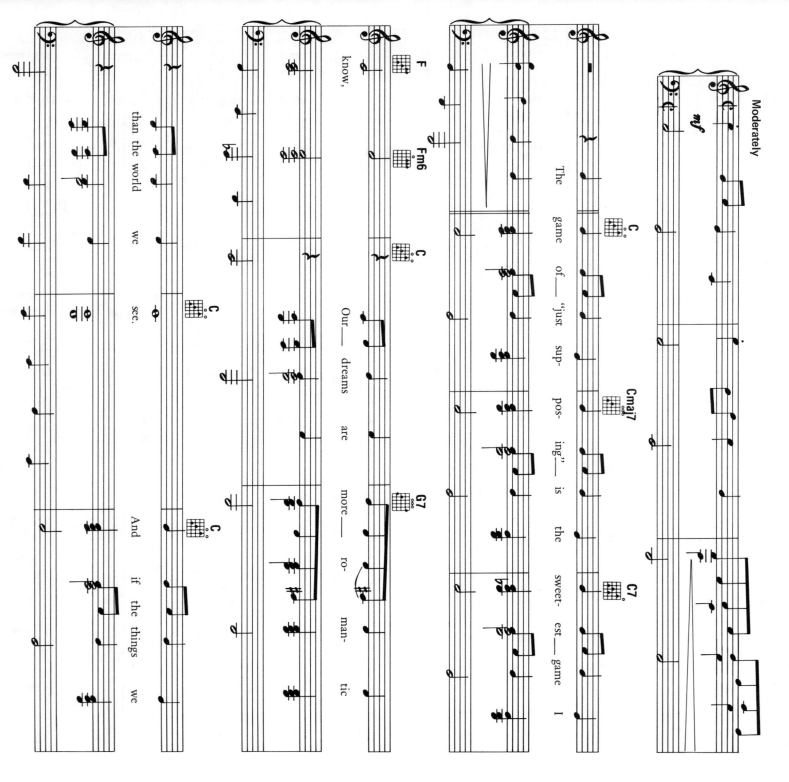

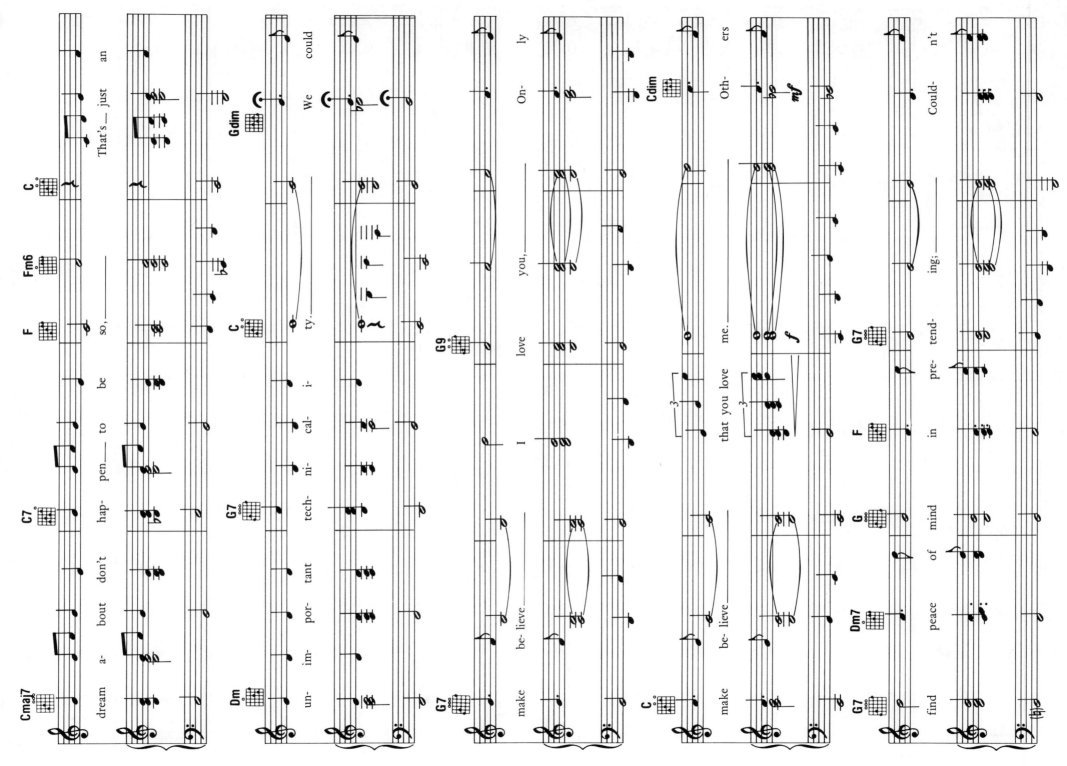

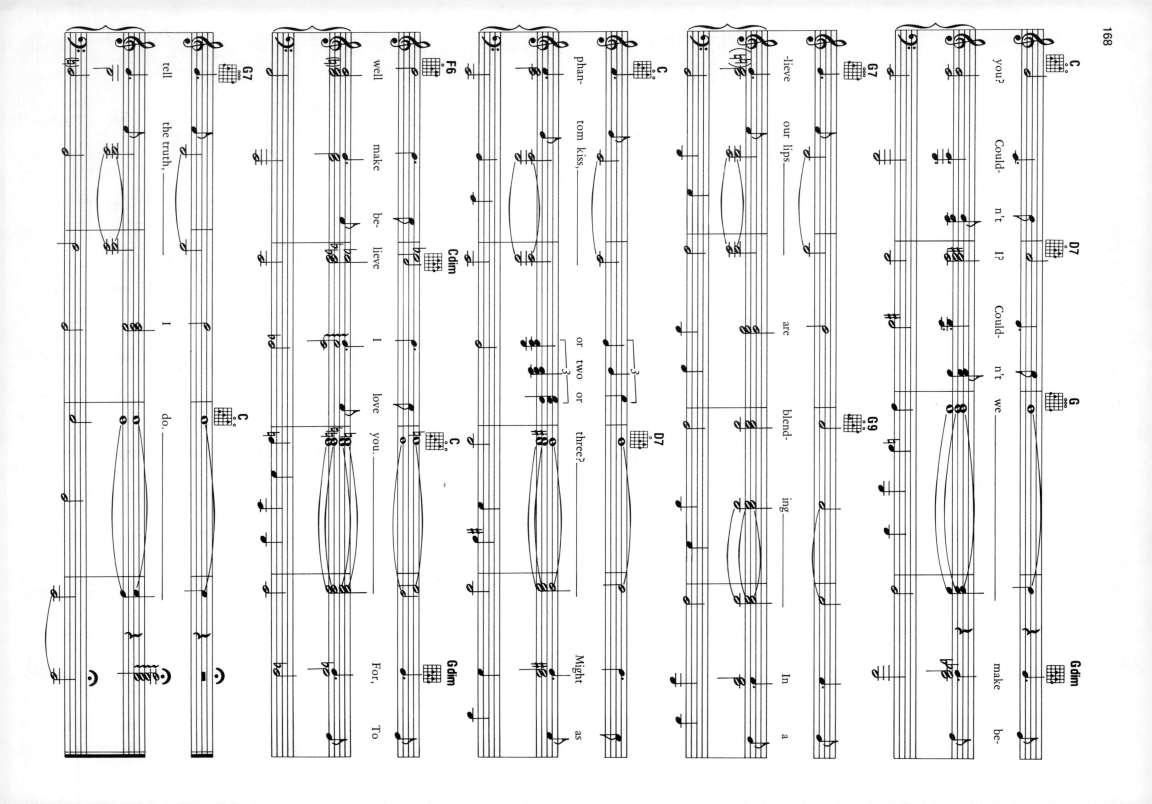

Make Someone Happy
(From "DO RE MI")

Words by BETTY COMDEN & ADOLPH GREEN
Music by JULE STYNE

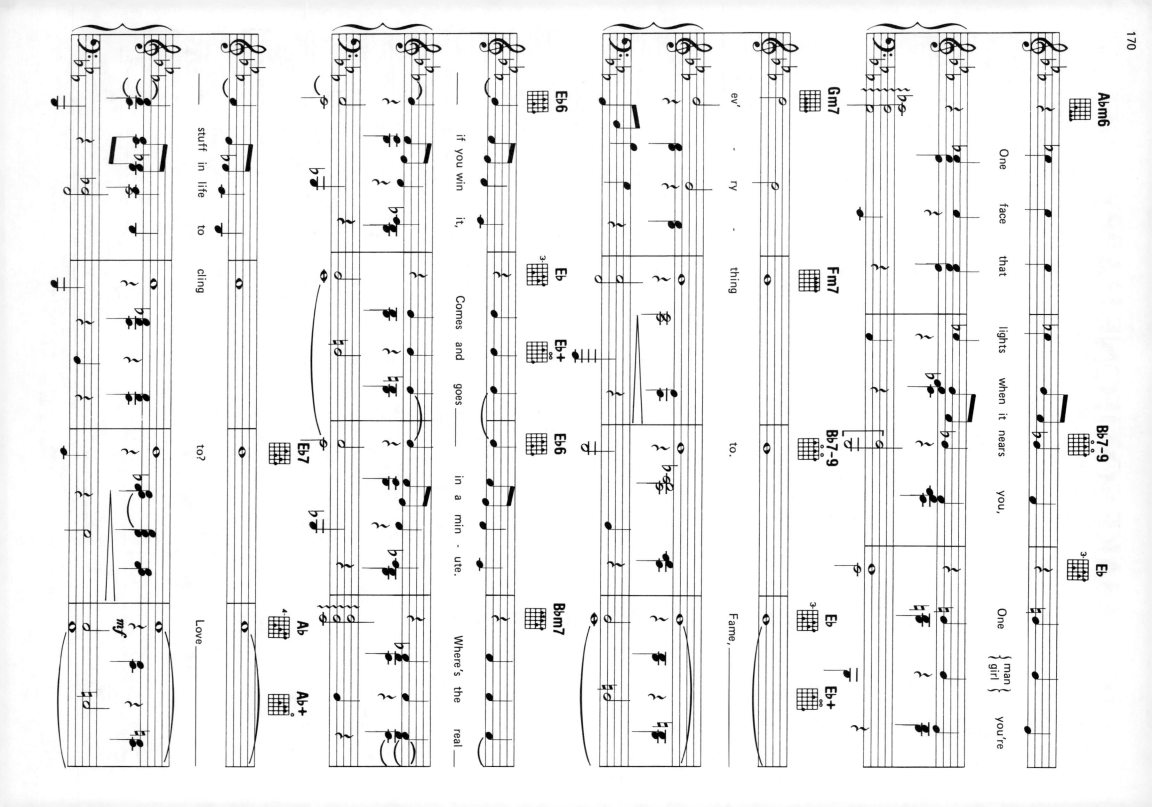

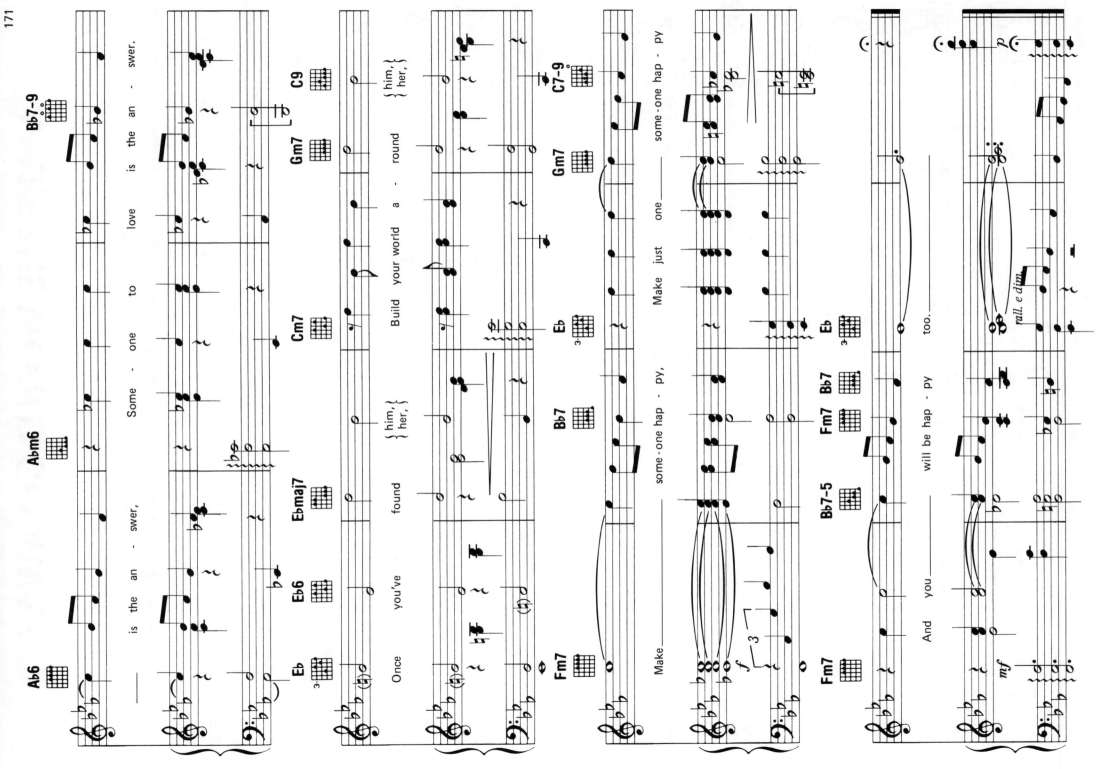

MAKE THE WORLD GO AWAY

By HANK COCHRAN

Moderately slow

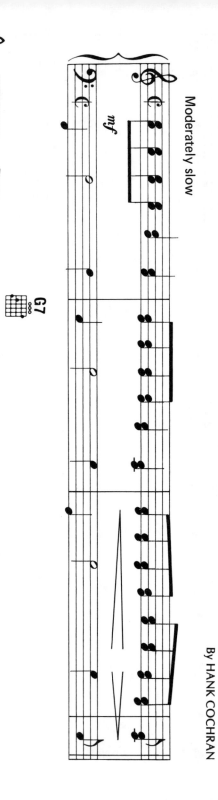

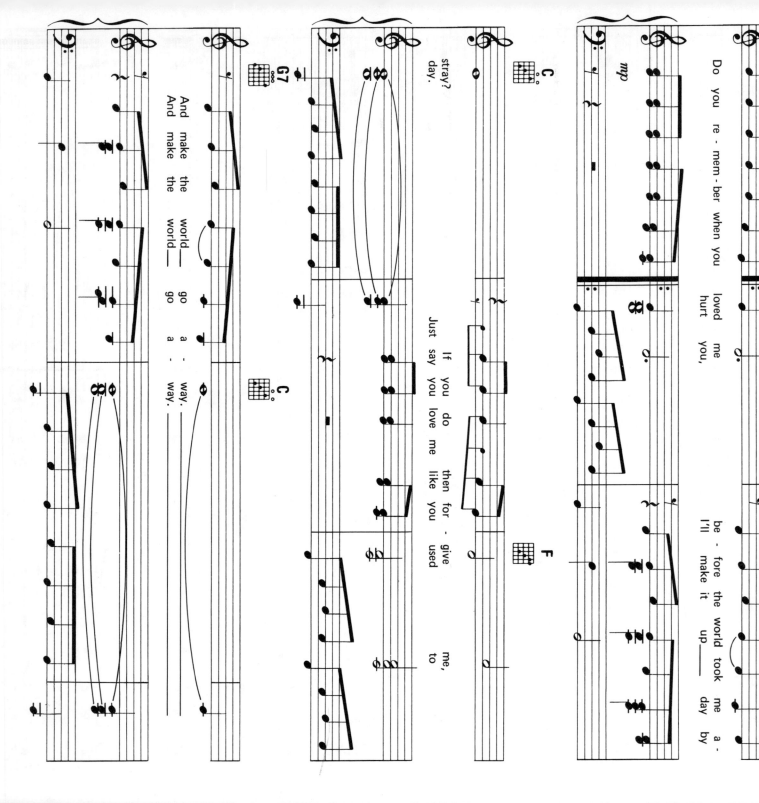

Do you re - mem - ber when you loved me be - fore the world took me a - day by

hurt you, I'll make it up____ day by

If you do then for - give me, to

Just say you love me like you used

stray? day.

And make the world____ go a - way.

And make the world____ go a - way.

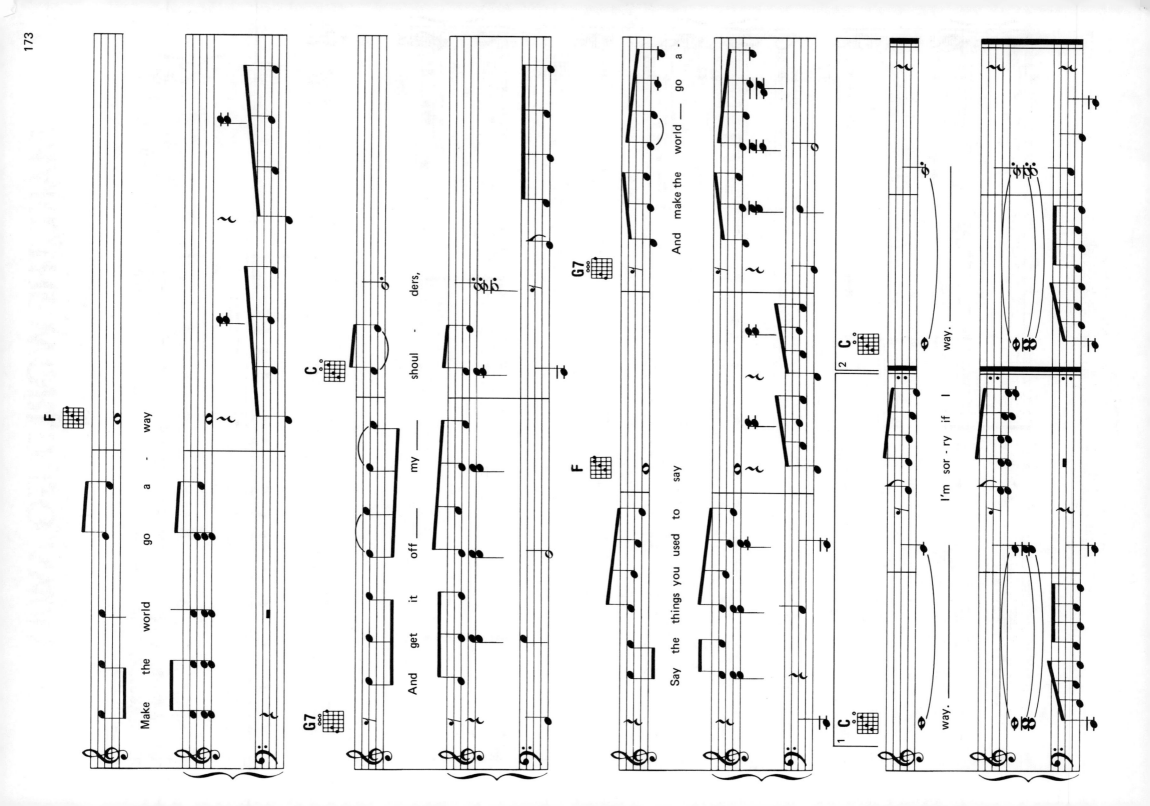

A MAN AND A WOMAN
(Un Homme Et Une Femme)

Original Words by PIERRE BAROUH
English Words by JERRY KELLER
Music By FRANCIS LAI

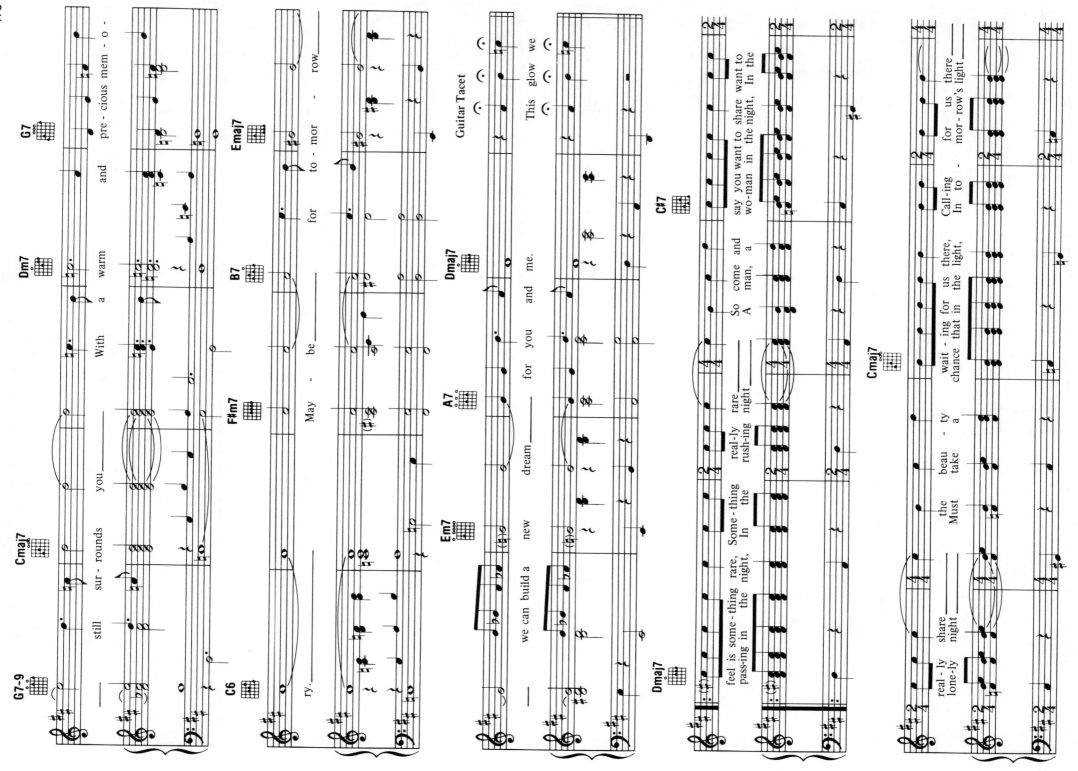

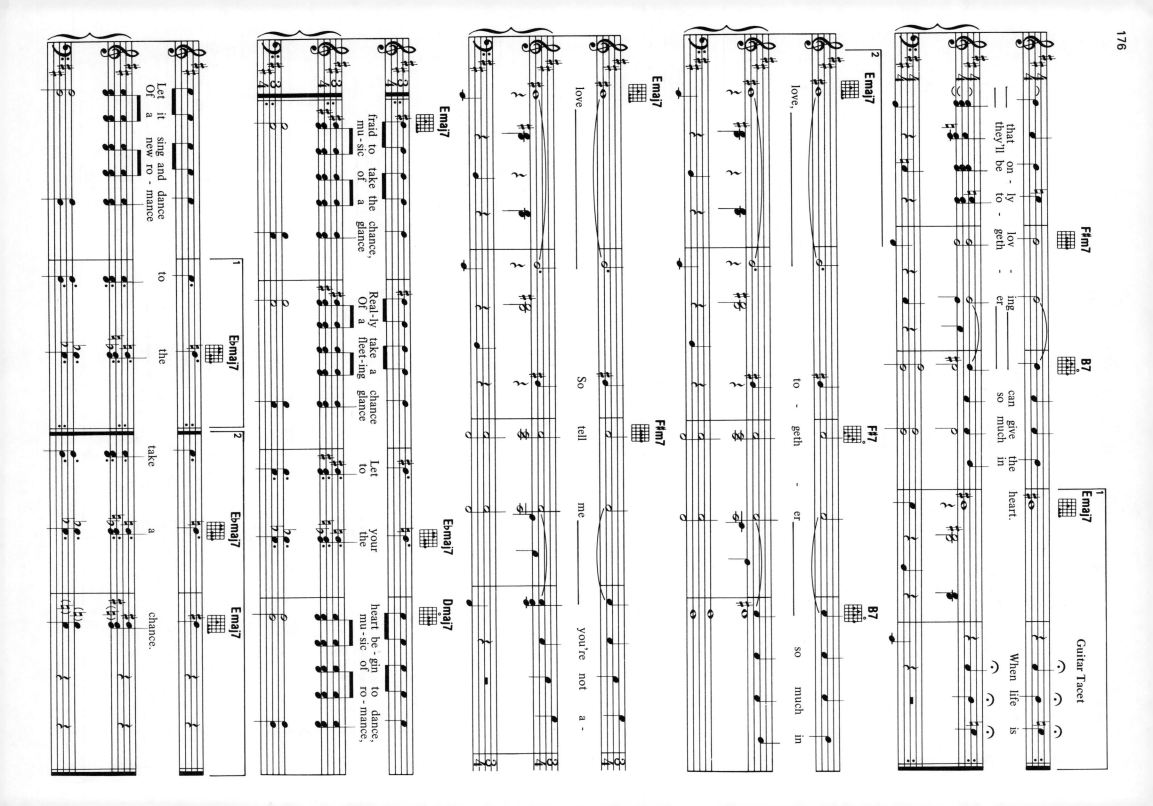

MARGIE

Words by BENNY DAVIS
Music by CON CONRAD and J. RUSSEL ROBINSON

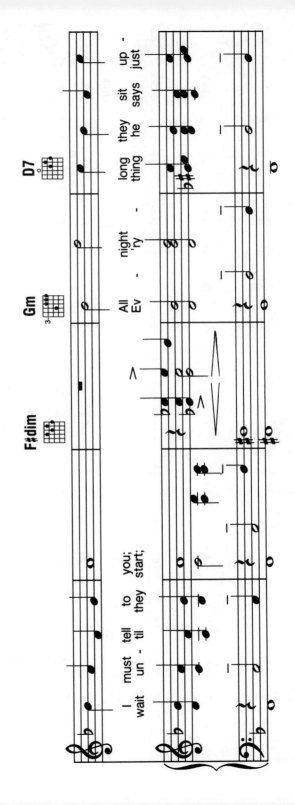

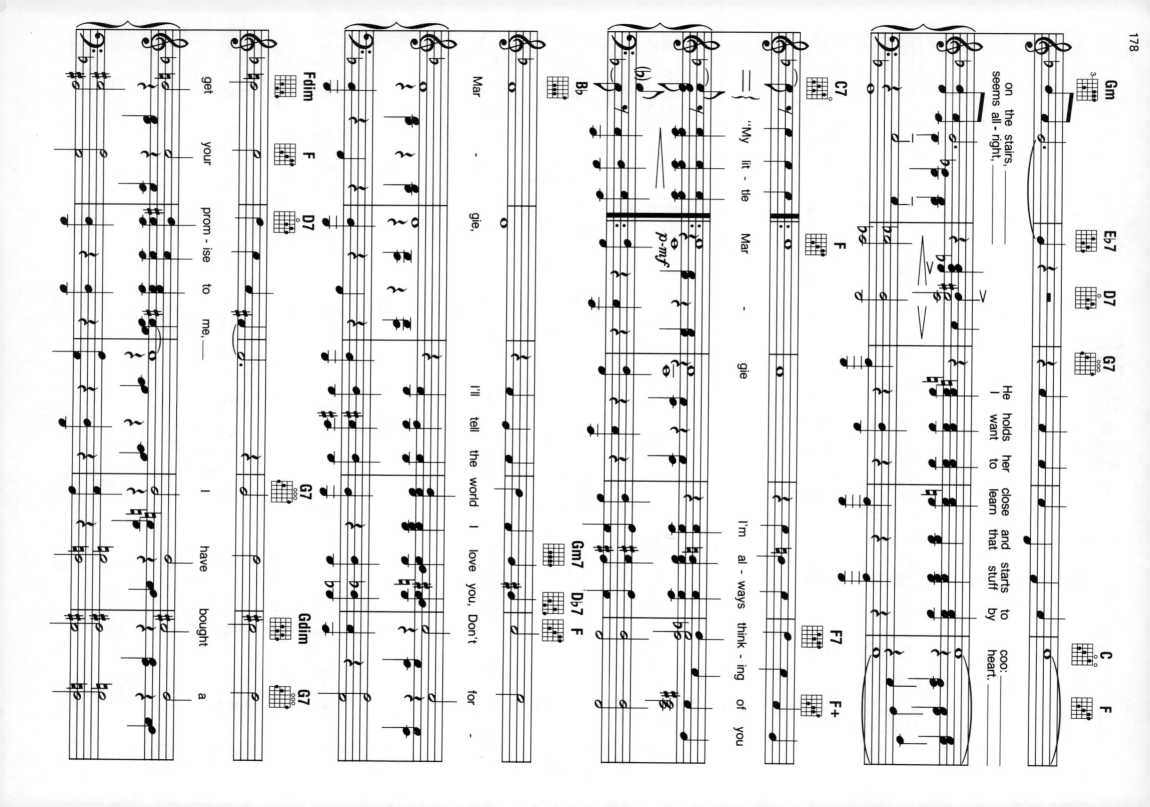

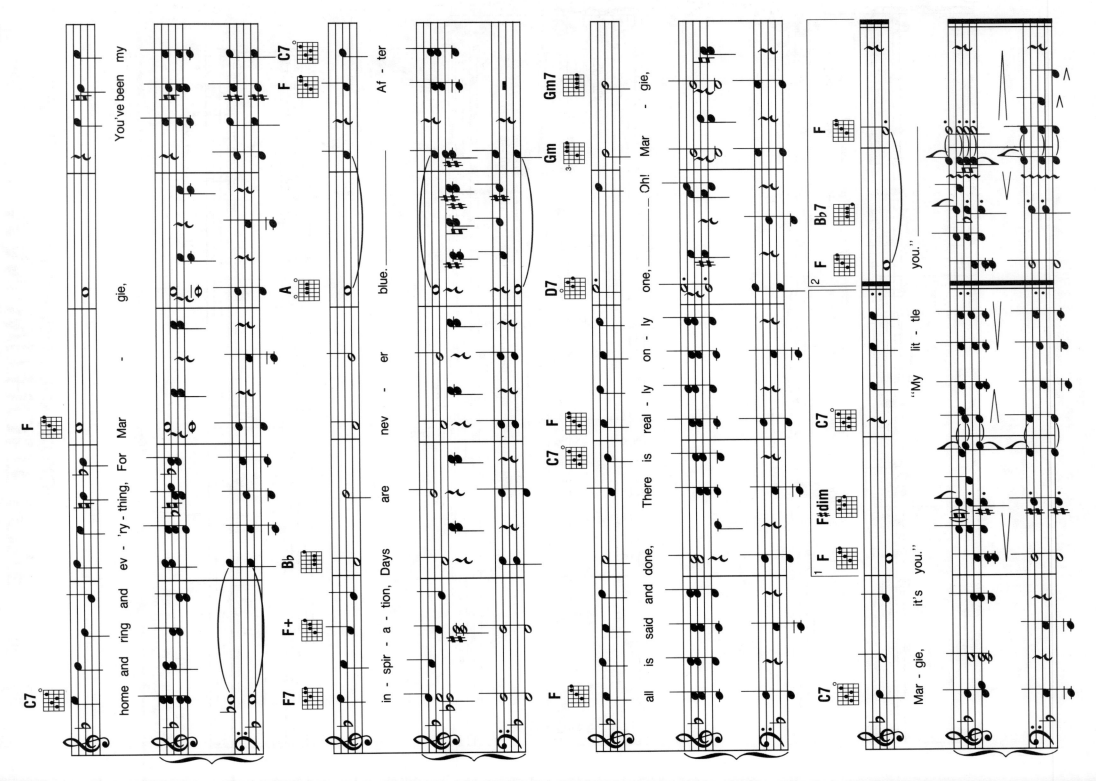

A MAN WITHOUT LOVE
(QUANDO M'INNAMORO)

English Words by BARRY MASON
Original Words and Music by D. PACE,
M. PANZERI, R. LIVRAGHI

Moderately

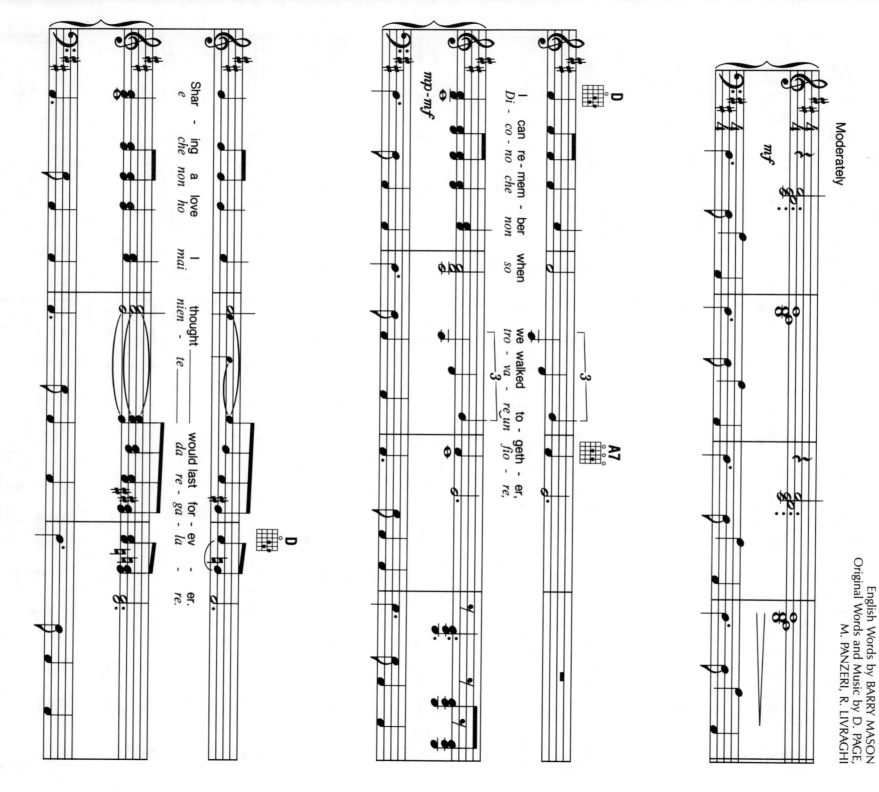

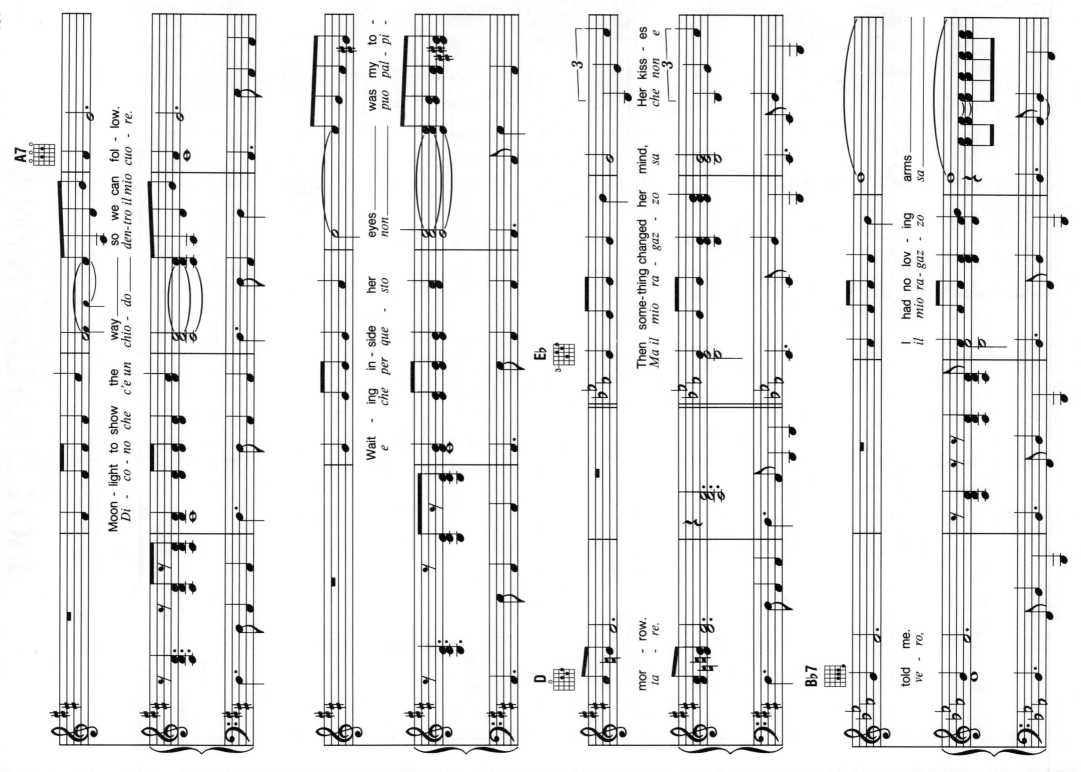

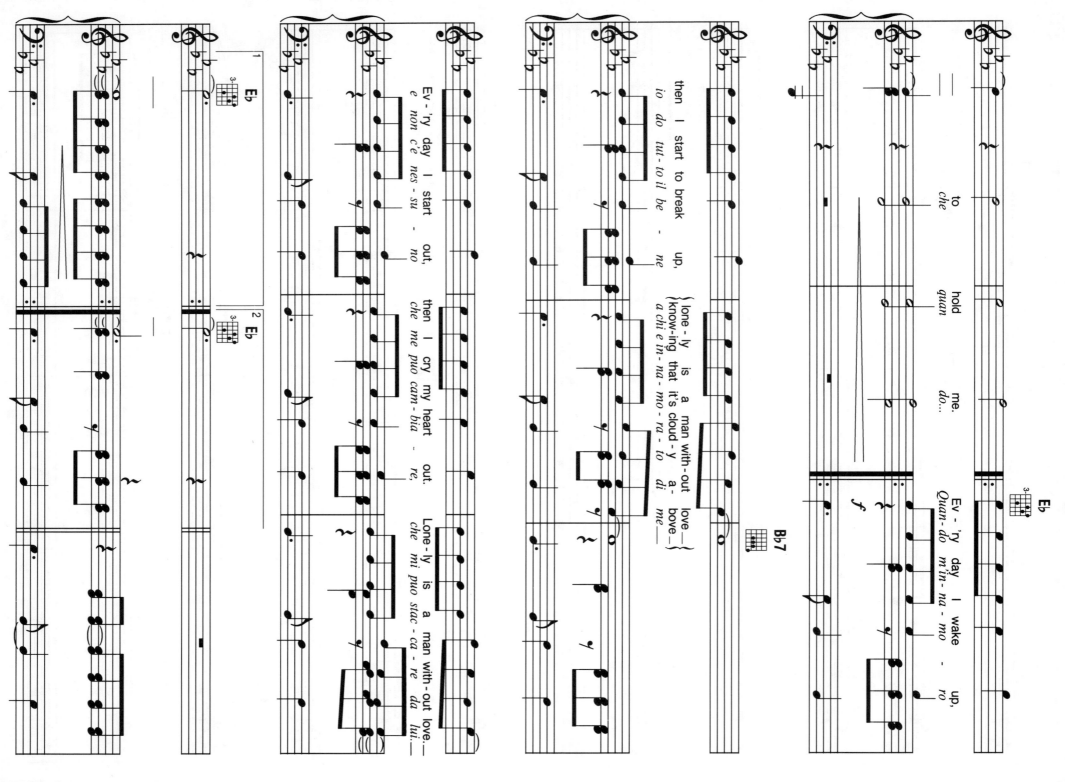

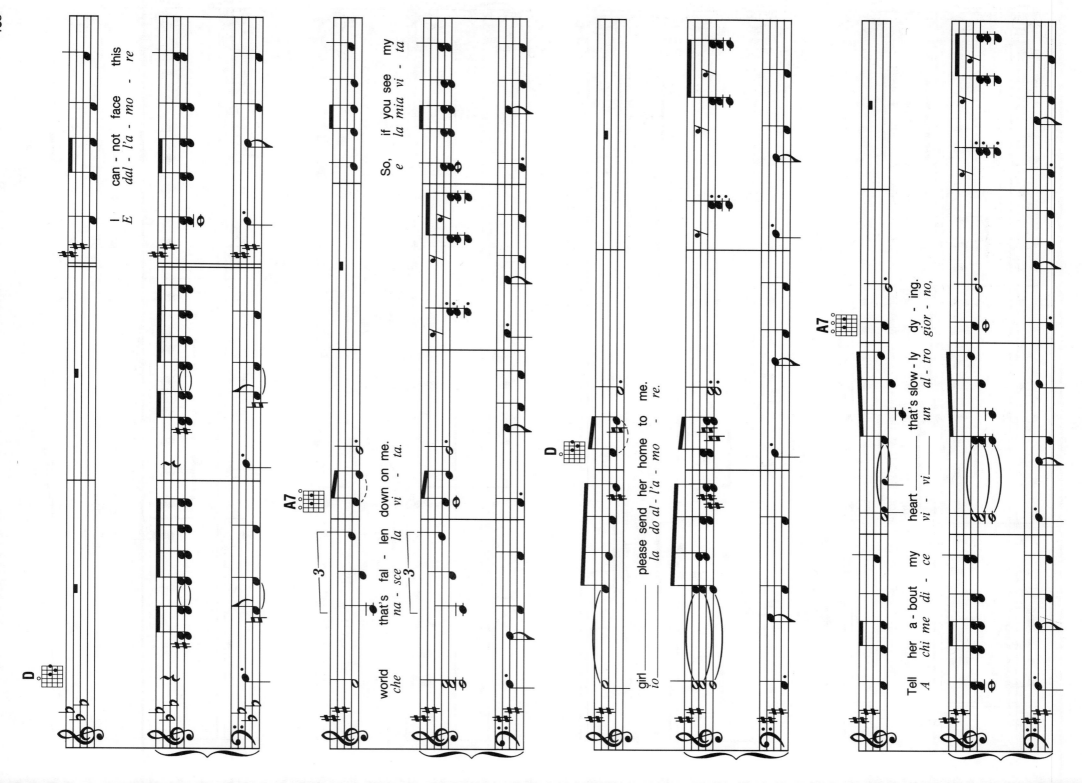

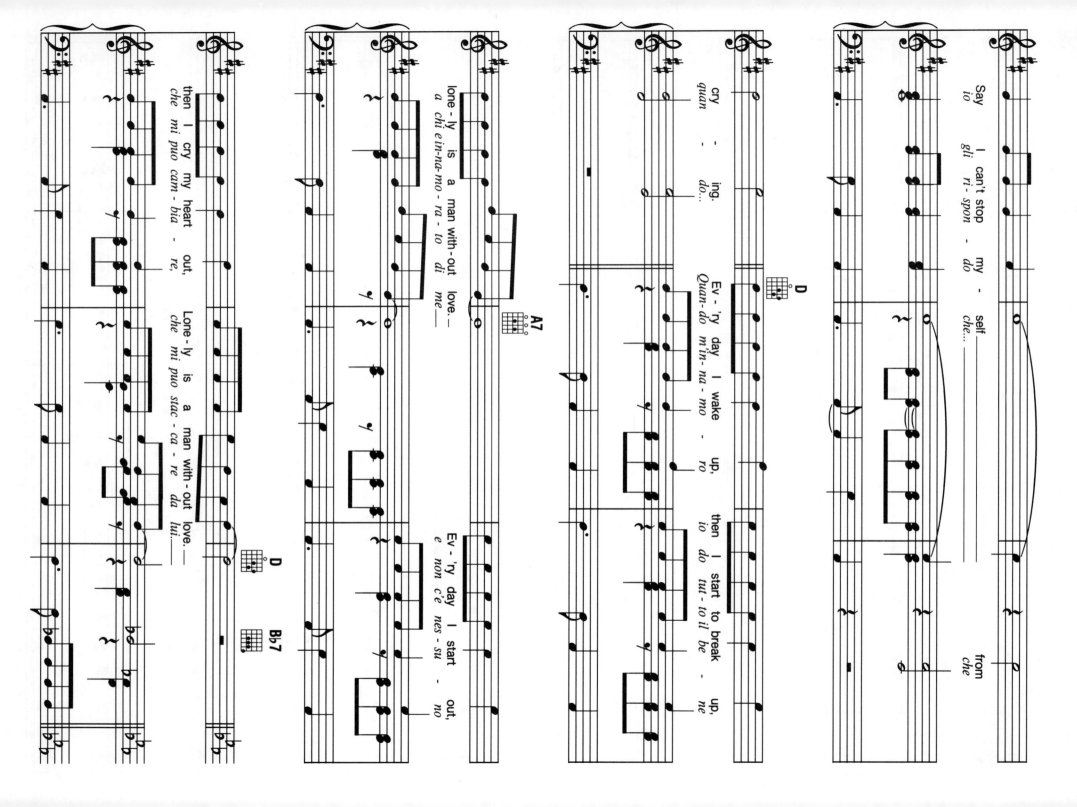

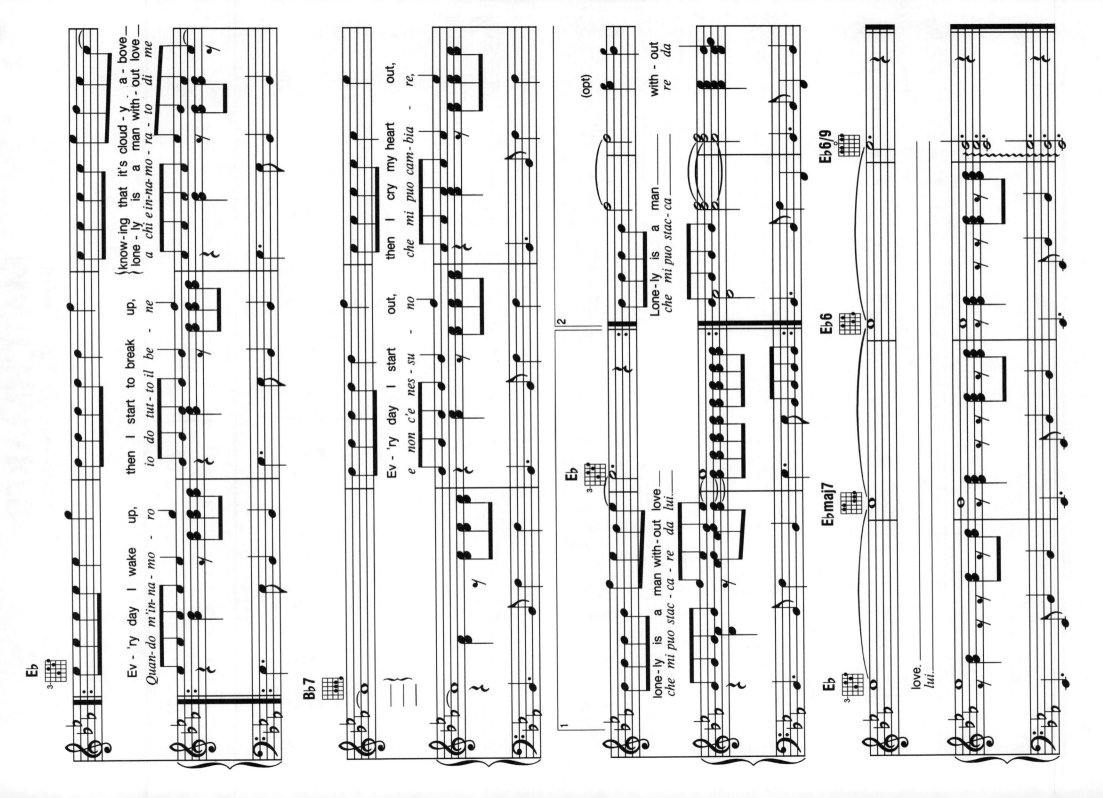

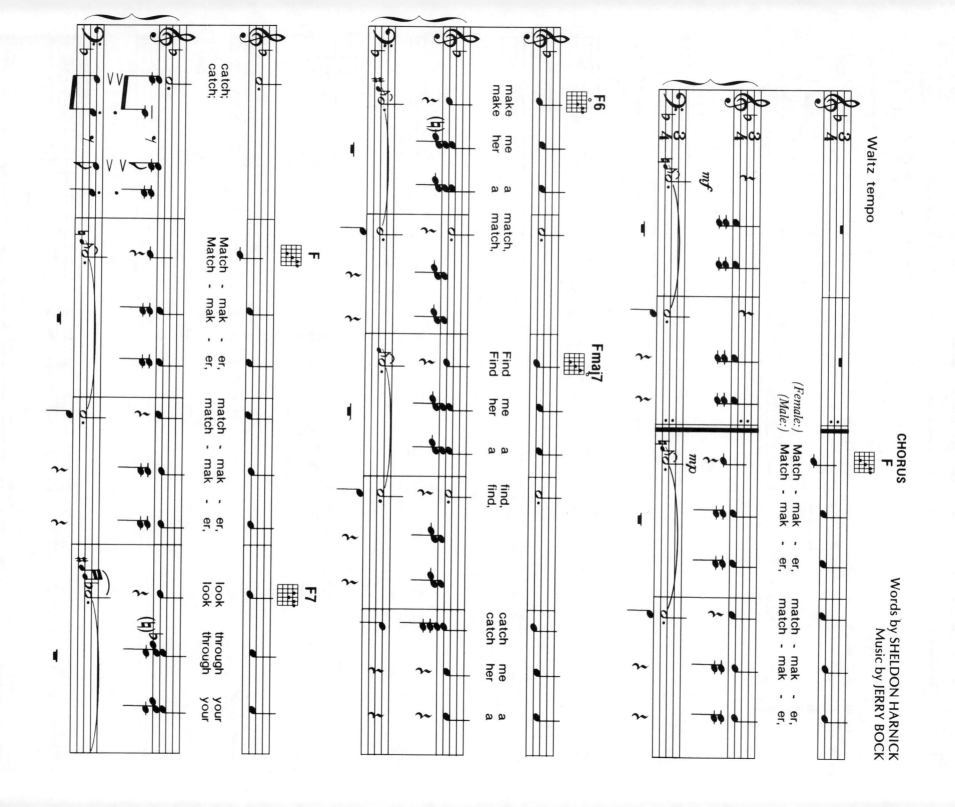

B♭ C11 C7 F C7-9
book And make me a per - fect match.
book And make her a per - fect match.
F F6 Fmaj7
1,2 Match - mak - er, match - mak - er, I'll bring the veil, You bring the
You know that I'm still ver - y
(M:) Match - mak - er, match - mak - er, We'll bring the veil, You bring the
F
groom, slen - der and pale; Bring me a ring, for I'm
young, Please take your time; Up to this min - ute, I
groom, slen - der and pale; Bring her a ring, for she's
F7 B♭ C11 C7 F F7sus F7
long - ing to be the en - vy of all I see. For
mis - un - der - stood that I could be stuck for good. Dear
long - ing to be the en - vy of all she'll see. For

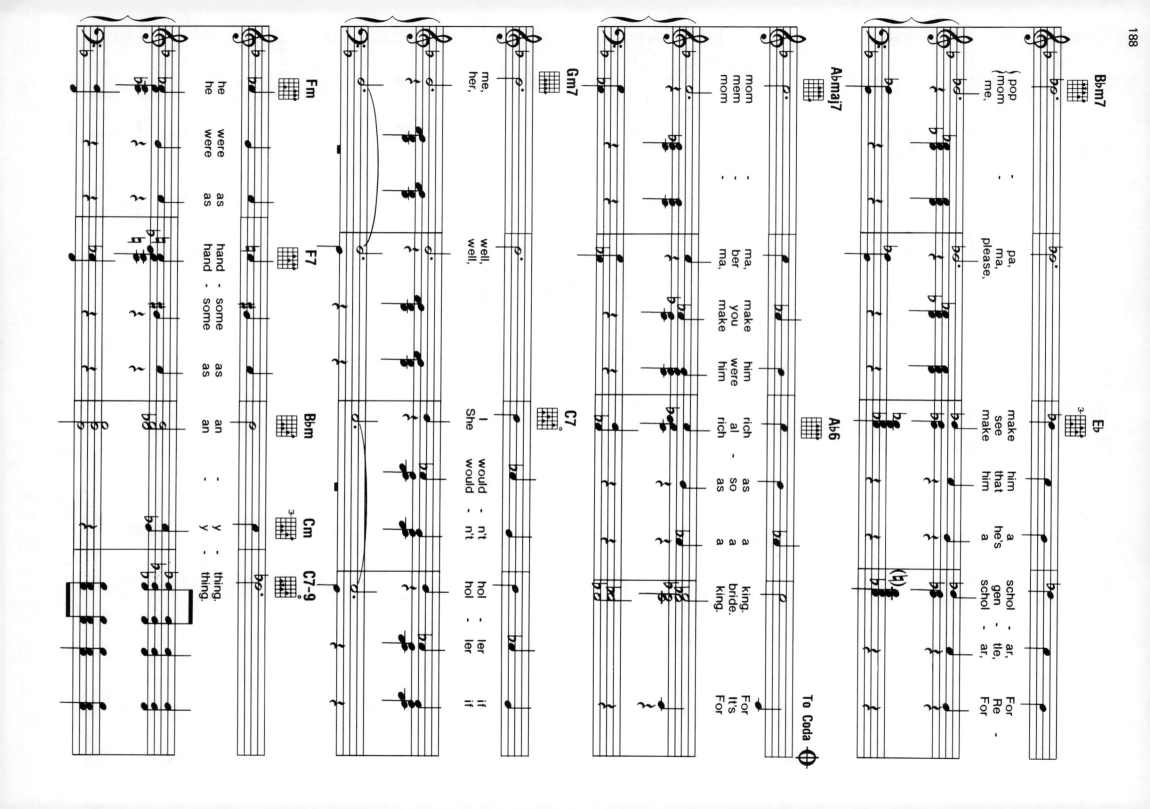

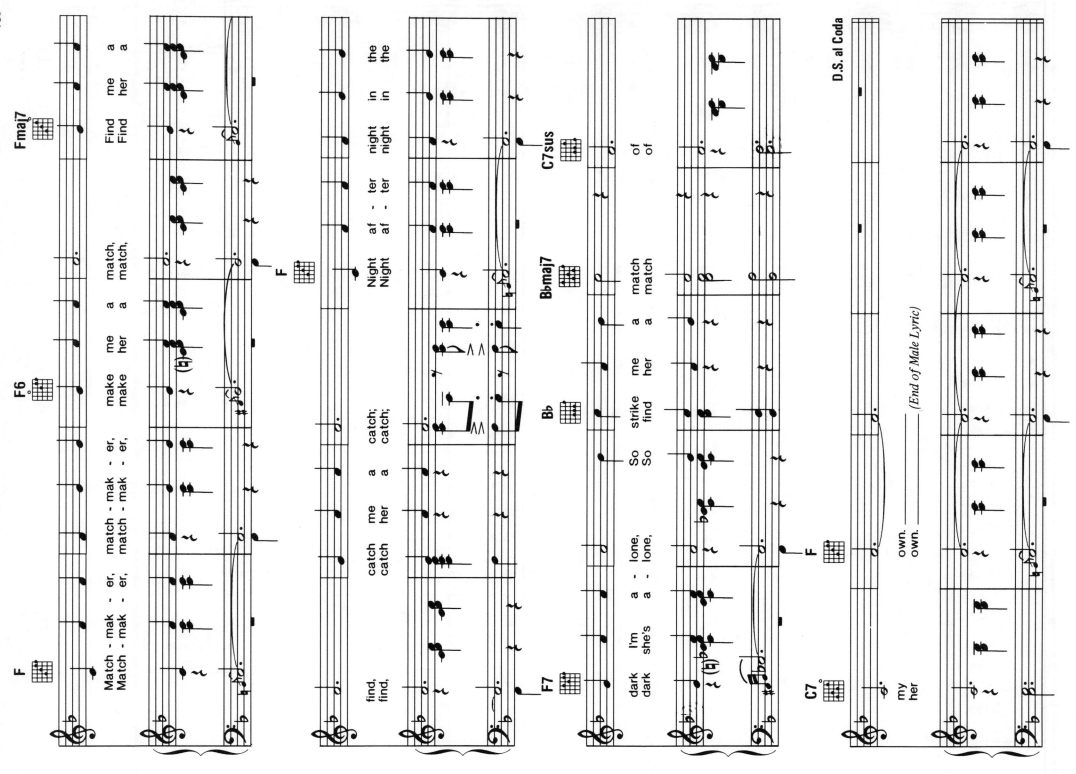

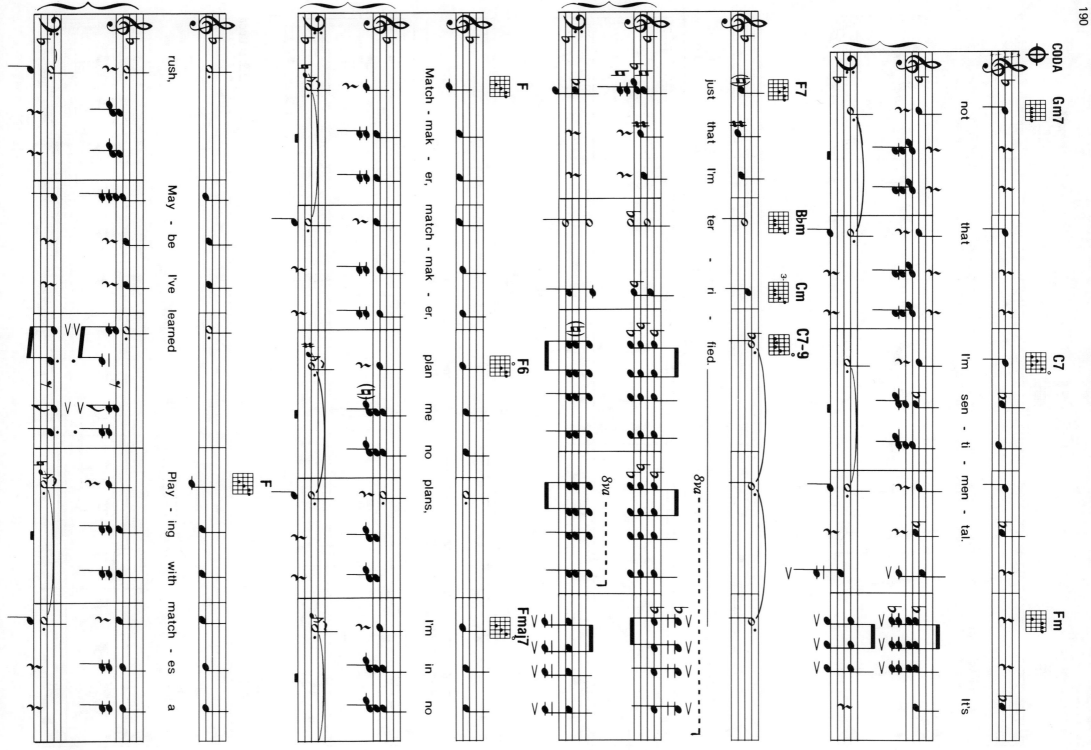

F7
B♭
B♭m
girl can get burned. So bring me no ring, Groom me no
(Male:) So bring her a ring, Groom her a
rit.
a tempo
F
G7
groom, Find me no find, Catch me no catch;
groom, Find her a find, Catch her a catch;
C11
C7+5
F
Un - less he's a match - less match!
And make her a match - less match!
8va

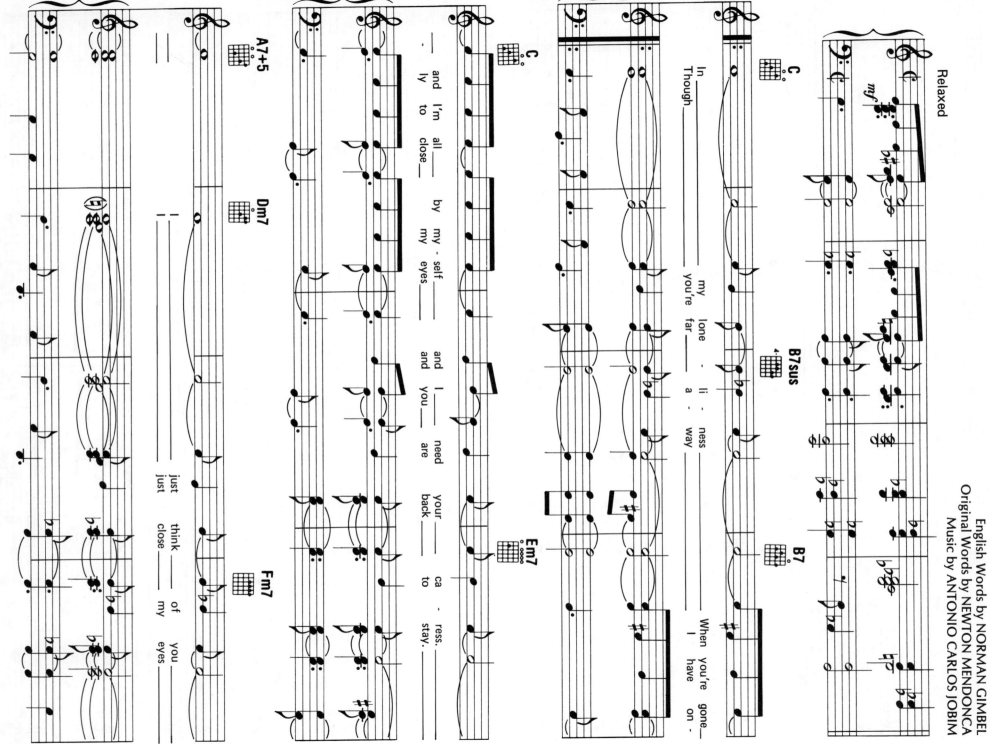

MEDITATION

English Words by NORMAN GIMBEL
Original Words by NEWTON MENDONCA
Music by ANTONIO CARLOS JOBIM

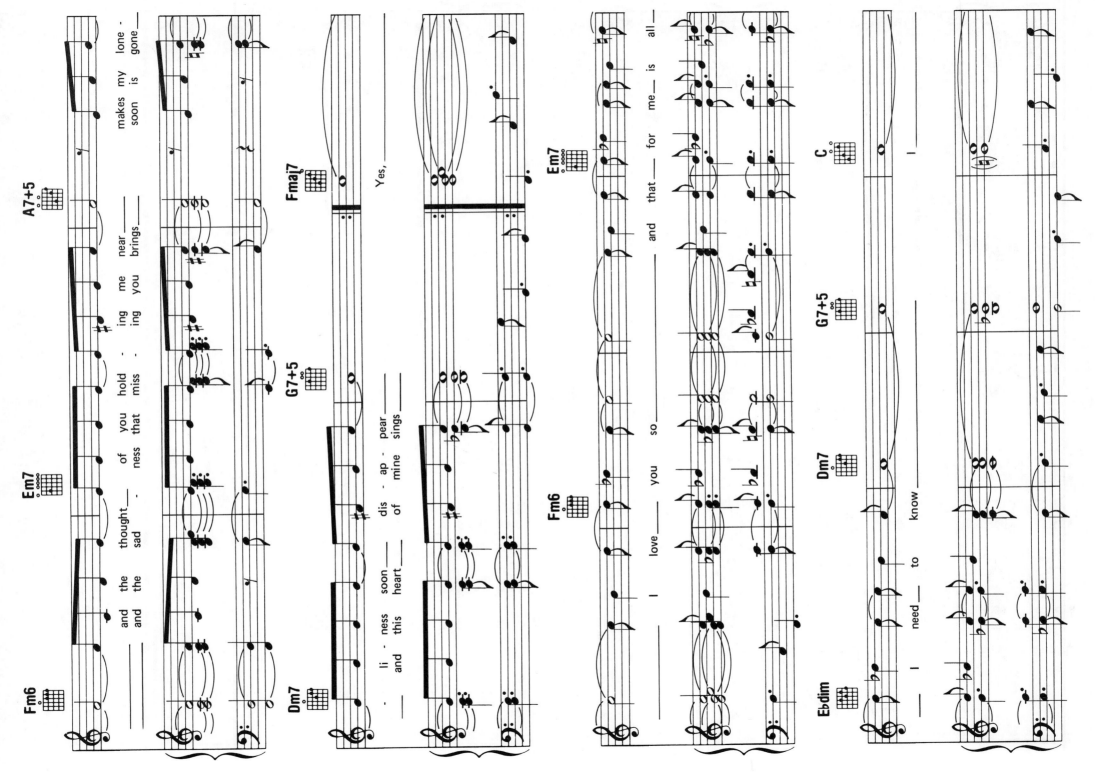

193

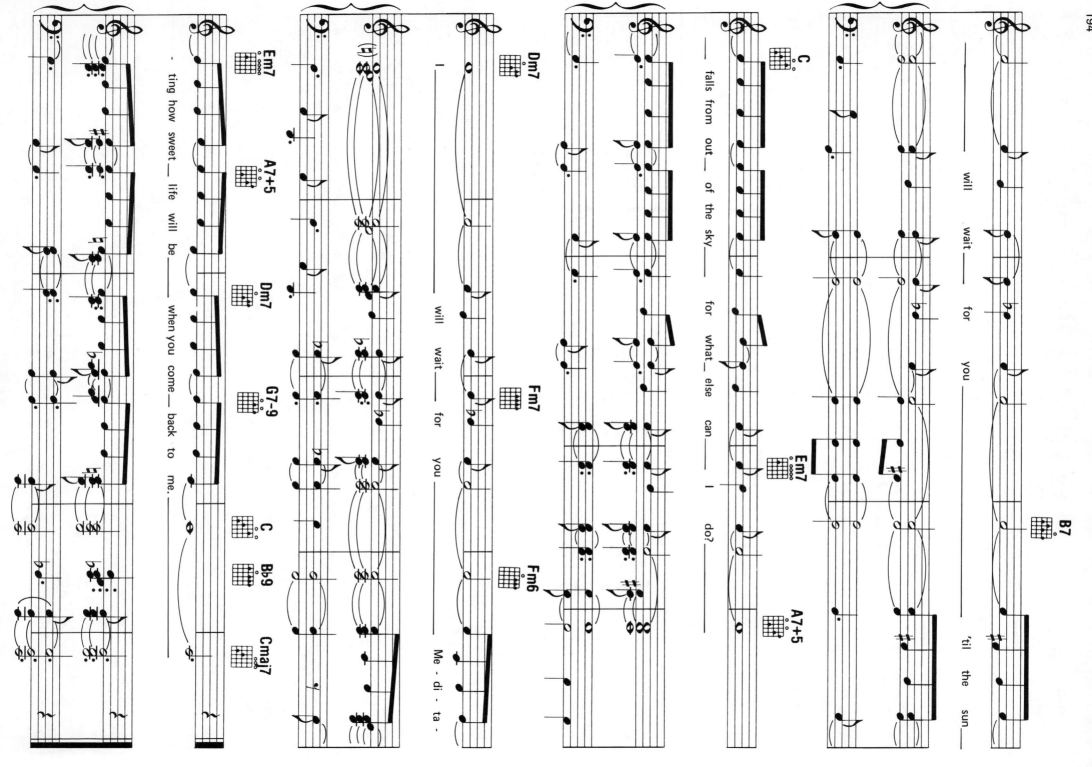

MEXICALI ROSE

Words by HELEN STONE
Music by JACK B. TENNEY

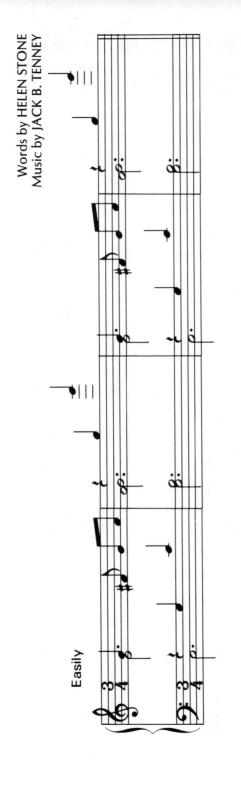

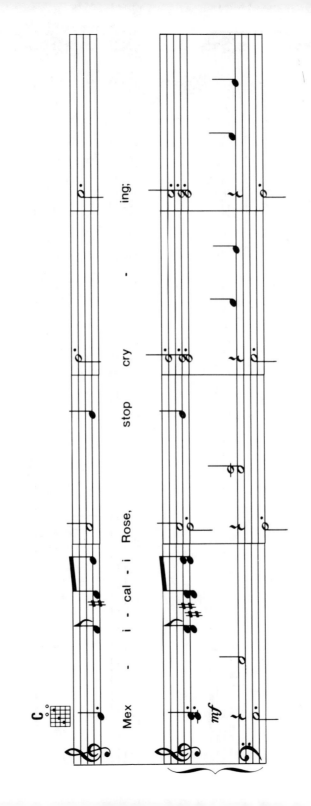

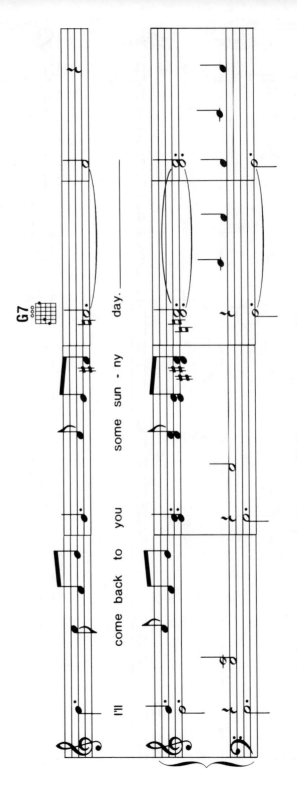

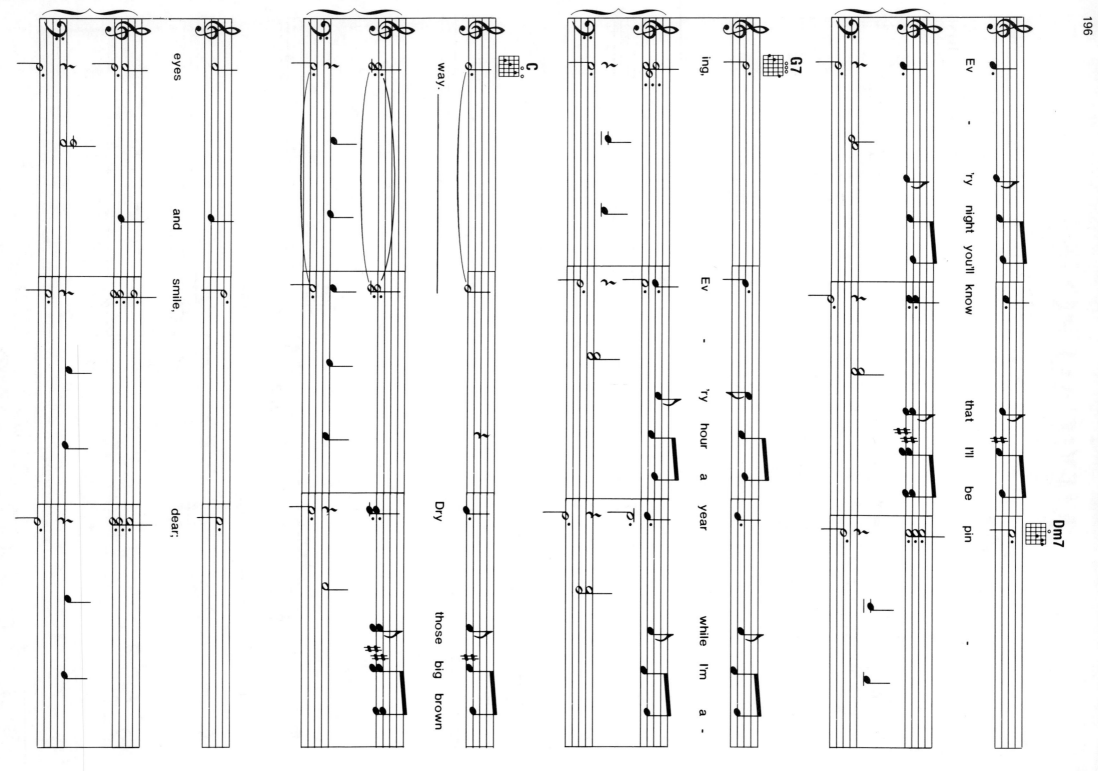

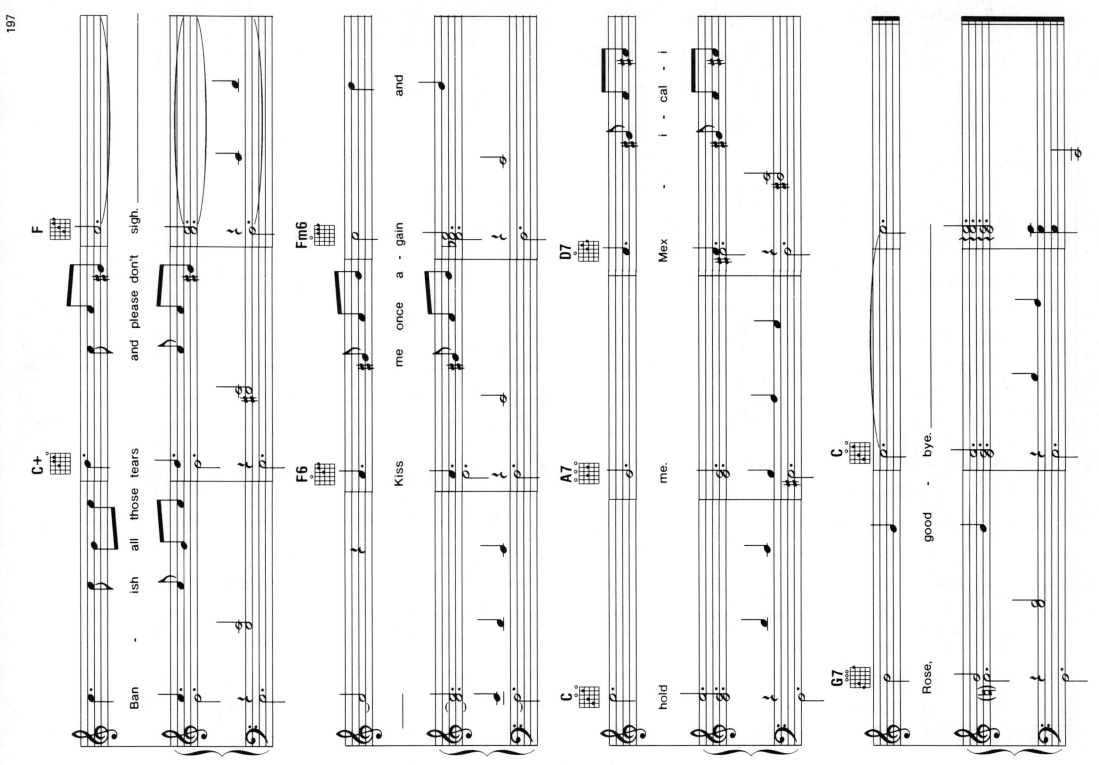

MEMORY
(From "CATS")

Text by TREVOR NUNN after T.S. ELIOT
Music by ANDREW LLOYD WEBBER

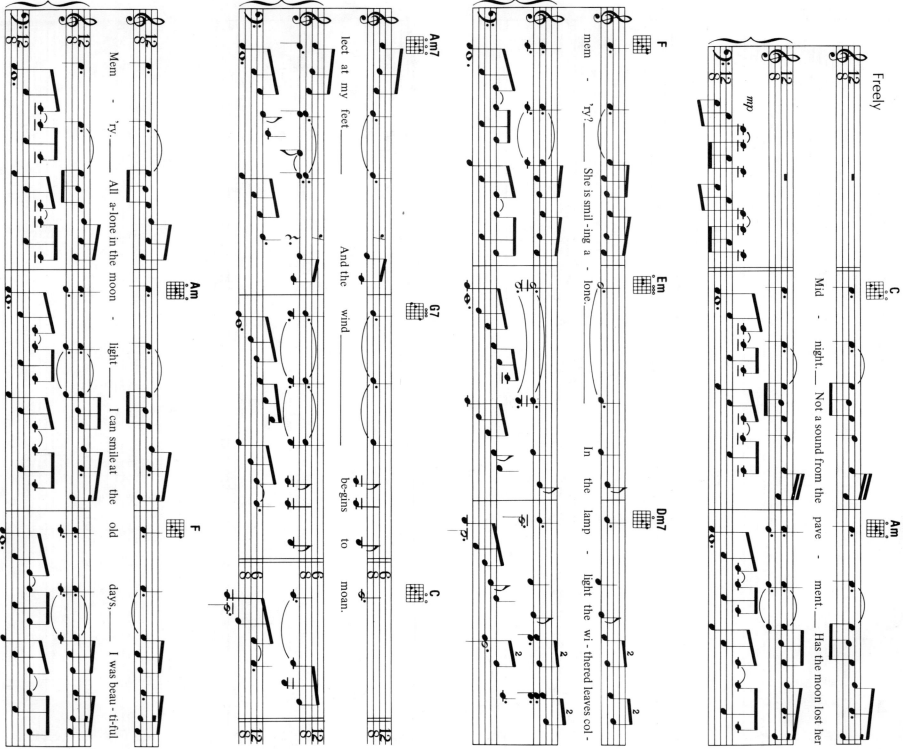
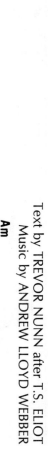

Mid - night.— Not a sound from the pave - ment.— Has the moon lost her

mem - 'ry?— She is smil-ing a - lone.— In the lamp - light the wi - thered leaves col -

lect at my feet.— And the wind— be-gins to moan.

Mem - 'ry.— All a-lone in the moon - light.— I can smile at the old days,— I was beau - ti-ful

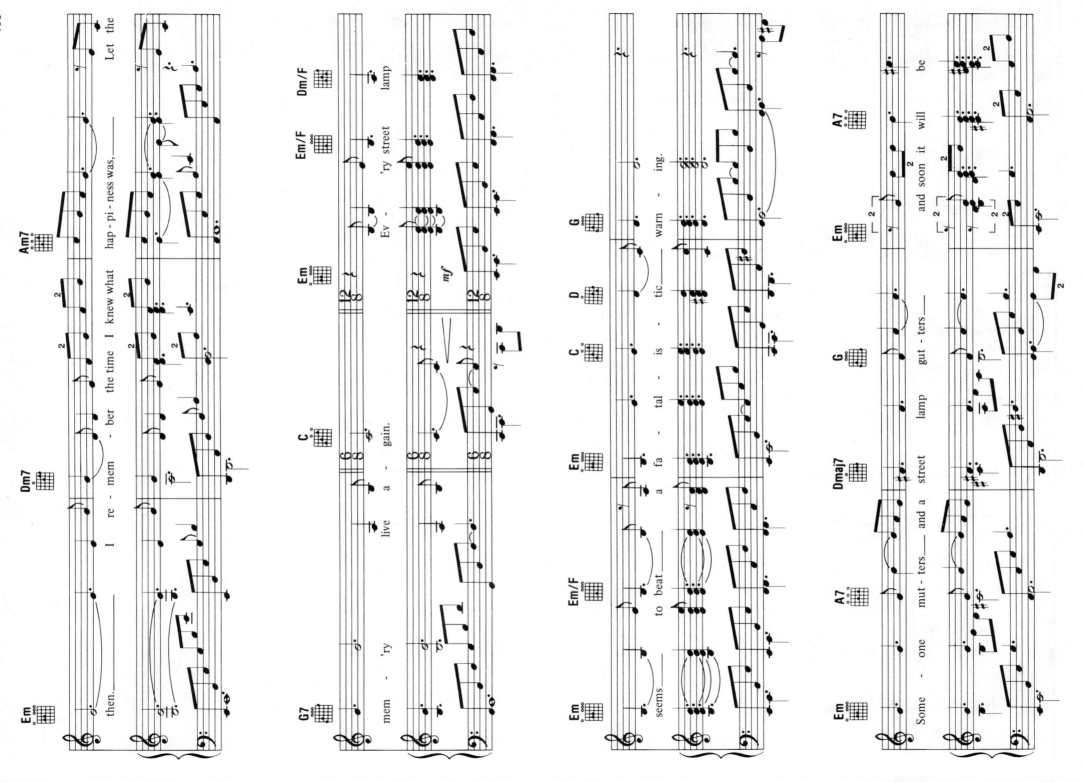

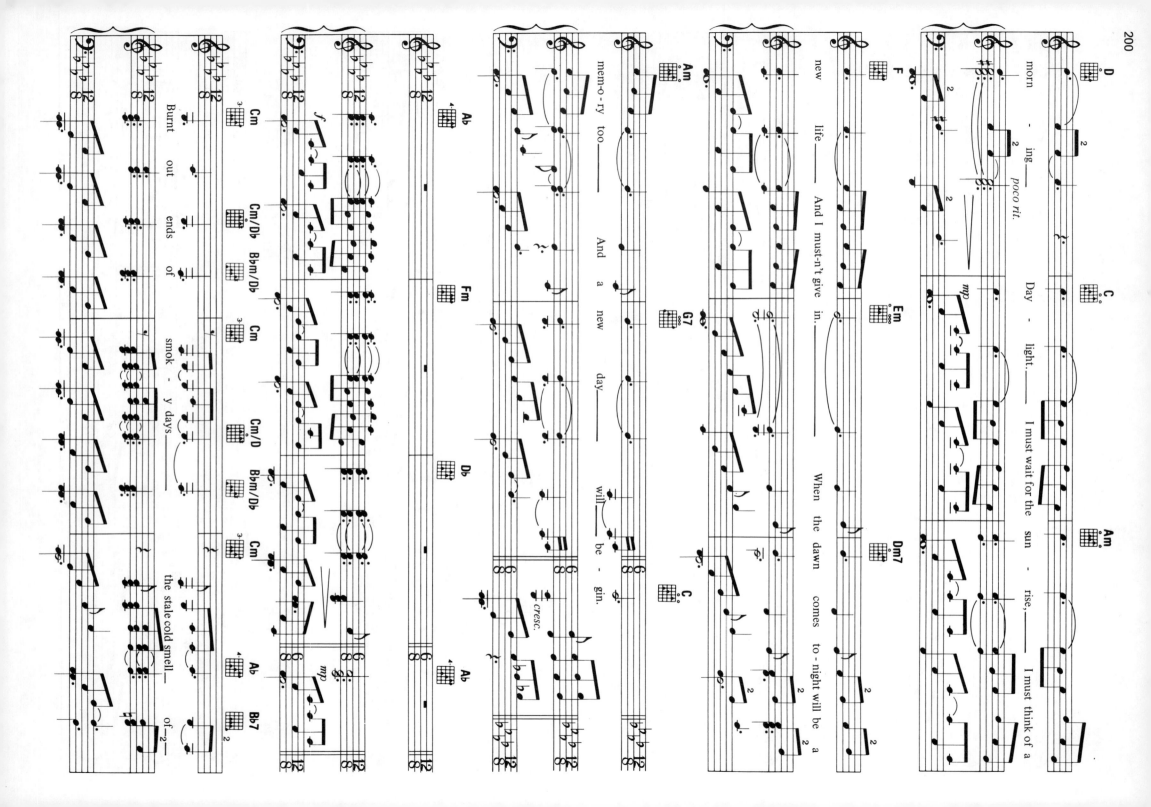

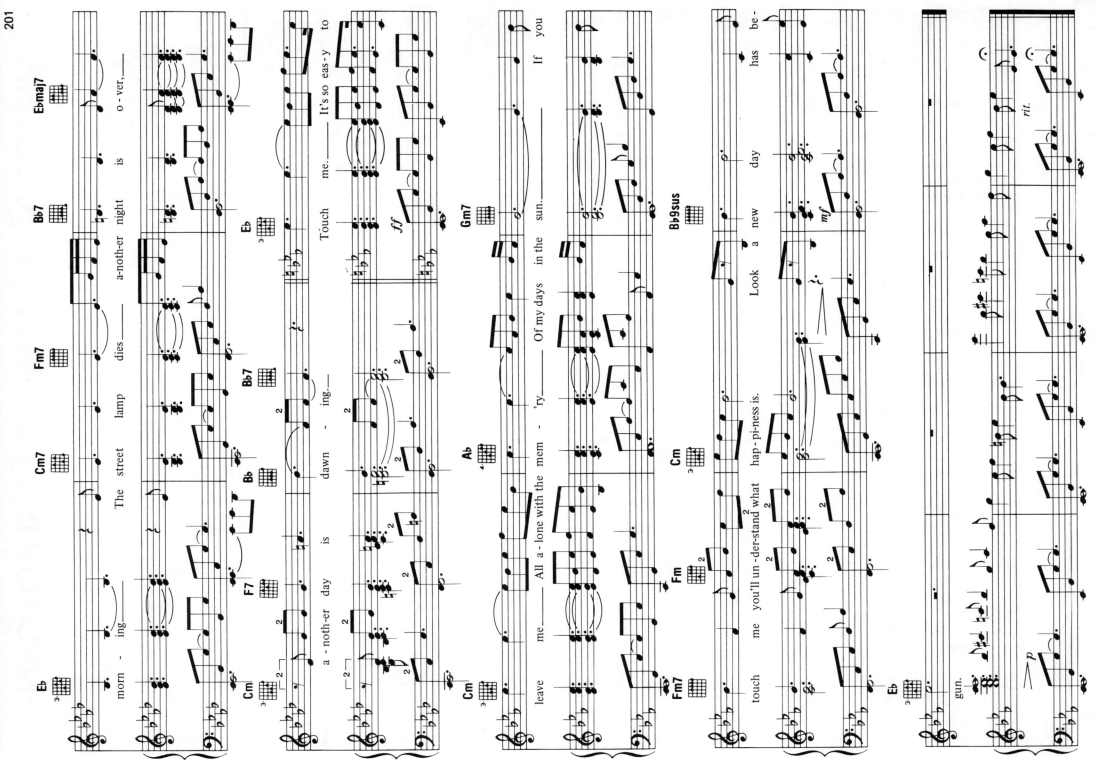

MENTION MY NAME IN SHEBOYGAN

Words and Music by BOB HILLIARD,
DICK SANFORD and SAMMY MYSELS

Bright tempo

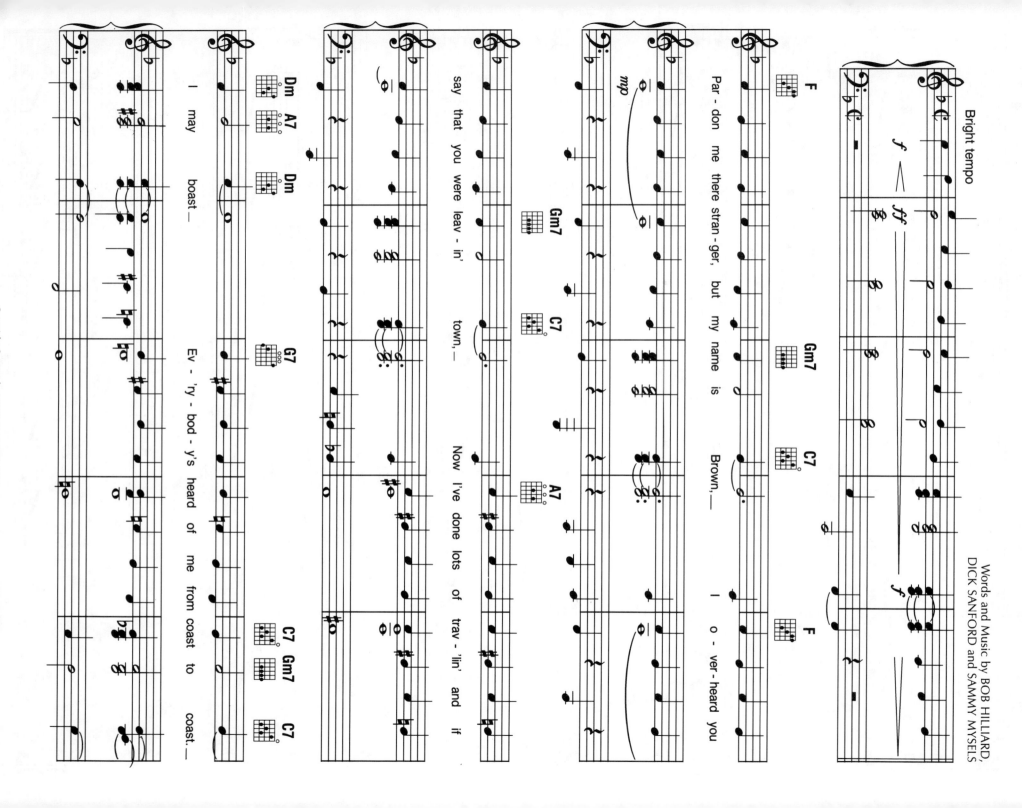

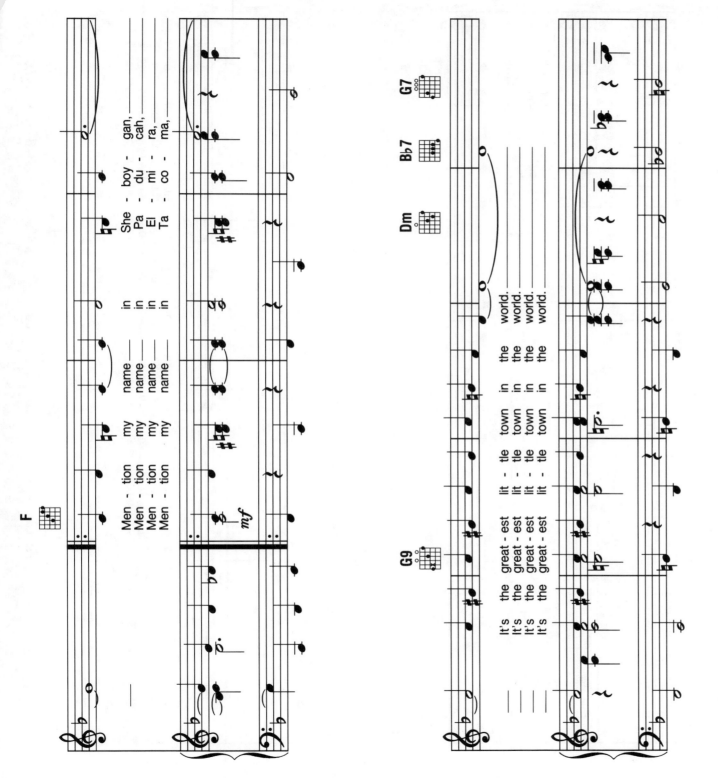
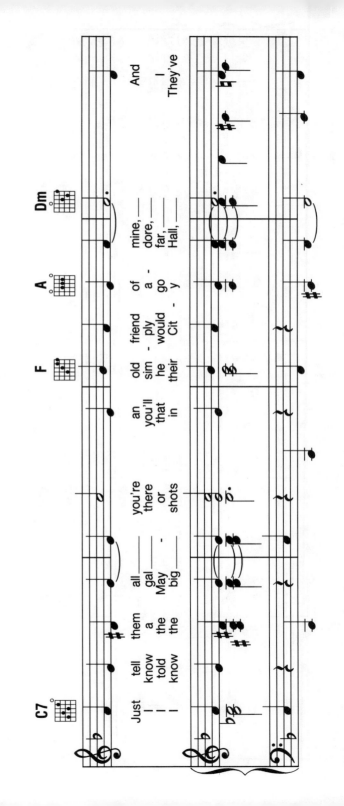

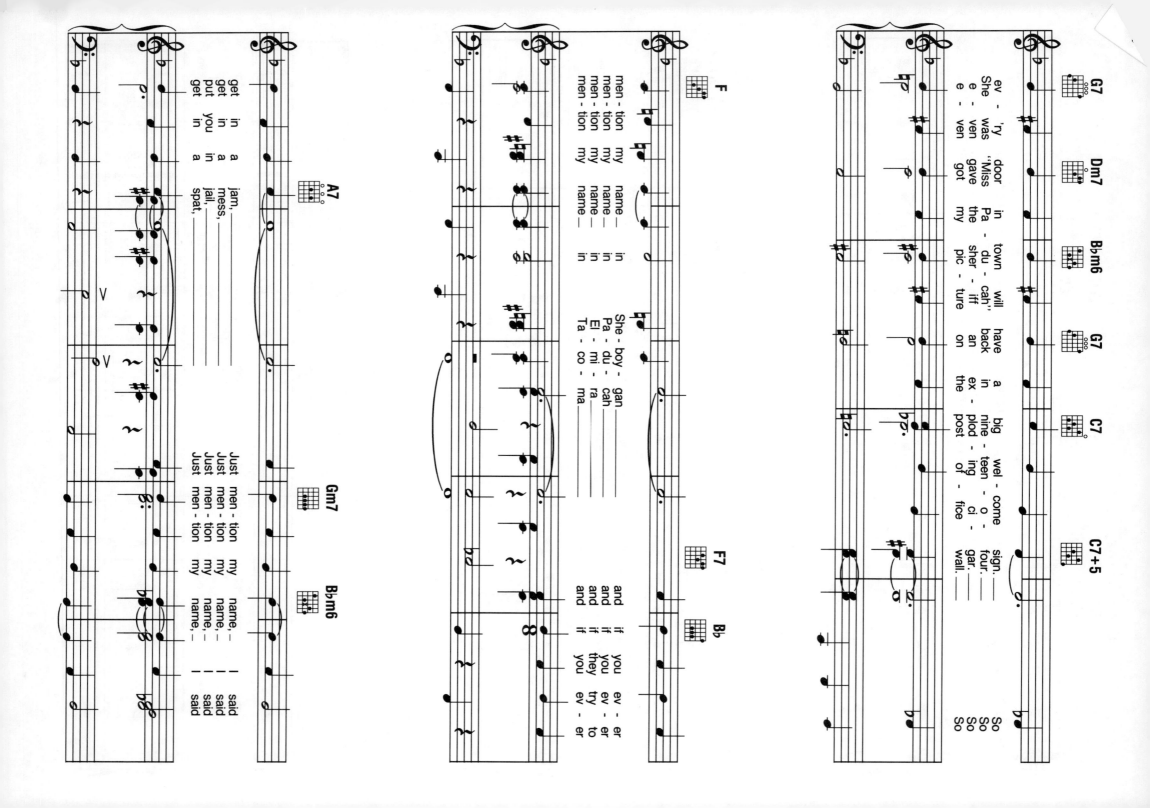

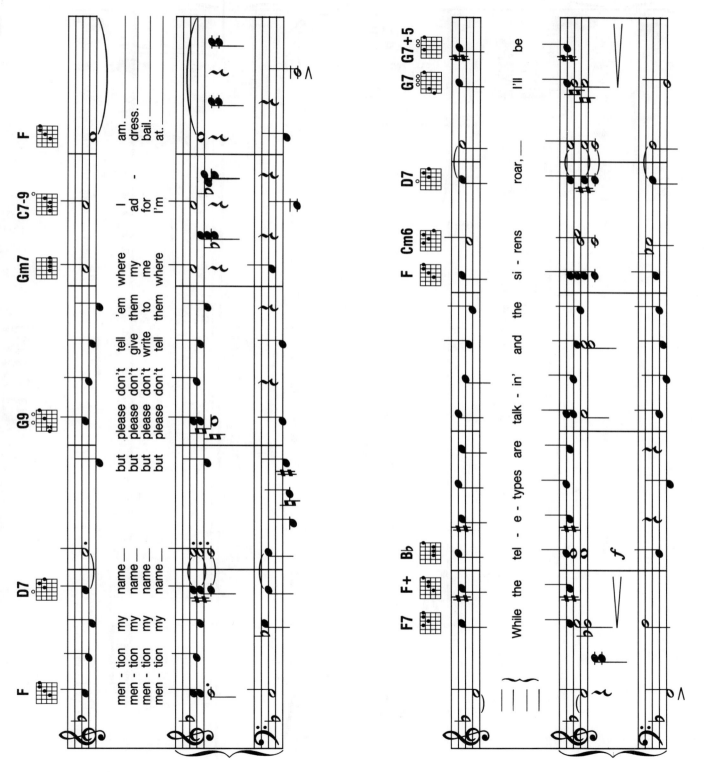

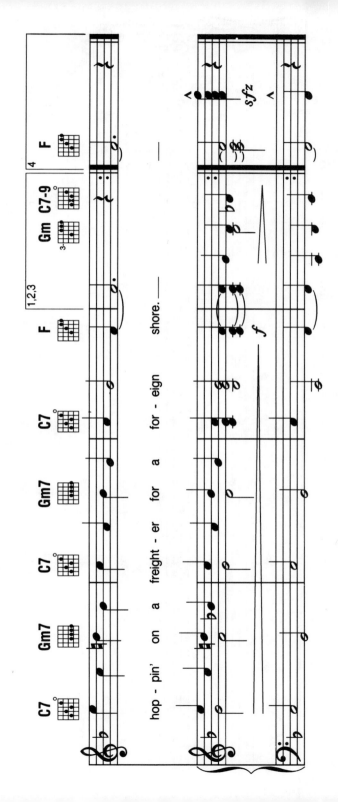

MISTY

Words by JOHNNY BURKE
Music by ERROLL GARNER

Slowly, with expression

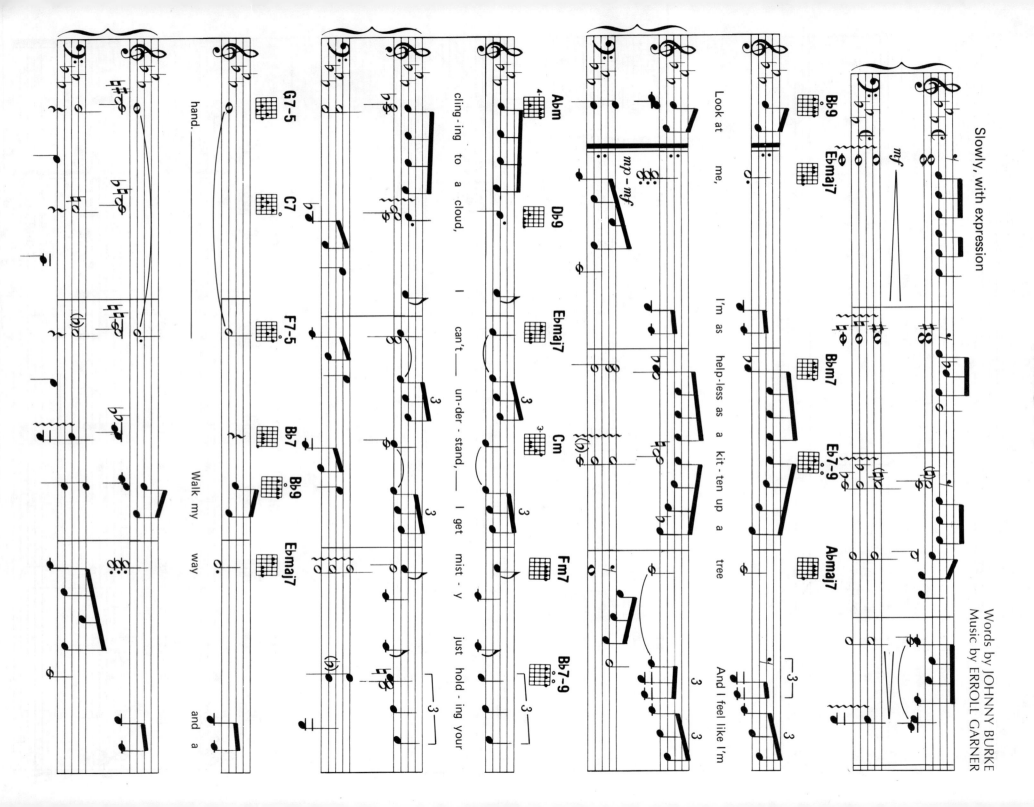

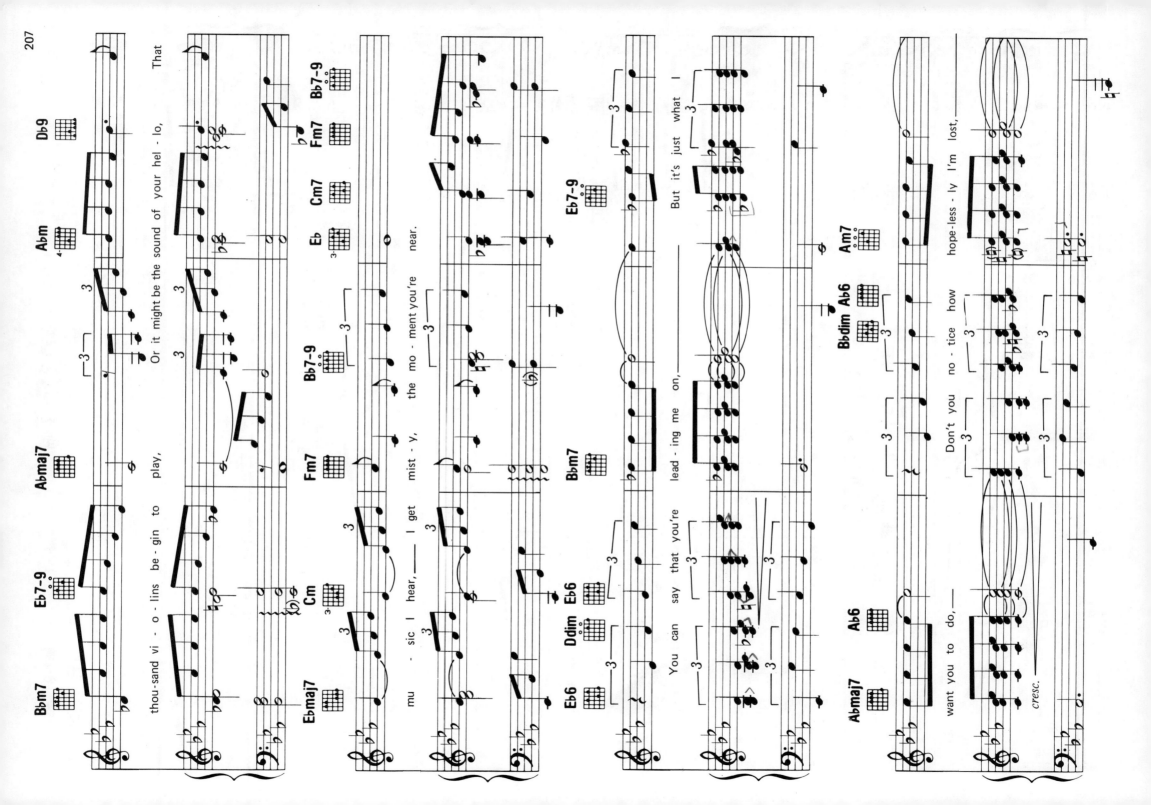

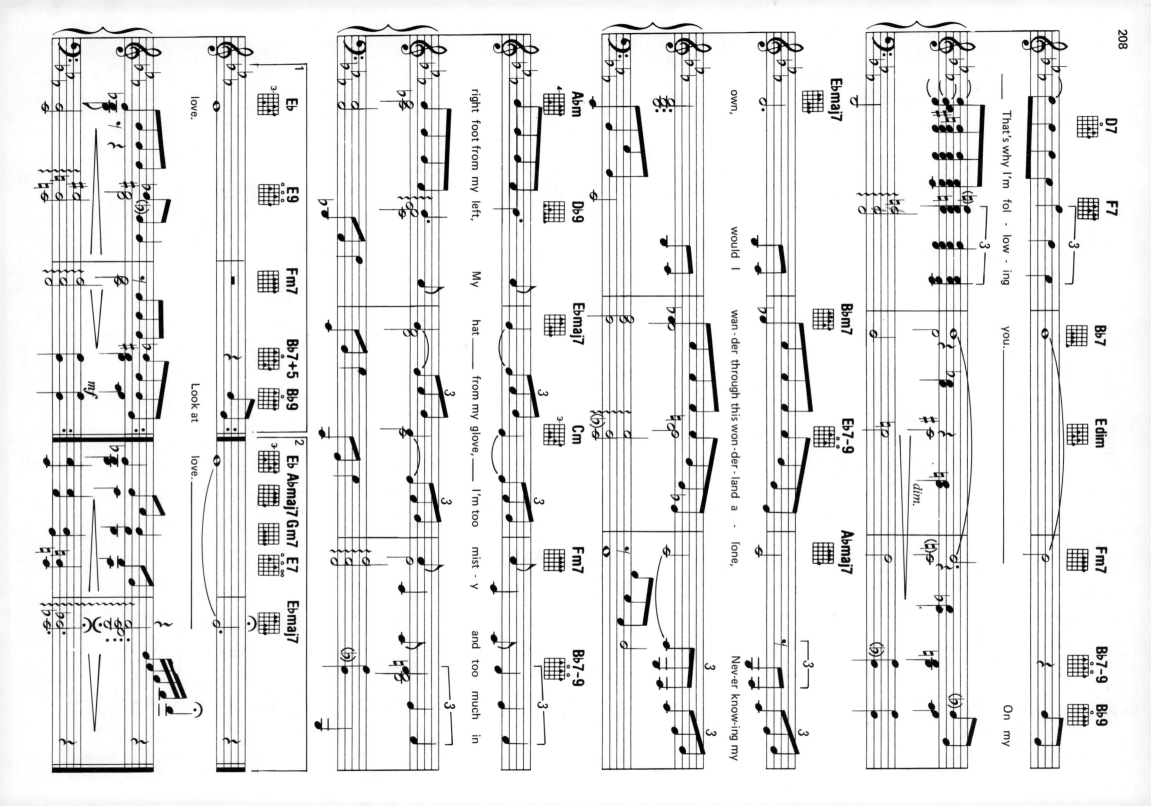

MORE
(Theme From MONDO CANE)

English Words by NORMAN NEWELL
Music by R. ORTOLANI and N. OLIVIERO

Moderately

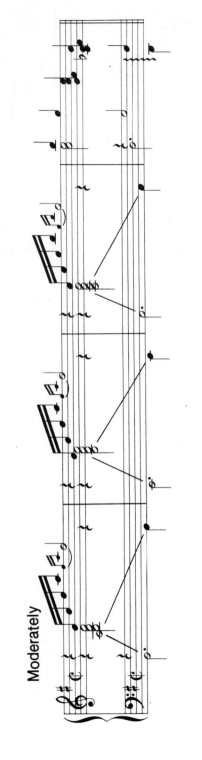

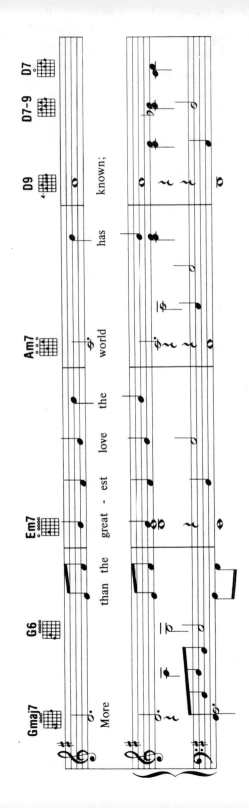

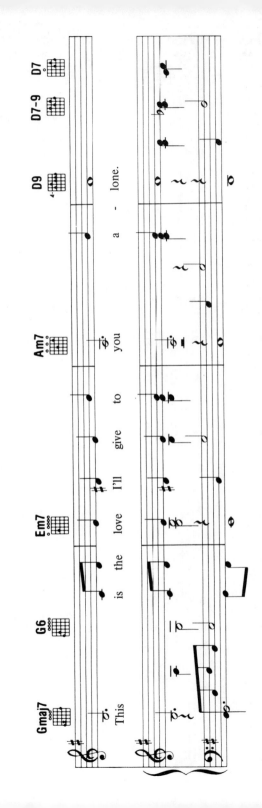

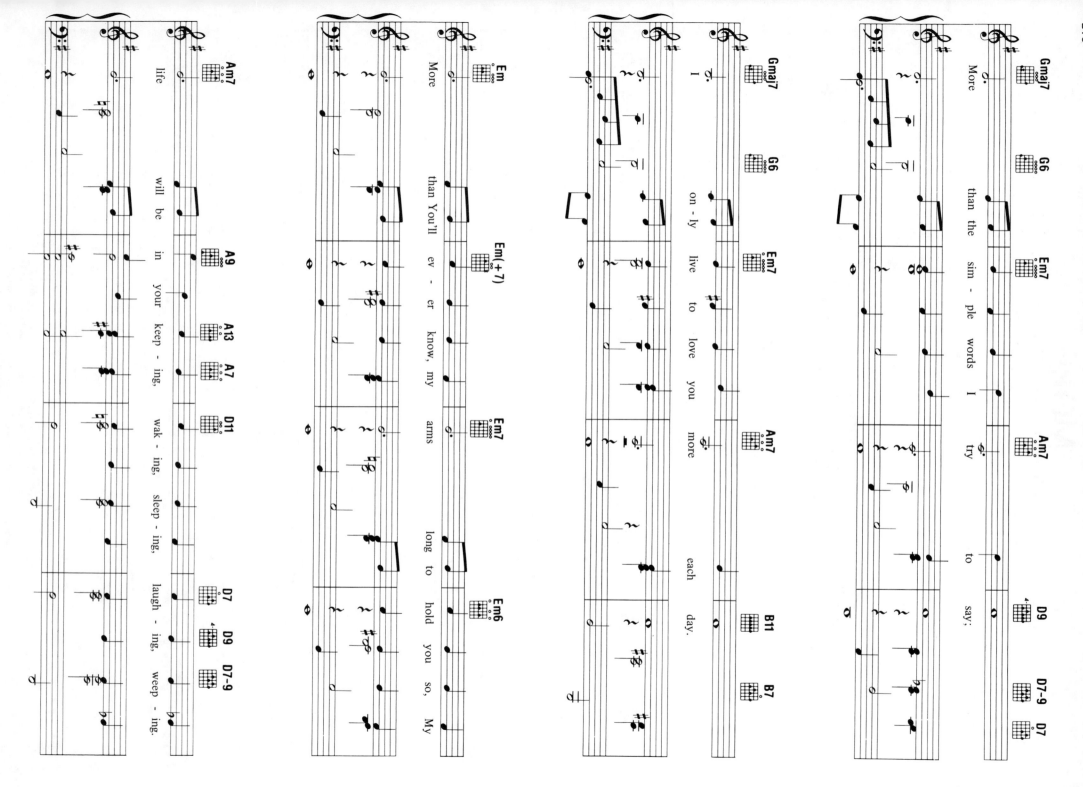

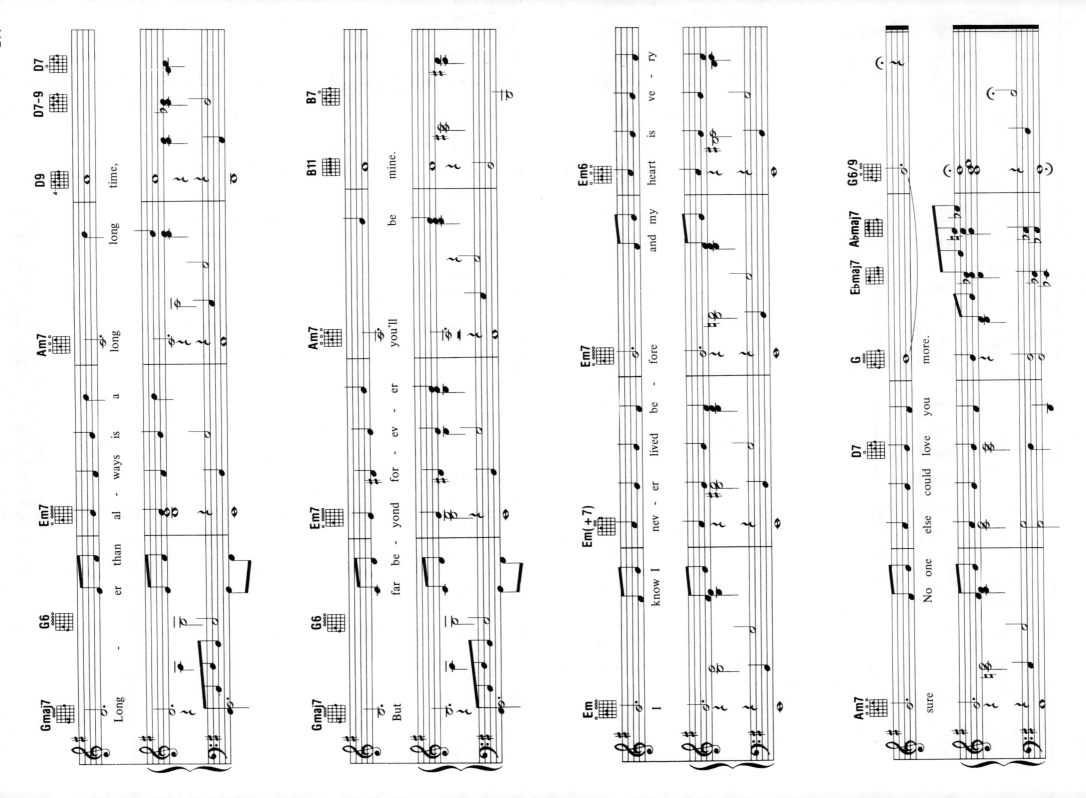

MONDAY, MONDAY

Words and Music by JOHN PHILLIPS

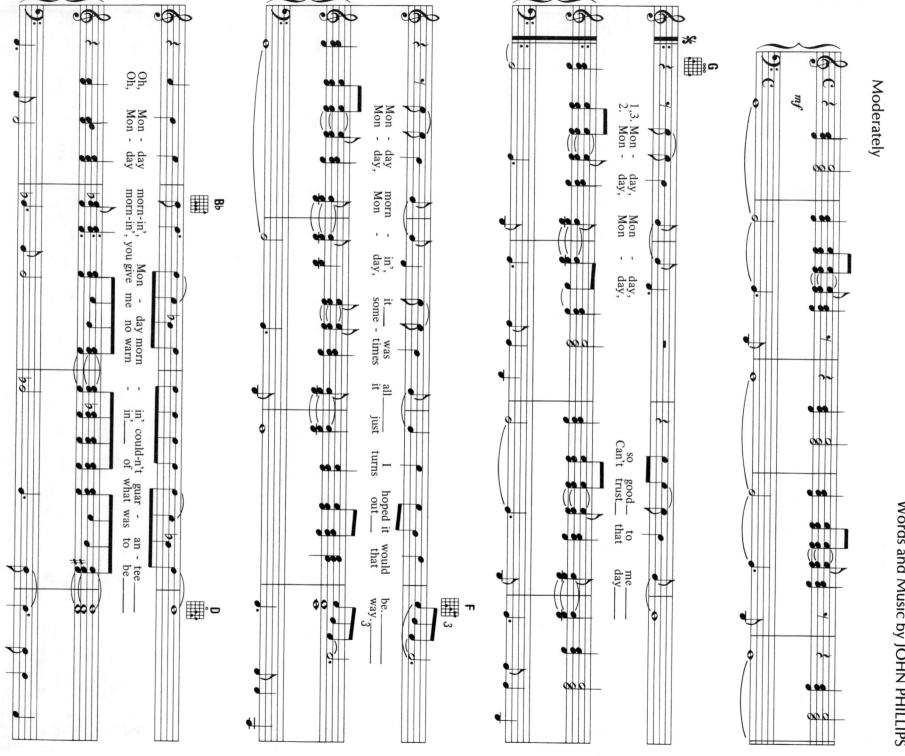

MCA MUSIC

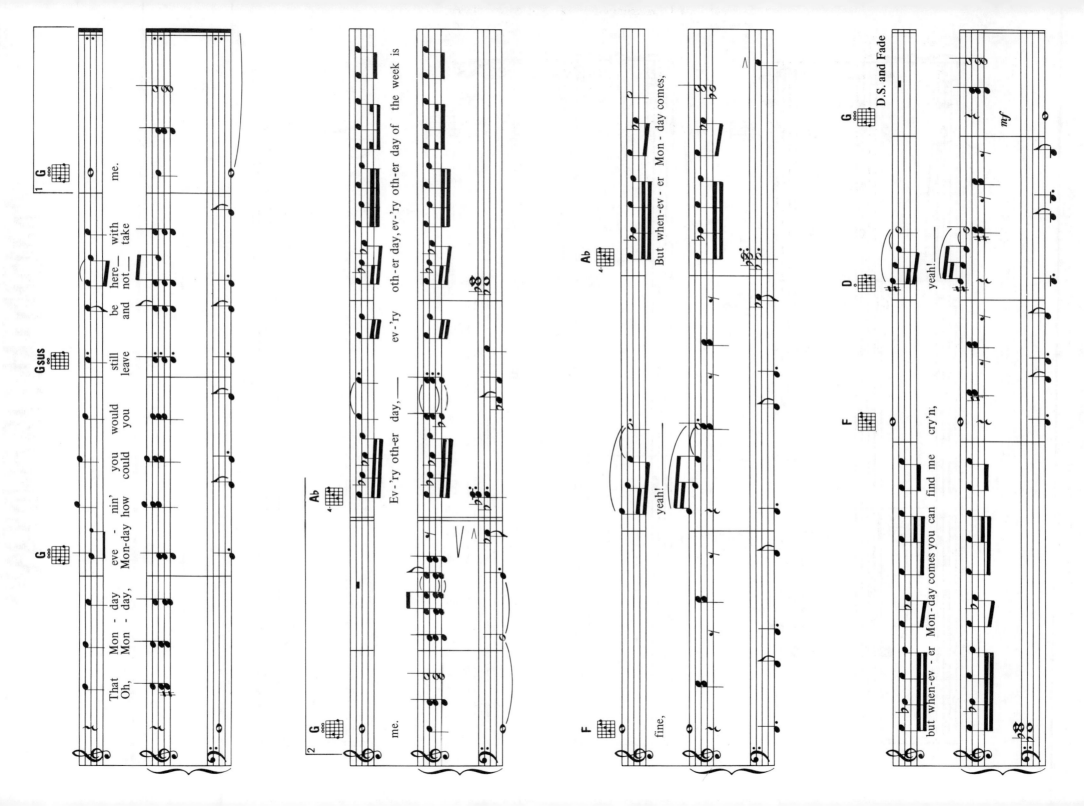

A MONTH OF SUNDAYS

Words by JOHNNY MERCER
Music by ROBERT EMMETT DOLAN

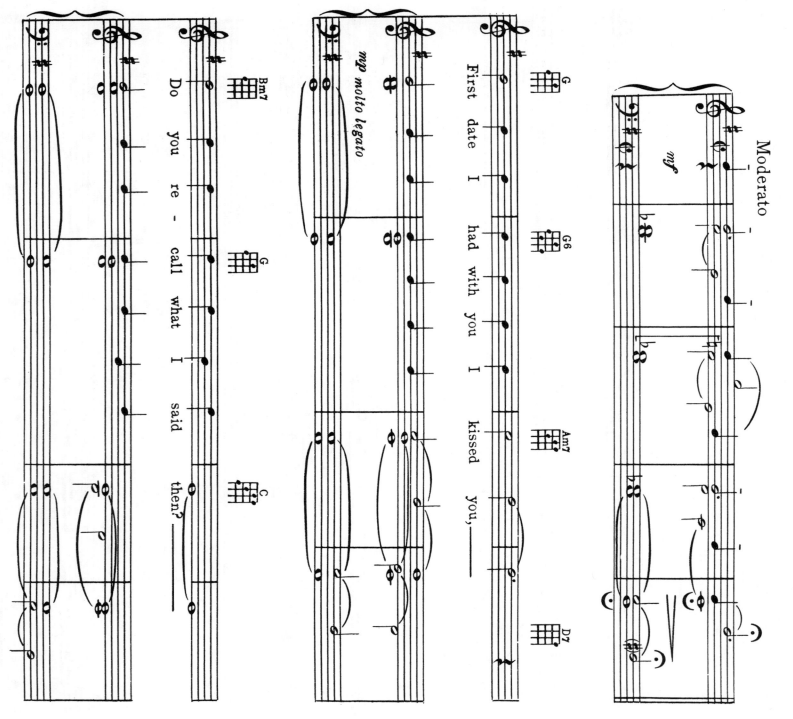

First date I had with you I kissed you,——

Do you re - call what I said then?——

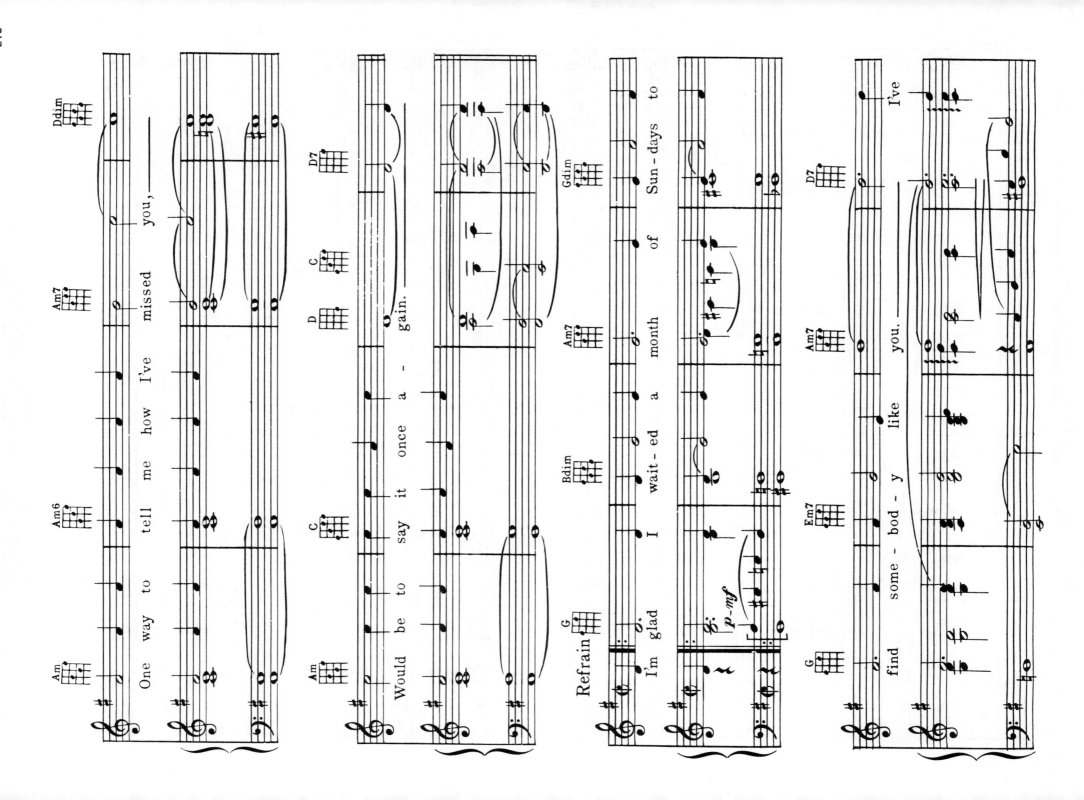

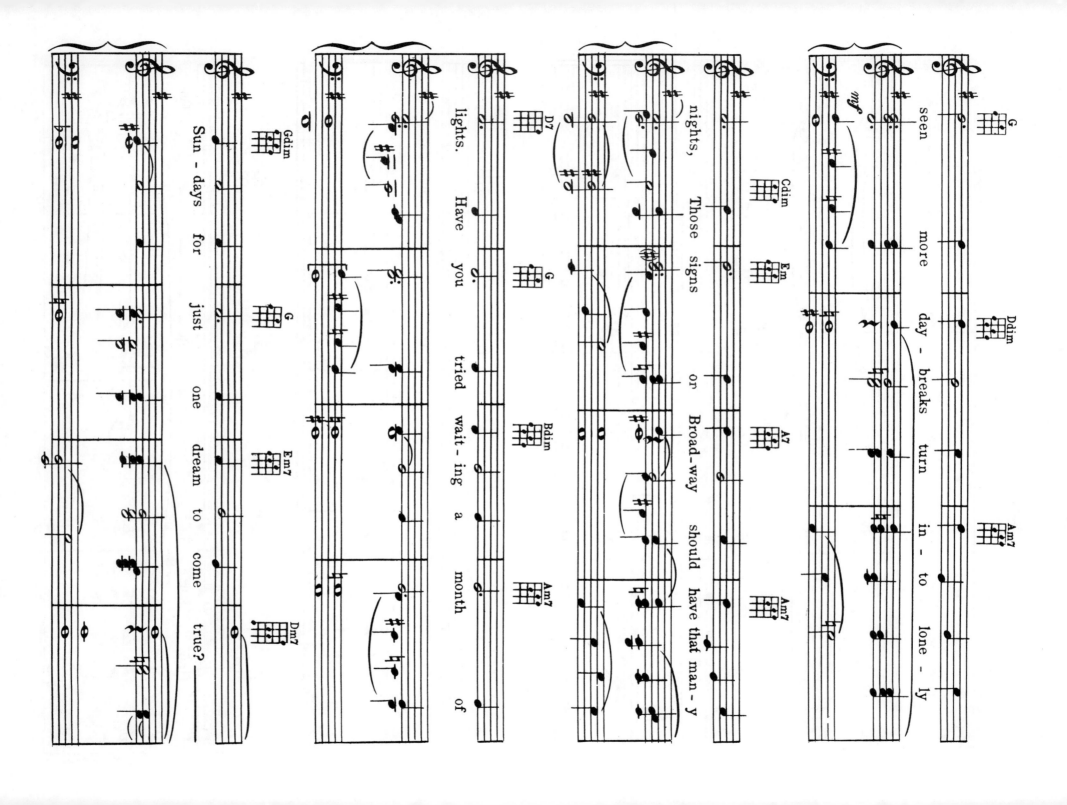

216

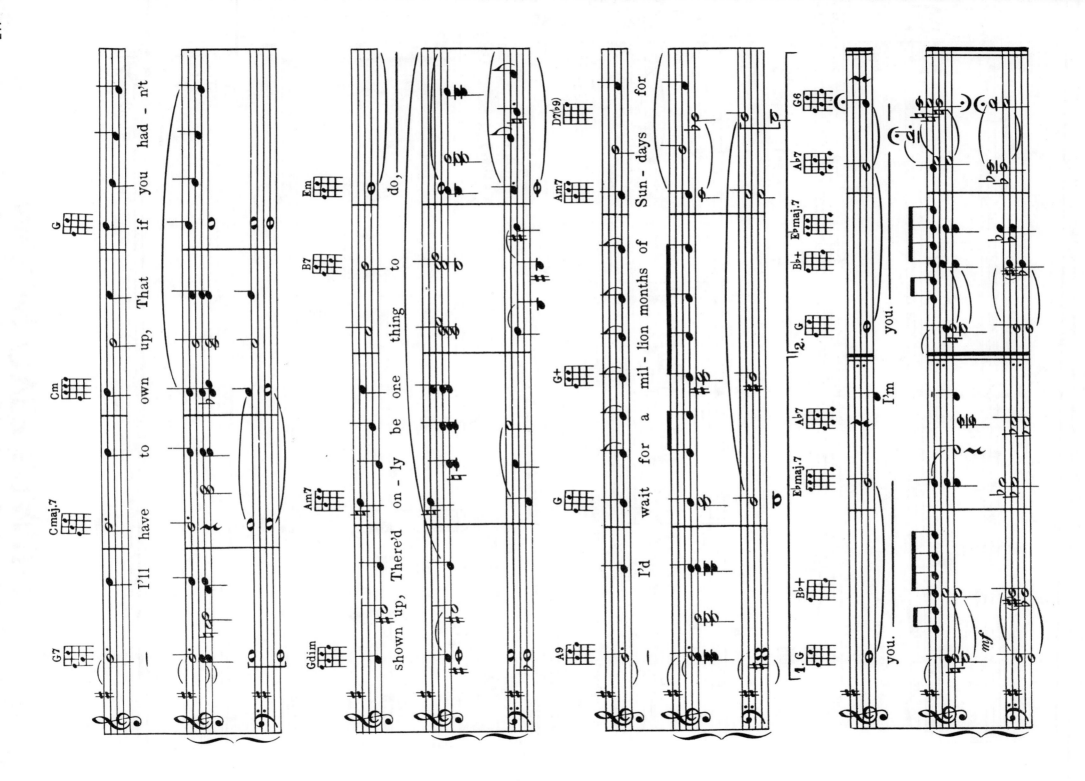

MOON OVER MIAMI

Words by EDGAR LESLIE
Music by JOE BURKE

Moderately Slow

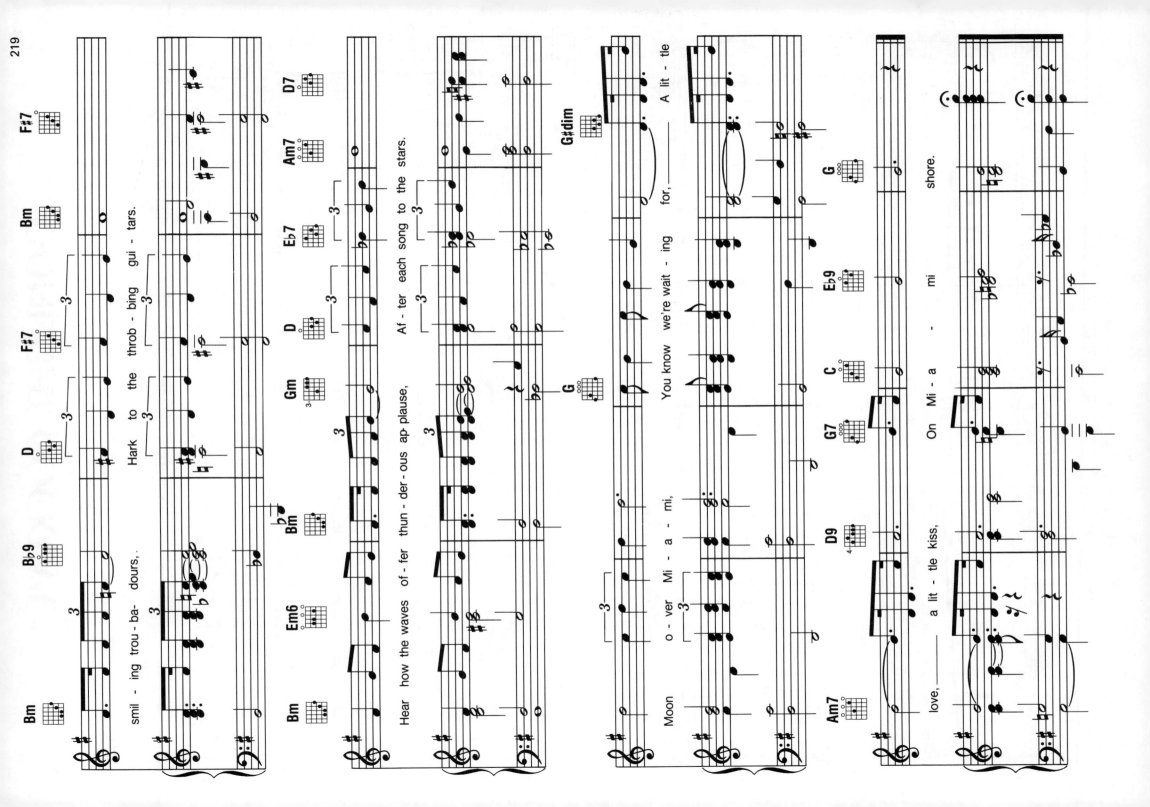

MOONLIGHT COCKTAIL

By LUCKY ROBERTS
and KIM GANNON

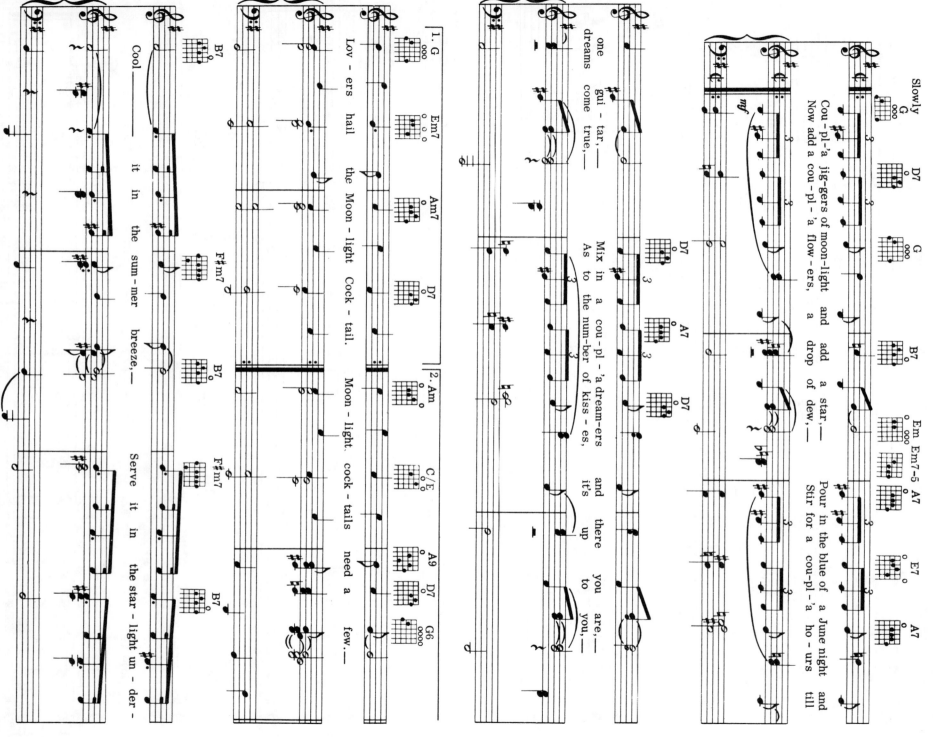

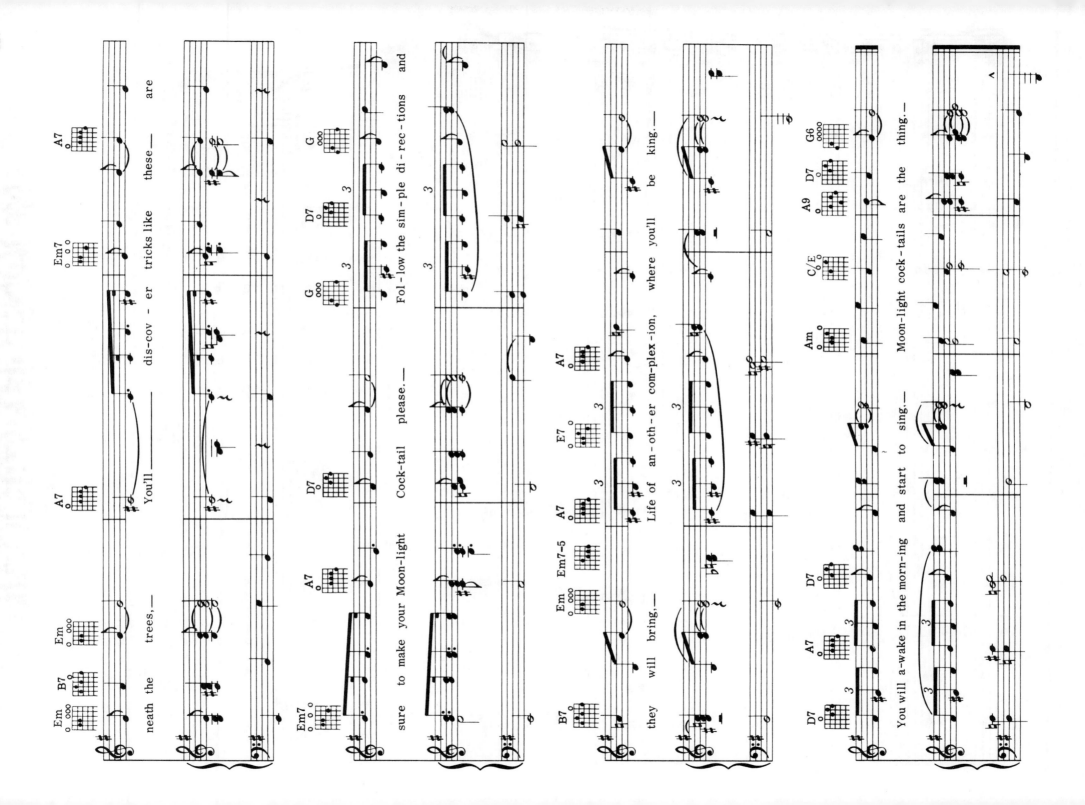

THE MOST BEAUTIFUL GIRL IN THE WORLD

(From "JUMBO")

Music by RICHARD RODGERS
Words by LORENZ HART

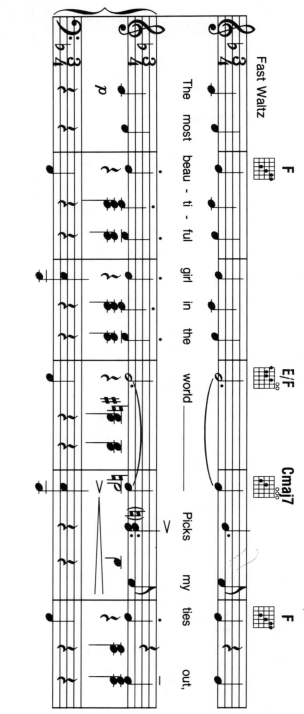

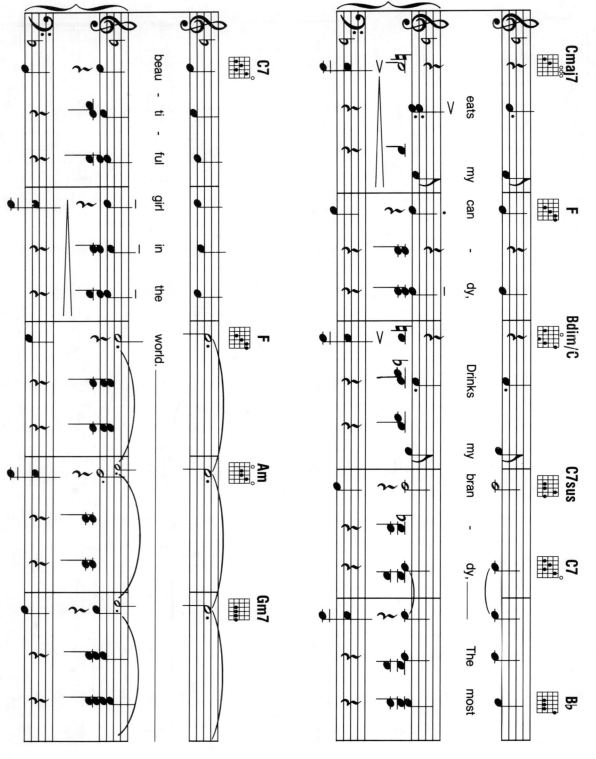

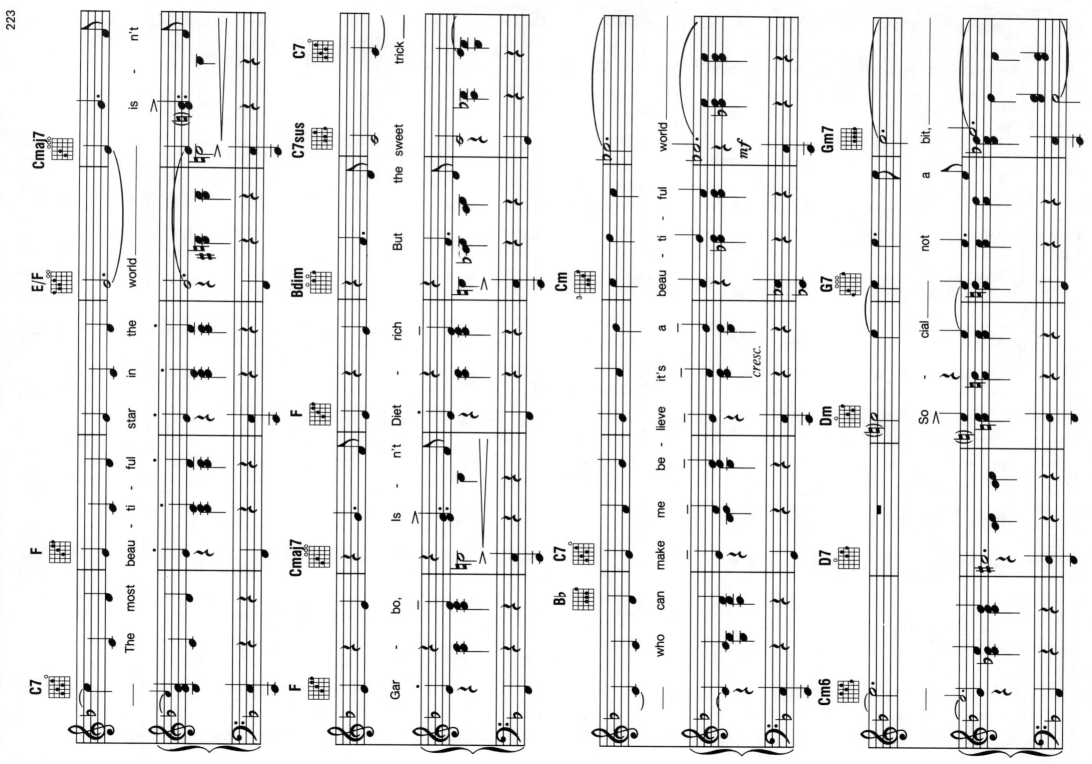

223

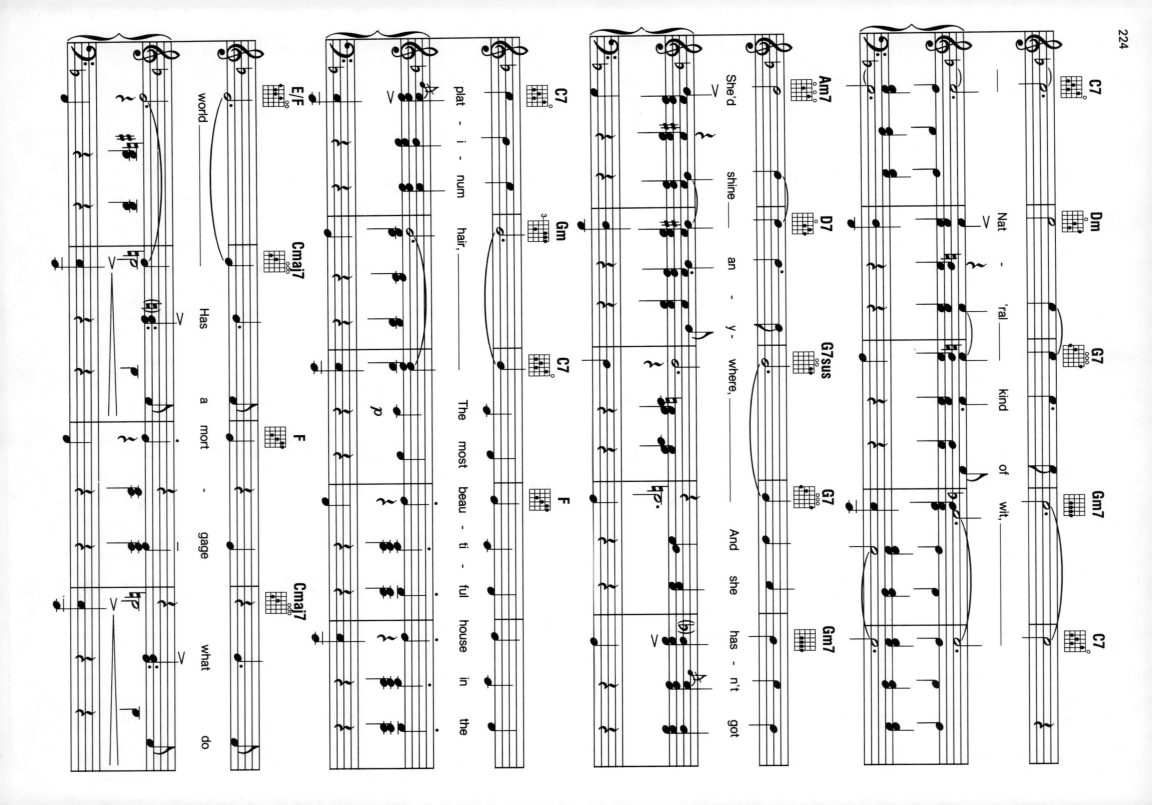

MY ELUSIVE DREAMS

Words and Music by CURLY PUTMAN and BILLY SHERRILL

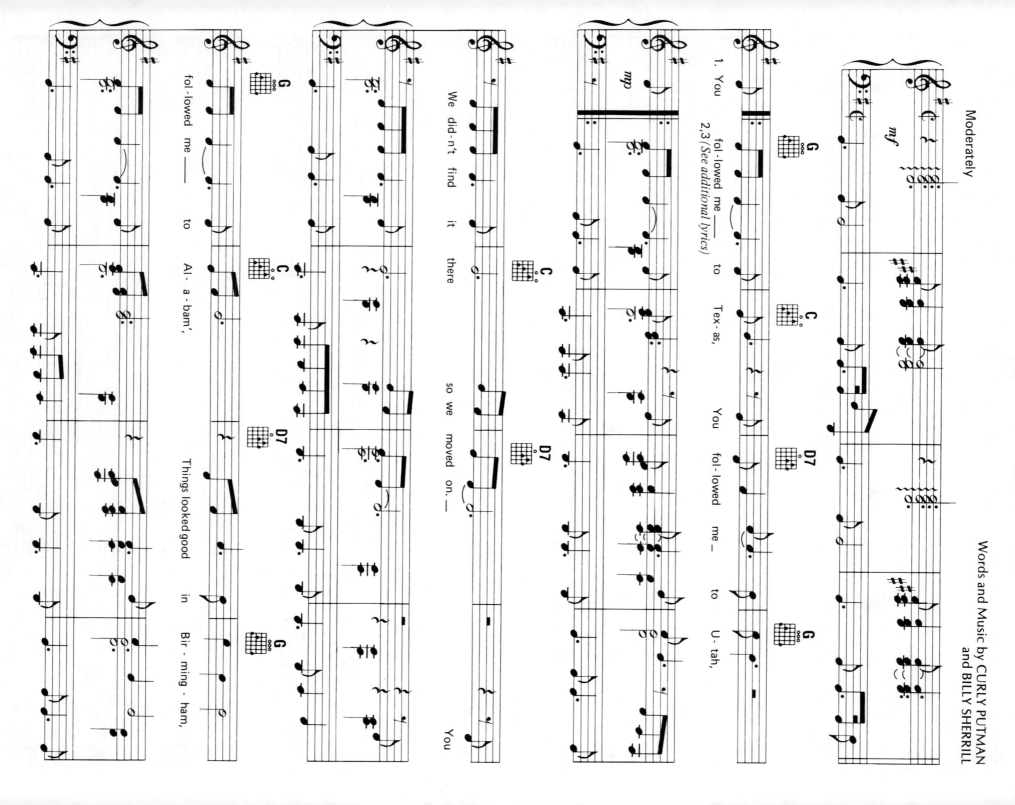

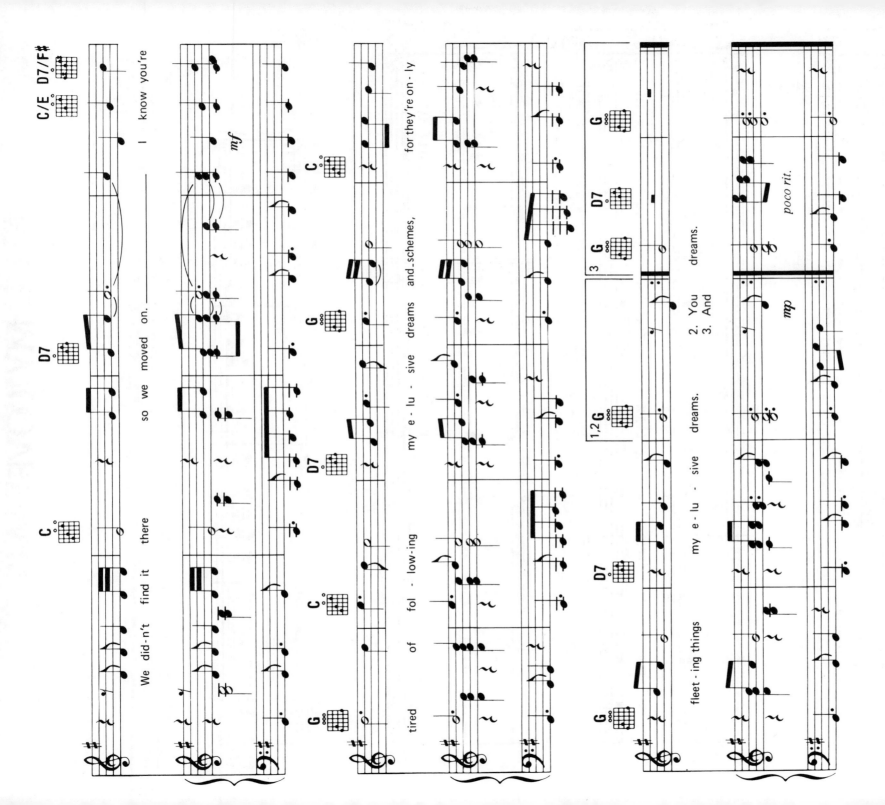

2. You had my child in Memphis, I heard of work in Nashville,
   We didn't find it there so we moved on.
   To a small farm in Nebraska to a gold mine in Alaska,
   We didn't find it there so we moved on. (Chorus)

3. And now we've left Alaska because there was no gold mine,
   But this time only two of us move on.
   Now all we have is each other and a little memory to cling to,
   And still you won't let me go on alone. (Chorus)

MY LOVE

Words and Music by
TONY HATCH

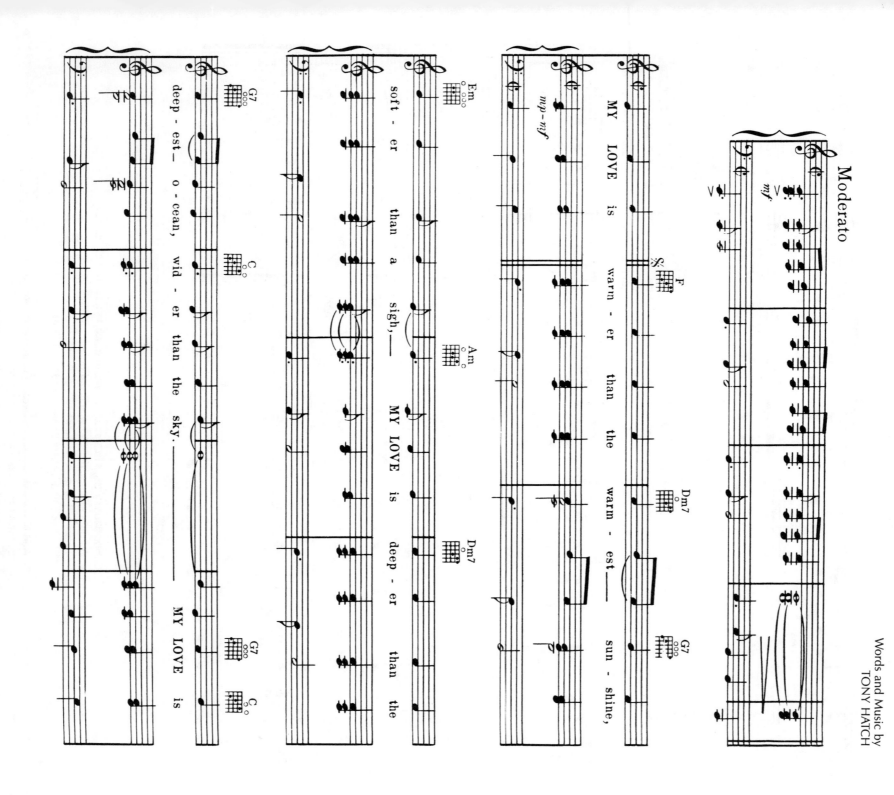

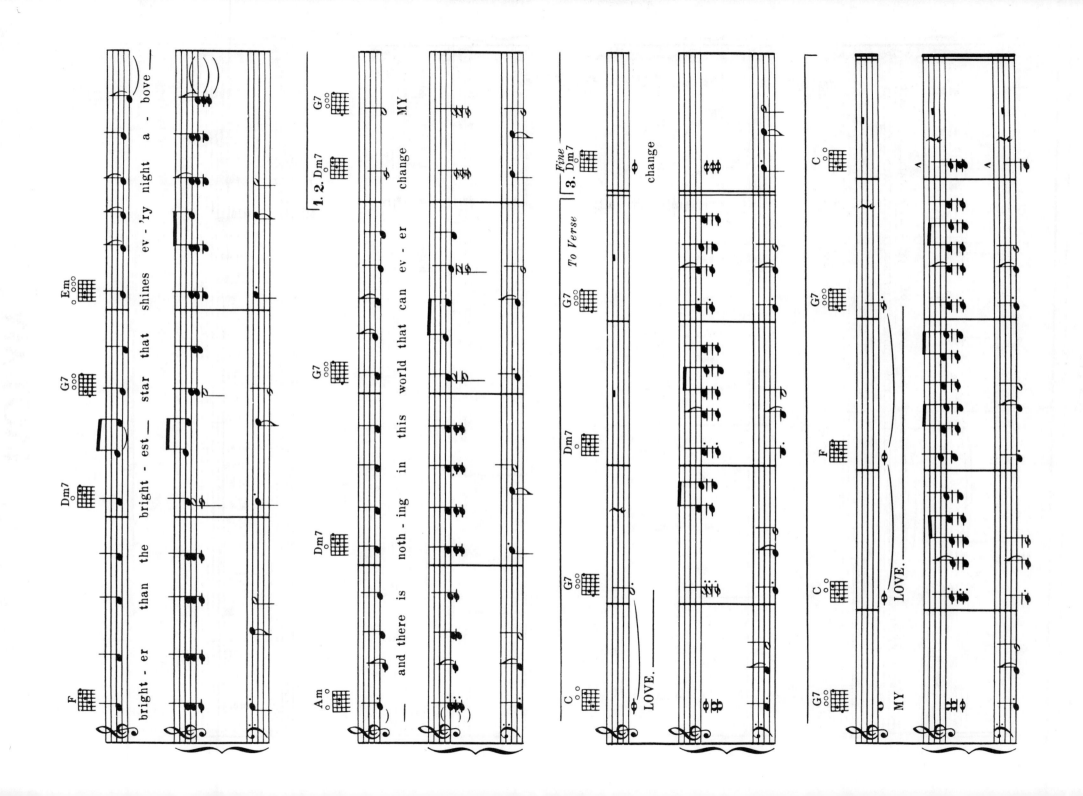

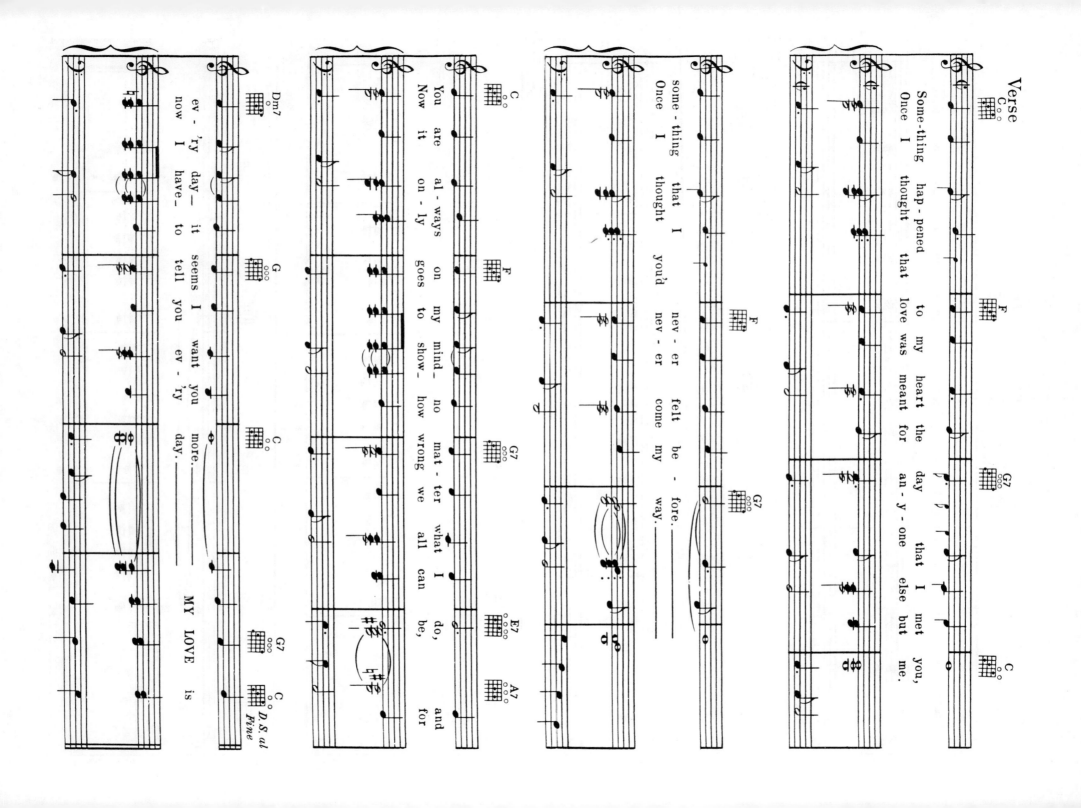

MY OH MY

Slow and steady rock

Words and Music by N. HOLDER
and J. LEA

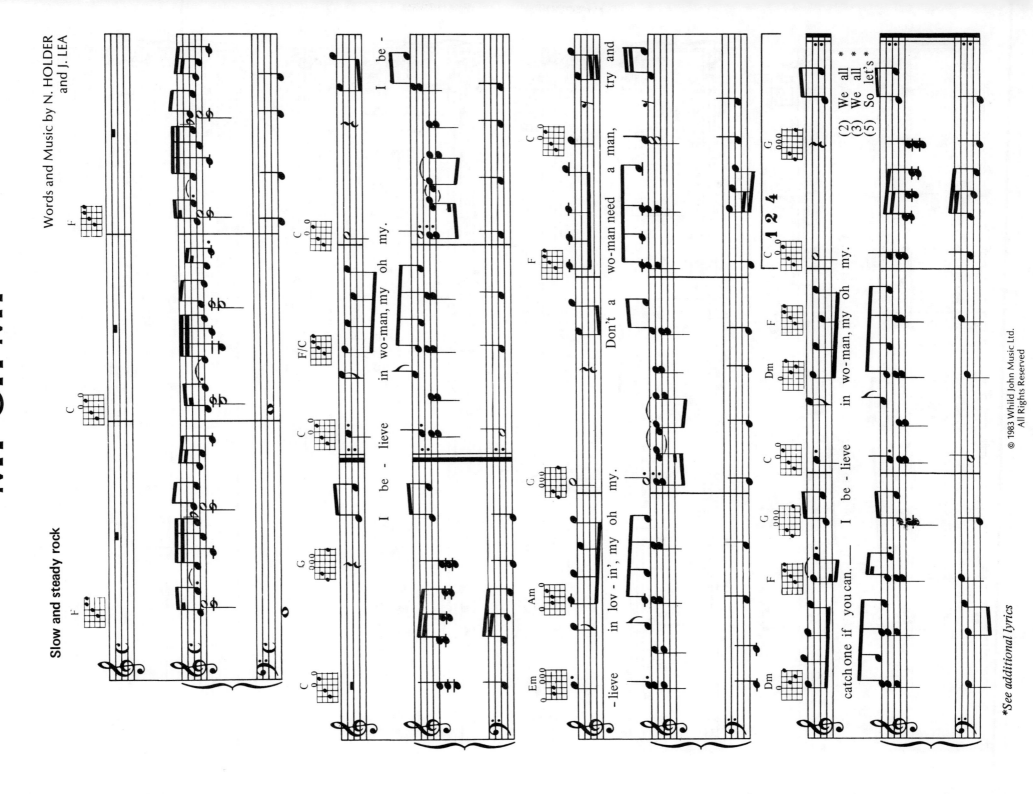

*See additional lyrics

2 We all need someone to talk to My Oh My
We all need someone to talk to My Oh My
You need a shoulder to cry on
Call me I'll be standing by
We all need someone to talk to My Oh My

3 We all need a lotta lovin' My Oh My
Yeah a whole lotta lovin' My Oh My
I can lend a helping hand
If you ain't got nothing planned
We all need some lovin' My Oh My

4 So let's all swing together My Oh My
We can all swing together My Oh My
You've got troubles of your own
No need to face them all alone
We can all swing together My Oh My

5 So let's all pull together My Oh My
Yeah let's all pull together My Oh My
We can ride the stormy weather
If we all get out and try
So let's all pull together My Oh My

MY ROMANCE
(From "JUMBO")

Words by LORENZ HART
Music by RICHARD RODGERS

Moderato

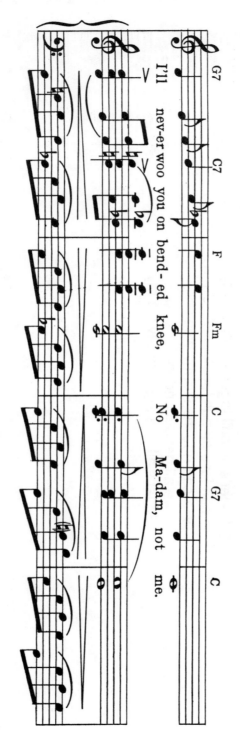

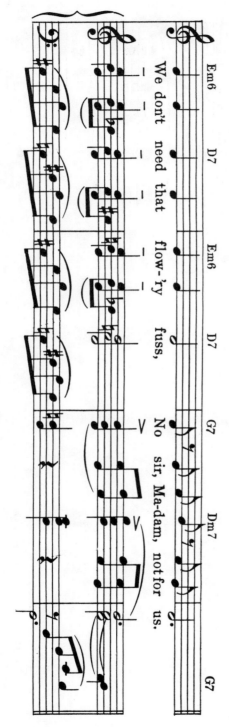

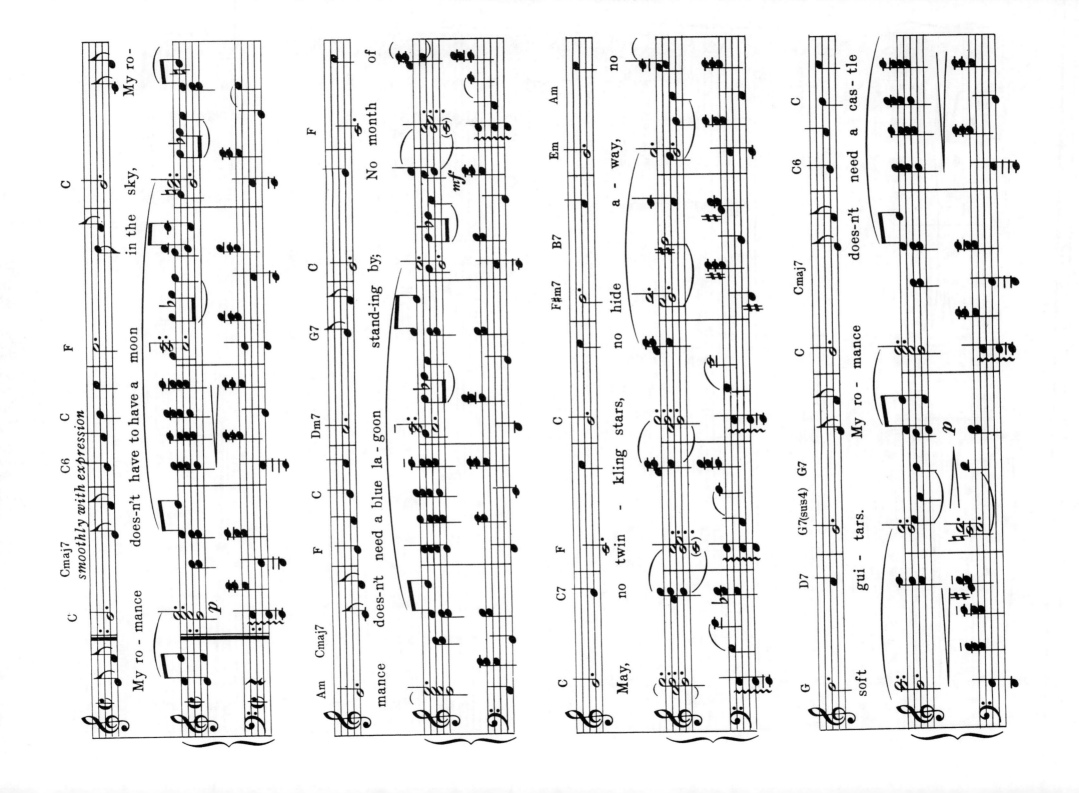

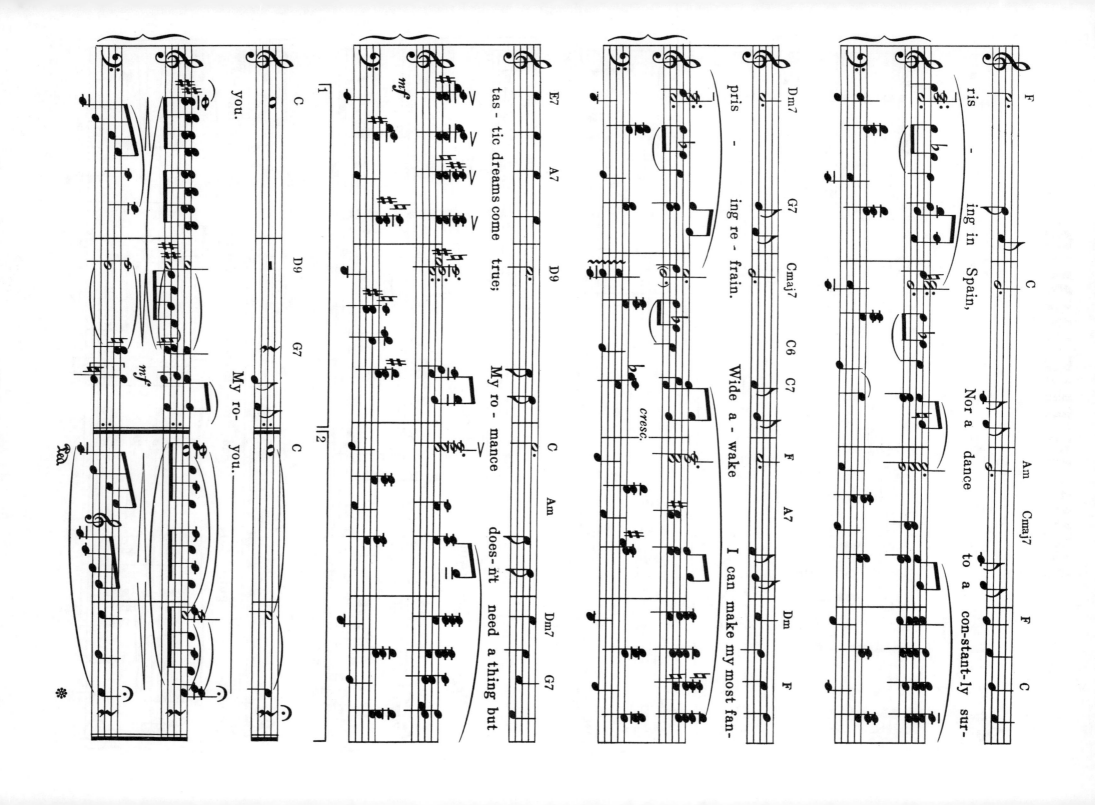

236

NOW IS THE HOUR

by MAEWA KAIHAN, CLEMENT SCOTT,
& DOROTHY STEWARD

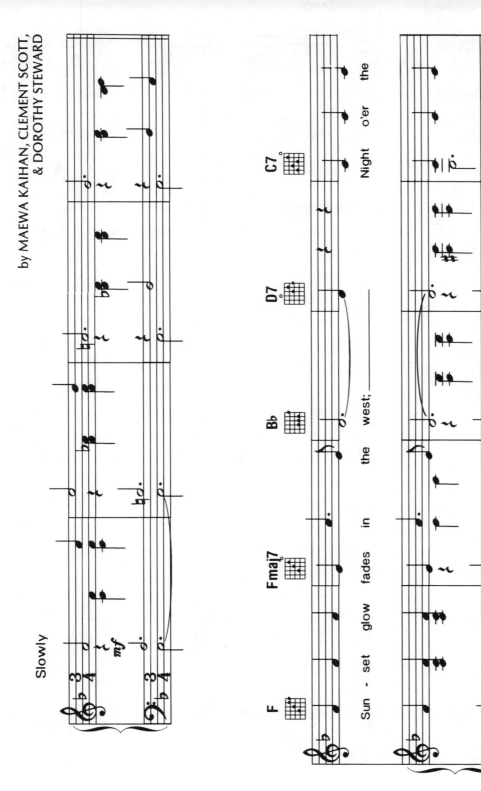

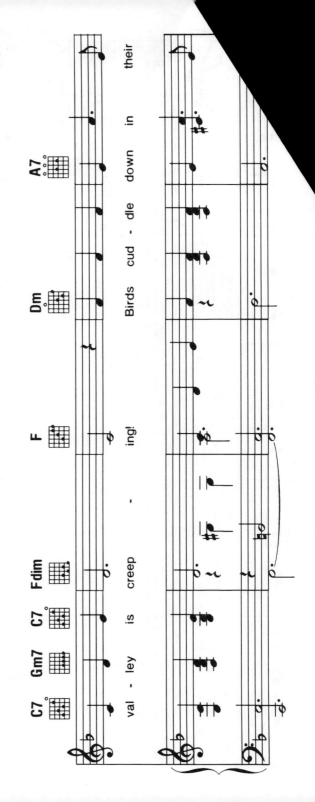

MCA MUSIC

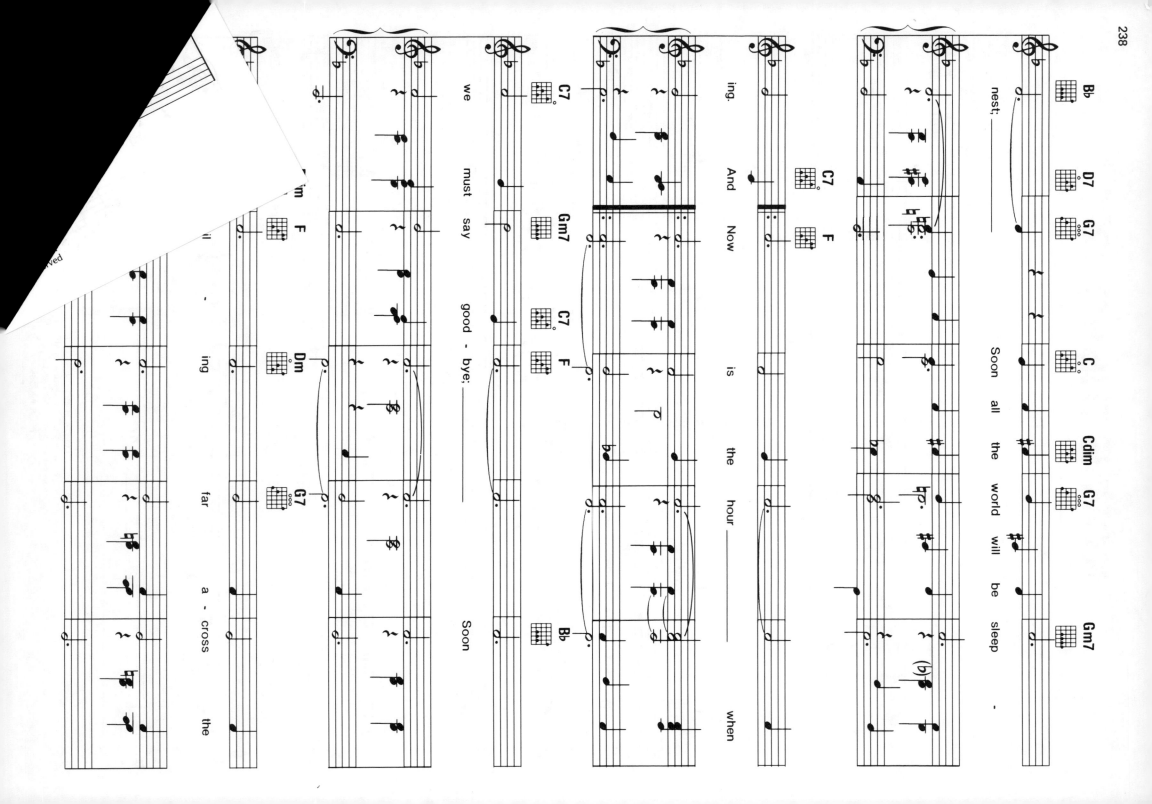

239

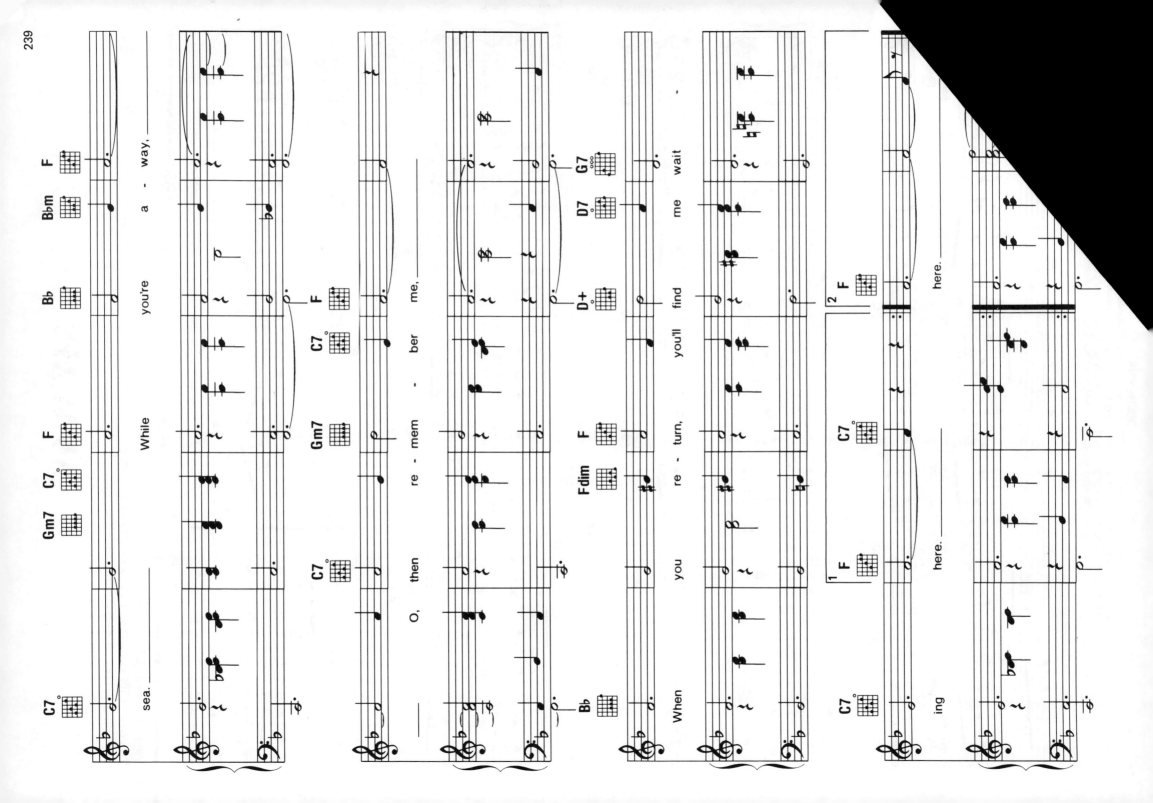

MY WAY

Orignial French Lyric by GILLES THIBAULT
Music by CLAUDE FRANCOIS and JACQUES REVAUX
English Lyric by PAUL ANKA

Moderately Slow

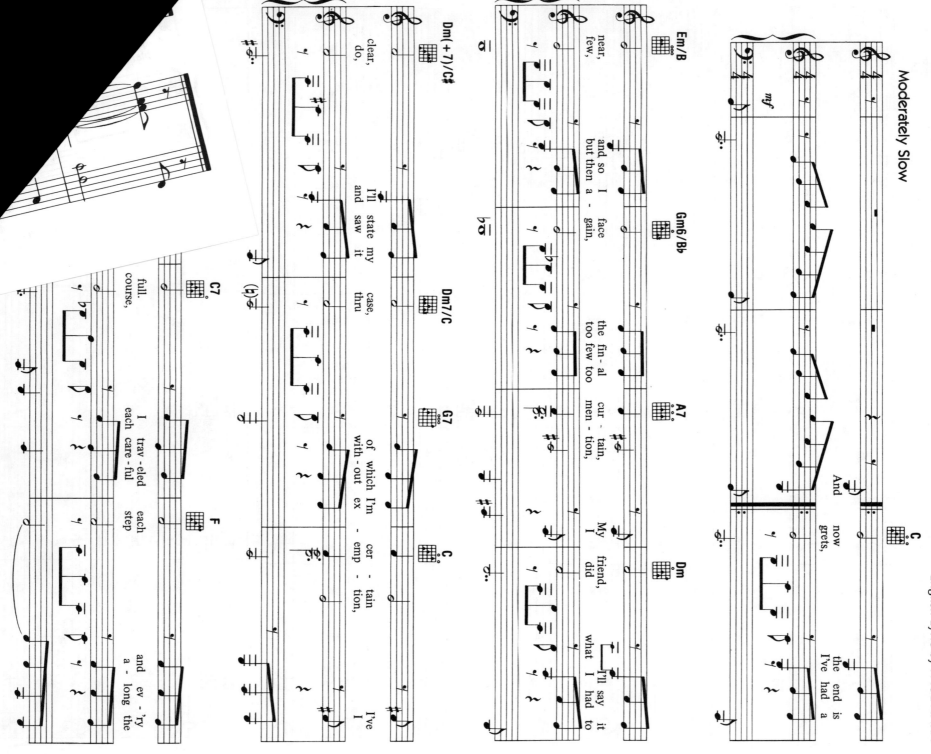

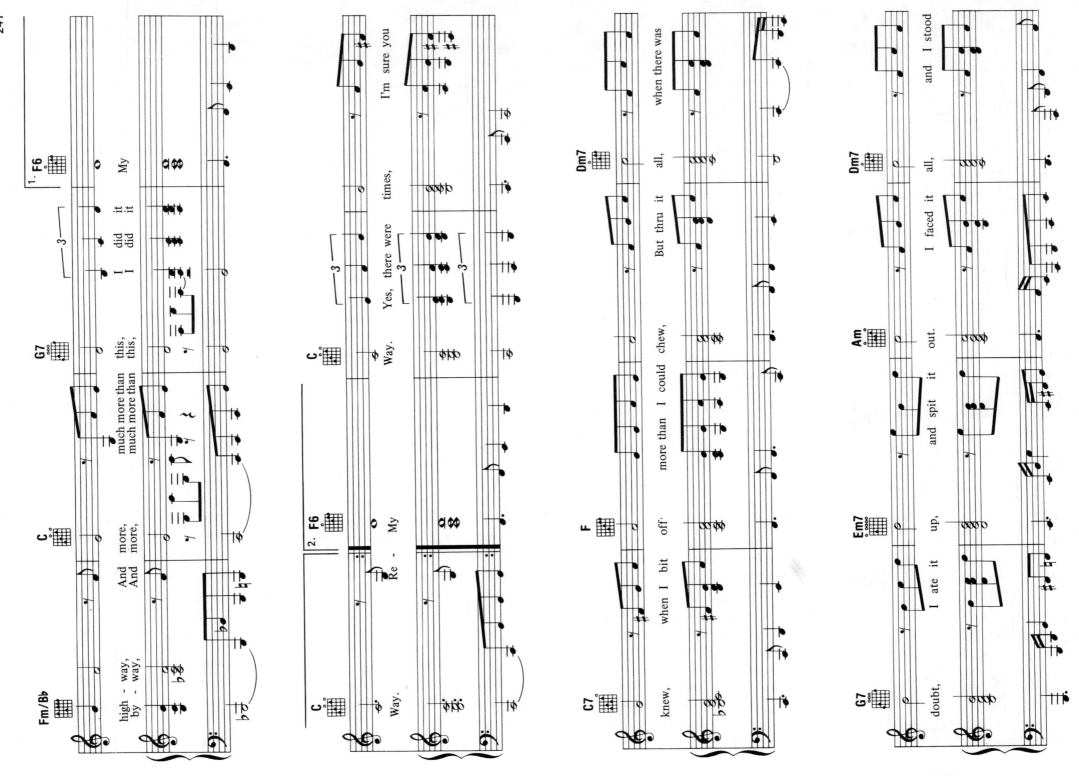

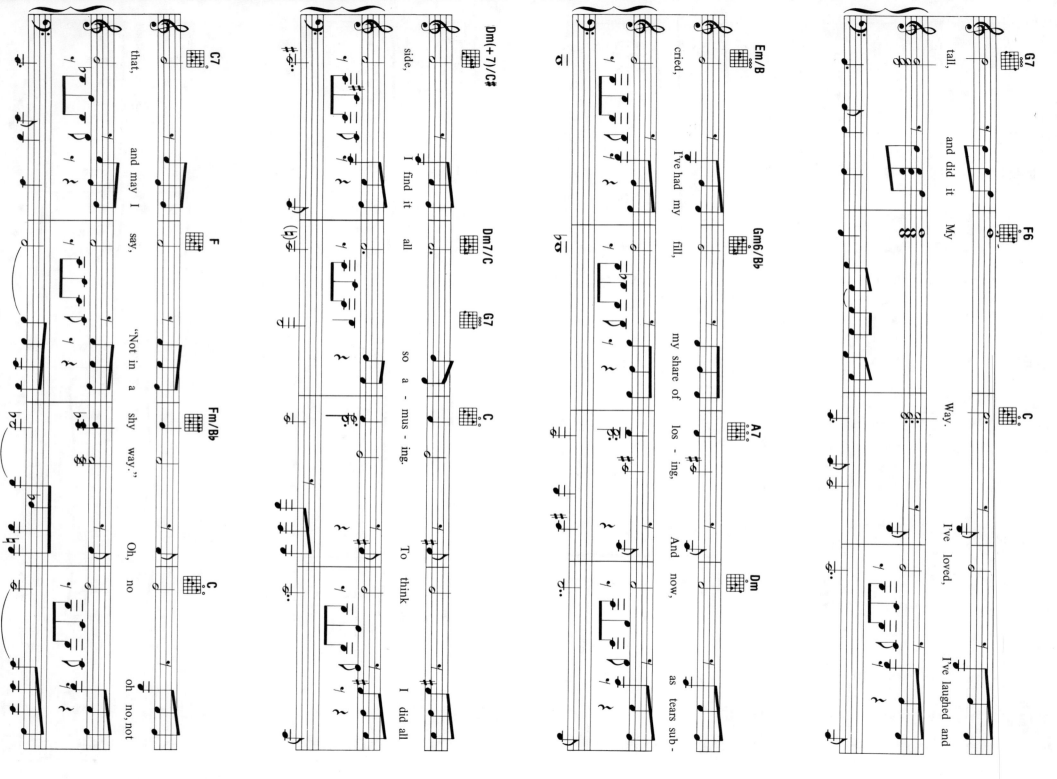

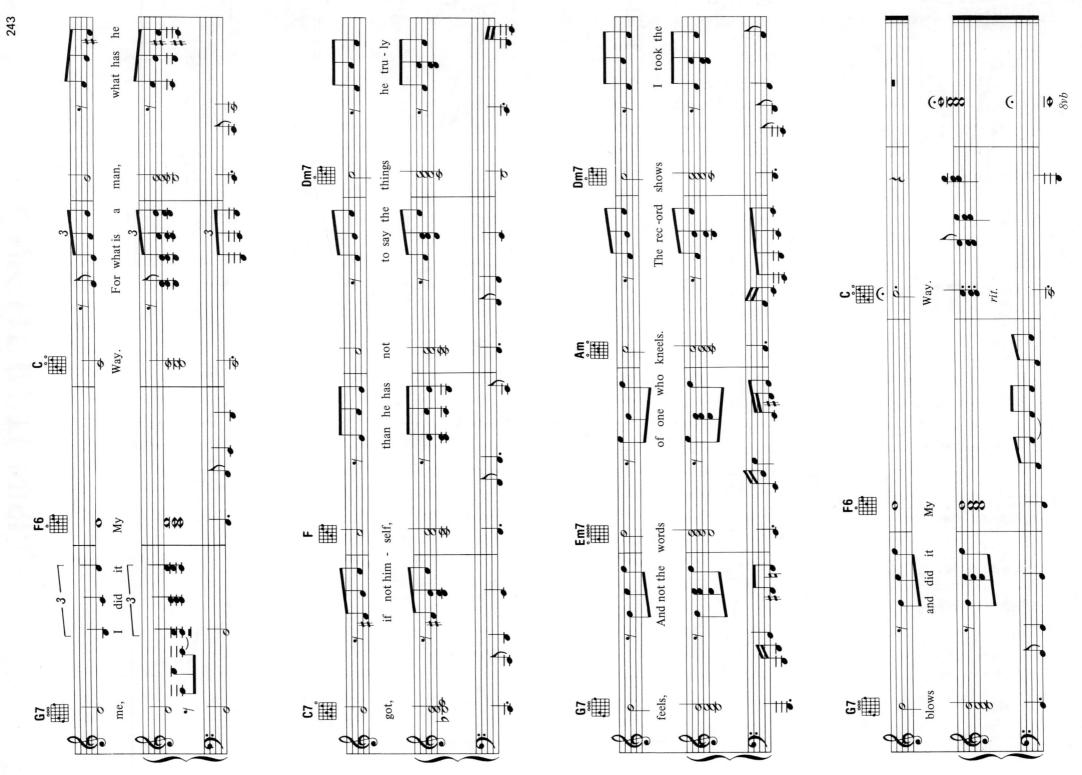

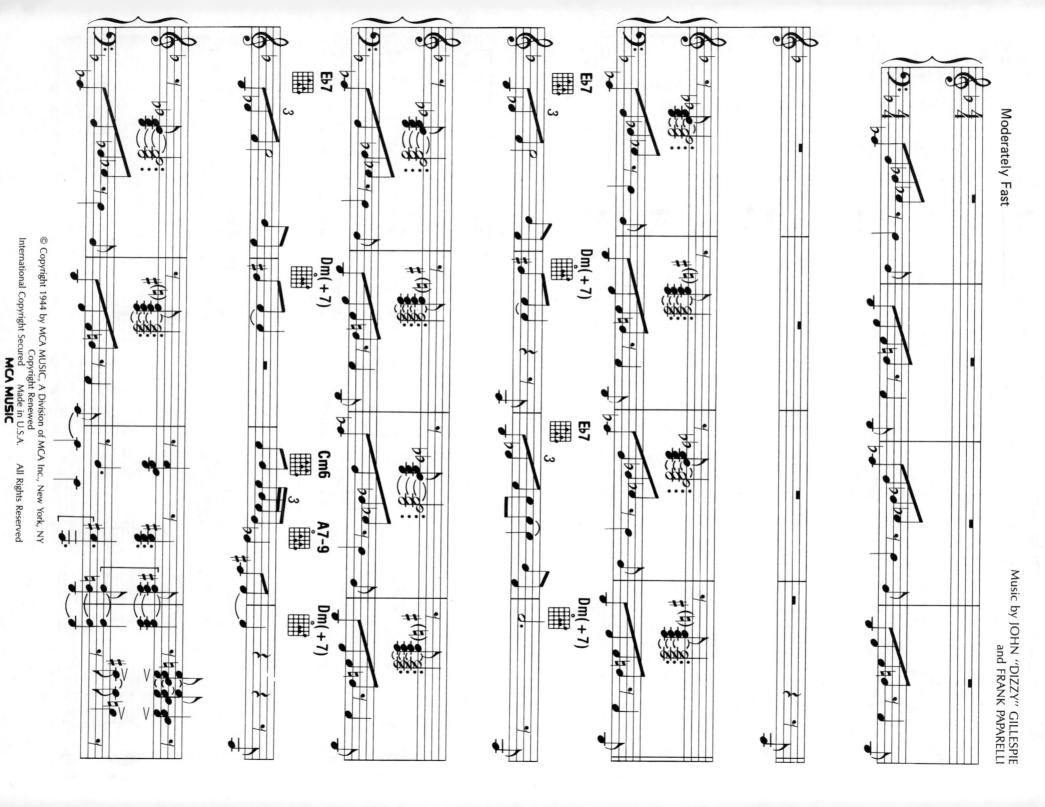

Eb7
Dm(+7)
Eb7
Dm(+7)
Eb7
Dm(+7)
Gm6
A7-9
Dm(+7)
Adim
D7-9
Gm6
D7-9
Gm(+7)
Gm6
Bbm6
C7-9
Fmaj7
Fm7
Edim
A7-9

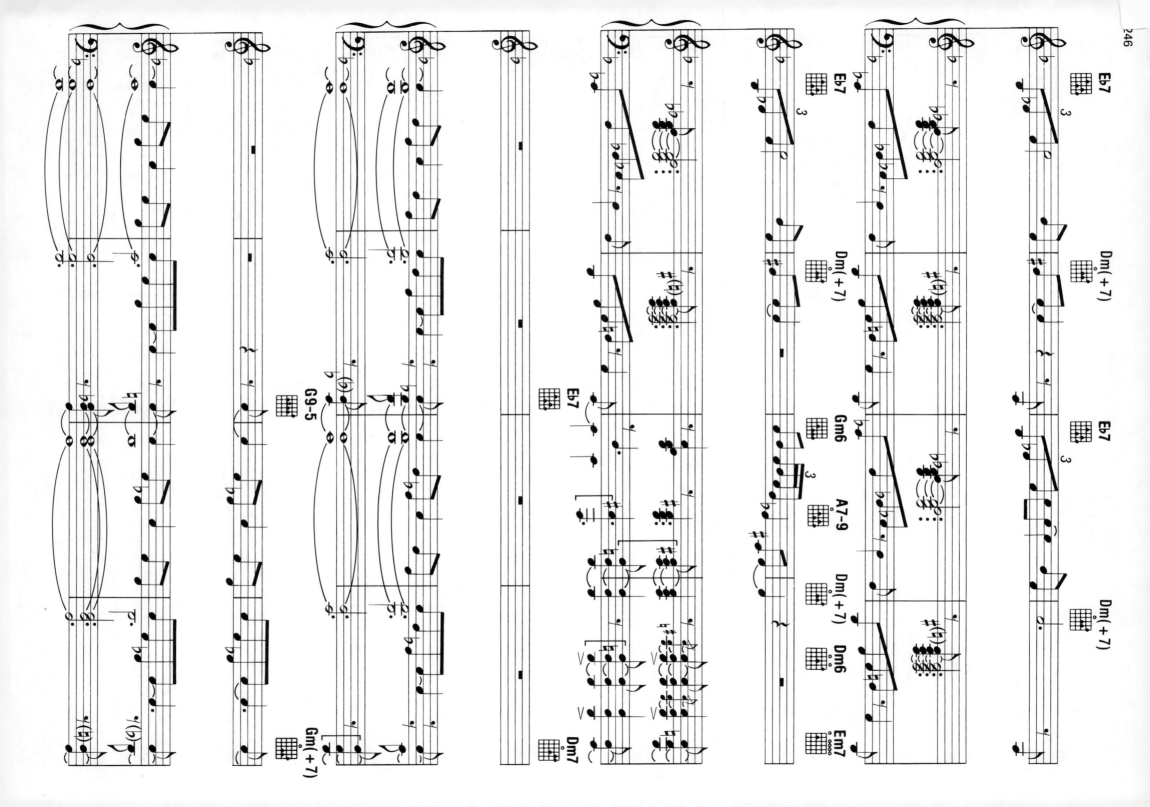

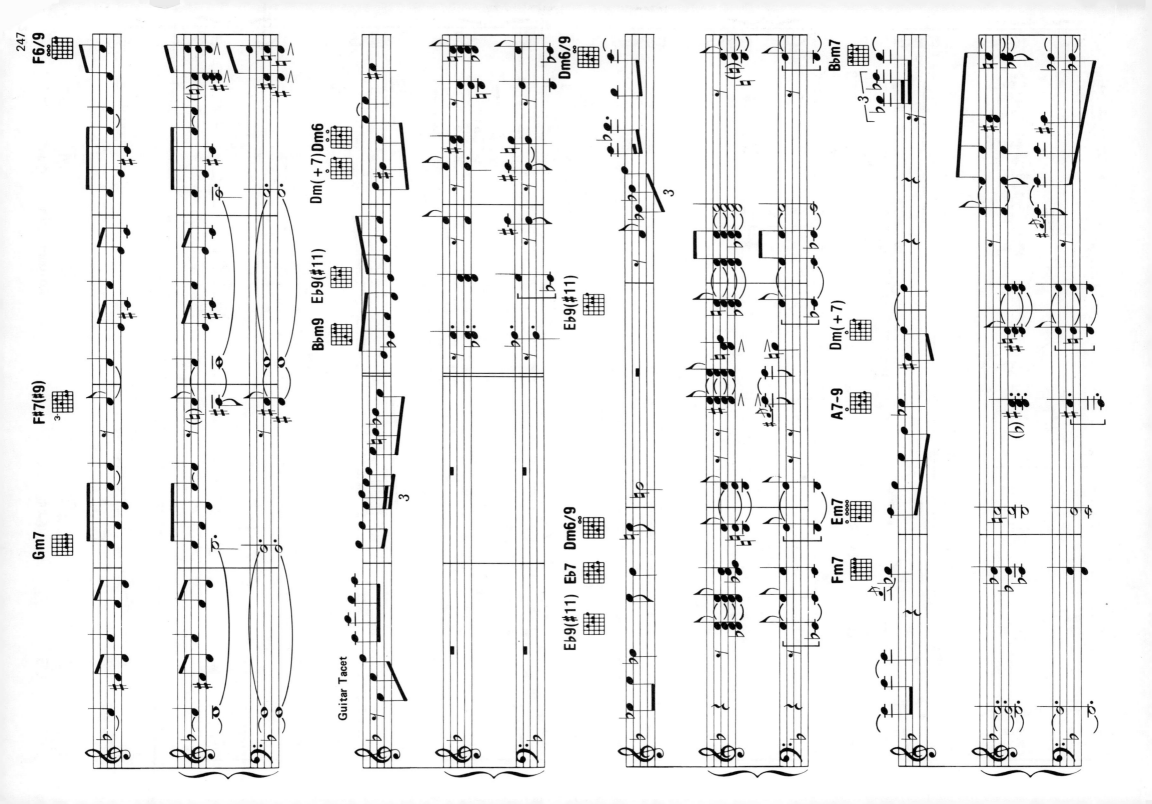

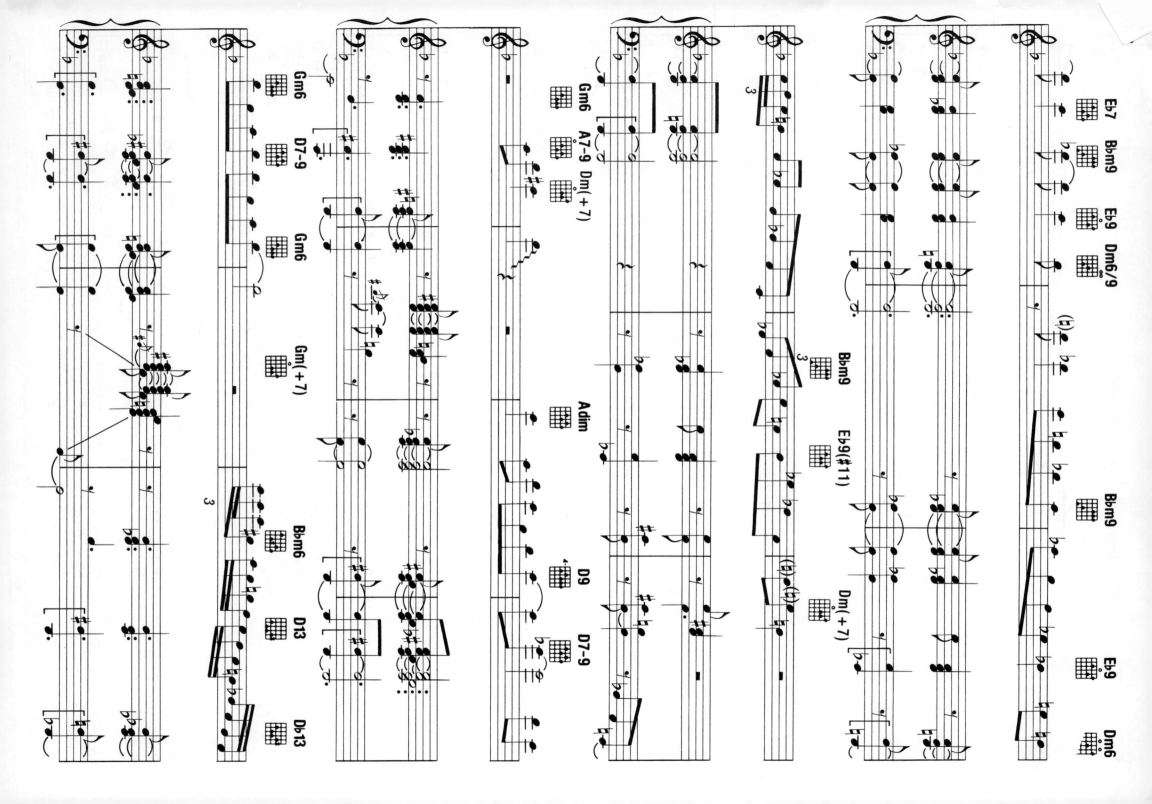

C9
Gb13
F6/9
Edim
A7-9
Bbm7
Eb9(#11)
Dm(+7)
Eb9
Eb9(#11)
Dm6/9
Eb9(#11)
Dm6/9
Eb9(#11)
Edim
A7-9
Dm6/9
Dm(+7)

NO OTHER LOVE

(From "ME AND JULIET")

Words by OSCAR HAMMERSTEIN II
Music by RICHARD RODGERS

Moderately

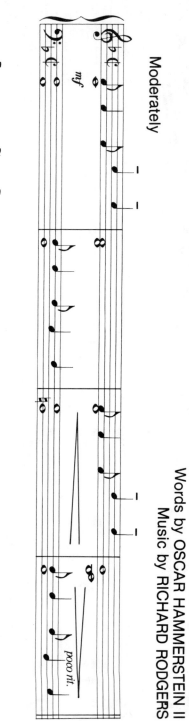
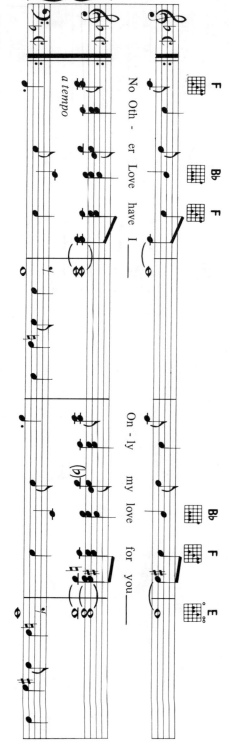
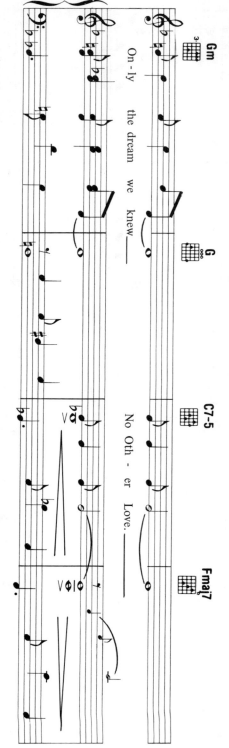
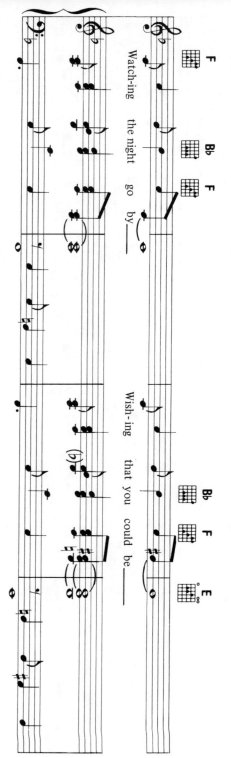

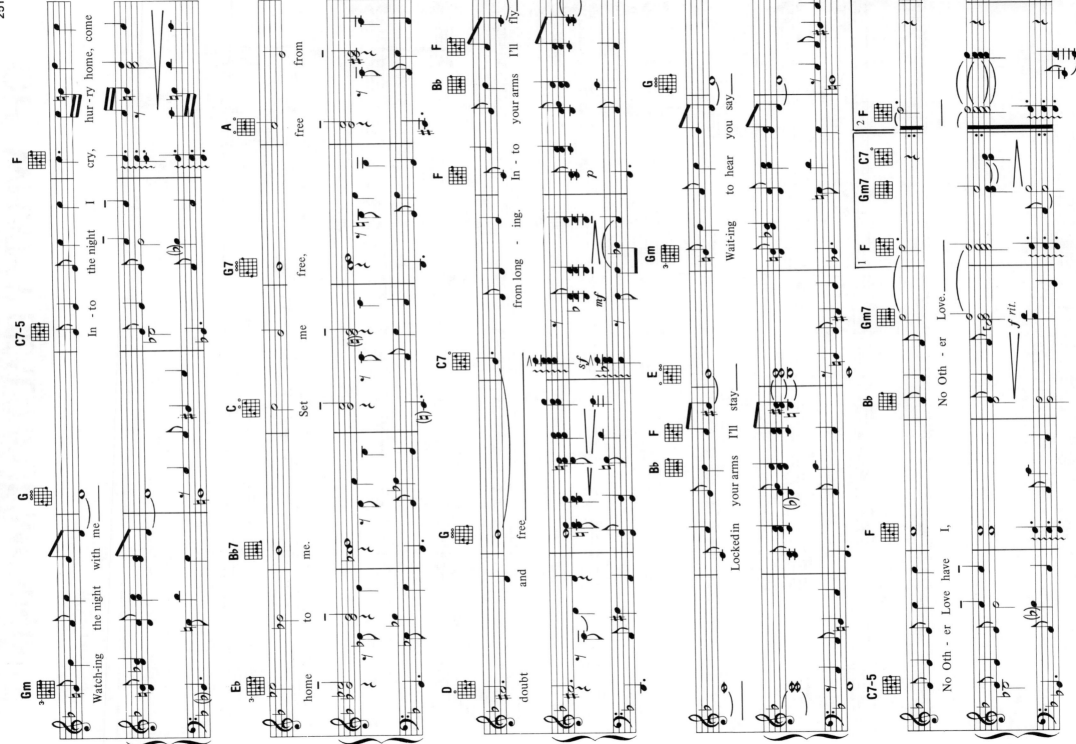

OH, WHAT A BEAUTIFUL MORNIN'
(From "OKLAHOMA!")

Words by OSCAR HAMMERSTEIN II
Music by RICHARD RODGERS

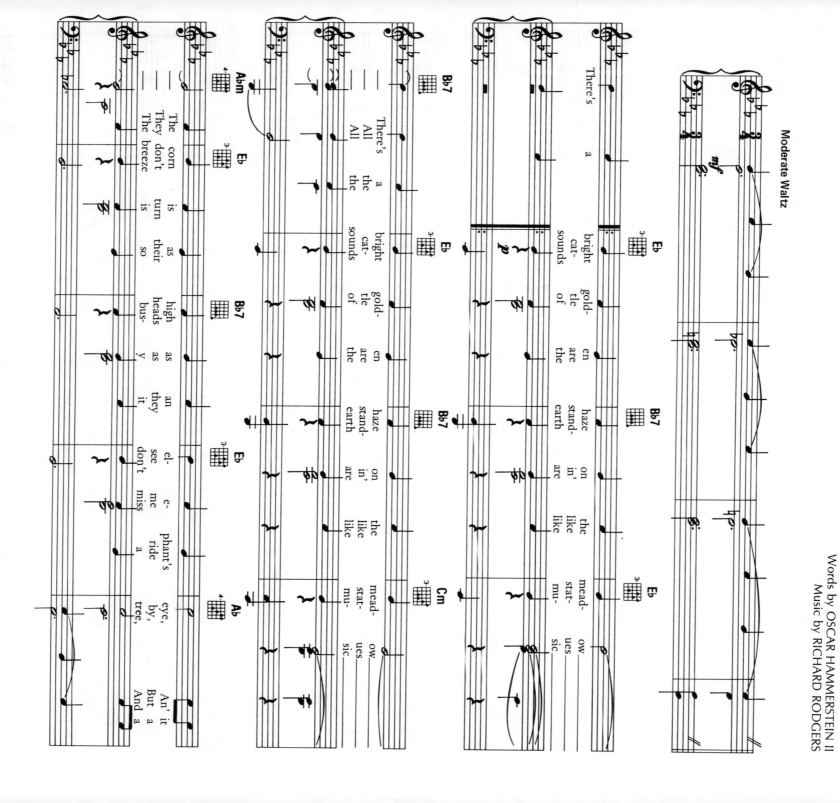

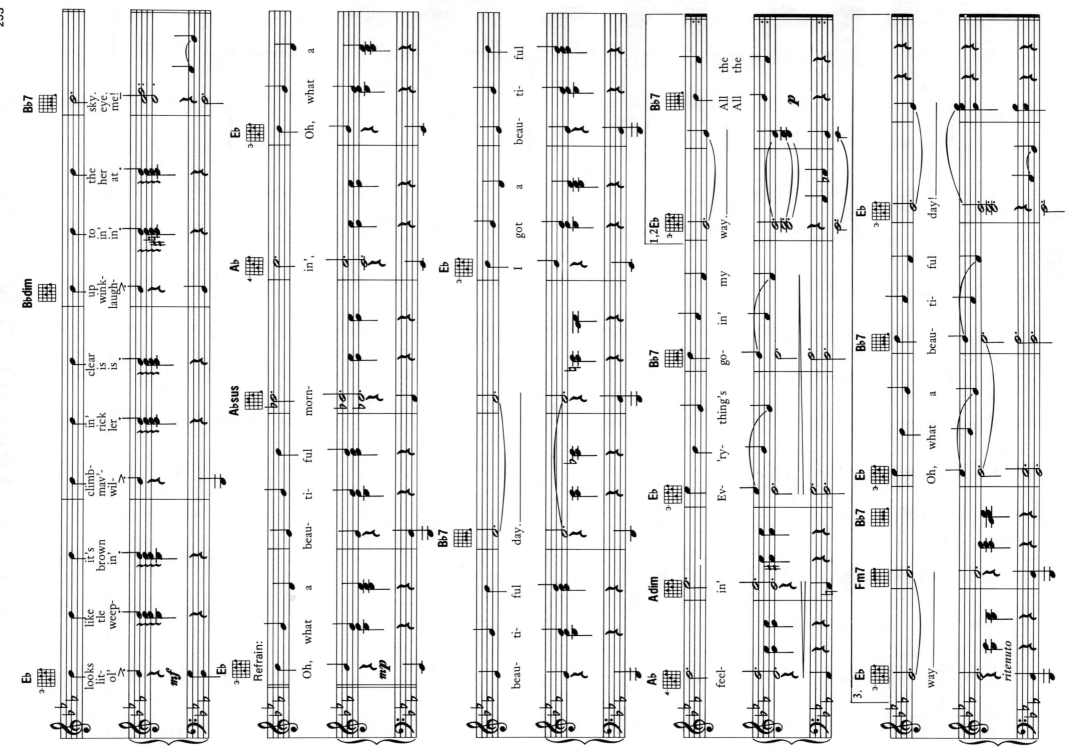

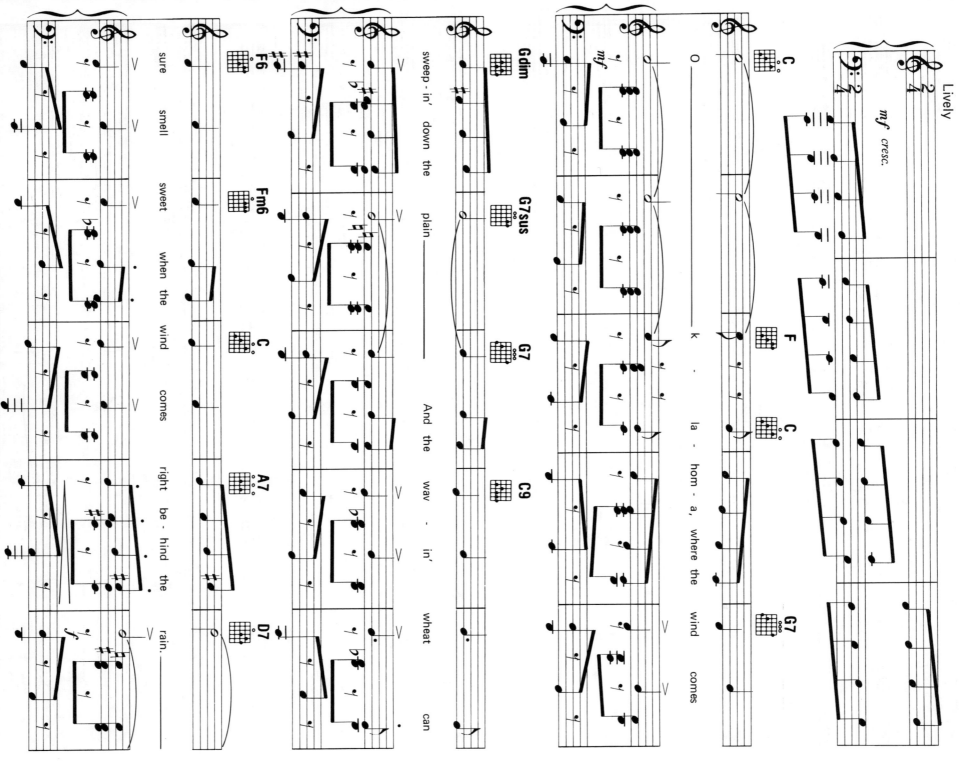

OKLAHOMA
(From "OKLAHOMA!")

Words by OSCAR HAMMERSTEIN II
Music by RICHARD RODGERS

G7 C F C
O k - la - hom - a, Ev - 'ry
G7 Gdim G7sus G7 C9
night my hon - ey lamb and I sit a - lone and
F6 Fm6 C G7
talk and watch a hawk mak - in' laz - y cir - cles in the
C F C
sky. We know we be - long to the land

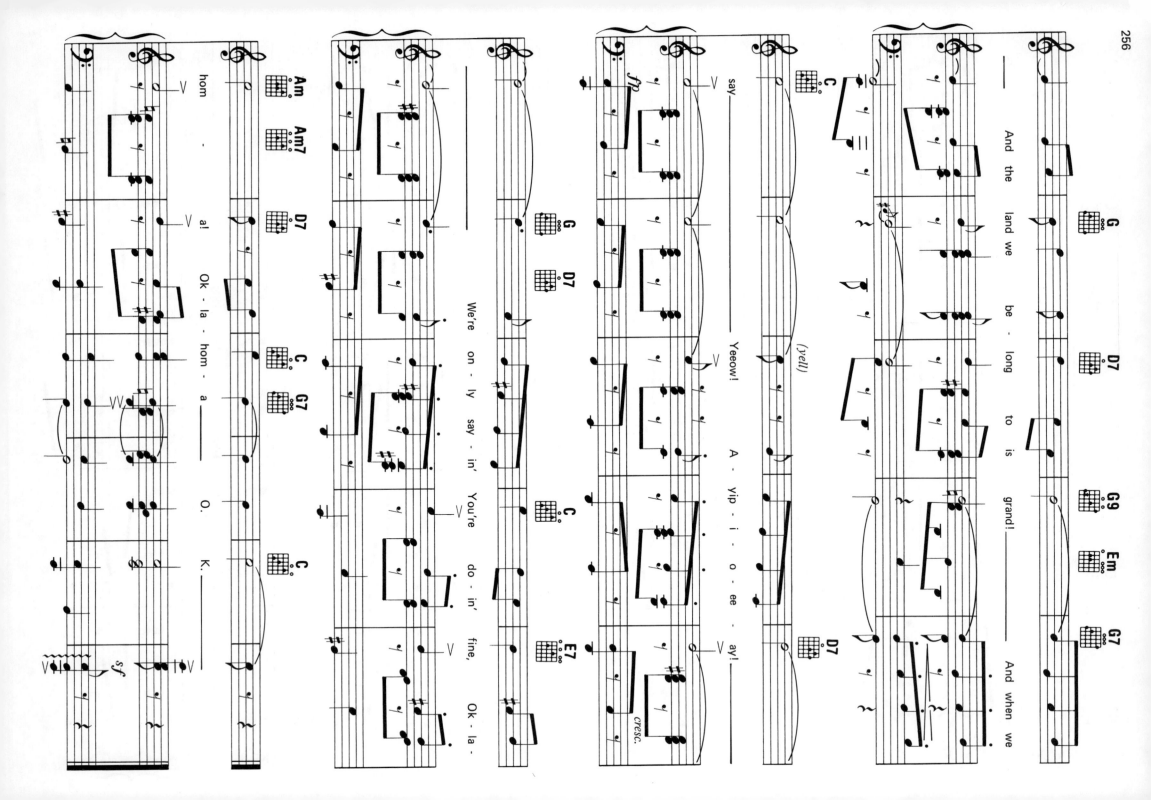

THE OLD LAMPLIGHTER

Words by Charles Tobias
Music by Nat Simon

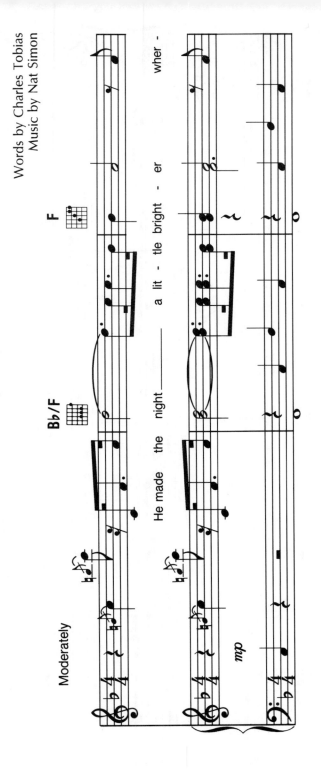
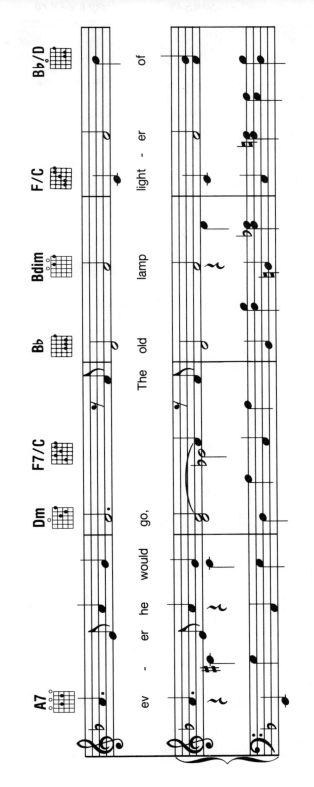
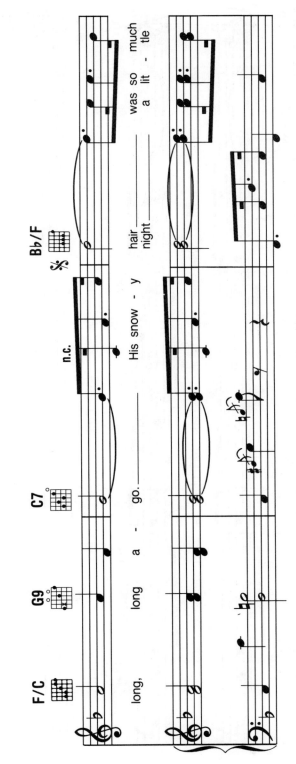

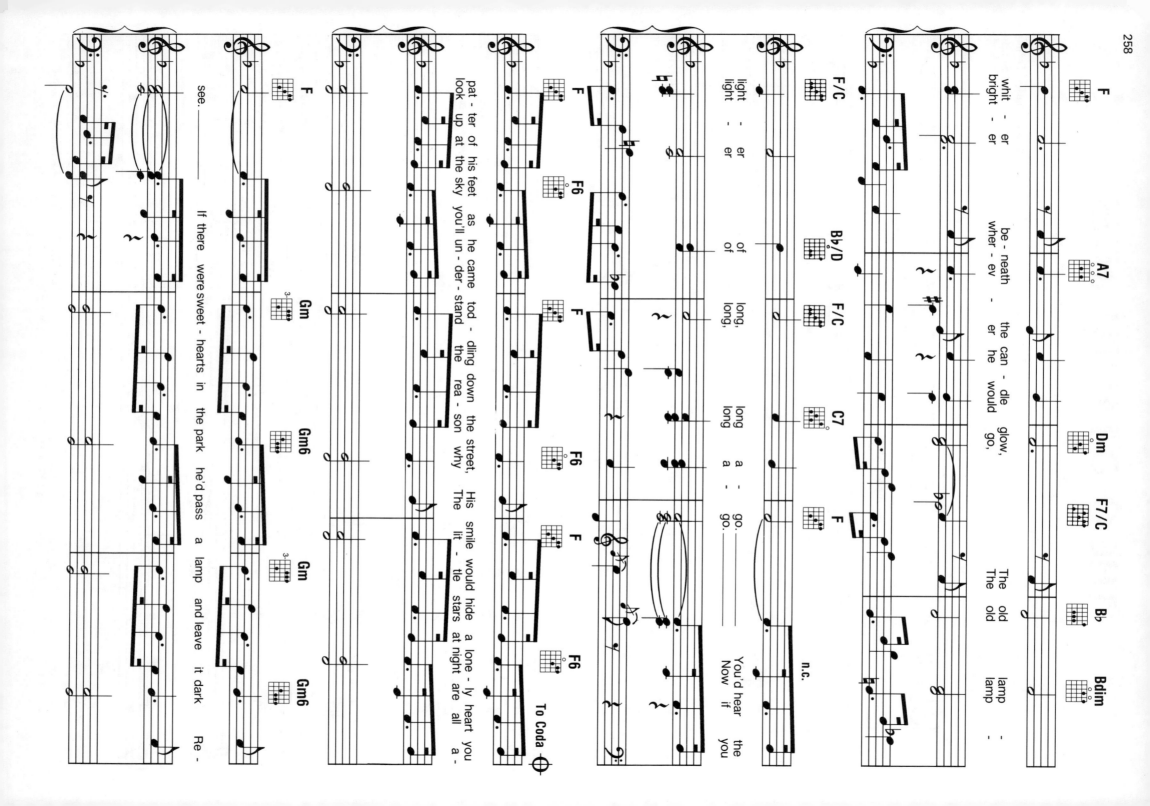

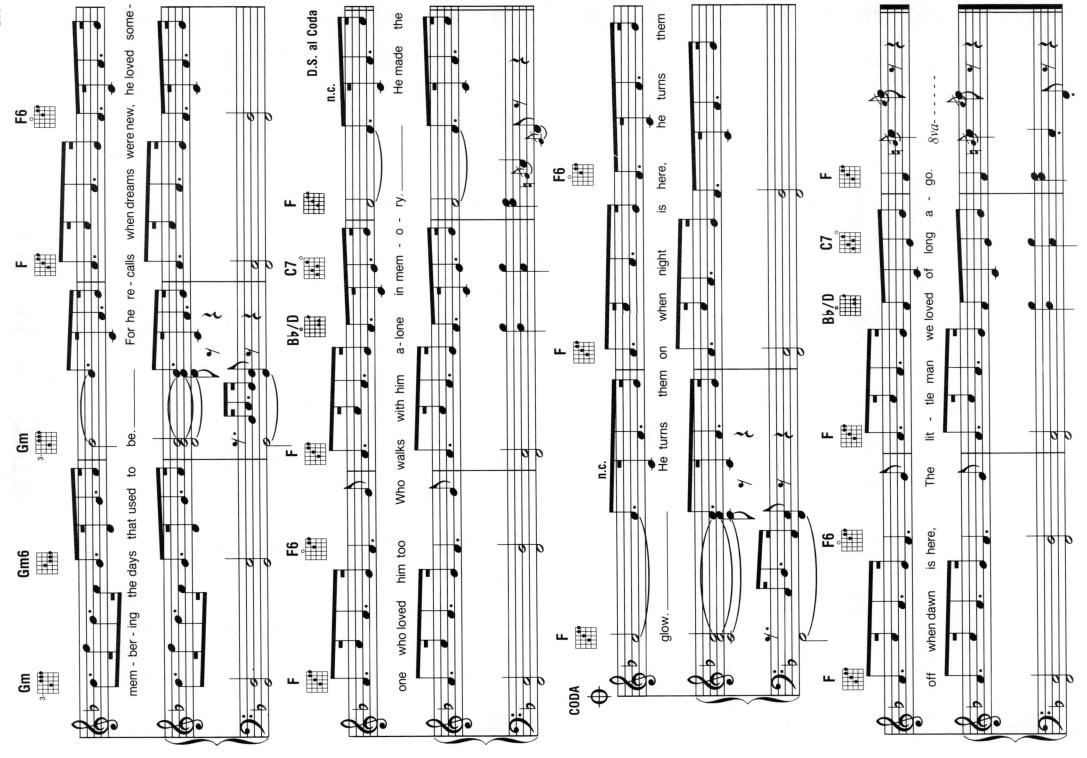

OL' MAN RIVER
(From "SHOW BOAT")

Words by OSCAR HAMMERSTEIN II
Music by JEROME KERN

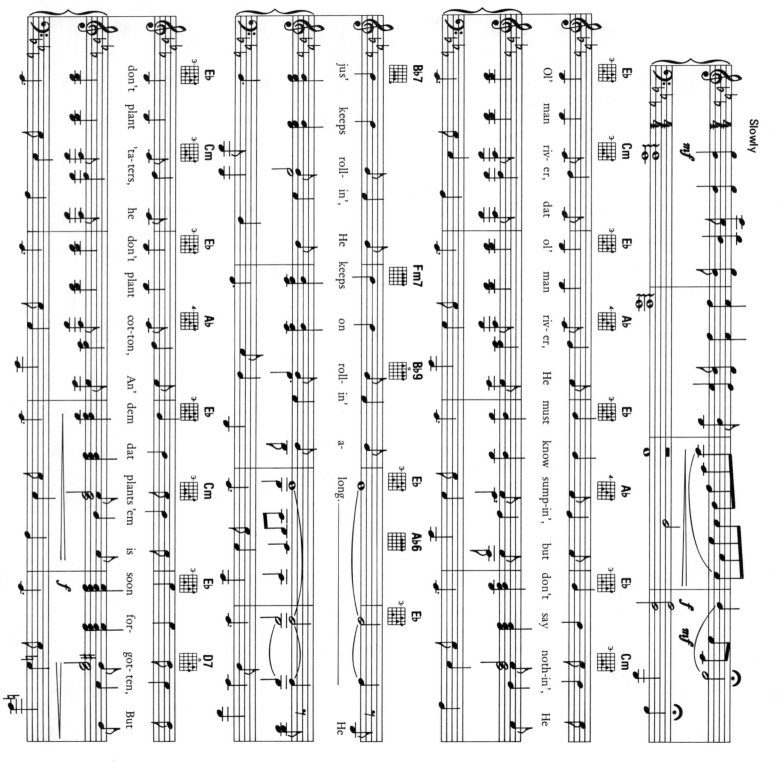

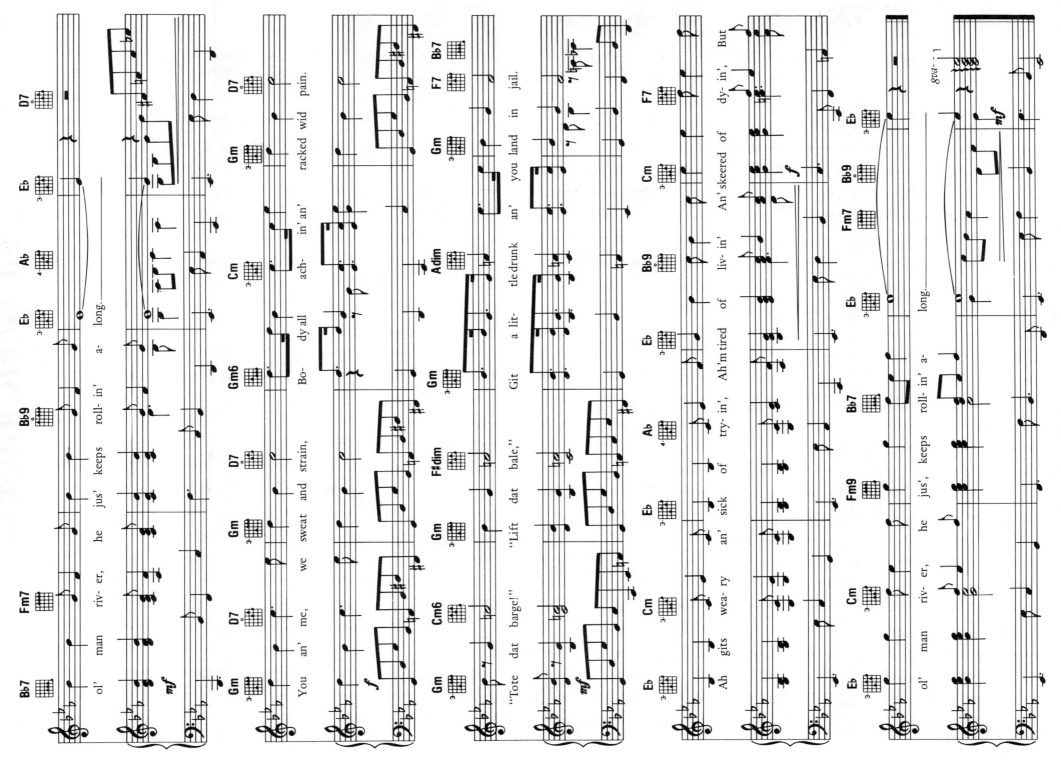

OLD DEVIL MOON

(From "FINIAN'S RAINBOW")

Words by E. Y. HARBURG
Music by BURTON LANE

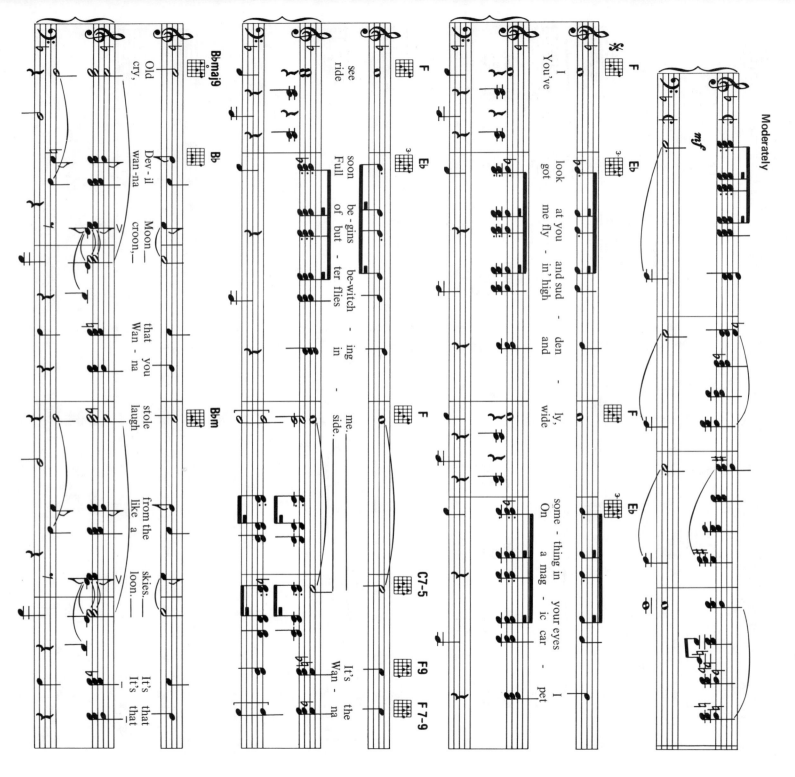

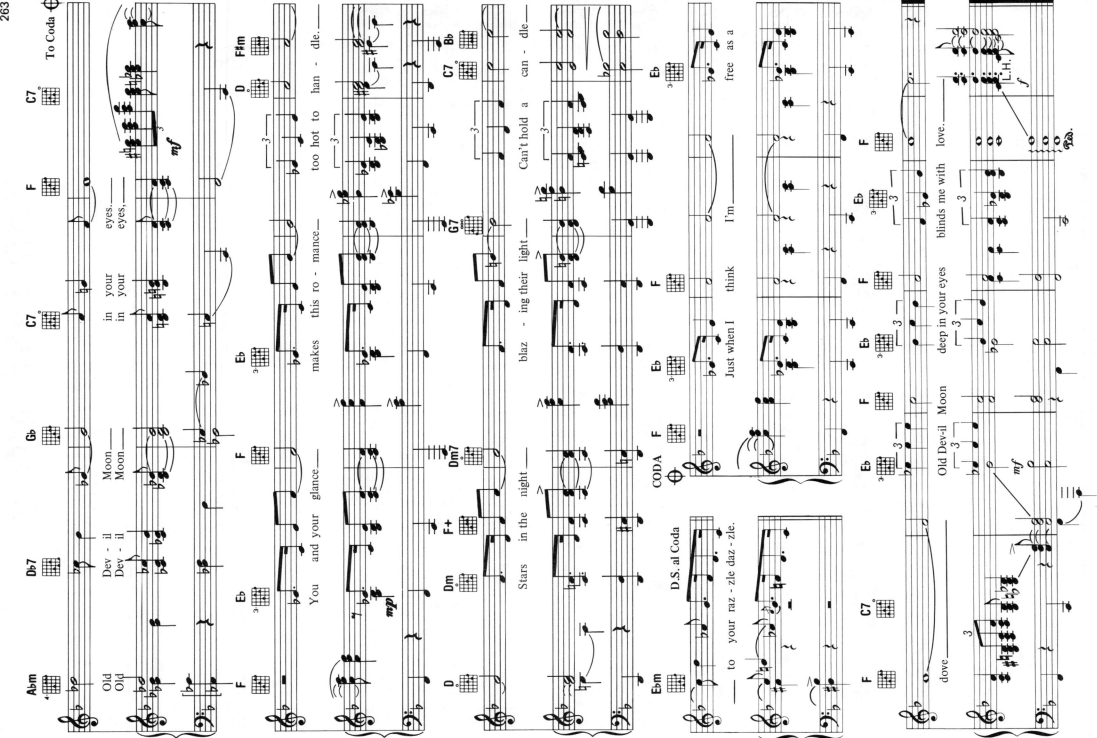

ON A CLEAR DAY
(YOU CAN SEE FOREVER)
(From "ON A CLEAR DAY YOU CAN SEE FOREVER")

Words by ALAN JAY LERNER
Music by BURTON LANE

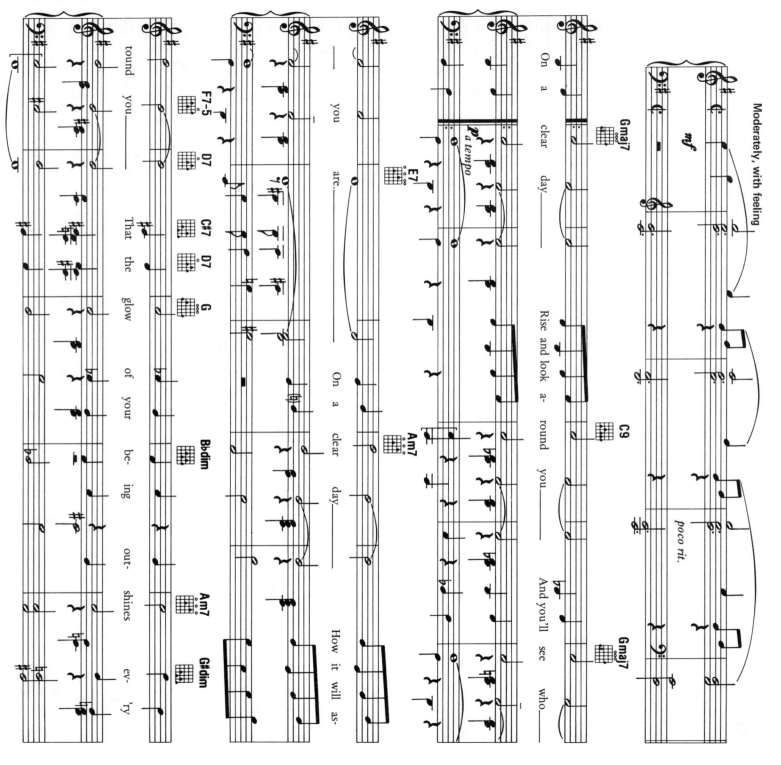

Moderately, with feeling

On a clear day —— Rise and look a- round you —— And you'll see who ——

On a clear day —— How it will as-

you are. —— That the glow of your be- ing out- shines ev- 'ry

round you ——

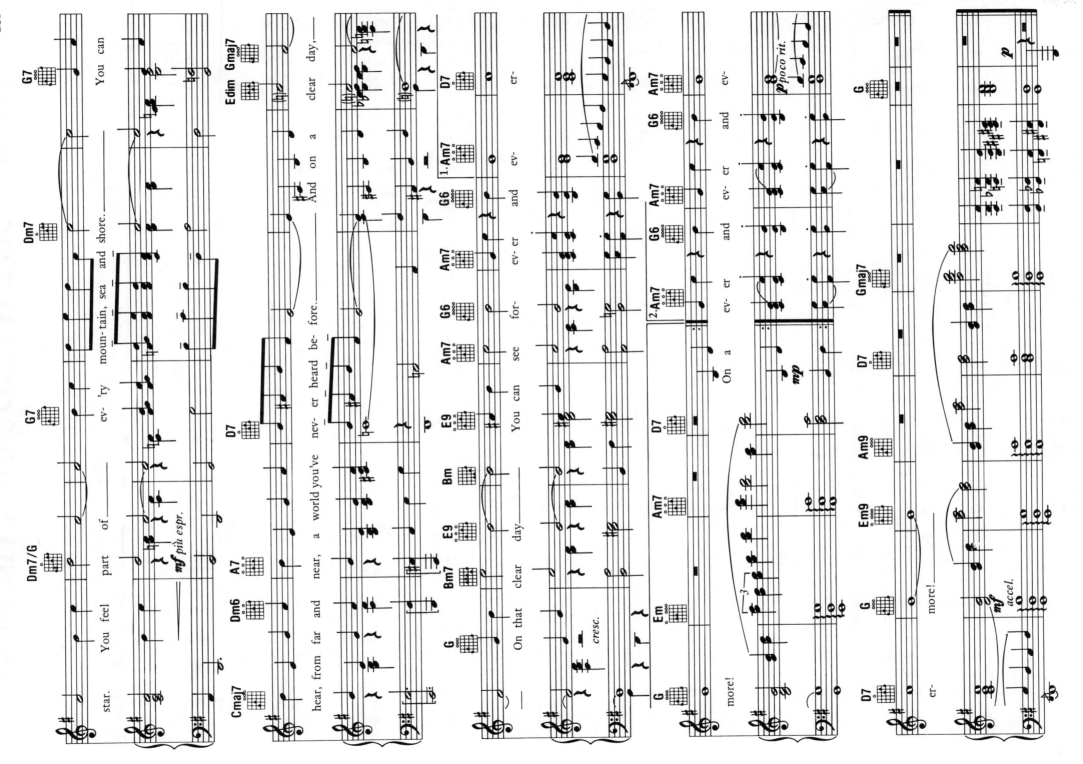

ON THE SOUTH SIDE OF CHICAGO

Words and Music by
PHIL ZELLER

Moderately

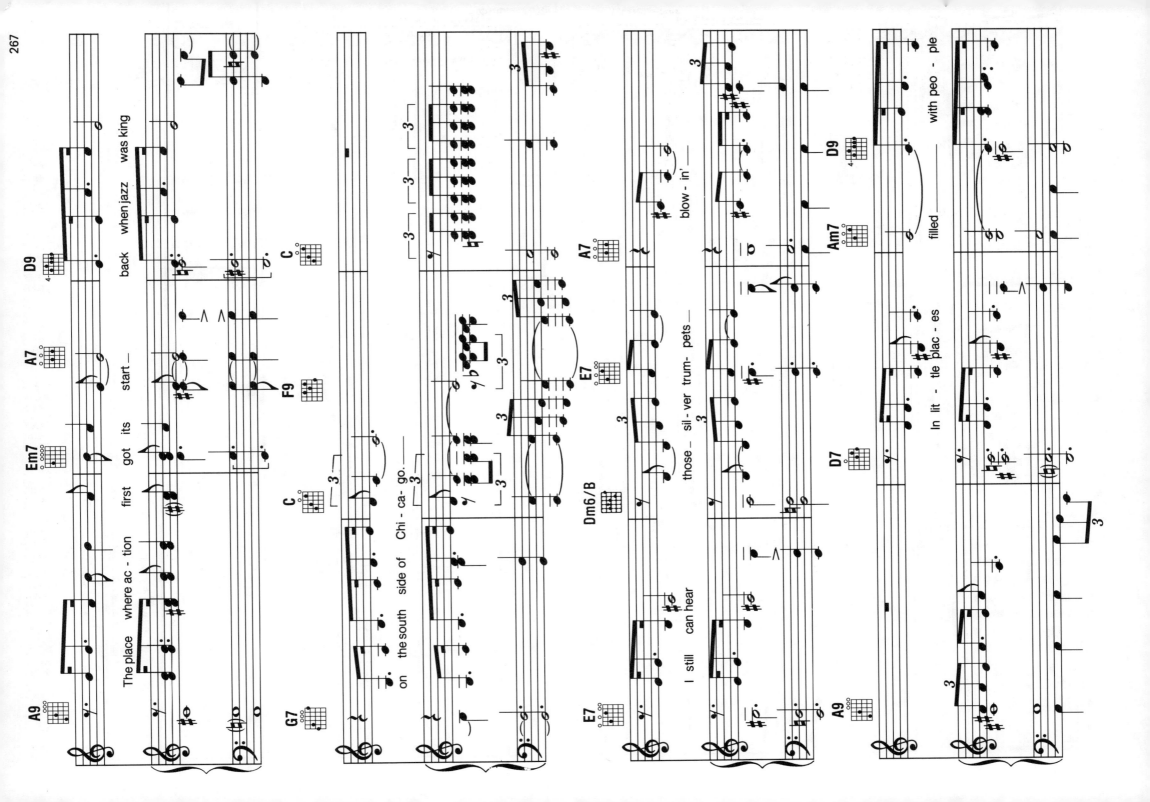

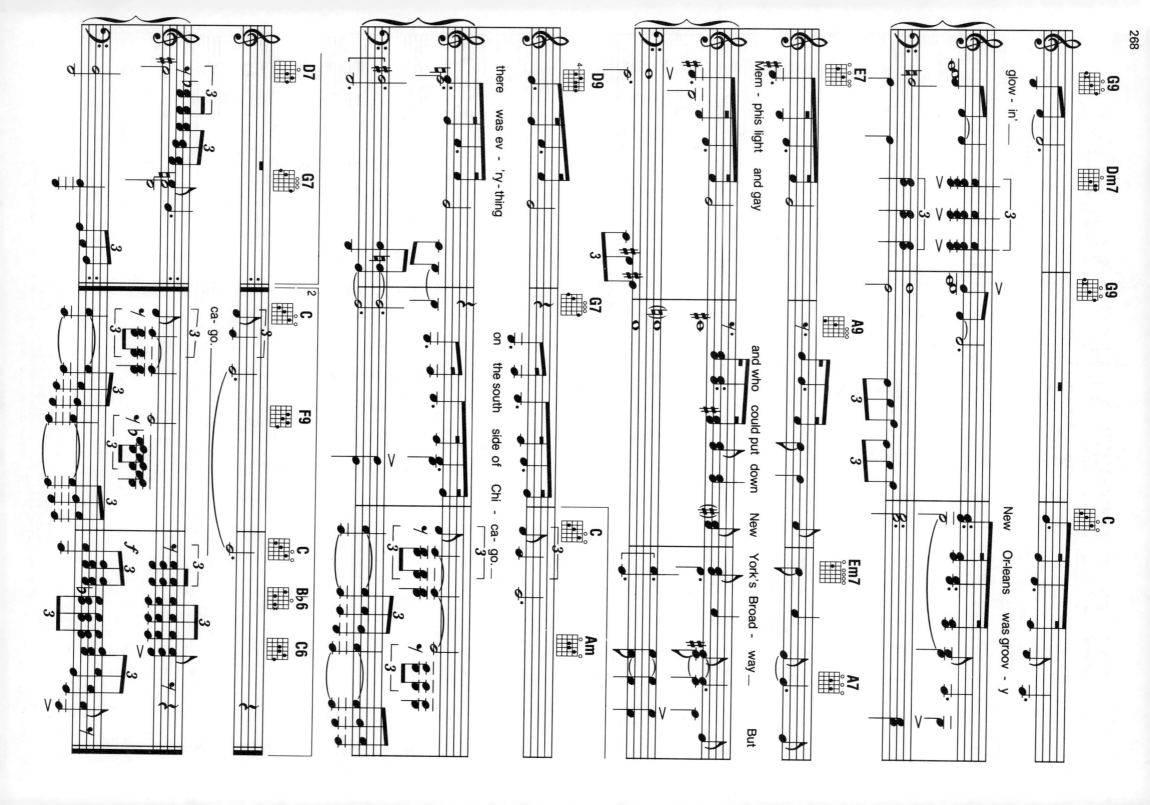

ON THE STREET WHERE YOU LIVE

(From "MY FAIR LADY")

Words by ALAN JAY LERNER
Music by FREDERICK LOEWE

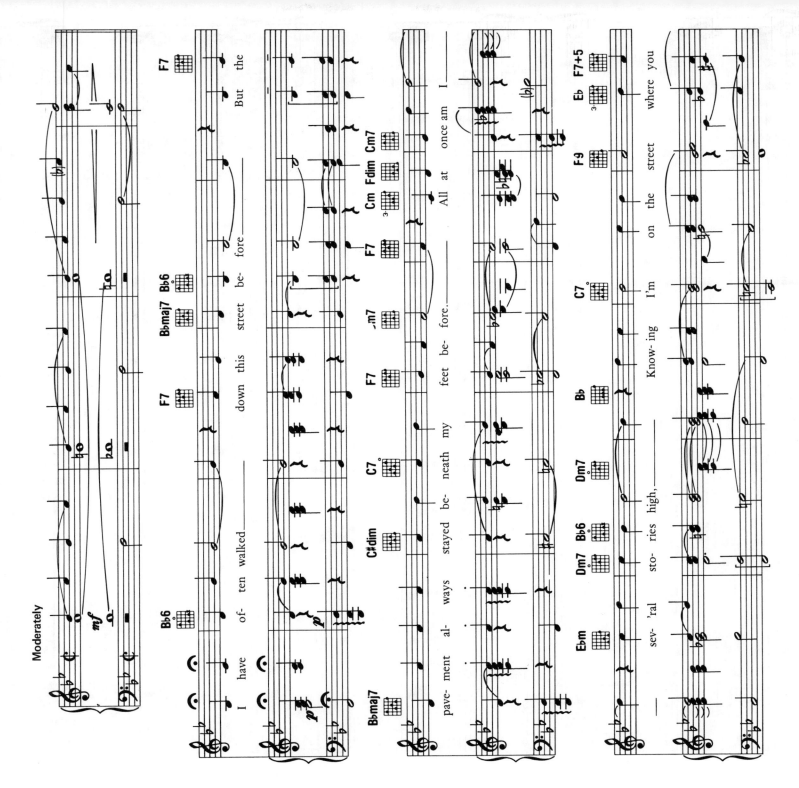

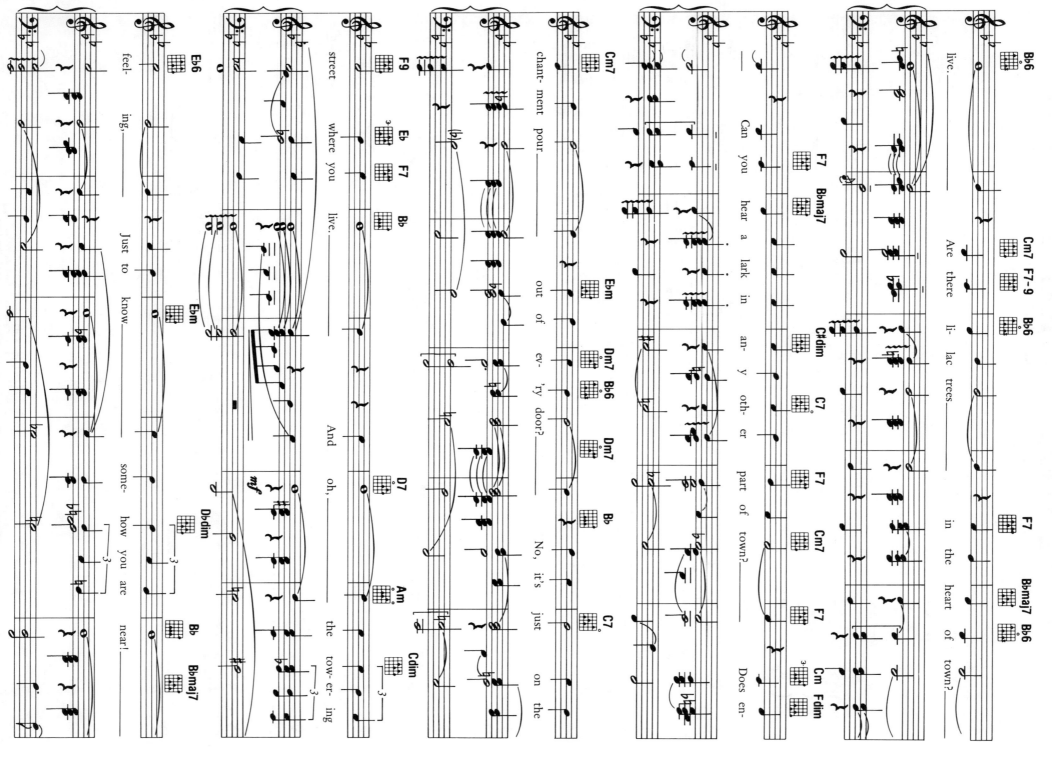

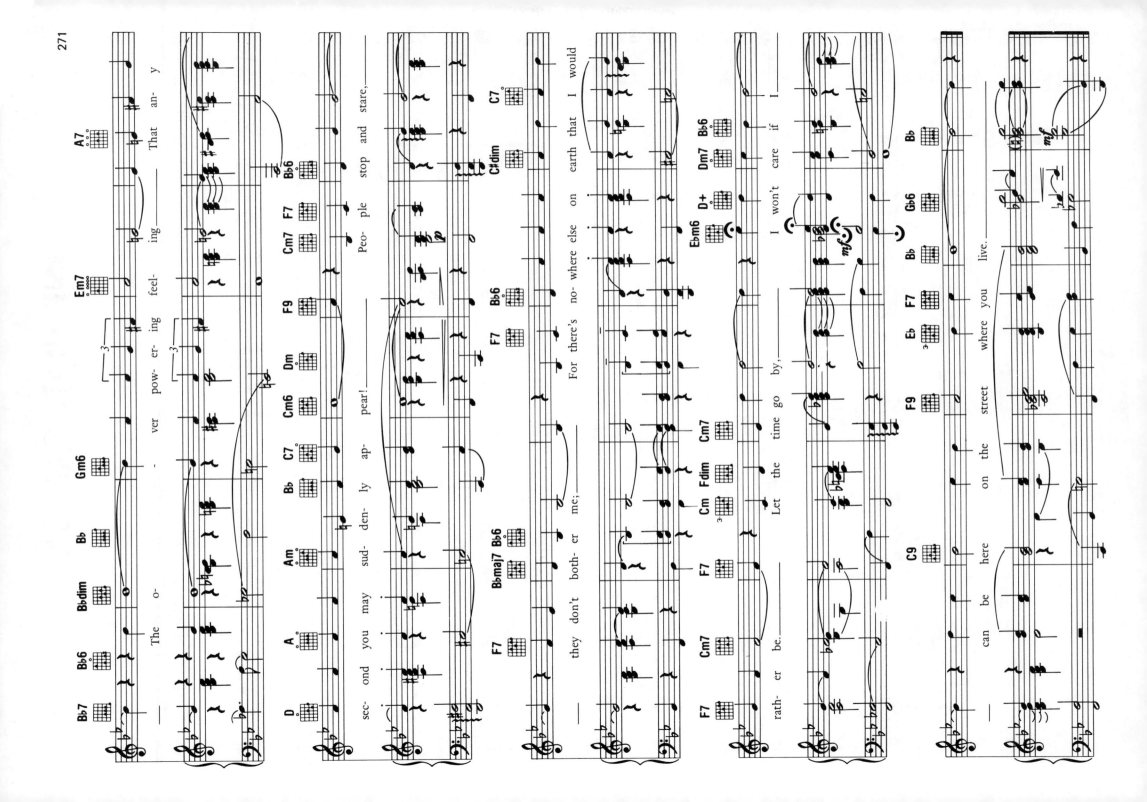

ONE NOTE SAMBA

Original Words by NEWTON MENDONCA
Music by ANTONIO CARLOS JOBIM

Lightly, with movement

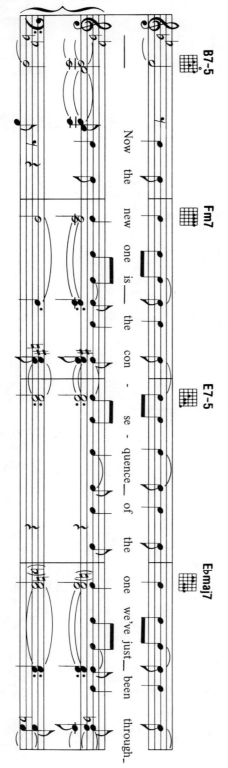
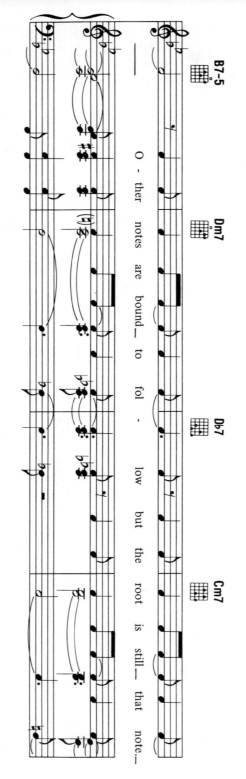
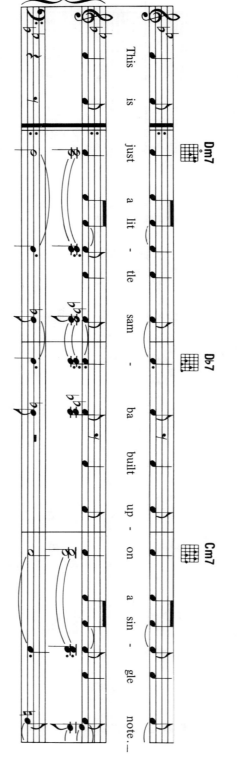
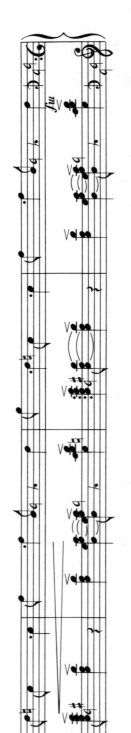

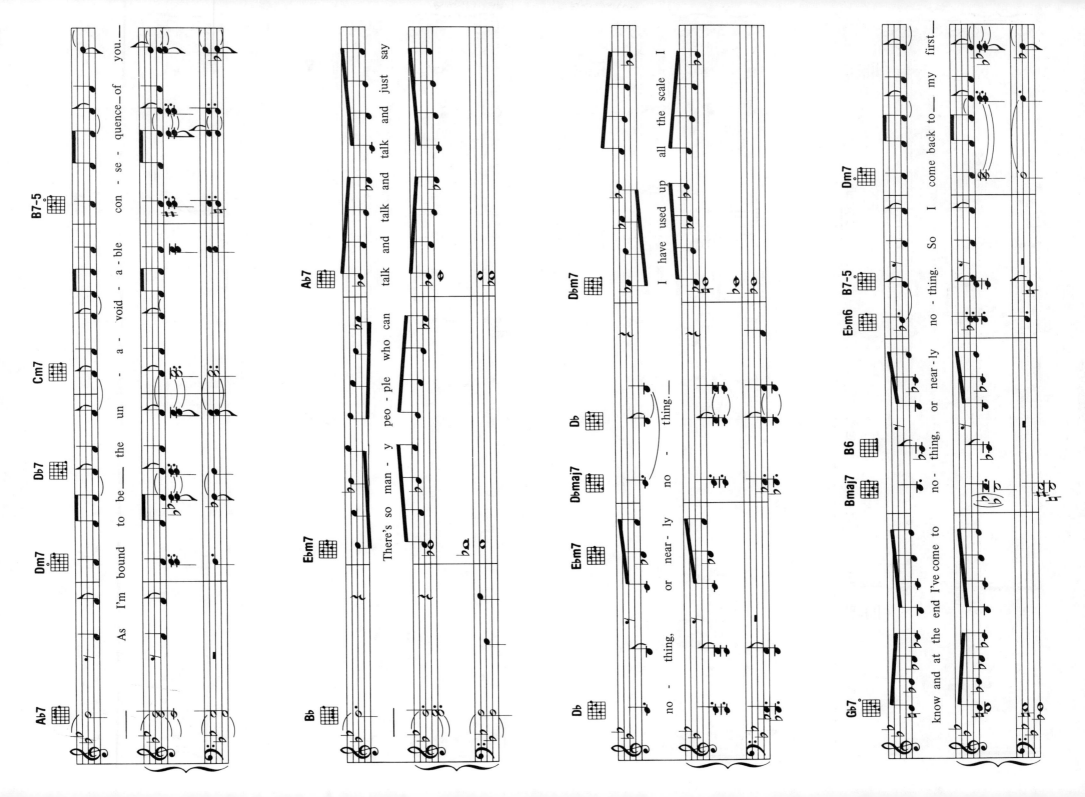

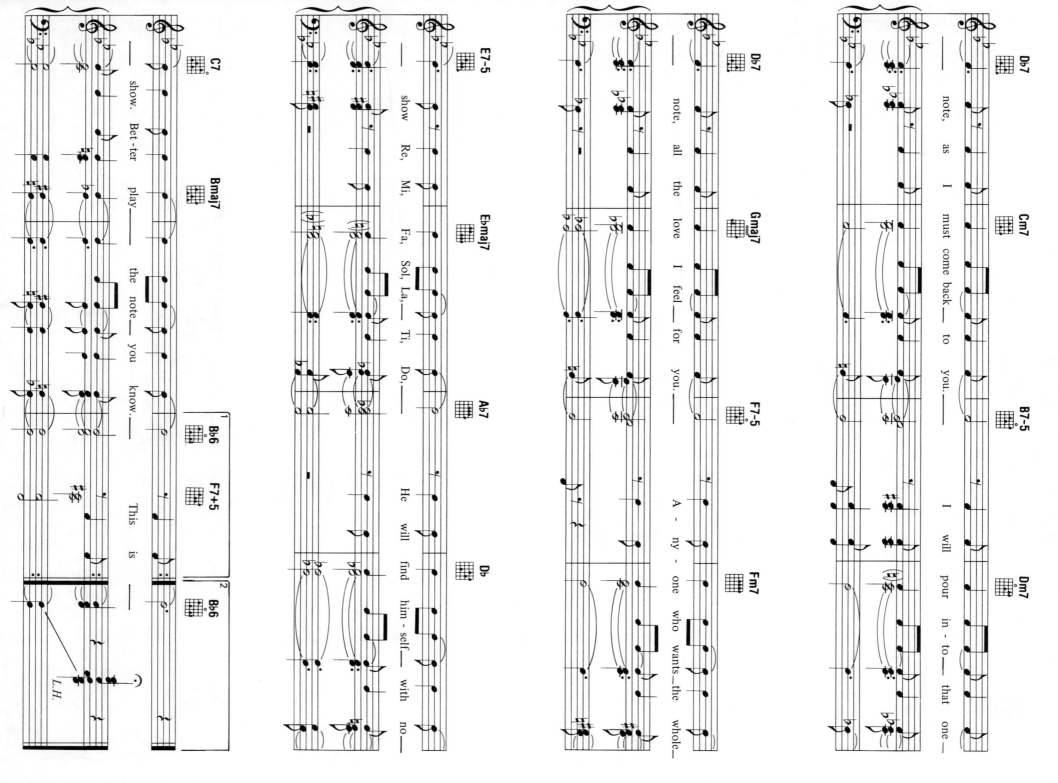

ONE TIN SOLDIER

Words and Music by DENNIS LAMBERT
and BRIAN POTTER

Moderately slow rock tempo

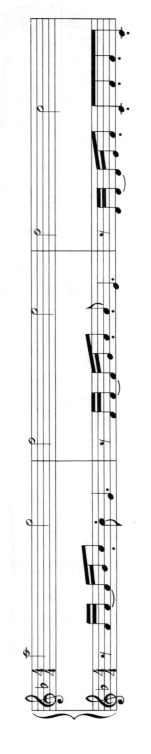

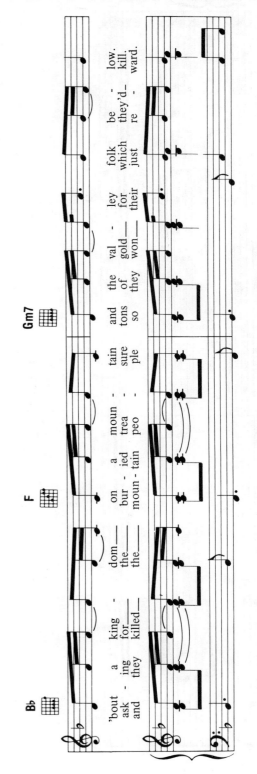

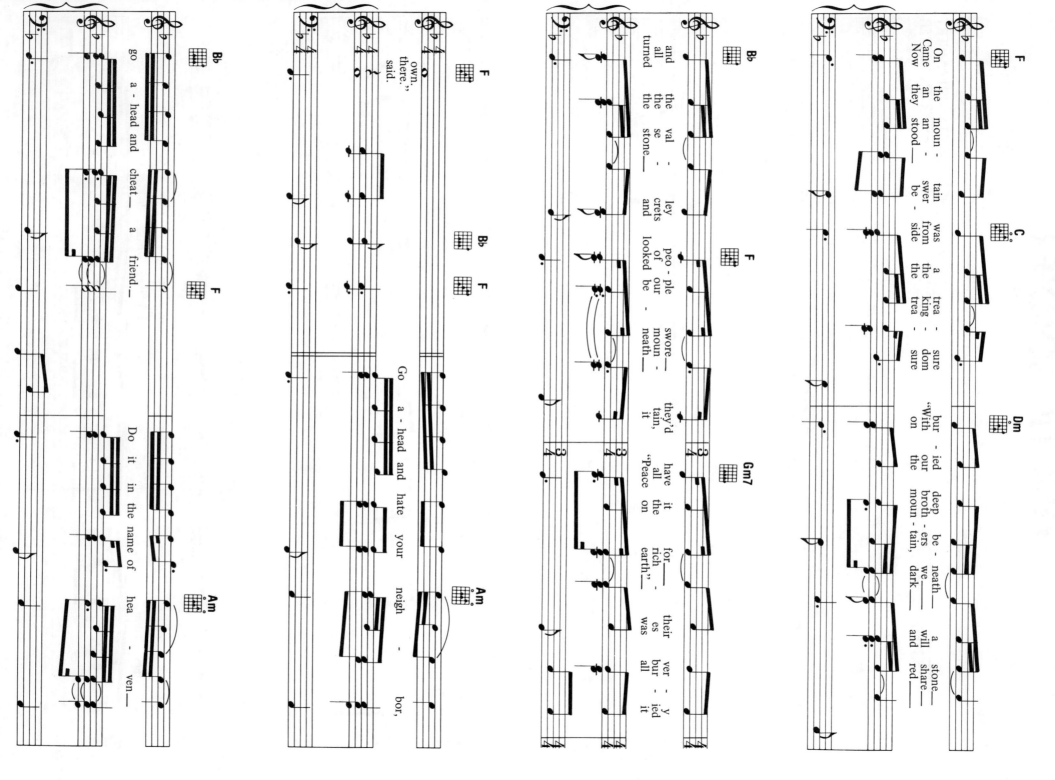

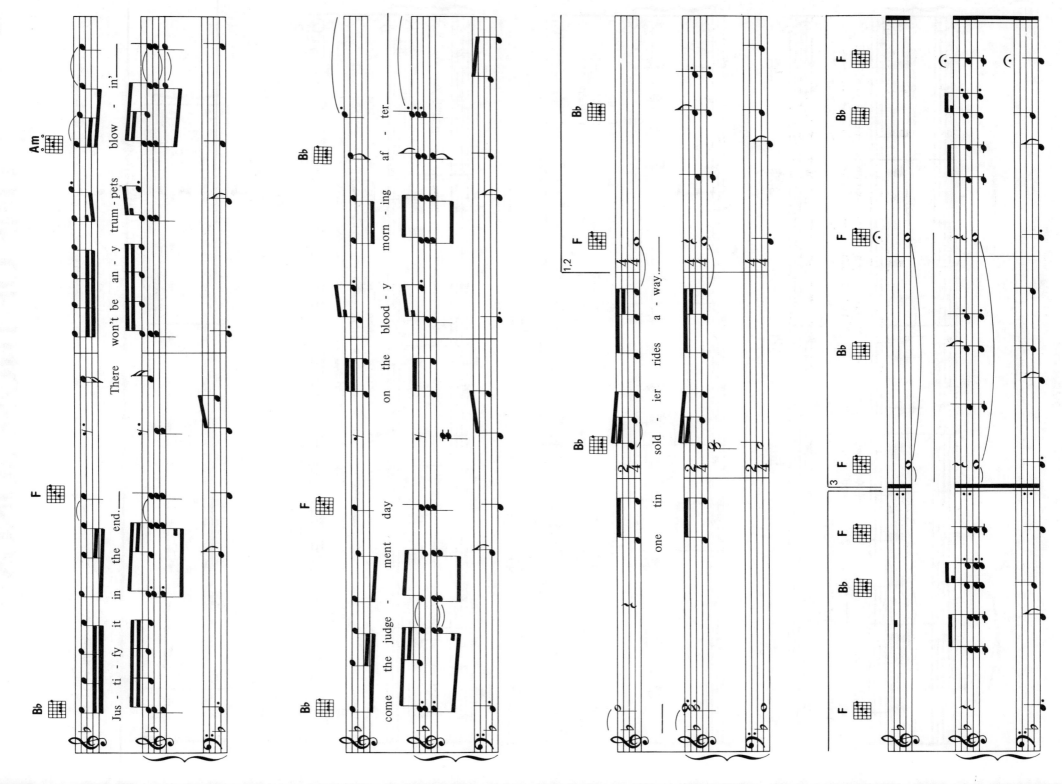

ONE OF THOSE SONGS

Words by WILL HOLT
Music by GERALD CALVI

Moderately bright

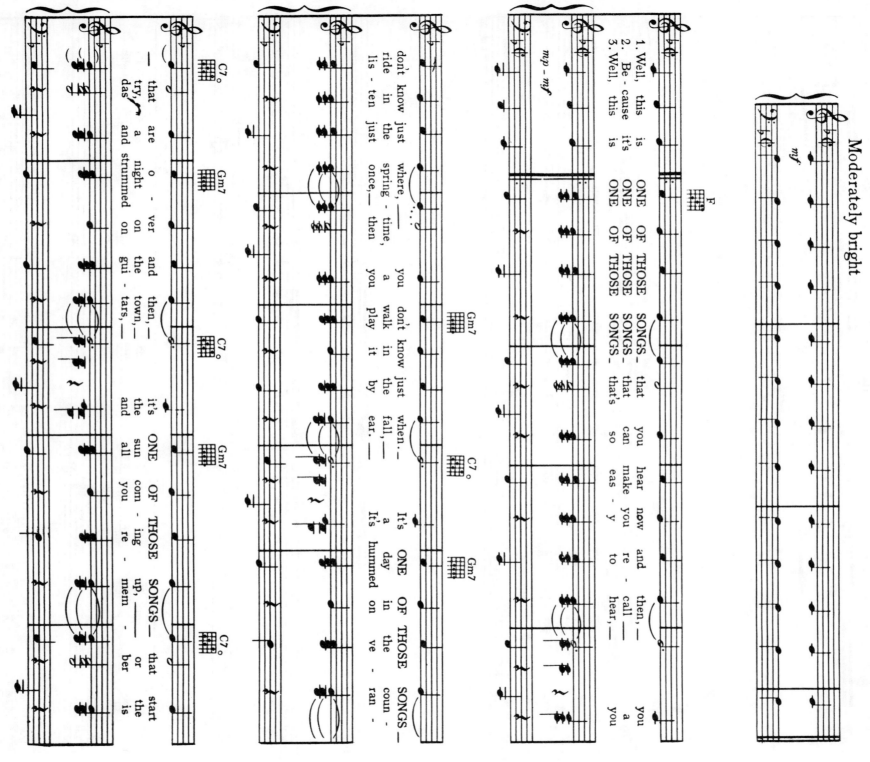

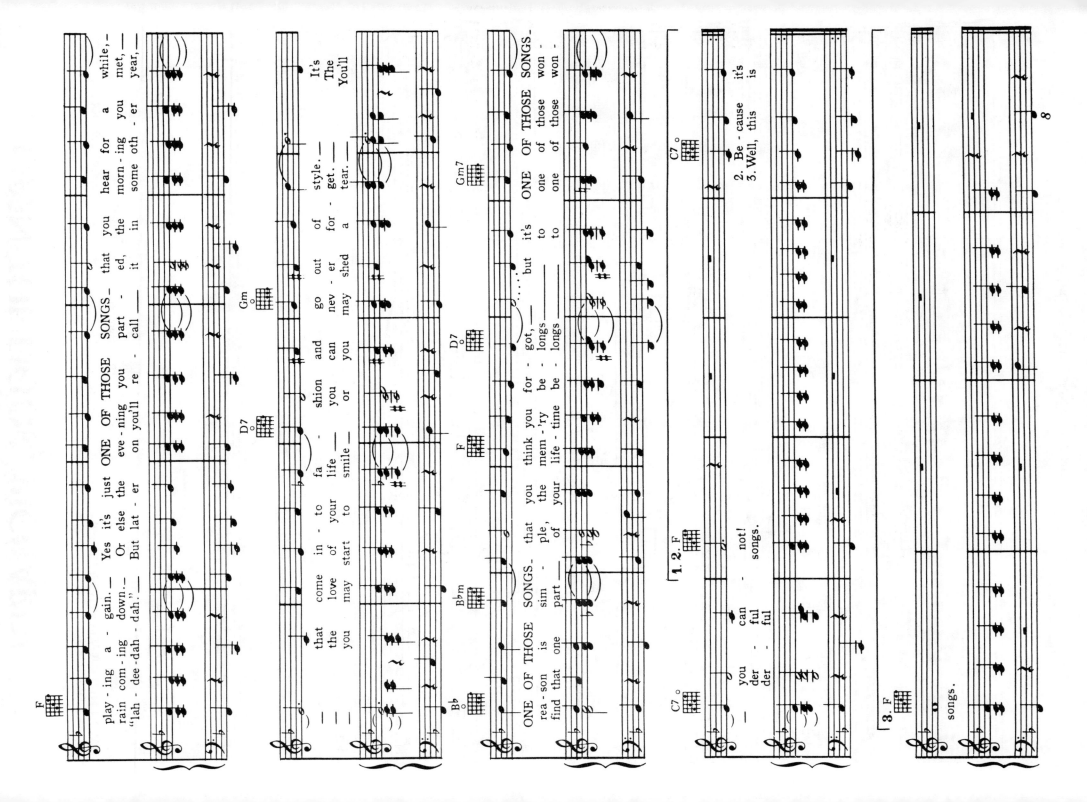

OPEN THE DOOR, RICHARD!

Words by "DUSTY" FLETCHER and JOHN MASON
Music by JACK McVEA and DAN HOWELL

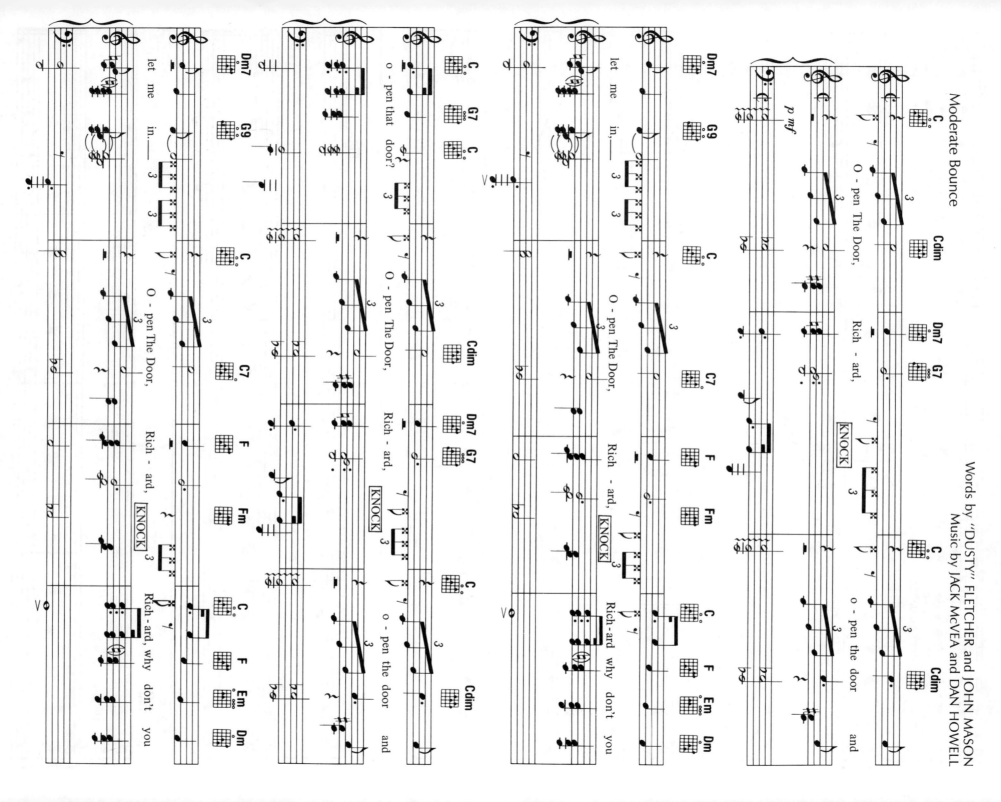

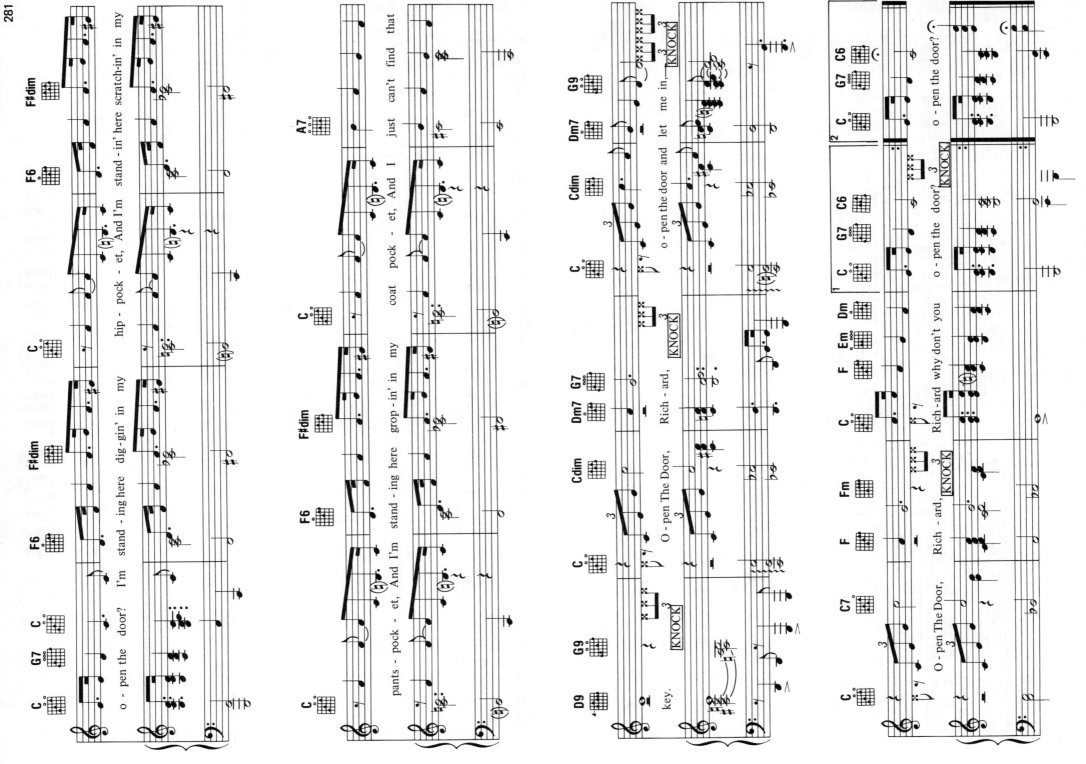

OUR DAY WILL COME

Words by BOB HILLIARD
Music by MORT GARSON

Slowly, with expression

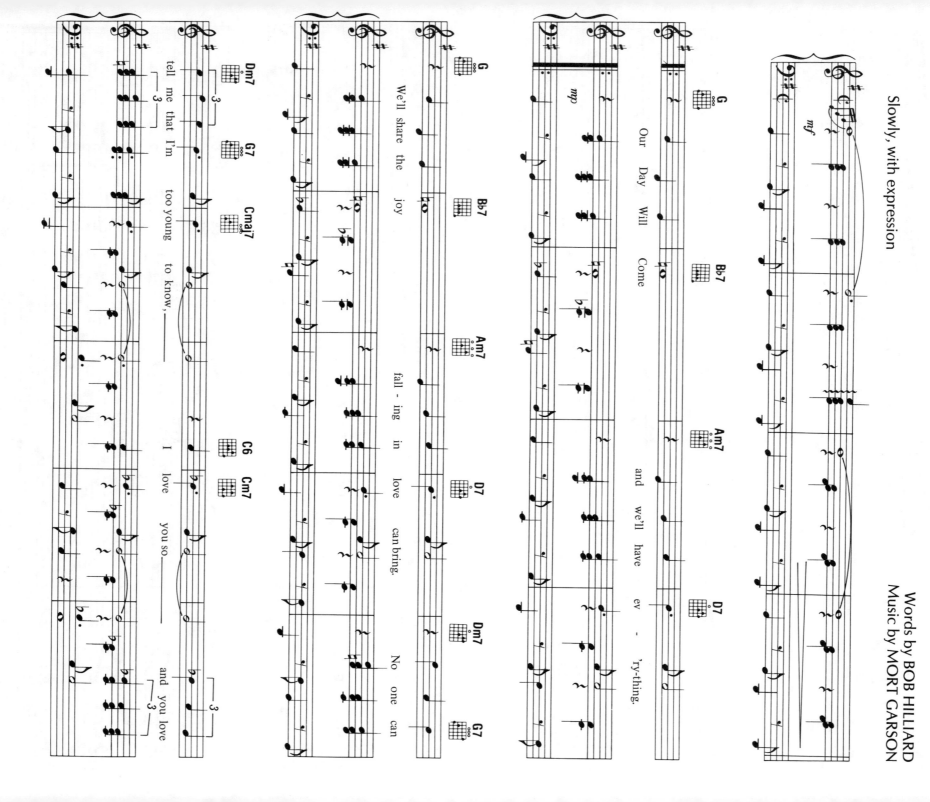

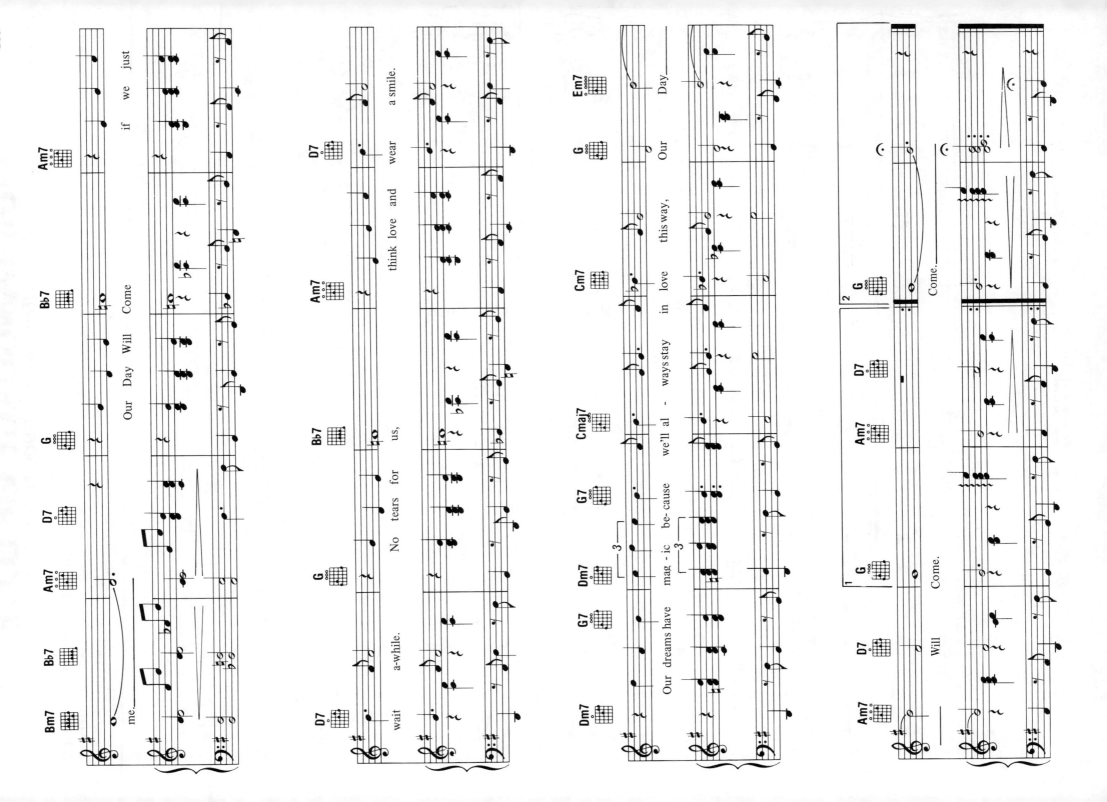

OUR LANGUAGE OF LOVE

(From "IRMA LA DOUCE")

Music by MARGUERITE MONNOT
Original French words by ALEXANDRE BREFFORT
English words by JULIAN MORE,
DAVID HENEKER and MONTY NORMAN

Moderately

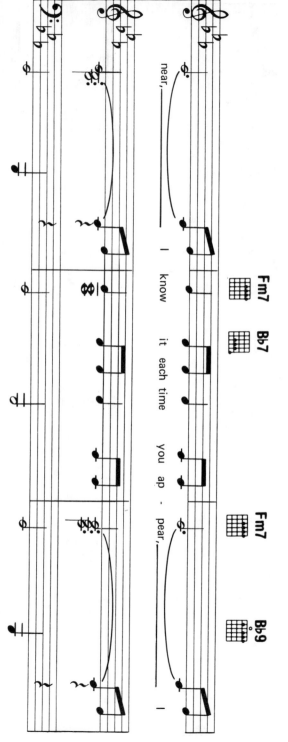

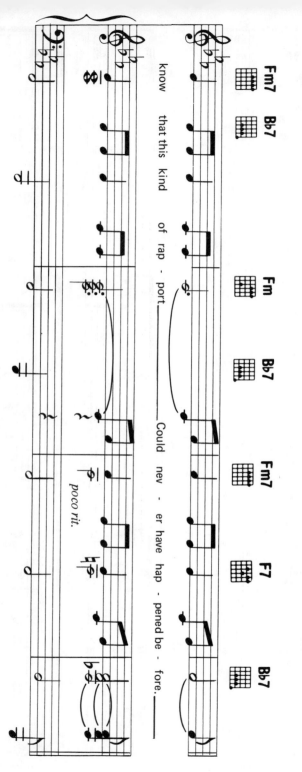

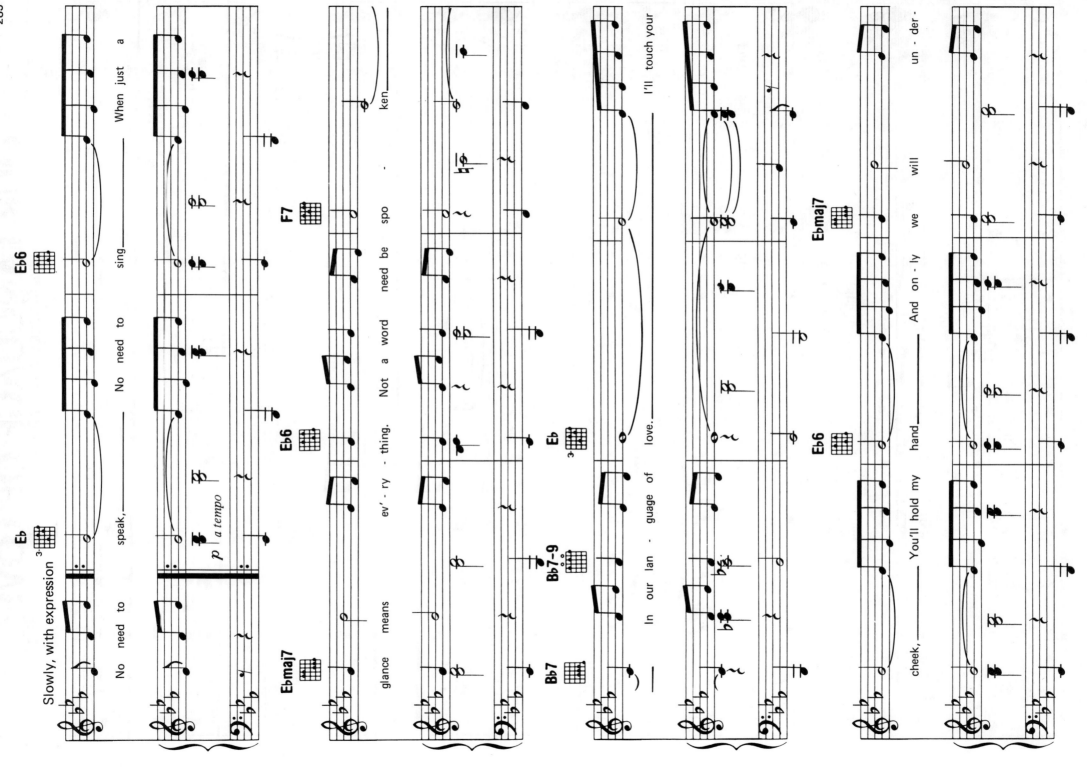

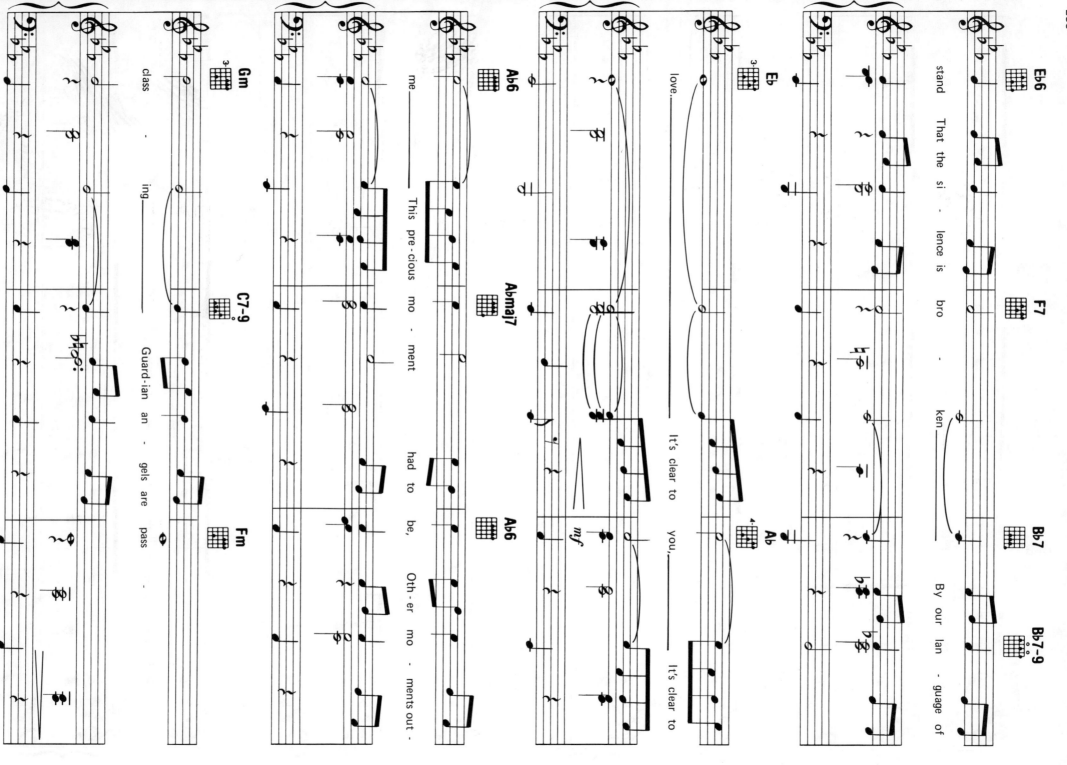

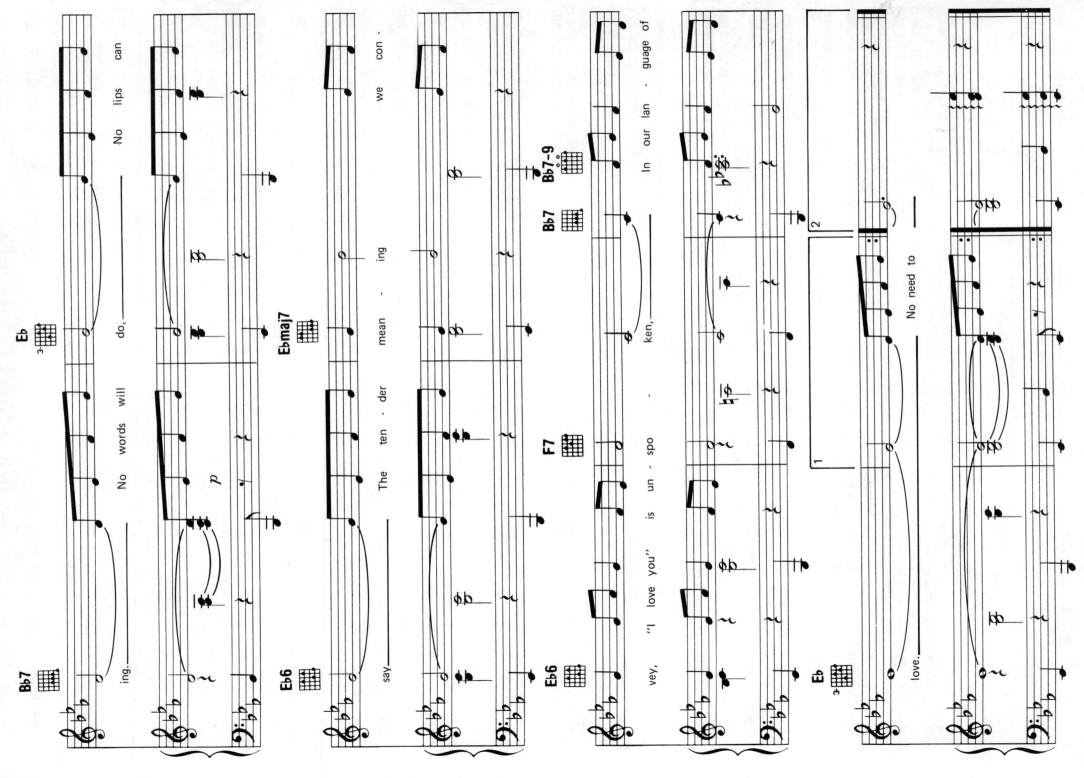

Piano/Vocal MIXED FOLIOS

Presenting the best variety of piano/vocal folios. Music includes guitar chord frames.

BEST BROADWAY SONGS EVER 00309155
Over 70 tunes featuring: All The Things You Are • Bewitched • Don't Cry For Me Argentina • I Could Have Danced All Night • If Ever I Would Leave You • Memory • Ol' Man River • You'll Never Walk Alone • and many more.

BEST CONTEMPORARY SONGS — 50 Top Hits 00359190
Some of the best, most recent hits, featuring: Any Day Now • Deja Vu • Endless Love • Flashdance . . . What A Feeling • I.O.U. • Islands In The Stream • September Morn • Through The Years • You Needed Me • and many more.

BEST COUNTRY SONGS EVER 00359498
Over 79 all-time country hits including: Always On My Mind • Could I Have This Dance • God Bless The U.S.A. • Help Me Make It Through The Night • Islands In The Stream • and many more.

THE BEST EASY LISTENING SONGS EVER 00359193
Over 100 beautiful songs including: Around The World • Candle On The Water • Day By Day • A Foggy Day • I'll Never Smile Again • Just In Time • Manhattan • Strangers In The Night • and many more.

BEST KNOWN LATIN SONGS 00359194
A fabulous selection of over 50 favorite Latin songs including: Blame It On The Bossa Nova • A Day In The Life Of A Fool • The Girl From Ipanema • Poinciana • Quando, Quando, Quando • Spanish Eyes • Watch What Happens • Yellow Days • and many more!

THE BEST SONGS EVER 00359224
75 all-time hits including: Climb Ev'ry Mountain • Edelweiss • Feelings • Here's That Rainy Day • I Left My Heart In San Francisco • Love Is Blue • People • Stardust • Sunrise, Sunset • Woman In Love • many more.

THE BEST STANDARDS EVER Volume 1 00359231
and Volume 2 00359232
A two volume collection of 140 vintage and contemporary standards including: All The Things You Are • Endless Love • The Hawaiian Wedding Song • I Left My Heart In San Francisco • Misty • My Way • Old Cape Cod • People • Wish You Were Here • Yesterday's Songs • and many more.

THE BIG BAND ERA 00359260
Over 90 top songs from the time of the big bands including: Harbor Lights • I Can't Get Started • In The Mood • Juke Box Saturday Night • Moonglow • Paper Doll • String Of Pearls • Tuxedo Junction • Amapola • Jersey Bounce • and many more.

THE BIG 80 SONGBOOK 00359265
80 Recent hits and favorite standards including: Autumn Leaves • Can't Smile Without You • Ebony And Ivory • Midnight Cowboy • More • Riders In The Sky • Sentimental Journey • She Touched Me • Stormy Weather • You Don't Bring Me Flowers • and much more.

BROADWAY DELUXE 00309245
126 Smash Broadway songs including: Cabaret • Edelweiss • I Could Have Danced All Night • Memory • Send In The Clowns • Seventy Six Trombones • Sunrise, Sunset • Try To Remember • What Kind Of Fool Am I? • A Wonderful Guy • and many, many more.

CONTEMPORARY HIT DUETS 00359501
14 hit duets from today's biggest pop stars includes Don't Go Breaking My Heart • Endless Love • Ebony And Ivory • Say, Say, Say • You Don't Bring Me Flowers • and more.

CONTEMPORARY LOVE SONGS 00359496
A collection of today's best love songs including Endless Love • September Morn • Feelings • Through The Years • and more.

80's GOLD UPDATE 00359740
Over 70 Hits from the 80's including: All Through The Night • Endless Love • Every Breath You Take • Fortress Around Your Heart • Memory • Miami Vice • One Night In Bangkok • Sentimental Street • What's Love Got To Do With It • Total Eclipse Of The Heart • and more!

FAVORITE HAWAIIAN SONGS 00359852
30 island favorites including Aloha Oe • One Paddle, Two Paddle • Red Sails In The Sunset • Tiny Bubbles • and many more.

GOLDEN ENCYCLOPEDIA OF FOLK MUSIC 00359905
A giant collection of more than 180 classic folk songs including songs of true love, unrequited and false love, spirituals, songs of the west, jolly reunions, international songs and singing the blues.

GRANDMA MOSES SONGBOOK 00359938
A beautiful collection of over 80 traditional and folk songs highlighted by the fascinating paintings of Grandma Moses. Features: America The Beautiful • The Glow Worm • Honeysuckle Rose • I'll Be Home On Christmas Day • Look To The Rainbow • Suddenly There's A Valley • Sunrise, Sunset • Try To Remember • and many, many more!

No. 1 SONGS OF THE 80's 00310666
Arthur's Theme • Everything She Wants • Everytime You Go Away • Careless Whisper • Sailing • What's Love Got To Do With It • The Reflex • Time After Time • and more.

#1 SONGS FROM THE 70's & 80's 00310665
60 of the top songs from the Billboard Hot 100 charts of the 70's and 80's, featuring: Every Breath You Take • How Deep Is Your Love • Joy To The World • Laughter In The Rain • Love Will Keep Us Together • Love's Theme • Maneater • Maniac • Morning Train • Stayin' Alive • and more.

150 OF THE MOST BEAUTIFUL SONGS EVER
Perfect Bound - 00360731   Plastic Comb Bound - 00360734
Bali Ha'i • Bewitched • Could I Have This Dance • I Remember It Well • I'll Be Seeing You • If I Ruled The World • Love Is Blue • Memory • Songbird • When I Need You • and more.

ROCK ON! 00360932
A collection of 50 top rock hits spanning the decades from the 60's to the present. Includes such rock classics as Free Bird • A Whiter Shade Of Pale • Sunshine Of Your Love • Maggie May • and many, many more.

70 CONTEMPORARY HITS 00361056
A super collection of 70 hits featuring: Every Breath You Take • Time After Time • Memory • Wake Me Up Before You Go-Go • Endless Love • Islands In The Stream • Through The Years • Valotte • and many more.

23 AWARD WINNING POP HITS 00361385
23 of the best including Don't Cry Out Loud • Flashdance . . . What A Feeling • Memory • You Needed Me • and more.

VIDEO ROCK HITS 00361456
A collection of hits by today's biggest video artists — Cindy Lauper, Twisted Sister, Tina Turner, Wham! and others. 21 songs including: Careless Whisper • Hungry Like The Wolf • She Bop • What's Love Got To Do With It • and many more.

YOUNG AT HEART SONGBOOK 00361820
101 light hearted, fun loving favorites: Alley Cat • Bandstand Boogie • Bye Bye Blues • Five Foot Two, Eyes Of Blue • I Could Have Danced All Night • Let Me Entertain You • The Sound Of Music • Tiny Bubbles • True Love • Young At Heart • and more.

ALSO AVAILABLE . . .

HAL LEONARD CHARTBUSTER SERIES
frequently released books of chart songs which include the top recorded hits from Billboard's Top 100 Chart.

PIANO ALPHABETICAL SONGFINDER 72000004
Complete listing of the thousands of songs included in the Easy Piano and Piano/Vocal/Guitar books. Song titles are cross-referenced to the books in which they can be found. Available free of charge from your local music store. Or, write to: HAL LEONARD PUBLISHING CORP. P.O. Box 13819, Milwaukee, WI 53213

HAL LEONARD PUBLISHING CORPORATION
8112 West Bluemound Rd. P.O. Box 13819 Milwaukee, WI 53213

For more information, contact your local music dealer, or write directly to: